A CULTURAL HISTORY OF FURNITURE

VOLUME 6

A Cultural History of Furniture
General Editor: Christina M. Anderson

Volume 1
A Cultural History of Furniture in Antiquity
Edited by Dimitra Andrianou

Volume 2
A Cultural History of Furniture in the Middle Ages and Renaissance
Edited by Erin J. Campbell and Stephanie R. Miller

Volume 3
A Cultural History of Furniture in the Age of Exploration
Edited by Christina M. Anderson and Elizabeth A. Carroll

Volume 4
A Cultural History of Furniture in the Age of Enlightenment
Edited by Sylvain Cordier, Christina M. Anderson, and Laura Houliston

Volume 5
A Cultural History of Furniture in the Age of Empire and Industry
Edited by Catherine L. Futter and Christina M. Anderson

Volume 6
A Cultural History of Furniture in the Modern Age
Edited by Claire I. R. O'Mahony

A CULTURAL HISTORY OF FURNITURE

IN THE MODERN AGE

Edited by Claire I. R. O'Mahony

BLOOMSBURY ACADEMIC

LONDON • NEW YORK • OXFORD • NEW DELHI • SYDNEY

BLOOMSBURY ACADEMIC
Bloomsbury Publishing Plc
50 Bedford Square, London, WC1B 3DP, UK
1385 Broadway, New York, NY 10018, USA
29 Earlsfort Terrace, Dublin 2, Ireland

BLOOMSBURY, BLOOMSBURY ACADEMIC and the Diana logo are
trademarks of Bloomsbury Publishing Plc

First published in Great Britain 2022

Series design: Raven Design.
Cover image: Visitors sit on Heatherwick Studio's Spun Chairs outside the
"Inside Heatherwick Studio" exhibition showcasing the work of British Designer
Thomas Heatherwick at the PMQ Qube gallery in Hong Kong on September 17, 2015.
(© ANTHONY WALLACE/AFP/Getty Images)

A catalogue record for this book is available from the British Library.

A catalog record for this book is available from the Library of Congress.

ISBN: Pack: 978-1-4725-7789-4
        HB: 978-1-4725-7788-7

Series: The Cultural Histories Series

Typeset by Integra Software Services Pvt. Ltd.
Printed and bound in Great Britain

To find out more about our authors and books visit www.bloomsbury.com
and sign up for our newsletters.

For Marjan Hester Groot (1959–2019)
Scholar Teacher Friend

CONTENTS

LIST OF ILLUSTRATIONS

PLATES

FIGURES

SERIES PREFACE

A Cultural History of Furniture is a six-volume series examining the changing cultural framework within which furniture was designed, produced, and used, as well as the cultural construction of furniture itself, from antiquity through to the present day in the Western tradition. All the volumes follow the same structure: an editorial overview of the historical context of the period under consideration is followed by chapters written by specialists that each correspond to one of the following themes: design and motifs; makers, making, and materials; types and uses; the domestic setting; the public setting; exhibition and display; furniture and architecture; visual representations; and verbal representations. The configuration of the series means that readers can use the material synchronically or diachronically: an individual volume provides a thorough grounding in the furniture of a particular period while following one distinct theme across all volumes presents the reader with the evolution of a specific aspect of furniture over time. The six volumes divide the history of furniture in this way:

Volume 1: A Cultural History of Furniture in Antiquity (From the beginnings to 500 CE)

Volume 2: A Cultural History of Furniture in the Middle Ages and Renaissance (500–1500)

Volume 3: A Cultural History of Furniture in the Age of Exploration (1500–1700)

Volume 4: A Cultural History of Furniture in the Age of Enlightenment (1700–1800)

Volume 5: A Cultural History of Furniture in the Age of Empire and Industry (1800–1900)

Volume 6: A Cultural History of Furniture in the Modern Age (1900–twenty-first century)

Christina M. Anderson
General Editor

CONTRIBUTORS

Anja Baumhoff is Associate Professor of History of Art and Design in the Department for Theory at Hannover University, Germany. Her research explores the history of Modernism in the twentieth century and its gender relations, published in *The Gendered World of the Bauhaus: The Politics of Power at the Weimar Republic's Premier Art Institute, 1919–1932* (2001). Together with Magdalena Droste she edited *Mythos Bauhaus. Zwischen Selbsterfindung und Enthistorisierung* (2009). Her new book is called *Der Neue Mann und das Bauhaus. Männlichkeitskonzepte der klassischen Moderne* (forthcoming).

Antony Buxton is a practising furniture designer-maker and has taught for the Department for Continuing Education, University of Oxford, UK, since 1998 as tutor on weekly classes, international programs and the M.St. in Literature and Arts. His D.Phil. exploring non-elite domestic culture as revealed by seventeenth-century probate inventories from the Oxfordshire market town of Thame was subsequently published as *Domestic Culture in Early Modern England* (2015). He was coeditor (with Linda Hulin and Jane Anderson) of the interdisciplinary volume *InHabit: People, Place and Possessions* (2017).

Helena Chance is Associate Professor in Design Studies at Buckinghamshire New University, UK. Her research focuses on landscapes and interiors published in Laura Rattray (ed.), *Edith Wharton in Context* (2012), and on corporate landscapes in her book *The Factory in a Garden: A History of Corporate Landscapes from the Industrial to the Digital Age* (2017) and in *The International Journal of the History of Sport* and *Studies in the History of Gardens and Designed Landscapes*. She is currently researching the social landscape of industry in High Wycombe and district, which until recently was a leading center for furniture making.

Clive Edwards is Emeritus Professor of Design History at Loughborough University, UK. He has particular interests in furniture and interiors of the nineteenth and twentieth centuries. His works include monographs, as well as contributions to multiauthored works and journals on interiors, architecture, and home furnishings including *Victorian Furniture: Technology and Design* (1993); *Twentieth Century Furniture: Materials, Manufacture and Markets* (1994); *Furniture Materials, Trades and Techniques* (2001); *Turning Houses into Homes* (2005); *Le Commerce du Luxe* (2015), and Deirdre H. McMahon and Janet C. Myers (eds.), *The Objects and Textures of Everyday Life in Imperial Britain* (2016).

†**Marjan Groot** was Associate Professor at Vrije Universiteit Amsterdam, the Netherlands, where she taught the history and theory of design and decorative arts. Some recent publications are *MOMOWO: Women Designers, Craftswomen, Architects and Engineers between 1918 and 1945* (e-book 2017, with Helena Seražin); *Living in the Amsterdam School. Designs for the Interior 1910–1930* (2016, with Ingeborg de Roode); and "Tokyo Halloween on the Street: Japanese Dressing Up between Bricolage and Authenticity," in *Dress: Journal of the Costume Society of America* (2017, with Takagi, Yoko).

Trevor Keeble is Professor and Dean in Faculty of Creative and Cultural Industries at the University of Portsmouth, UK. His research and supervision focus on nineteenth- and twentieth-century design, architecture, and material culture. As a founding member of the Modern Interiors Research Centre (Kingston University), he has contributed to a number of international conferences and publications including *Fashion, Performance and the Modern Interior* (2011), *Designing the Modern Interior* (2008), and *The Modern Period Room* (2006). Recent publications have explored the relationship between objects, narrative, and homemaking; the rise of Victorian furnishers and furniture shops; and furniture design since 1900.

Claire I.R. O'Mahony is Associate Professor of History of Art and Design in the Department for Continuing Education, University of Oxford, UK, where she founded and directs the M.St. in the History of Design. She is Chair of the Design History Society and an Editor of the *Journal of Design History*. Her research explores French decoration since 1870, published in *Brunel and the Art of Invention* (2006); *Symbolist Objects: Materiality and Subjectivity at the Fin de siècle* (2009); David Evans and Kate Griffiths (eds.), *Institutions and Power in Nineteenth-Century French Literature and Culture* (2011); Marta Filipová (ed.), *Cultures of International Exhibitions 1840–1940: Great Exhibitions in the Margins* (2015); and articles in *The Journal of War and Culture Studies* and *The Journal of Modern Craft*.

Penny Sparke is Professor of Design History at Kingston University, London, UK. She studied French Literature at the University of Sussex from 1967 to 1971 and was awarded her Ph.D. in Design History from Brighton Polytechnic in 1975. She taught Design History at Brighton Polytechnic (1975–82) and the Royal College of Art (1982–99). She has given keynote addresses, curated exhibitions, and broadcast and published widely. Her publications include *As Long as It's Pink: The Sexual Politics of Taste* (1995); *Elsie de Wolfe: The Birth of Modern Interior Decoration* (2005); and *The Modern Interior* (2008).

Gregory Votolato is an architect, curator, teacher, and writer on design, technology, and culture. He trained as an architect at the Rhode Island School of Design and took degrees at Boston University and Pratt Institute before gaining his doctorate at Teesside University, UK. He is Emeritus Professor of Design History at Buckinghamshire New University and lectures at the Royal College of Art and the Victoria and Albert Museum in London and the University of Oxford. His publications include *American Design in the Twentieth Century* (1998), *Transport Design: A Travel History* (2007), *Ship* (2012), and *Car* (2015).

Introduction

CLAIRE I.R. O'MAHONY

PRIVATE AND PUBLIC PARADIGMS

It is so practical; everything connects.
—Mme Arpel in *Mon Oncle* (Dir. Jacques Tati, 1958)

How we furnish where we dwell, toil, and play provides evocative traces of both the individual personalities who inhabit these places and wider society. Furniture in the twentieth century embodies the transformations of private and public life in the modern age brought about by adjustments in social conditions, new materials and manufacturing techniques, and shifting meanings of historical and new styles. Why we choose our furniture and how we use it, its representation in words and images, reveal the inheritance and rejection of cultural habits and conventions as well as new fashions, personal taste, and repurposing. In the 1958 film *Mon Oncle*, when Monsieur and Madame Charles Arpel return to their modern suburban villa after an evening out they discover that their relative Monsieur Hulot has disrupted the mid-century chic of their bourgeois lifestyle, literally turning their contemporary sofa on its side in a search for comfort in this sterile modernist interior.[1] The imaginative parodies of furniture invented by Jacques Lagrange (1917–95) in dialogue with the director Jacques Tati (1907–82) for the film suggest some of this volume's frameworks for undertaking a cultural history of furniture design in the twentieth century and beyond (Plate 1). *Mon Oncle* satirizes not only the typologies and appearance of contemporary furniture, but also the social mores and geopolitics these furnishings force sitters to negotiate. Whilst looking after the Arpel's son Gérard, the eponymous uncle humanizes the soulless elegance of their fashionable residence. In its improvised, inverted position, the "green bean" sofa upon which the uncle sleeps with abandon achieves a genuinely ergonomic organicism resonant with the famous modernist photograph of Charlotte Perriand (1903–99) at her ease on the "B306" chaise longue that she designed with Le Corbusier (1887–1965). Skeletal contemporary chairs and a lamp are clothed in the nostalgia of Hulot's archetypal bedraggled mackintosh, hat, and umbrella, whilst one imagines that the clutter of his informal pleasures suffuse this clinical space with the pervasive earthy scent of his pipe's fading embers and his striped-stocking feet alongside cast-off shoes. The rumble of the uncle's snores and his carefree dreaming posture contrasts with the staccato metallic clack of Madame's disapproving high-heeled march across her hygienic, white floor tiles. The film inspired international popularity and controversy in equal measure, winning the Best Foreign Film Oscar in 1959 alongside accusations of Tati's anticlerical and left-wing tendencies (Bellos 2012: 212–39).[2] Contemporary audiences recognized the serious play of these insightful spoofs of iconic furnishing. Expressing more than period style, they wistfully embodied anxieties about the increasing permeability of public and private life as well as the complexity of postwar relations between Europe and America.

The villa Arpel revels in imagining the challenges of attempting to reside in the "machine for living in" theorized by Le Corbusier. The landscape design dictates circumambulation rather than welcoming entry to the house. The anxieties of American technocracy are sounded in the clanging, automated furnishing of kitchen cabinets and a garage door that terrorize and imprison the family, whilst the silhouettes of the Arpels in the ocean-liner style porthole windows become eyes of searchlight surveillance at night (Chion 2006: 86–8). Only metal chairs with "Eiffel Tower" substructures and wire-mesh seats popularized by American contemporary chair designers travel easily between the villa's interior and exterior zones.[3] The spoof villa Arpel models three paradigms of modern furnishing that inform this volume: early twentieth-century modernist prototypes and their utopian tropes; mass-produced product consumption at mid-century; and finally, postmodern homages and parodies of both precedents. A spate of twenty-first-century exhibitions inspired by *Mon Oncle*'s gentle satire of modern furnishing demonstrates the persistence of its meditations upon modern interiority.[4]

Despite Madame Arpel's proud assertion to all guests upon entering the house "C'est si pratique; tout communique" (It is so practical; everything connects), the fashionably uncomfortable furnishing achieves neither streamlined, modernist functionality nor the intimate connection associated with the elaborate inherited furniture of a traditional family home. The low, open-seated, wire-mesh chairs in which guests flail about gracelessly also appear in the director's office at Plastac, Monsieur Arpel's employer, where their awkwardness reinforces Monsieur Arpel's lesser middle-management status in an American-style corporate hierarchy. The controlling structures of the modern workplace and home coalesce in the performance of social rituals of domination between corporate ranks as well as rival feminine neighbors amidst this vertiginous furniture. The addition of feminized features to Monsieur's chair, a rocking base and over-bright canary upholstery, ensures it fails to express the identity of the *pater familias* traditionally imbedded in the easy chair; he never appears truly at home. Erving Goffman's 1959 sociological study, *The Presentation of Self in Everyday Life*, illuminates how furnishings were recognized as vital elements in the performance of personality in twentieth-century society: "furniture, décor, physical layout and other background items [...] supply the scenery and stage props for the spate of human action played out before, within, or upon it" (cited in Lees-Maffei 2014: 90). The furniture of the villa Arpel tells us a great deal about postwar reconstruction and contemporary society during what the economist Jean Fourastié (1907–90) called France's "30 glorious years" proposing questions that a cultural history of furniture should investigate (Fourastié 1979; Rudolph 2014, 2015). To what extent did modernity or historicism dominate the furnishing tastes of the twentieth century? How did furniture help to negotiate rival longings for privacy and community both in contemporary dwelling and public space? What identities and ideologies did furniture communicate and by what material and discursive means?

For the French Pavilion at the 2014 Venice Biennale devised under his aegis, the architectural historian Jean-Louis Cohen (1949–) responded to the overall brief of "Fundamentals" by curating a four-room installation entitled "Modernity: promise or a menace?" (Larrochelle 2014). In devising homages to *Mon Oncle*'s glacial, parodic inventions alongside Jean Prouvé's (1901–84) austere yet humane furniture designs for mass production in war-torn Europe and Africa, Cohen attended to modern furniture's utopian aspirations and the limits of their realization. The multimedia installation also deployed diverse modes of historical evidence from the archive, library, marketplace, cinema, and web that underpin such interpretations. This volume investigates how the conception, production, dissemination, and consumption of furniture affords distinctive insights into the cultural history of the twentieth century, demonstrating that the materiality, aesthetics, and ideologies of furnishing were manifestations of the transforming social conditions of the modern age (Walker 1989).

TOWARD A CULTURAL HISTORY OF FURNITURE

The cultural history of furniture draws upon analysis of the embodied experience of physical artifacts and scholarship from a gallimaufry of contrasting academic disciplinary traditions. Each of the chapters in this volume juxtaposes the material effects of objects with the intellectual propositions of primary and secondary sources by and about designers, makers, and users, studies of period and national style traditions, investigations of furniture typologies and theorizations of consumption and society to inform our understanding of how furniture embodies the character of our age. This project builds upon the work of esteemed forebears, not only invoking but also questioning the efficacy of these intellectual traditions to the task at hand. Before delving deeper into preliminary examples of the thematics that frame the volume, it behooves the cultural historian of furniture to reflect upon what core sources and research methods best support its specific aims and case studies.

The historical particularity of the primary source, be it textual or tangible, affords the most immediate glimpse of the past (Burke 2001, [2004] 2015). Essential, if instrumental, evidence about materials, costs, distribution, and consumption resides in the objects themselves and the archives of makers, sellers, and public and private custodians of furniture. The rhetoric used to characterize furniture in designers' own theorizations of their practice, critics' discourse as well as its popular dissemination and subversion through advice literature, fictional writing, cinematography, and advertising also offer "eyewitness" perspectives on a case study often with the added enrichment for the cultural historian of denser textures of interpretable language. By way of example, the machine age is a defining conceptualization of the cultural history of modernity; how might modern furniture have expressed, disguised, rebuffed, or ignored such a construct (Smith 1993; Rutsky 1999; Wilk 2006a)? Considering the terminology deployed or invented by designers, manufacturers, or retailers to identify their furniture can illuminate how the object manifests cultural histories of the shifting reception of modern technology. Josef Hoffmann (1870–1956) named a design for an adjustable steam-bent beech wood frame armchair with geometric turned elements and punched plywood panels: "model 670: *Sitzmaschine* (a machine for sitting in)" (Museum of Modern Art [1999] 2004: 56) (Plate 2). Reclining chairs had been made for ease and convalescence since the seventeenth century; the "Morris" chair designed by Philip Webb (1831–1915) after Morris, Faulkner and Co. manager George Warrington Taylor's (1838–70) sketch of an example found in Ephraim Colman's carpenter's shop is also usually cited as a precedent (Campbell 1999: 335; Andrews 2005: 32). Hoffmann's 1904 design commissioned for the Purkersdorf Sanatorium sits within this historical typology. Its nomenclature, manufacturing, and exhibition history also captures the multivalence of psychiatric and design debates particular to *fin de siècle* Vienna (Schorske 1980; Gronberg 2007). The invocation of "machine" distanced period associations with the typology of a reclining chair, instead bestowing a technological and medical aura upon it, which resonated with the somatic psychiatric methodologies of Richard von Krafft-Ebing (1840–1902), Director of the Purkersdorf Sanatorium and author of *Pychopathia Sexualis* of 1886

(Topp 1997). The chair's hygiene, stabilizing rationality and elegance formed part of the Purkersdorf curative process. The sanatorium was a *gesamtkunstwerk* (total project) for which the Wiener Werkstætte workshops provided every element of furnishing from public spaces for leisure, dining, and treatment to private bedrooms. The *Sitzmaschine* declares its alliance with bentwood mass-production techniques originally proliferated by the firm of Michael Thonet (1796–1871), discussed in more detail in the preceding volume, but its specific manufacture by Jacob and Joseph Kohn for the sanatorium involved handwork to create the elegant simplicity of the ball stops that control the back's position (Lizon 1997: 131–2). When shown in the 1909 *Kunstschau* (Vienna Arts Show), the chair was not presented as a medical tool but rather was designated as being destined for a "country house" signaling the fluidity of inflections the same piece of furniture could connote. Thus, the material and immaterial primary evidence of the physical properties and nomenclature of the *Sitzmaschine* suggest the interconnectedness between reputedly polarized rival cultures of technology and craft in early twentieth-century furniture design and manufacturing nuancing our understanding of not only this particular chair and the Wiener Werkstætte workshops but also the ways in which furnishing imparts a cultural history of debates about mental health.

In comparable ways, many interwar and mid-century designers and manufacturers utilized a technical nomenclature of acronyms for their furniture designs such as the Eames's molded plywood "LCW" (lounge chair wood) of 1945 (Victoria and Albert Museum [hereafter V&A], W.17-1989) (Figure 2.3) or Marcel Breuer's (1902–81) tubular steel "B3" of 1925 (V&A, W.2-2005). Breuer's use of an acronym is evocative of his claims for the spatiality of metal furniture in the creation of new ways of life: "It is styleless [...]. The new space should not represent a self-portrait of the architect nor from the outset the composure of the soul of its individual user" (Breuer [1928] 2012: 224). However, having been associated with the Masters' houses at the Bauhaus, the "B3" was reissued in the 1960s by the firm Gavina and marketed as the "Wassily" chair in honor of Breuer's colleague at the Bauhaus and early advocate for the chair, the painter Wassily Kandinsky (1866–1944). Despite Breuer's admonitions against furniture representing the designer or user, the name "Wassily" has fundamentally supplanted Breuer's original depersonalizing acronym. The "B3" acronym also implied that serial mechanized production had replaced handicraft. However, the various early permutations of the chair's actual manufacture in the interwar years were still reliant upon bespoke shaping (by Mannesmann rather than the industrial processes of the Adler bicycle firm that Breuer originally approached) as well as hand welding and polishing by a local plumber. The work flow was streamlined and simplified with the use of screws and fewer repositioned elements when manufactured in 1926 by Standard Möbel and in 1929 by Thonet (Vegesack 1996: 25). The advent of the name "Wassily" relocated the allure of the chair in heroic modernist biography rather than the utopian, if stark, anonymity of the "B3" acronym. Such rhetorical effects extend beyond the realm of designers' pronouncements; traditions of scholarly vocabulary about furnishing also continue to play an important part in the cultural history of modern furnishing. A contested mobility implicit within the French vocabulary for furnishing ("meubles" are movable objects within unmovable buildings, "immeubles") became infused with the liberation and exigencies of twentieth-century nomadic lifestyles, which abandoned nineteenth-century tastes for upholstered solidity and historicist style in favor of an "inherent potential for disassembly, mobility, conversion and re-use" (Frampton 1998: 58).

Archival and physical evidence, individualist biography, and aesthetic writing attest to the legacy of monographic traditions of historical, art historical, and literary scholarship that underpin the task of cultural history. Learned societies and their journals have complemented the work of museum curators and auction houses in documenting modern furniture.[5] This groundwork of establishing features of period style and authorship inform this volume (Praz 1964). However, it attempts to locate these knowledges within the methodological reconceptualizations proposed by design history in the last decades of the twentieth century (Forty 1986; Walker 1989; Fallen 2010; Sparke and Massey 2013). Furniture scholarship in the hands of design historians has progressed connoisseurship and biography into the aims of cultural history (Sparke 1986b; Auslander 1998; Cranz 2000; Massey 2011). Analysis of the role of networks of making and use in the life of the furnished object in the chapters that follow demonstrates the pertinence of sociological research methods particularly associated with both technology and material culture studies for a cultural history of furniture (Miller 1987; Brown 2004; Latour 2005; Bijker 2012).

This interdisciplinary strategy encourages the search for critical discourses about furniture across a wide variety of textual forms and a spectrum of elite and populist sites of dissemination. To return to our task of assessing the relationships between the machine age and furniture, the theorizations published by iconic modernists such as Le Corbusier (Charles Jeanneret, 1887–1965) do provide vital insights into how this dialogue was conceived. His polemics about modern furniture were first disseminated in the journal he founded with Amedée Ozenfant (1886–1966) and Paul Dermée (1886–1951) *L'Esprit Nouveau* (The New Spirit) then collected as an anthology *The Decorative Art of Today* of 1925 (Le Corbusier 1925; Eliel et al. 2001). Modernity of conception, materials, and production techniques were promulgated through international exhibitions and publications, which shaped the dominant frameworks of histories of twentieth-century design. Canonical sources, such as *Pioneers of the Modern Movement: William Morris to Walter Gropius* (1936) by Nikolaus Pevsner (1902–83) and *Theory and Design in the First Machine Age* (1960) by Reyner Banham (1922–88), constructed evolutionary historical models of exemplary designers progressing toward the modernist ideal of "The International Style," a nomenclature deriving from a paradigmatic architecture exhibition of 1932 curated by Alfred H. Barr (1902–81) at New York's Museum of Modern Art (Whiteley 2003). However, these teleological paradigms and their canon of machine age case studies have occluded so much fascinating modern furniture production: surviving predilections for historical pieces, period styles, handicraft, anonymous mass production, recycling, etc. The ascendancy of late twentieth-century feminist design history and new perspectives within the history of interiors ensured that the gender politics of design, consumption, and taste has gained a more secure place in the canon and research methods of cultural history (Sparke 2005; Lees-Maffei 2014). Although many careers still await examination, cooperative international research projects such as "Women's creativity since the Modern Movement (Mo Mo Wo)" co-funded by the Creative Europe Programme continue to progress knowledge and analysis of femininity and furnishing (Mo Mo Wo n.d.). Business history, anthropology, and social geography have also made important contributions in redressing the balance of attention from elite named designer pieces to a diversity of case studies illuminating the vital role of anonymous makers and industrial production (Sharp, Benton, and Campbell Cole 1977; Edwards 1994, 2014; Jackson 2013; Reimer and Pinch 2013). More global perspectives, analyses of amateur craft, recycling, and homelessness are opening up new frameworks for the cultural history of furniture amidst the reformulation of university syllabi and publishers' lists to embrace world history, everyday things, and sustainability in the twenty-first century (Carlano and Sumberg 2006; Sand 2013; Knott 2015; End Furniture Poverty n.d.) (Plate 17).

Governmental reports, advice on furnishing in popular books, magazines, radio and television programs as well as the fictive realms of literary or cinematic representations provide rich evidence of a broader spectrum of identity politics manifested in twentieth-century style and taste. A negotiation of the dialectics between industry and craft and the persistence of historicism coexisted alongside machine-age paradigms. Furnishing taste is positioned as a pedagogic task of dissemination as much as a national character or innate personality trait. Roger Fry's "Scheme for Workshops of Decorative Design in Industry," an appendix in the Board of Trade report on the Royal Academy Art and Industry exhibition, called for "Laboratories for Design" (1932: 44–9) where a new alliance of artists, craftsmen, and manufacturers would foster contemporary furniture design. He proposes that this industrial cooperation operate in tandem with the creative education of school children to instill an understanding of modern design taste and color from their earliest years. Gordon Russell and Jacques Groag even contributed the children's book *The Story of Furniture* to the task (1947). An American popular advice book, *Priscilla Home Furnishing Book*, opens with an analogous meditation that "The only way is by education [...] good taste is never a natural endowment,—it is always acquired" (Priscilla Publishing Co. 1925: 1).[6] Homemakers are instructed to create an environment of "suitability and simplicity" for their children and husbands. The Arpel household could have benefited from *Priscilla*'s advice on the selection of an "easy chair" for the living room that could fulfill the goals of home furnishing: "[to] express two dominant qualities,—comfort and individuality." The gender politics of the discussion is intriguing. Whilst recognizing that the head of house in this interwar moment might not be a patriarch, "we'll assume that in this one instance the head of home is 'father',", nonetheless, the admonishments are largely against any feminine predilections to prioritize decorative unity by purchasing a "three piece suite" or an "adorable antique," at the cost of comfort (given the taller proportions and informal posture of modern bodies). The genuine easy chair must be individually suited:

> That chair is surcharged with the personality of the user [...]. It was chosen for father and by father and so it possesses the individuality of "father." Here in this one chair you may mark the beginnings of both comfort and individuality in this living room.
>
> (Priscilla Publishing Co. 1925: 102)

This urge for individual comfort and the projection of identity remained an imperative for modern furniture throughout the twentieth century, but was conceived in many contrasting ways, embracing inherited period pieces as well as the integrated suites against which *Priscilla* admonished (Plate 31).

Priscilla's recognition of the performance of identity through furnishing would be well served by the surveying techniques and assessments of the embodied nature of experience proposed by sociological methodologies seeking to extend cultural history beyond quantitative data and elite discourse. Pierre Bourdieu's influential juxtaposition of qualitative and quantitative research in his investigation of "distinction" also informs the multivalent approaches adopted in this volume:

> If a group's whole lifestyle can be read off from the style it adopts in furnishing or clothing, this is not only because these properties are the objectification of the economic and cultural necessity which determined their selection, but also the social relations objectified in familiar objects, in their luxury or poverty, their "distinction" or "vulgarity", their "beauty" or "ugliness", impress themselves through bodily experience which may be as profoundly unconscious as the quiet caress of beige carpets or the thin clamminess of tattered garish linoleum.
>
> (Bourdieu 1979 cited in Lees-Maffei 2014: 92)

Bourdieu's admonition about the importance of seeking to capture the ephemerality of "social relations" and "bodily experience" alerts the cultural historian of furniture to the pursuit of interpretation, which may elude exclusively factual historical methods. The model of cultural history proposed in this volume explores the intersections of private and public forces; financial and ideological power as well as psychological and corporeal sensations to which furniture is a testament.

MEMORY AND MASS CULTURES

The projection of identity was a leitmotif of twentieth-century aesthetic discourse about furnishing. "On Reading Ruskin," the preface to Marcel Proust's (1871–1922) French translation of John Ruskin's (1819–1900) *Sesame and Lillies* (1865) proposes an arresting evocation of the ways in which memory inhabits inherited furnishings:

> all those things which not only could not answer any of my needs, but were even an impediment, however slight, to their satisfaction, which evidently had never been placed there for someone's use, people my room with thoughts somehow personal, with that air of predilection, of having chosen to live there and delighting in it, which often the trees in a clearing and the flowers on the road sides or on old walls have. They filled it with a silent and different life, with a mystery in which my person found itself lost and charmed at the same time.
>
> (Proust [1906] 1987: 105)

For Proust, the sympathetic mystery of ancestral personalities that inhabit admittedly ill-suited pieces create the sense of dwelling essential to domesticity. A contemporary German meditation on the place of modern handicraft aligned this animated character in furnishing to the task of nation-building through the family home. Artistic societies such as the Dürer League and *Kunstwart*, a cultural journal founded by a poet-publisher Ferdinand Avenarius (1856–1923), sought to educate the German public, especially women responsible for decorating the home, to recognize and to abhor "kitsch," be it penny-dreadful pulp fiction or hideous household ornaments (Jenkins 1996).[7] The journal's "Masterpieces for the German Home" albums were launched in 1900, providing Old Master and modern artworks with accompanying edifying text for 25 pfennig (or free to poorer households) to educate the German public about art (by 1906 a choice of 156 images were available). The aesthetically principled liberal politician Friedrich Naumann (1860–1919) wrote an accompanying pamphlet entitled "The Spirit in the Furniture" in 1909, which adopts the form of an epistolary exchange between a newlywed niece and her uncle about how to furnish the marital home. The avuncular advice warns against mass-produced factory furniture:

Only one thing would be missing, the spirit in the furniture. The things have no soul. They don't speak; they don't love us, they can stand tomorrow in someone else's living room, they don't impress anything on our children, they are nothing but "furniture" that means objects that are meant to be shoved here and there.

(Naumann 1909 quoted in Jenkins 1996: 139)

Guided by this wisdom, her bridegroom Ernst discerns the appropriate pieces typified by the advertisements for furniture designed by Richard Rimmerschmid, which appear at the end of the pamphlet. The uncle praises the couple's agency in understanding and forging a cultural public sphere for the nation through the furnishing of their future home: "You have understood something many older people than you have not yet understood: the deep connection between the character of the furniture and the character of the people" (Naumann 1909 quoted in Jenkins 1996: 139–40). Where Proust wistfully embraces the traces of family memory inhabiting his inherited furniture, Naumann's newlyweds participate in the "invention" of the nation through their discerning consumption of well-made, new German furniture (Hobsbawm and Ranger 1983).

The role of furnishing in the projection of national identity and political ideology in the twentieth century would take on particular acuity amidst the pressures of economic depression and global conflict. As the program of a 1940 Museum of Modern Art competition for "organic" furniture design recognized whilst Europe plunged into another world war: "Economics and politics and the fate of nations in war and peace are all affected by the vast recent changes in the equipment of man [...] the forms of our furniture should be determined by our way of life" (Noyes 1941: 4). Fascist regimes employed spectacular display to enhance the persuasiveness of their ideology. Both Benito Mussolini (1883–1945) and Adolf Hitler (1889–1945) embraced modernist classical idioms to furnish their regime's new architecture be it a sport's ground, government bureaucratic building, or an official residence. Through elaborate temporary installations, such as the 1933 "Away with Kitsch" exhibition designed by the Deutsche Werkbund in Cologne or the displays organized by the Beauty of Labor Bureau directed by Albert Speer (1905–81) celebrating ideal factory environments as well as the notorious juxtaposition of Nazi and Soviet pavilions in the 1937 Paris exposition, modern commodities including furniture articulated the cultural credentials of brutal oppressive fascist regimes (Hayward Gallery 1995: 58–119; Betts 2007: 23–72). An Italian fascist variation of the elegant tubular furniture typically associated with the utopian politics and aesthetics of the Bauhaus proved equally effective in bridging tensions between the assertion of total state authority and the seduction of a mass public through consumer opportunities promulgated by the regime. The constraints of autarchy resulting from the League of Nations' sanctions imposed after Mussolini's invasion of Abyssinia meant the bauxite-rich regime celebrated aluminum as a particularly attractive material through which to imagine a shiny, modern industrial future for the new fascist empire. Both luxury, modernist furnishing, and more attainable standardized designs were displayed in the Italian Housing and Interior Design exhibitions of 1933 and 1936, exemplifying the regime's astute determination to encompass rival constituencies (Rusconi and Zanchetti 2013: 158–9, 164–7).

The furnishings designed by the architect Giuseppe Terragni (1904–43) for the offices and meeting rooms of the Casa del Fascio (1932–6), the party headquarters in Como, embodied the contradictory ideological associations of styles, materials, and spatiality at the heart of Italian fascism (Schumaker 1991; Rifkind 2012) (Plate 3). This spectacular modernist building designed by Terragni positioned Fascist Party users within a didactic environment that sought to reconcile the regime's ideological fiction of a collectivist dictatorship. Terragni and Mario Radice (1898–1987) negotiated these geopolitical problematics through their design solutions that integrated the regime's rival obsessions with ancient imperial precedents, devotional practice, and technological futures. The transparency of the building's glass walls and fenestration fostered the illusion of openness and belonging, immersing the crowd, the party, and the leader into a universalizing Futurist energy articulated in the quotations from Mussolini's 1932 *The Doctrine of Fascism*, which Terragni and Mario Radice (1898–1987) had incised into the marble walls (Radice 1936 cited in Rifkind 2012: 183). A special issue of the architectural journal *Quadrante* in 1936 provides unique visual and textual primary evidence about the site and its furnishing. In the director's conference room, modernity and craft skill are both demonstrated in the technical miracles of the conference table. A one centimeter thick crystal top encased in a rosewood frame (with niches for fascist relics) glided above a seven meter chromed white copper tubular substructure. Integrated into the wall directly opposite the head of the director's table (where no chair is positioned and the aluminum foot rest bar is interrupted), a larger than life photomontage of Mussolini ensured the leader was always symbolically present, standing actively in control of the room's meetings (Schumaker 1991: 163; Rifkind 2012: 181–3). In his article in *Quadrante*, Terragni (1936: 5–27) champions the modern Italian artisans who made the windows, tables, and chairs of the Casa del Fascio as a microcosm of fascist collective selfhood under autarchy. He rejoices that "the unexpected and glorious event, the war in Africa (and consequent economic siege)" meant he relied solely upon local workmen who created the "incredible crystal which is the table surface in the director's salon." Having "asked for materials in dimensions or thicknesses that would have tried the best and most organized foreign industries" he affirms how the materiality of making and furnishing connect the artisan, the crowd, and the Duce:

> The moving quality of the work is no longer the rhetorical figure with a spade or pick on his shoulder [...]. It resides rather in acknowledging the thousands and thousands of black-shirted citizens amassed in front of the Casa del Fascio to hear the voice of their leader announce to Italians and foreigners the advent of Empire. It is the throng where a fellow smiling, indicates to his comrades that particular window or slab of marble; and surely he is confiding with simplicity and satisfaction that he, too, worked there, and the Casa del Fascio, if only in small part, is to his credit too.
> (Schumaker 1991: 151, translated by Deborah Dolinski)

This physical integration of the state and the individual within the Casa del Fascio and its interiors was also expressed in the embodied interactions required by the furniture. The intrinsic subjugation of the individual to authority was expressed through the hierarchical taxonomy of the furnishing for the functions of distinct spaces. The authority of the leader and its dissemination through party officials in the director's conference room was signaled in the naming of the *Benita* chair. Its luxurious green-leather upholstery referenced historical traditions of elite seating types, but the metal substructure reconfigures the experience of sitting on the chair to the demands of fascist ideology. The mass and scale of the *Benita* club chair perhaps occludes awareness of the suspended space between the tubular frame of the back and the seat. Both the *Benita* and the *Lariana*, a more modest high-backed desk chair utilized by lesser ranks in office spaces, required a tensed, upright posture from its sitters, imposing the regime's prescriptions to physical dynamism even on the corporeal act of sitting (Armanni 1998: 121–5).[8]

The efficacy with which furniture can project internal selves and external relationships extends beyond Proustian reverie or political ideology into the dystopian cultures of anonymity and consumerist spectacle of the twenty-first century. As "IKEA Boy," the protagonist in Chuck Palahniuk's 1999 *Fight Club*, divulges, the multinational corporation's furniture catalog had replaced pornography as the diversion found in his bathroom: "I'd flip through catalogs and wonder [...] which dining set defines me as a person?" The mourning he expresses when his apartment is destroyed articulates the equation of the consumption of furnishing and selfhood: "I loved every stick of furniture. That was my whole life. Everything, the lamps, the chairs, the rugs were me [...]. It was me that was blown up" (cited in Kristoffersson and Jewson 2014: 166) (Plate 32). Balanced vertiginously between individual expression and collective societal relations, furniture captures the volatility of identity intrinsic to modernity.

THE POWER OF PLAY: FURNISHING PRIVATE AND PUBLIC ENVIRONMENTS

The ways in which furniture signifies power and responsibility is encoded in language, space, and corporeality. To be a "Chair" is to manage a group meeting or to have garnered academic rank. In an interactive public sculpture to commemorate the 800th anniversary of the signing of the Magna Carta at Runnymede, Hew Locke's *The Jurors*, a set of twelve bronze chairs, are incised with representations of "struggles for freedom, rule of law and equal rights" (Art at Runnymede n.d.). To sit upon them is to take part, responsibility, a position. Leisure activities such as dining also involve hierarchies or their disruption. The decision by the founders of Kellogg College to abandon the University of Oxford's tradition of the "High table" where the Master and Fellows sit aloof from their students, and instead to sit at communal tables dining together embodies the culture of inclusion striven for by this new graduate college. Furniture can also embrace the pleasures and perils of play to transform conventions. How might furniture provide traces of the cultural history of the ephemeral pursuit of play?. The many important furnishing projects for playgrounds, game rooms, cinemas, restaurants, and social zones within workplaces provide insights into how these environments mediate perceived polarities of domestic and public life (Plate 4). Modern designers, educators, governments, and industry wrestled with the questions of how the spaces and equipment of children's play might help to forge a better society (Kinchin and O'Connor 2012; Ogata 2013). One of many collaborations with Creative Playthings Inc. was a 1954 Museum of Modern Art playground sculpture competition that attracted 360 entries.[9] A new special division "Play Sculptures" marketed structures such as the biomorphic environment known as the "Egg" designed by Egøn Möller-Nielsen (1915–59) providing a place of safety and inspiration for urban children's play.[10]

Monsieur Hulot delights us by unwittingly undermining the technocratic constraint of contemporary furnishing intruding upon domestic mores; much contemporary furniture purposefully encourages his anarchic incapacity to internalize received codes of "distinction." Playful furnishing for adult spaces is a central manifestation of postmodernity where parody and unconventional spatiality invites us to reassesses the social boundaries that define the permeability of function and security within public interiors. Penson's 2012 designs for Google's Super HQ in London's Covent Garden propose a reconceptualization of creative work space where the booths of the "Hedge Your Bets" roof garden provide fresh air and private shelter whilst tassel-bedecked wing-chairs appropriate the intimate comfort of the "Granny flat." The stacked seating of upholstered built-in settles in some of the meeting rooms requires choices about privacy and sociability as in cinemas and the pub. The ironic claustrophobia of a green-padded wall treatment culminating in submarine-lock doors in a meeting room furnished with standard tables and chairs perhaps also acknowledges dystopian surveillance and containment within this corporate play environment (Penson n.d.). Such postmodern meditations on the quixotic tensions between individual and collective encounter in contemporary life resonate across much twentieth-century furniture.

Play and its furnishings provide evocative traces of the multivalent relationships between the modern self and society. The billiard table in the Villa la Sapinière embodies not only the creative partnerships between designers and patrons or style debates at the dawn of the twentieth century, but also how important examining the use of furniture is in researching its cultural history. The table resides amidst a symphony of white and gold neo-rococo decoration, the apogee of the elite "gesamtkunstwerk" championed by Art Nouveau designers and purchased by an affluent transnational clientele outwith traditional aristocratic circles (Long 2009).[11] The interior balances upon the stylistic cusp of 1900 where a rococo revival, Art Nouveau organicism and emergent modernist simplification vied for preeminence (Musée D'Orsay 2008: 154–8, 172–4). The design of the billiard room was coordinated by Félix Bracquemond (1833–1919) who devised the ornament of the sculpted wood and silk-embroidered wall treatments; the furniture was created by Alexandre Charpentier (1856–1909) surrounded by mural and ceiling painting by Jules Chéret (1836–1932) all in consultation with the Vitta family. The "bijou" eight foot billiard table is the focal point of the interior's decorative synthesis. However, this confection of wood, slate, marble, cloth, gilded bronze, and paint testifies not only to the networks of designers, crafts people, patrons, and critics involved in modern furniture but also to the overlooked cultural history of play enacted by the use of the table.

The billiard room furnishings were widely disseminated through display in national exhibitions as well as published illustrations. In numerous articles in the art press and a luxury commemorative volume issued in an edition of 200, Roger Marx argued these furnishings embodied a collaborative relationship between designers and patrons, which forged a "social art" suited to the modern age (Marx 1913; Froissart Pezone and Méneux 2006: 229; Bouillon 2014: 74–5). The artful interior design photography of the 1902 illustration in his article provides vital aesthetic insights but nonetheless also denatures the billiard table in the absence of players and play, neglecting the furniture's active use (Plate 5). To reintroduce traces of the animated domestic leisure enjoyed amidst these objects of play, one might look to the patron's family history found in public records, private correspondence, and oral history (Archives Nationales, Fanny Vitta Foà dossier n.d.). Examining the history of billiard furniture and its role in the sociability of the game can also help in repopulating these representations with the table's intended function.

The creative exchanges amongst the three artist-designers and Baron Joseph Raphaël Vitta (1860–1942) are well documented in secondary scholarship about the billiard room (Bouillon 1979; Weisberg 1979; Palais de Lumière 2014).[12] However, considering who used the table, whether it was the centerpiece of a preserve of exclusively male fantasy and creativity, or rather a space equally redolent with the imagination of the women of the family has yet to be attempted. Glimpses of the lives of the female members of the household, Baroness Hélène Vitta (née Oppenheimer 1837–1901), her daughter Fanny Foà (née Vitta 1870–1952), and Joseph Vitta's working-class companion, later wife, Malvina Bléquette (1881–1948), discernible in private correspondence and the official documentation of the rituals of marriage and death invites reflection about their role in the life of the table (Nimmen 2014). The marriage record of Fanny Vitta to the renowned explorer Edouard Foà (1862–1901) indicates an overlooked matrilineal dimension to the authorship and ownership of the villa, which invites a more inclusive interpretation of the sculpted feminine motifs of the billiard table.[13] In the certification of the ceremony held on September 18, 1899, in the Villa la Sapinière presided over by the Rabbi Lévy Kahn, Hélène Vitta attests as Fanny Vitta's surviving parent that her daughter would be the primary resident of Evian-les-Bains, indicative of Hélène's formal bequest of the Villa la Sapinière to her daughter upon her death in 1901 (Archives Nationales 1870).[14] If understood solely as elements of a private billiard room for the Baron, the tactility of the nude and draped female figures sculpted in high- and low-relief bronze by Charpentier for the doorplates and the billiard table's gilt-bronze scoring devices and leg ornaments perhaps speak with uncomfortable singularity to male erotic desire. However, the presence of a sculpture studio for Fanny in the villa, indicating her direct involvement in the medium and the agency of both Fanny and Hélène Vitta in commissioning other sculpted elements of the interior design, opens up an interpretation of the billiard room as space where men and women partake of communal authorship, ownership, and play. Chéret's murals and ceiling paintings of the theatrical carnival of Montmartrois "chérettes" and pierrots are suggestive of Malvina Vitta's aspirations to a life on the stage before her lifelong relationship with Joseph Vitta and their joint friendship with the artist (Bargiel 2014).

Examination of visual and verbal representations of the game and the specialist furniture it required provide better understanding of the billiard table's consumption and use around 1900. Billiards was not only an exclusively masculine leisure confined to elite gentleman's clubs or proletarian "pool" halls, but also an activity for women or where the genders mixed at home. In the frontispiece photograph to his 1901 volume *Billiards for Everybody*, Charles "Vivid" Roberts stands clasping a copy of his book beside a woman player with her cue poised beside a ball on a well-appointed traditional mahogany table ("Two Books on Billards" 1912: 20) (Figure 0.1).[15] The image represents the aspirations expressed in his concluding chapter that "this book is written for all, as the title indicates, and I hope that numerous lady cueists will benefit by my instruction" (Roberts 1901: 103). The temptation to equate the sensual femininity invoked in the neo-rococo decoration of the billiard room in the Villa la Sapinière with the gratification of masculine desire loses sight of the respectable virtues attributed to billiard playing for both men and women. The playing of billiards was a family pastime undertaken in reputable public spaces and elegant domestic settings. *Game of Billiards* (1807; State Hermitage Museum, Saint Petersburg), a painting by Louis Léopold Boilly (1761–1845), portrays how in the Napoleonic period mixed play was a respectable form of family recreation, if also perhaps intimating romantic narratives typical of his genre paintings (Siegfried 1995: 150–7; Bailey, Conisbee, and Gaehtgens 2003: 350–3). In the 1860s, the court portraitist Charles Édouard Boutibonne (1816–97) also painted scenes of women playing billiards in bourgeois interiors (artnet n.d.-a). An anonymous 1900 pantomime publicity photograph shows an actress cross-dressed as a curate playing billiards with the lady of this elegant household in her dressing gown.[16] In the watercolor sketch by the aristocratic Georgina Louise Berkeley (1831–1919), a queue and mace (utilized by men and women, respectively) are juxtaposed on a billiard table, animating the still life with intimations of mixed play.[17] Thus when the Vittas furnished their villa, the representation of billiards as a form of exciting but respectable feminine leisure was widespread.

Advice manuals and popular journals about billiards provide lengthy disquisitions about the benefits of play and the virtues of different billiard table types. Nineteenth-century sources align the elevated blend of intellectual and physical training required by the game of billiards with the grandeur of history. In his pamphlet on the moral virtues of billiards, Hirschler associates this "noble" game not only with the antique heroic pursuit of gymnastics and medieval jousting, but also with "a sort of philosophical dissertation because each play requires thought, reflection and reasoning" (1874: 1, 5). In his preface for his lengthy, illustrated poem "Le billard," Lalanne invokes François I and Louis XIV, kings of France who played this "king of games," also suggesting elevated ancestry in his use of the classical epic form of poetry for his homage (1866: iii). In the introductory chapter "Some account of the origin of billiards and an appeal to the wives and sisters of America in its favor," the Irish player, historian of the game and billiard hall proprietor Michael Phelan (1819–71) opens by reassuring his assumed female readership that Shakespeare was a billiard player. They would be joining an elite matriarchy from Cleopatra and Mary Queen of Scots and Madame de Stael by embracing this sport:

FIGURE 0.1 Frontispiece to Charles Roberts, *Billiards for Everybody* (1901).
Photograph courtesy of the Bodleian Libraries, University of Oxford.

The late Duchess de Berri [*sic*] was also very fond of the game, and highly
skilled in its execution; her example gave the tone to Parisian fashion, and
today the billiard room is regarded as an indispensable adjunction to every
chateau of any pretension on continental Europe.

(Phelan [1859] 1874: 24)

Hirschler extends his praise of the intellectual and physical training benefits of the game to women:

> Women of good society in France, as in foreign lands, find pleasure and an agreeable distraction in billiards. Its gentleness is revealed in the curvaceous grace of their movement. Let us avow in a whisper that a woman playing billiards in an adorable creature.
>
> (1874: 7)

This beautification of home and body was also championed in articles in the popular one-penny monthly London magazine launched in 1903, *The Billiard Player: A Journal for the Public and Private Billiard Room*, which counselled that billiards provides "necessary exercise," which both encourages "an easy graceful carriage" in women and slims the waist (1903a: 79).

The purchase of a billiard table for the home benefited all the family, providing a "domesticating influence" on the head of the house as well as a positive form of collective leisure (Hirschler 1874: 6):

> Our wives and children would be more healthy and happy, more affectionate and fond of home; for there is nothing which endears the family circle so intimately, as the recollection of amusements shared in common—of games in which we all took part.
>
> (Phelan [1859] 1874: 24)

The enhancement of social status, merit, and affordability of acquiring a piano is a frequent comparison (Lalanne 1866: i). Hirschler recommends the billiard table over the piano, not being so susceptible to damage and climatic conditions. By its presence, this piece of "luxury furniture" identifies "the proprietors of the house as intelligent, educated and up-to-date" (1874: 6). Hirschler even elevates the makers of billiard tables who "are artists not workmen" (4). *The Billiard Player* regularly deliberated on desirable features in tables and cues, on their care as well as strategies of play (Taylor 1903: 18–19; *Billiard Player* 1903b: 94–5). Full-page illustrated advertisements from firms such as J.W. Smart of 15 College Green Bristol (established 1880) reveal the global geographies of production and consumption. Declarations of regional prowess in a particular feature of manufacture (in this instance prized West Country covering fabrics) are juxtaposed with invocations of colonial markets in the reference to "suitable for any Climate" alongside an affidavit from a satisfied customer, one Philip Williams on behalf of the Marine Club of Swataw, China. An anonymous illustrated article elaborates upon the innovation of smaller "bijou" tables that can be rotated to double as dining tables; £5 and 5 shillings for a four-foot table to £9 for a seven-foot table (*Billiard Player*

1903c: 220–1).[18] In regular articles "bijou" tables are praised for facilitating women's play. Given "it is out of the question for a woman to get her billiards in a public room" and should she not yet be a member of a "ladies club," *The Billiard Player* advised commitment to the costs of a "bijou" table, payable in instalments as with a piano, "now that there is a small sized table on the market which is not a toy, mothers of families would do well to give the question of acquiring one" (1903a: 79). These images and texts capture a wider context of the aesthetics, gendering, and use of billiard tables reanimating the photograph of the "bijou" billiard table in la Sapinière with an intriguing cultural history of furnishing, family, and play.

The ensuing chapters in this volume deploy nine connected themes examined through case studies drawn from across the twentieth and twenty-first centuries. Considering the materials out of which furniture is made, its design and type, the impact of its destination for domestic or public use, its dissemination in display, images, and words provides a framework for the investigation of how furnishing embodies the arresting traces of the historical experience of how we work, play, and live in the modern age.

CHAPTER ONE

Design and Motifs

TREVOR KEEBLE

The realist object of utility is beautiful.
—Le Corbusier, *The Decorative Art of Today* ([1925] 1987: 188)

THE SURFACE, SUBSTANCE, AND STYLE OF FURNITURE SINCE 1900

The often-uncomfortable relationship between design and motifs has arguably been at the heart of critical discourses and practices of furniture design since the turn of the twentieth century. Most commonly viewed through the paradigmatic conceptions of Modernism and Postmodernism, the critical relationship between the form and the aesthetics of furniture, as part of the wider culture of design, was central to the ways in which design, as distinct from the fine, applied, and decorative arts, was formed within the industrial and cultural modernity of the twentieth century. Modernism and Postmodernism constitute the two broadly conceived philosophical and cultural movements most commonly used to explain art, communication, and cultural production, including design, throughout the twentieth century. Whilst both accommodate diverse explicit and underlying political and critical positions, they are each useful for thinking through the ways in which furniture design has been critically produced, considered, and evaluated in its formation as a modern, industrial profession. Importantly for this chapter, the critical fissure between modern and postmodern furniture discourses has most commonly centered upon the contested relationship between design, function, and aesthetics.

This chapter considers the broad arc of this critical relationship through the reevaluation of some key objects and moments of furniture design since 1900.

It uses the discourses and loose periodization of Modernism and Postmodernism to explore the tensions between these discourses and the actual objects of their concern, to suggest that the distinctions between modern and postmodern furniture design and thinking are in fact less marked than has often been suggested by the history of design because the practice of furniture design sustained core critical concerns with function, materiality, manufacture, and innovation throughout this period. This chapter does not therefore present a history of furniture since 1900 as it was experienced and lived by the masses but presents instead an account of canonical furniture that embodied and shaped the critical discourses and theories used to understand furniture design and style since that time.[1]

MODERNISM: FORM, FUNCTION, AESTHETICS

Whilst in its genesis Modernism accommodated a number of differing political and philosophical positions, at its heart it was consistently concerned with the relationship between form and function. The preeminent modernist architect Charles-Édouard Jeanneret (1887–1965), better known by his self-styled moniker "Le Corbusier," made perhaps the most cogent and subsequently influential case for "functionalism" in his 1925 book, *The Decorative Art of Today*. In a chapter entitled "Type-Needs, Type Furniture," Le Corbusier argued that designing objects according to their functional requirements was the only means by which design could rediscover "*human scale*, the human function" (Le Corbusier [1925] 1987: 71). Characterizing generic "type needs" as universal to the human condition, Le Corbusier made the physical requirements of the human body central to his conception of functionalism by proposing that objects such as furniture should be understood only in relation to the human body, and that as "human-limb objects" furniture should be viewed as tool-like extensions of the body.

Le Corbusier illustrated his discussion with numerous examples of functional office furniture such as steel desks, filing cabinets, and units. Having made his functionalist argument on solely physical grounds, he went on to assert that such a functionalist approach to furniture design would provide an aesthetic "art" appropriate to its time, one that would counter "sentiment" (Le Corbusier [1925] 1987: 73). In pursuit of its polemical thesis, *The Decorative Art of Today* makes repeated links between decoration, emotion, and sentiment, which it argues lead to "adorning one's surroundings to make life less empty" (186). By contending that the desire to do what's thought socially appropriate and fitting constitutes a form of oppression preventing one from being "master of yourself" (188), Le Corbusier made authenticity and artifice the polarized terms through which progressive modern design would be judged.

Le Corbusier was certainly not the first theorist to argue against decoration on the basis that it encumbered modern man. In his 1908 essay "Ornament and Crime," the Viennese architect and designer Adolf Loos (1870–1933) made clear links between decoration, the tattooed savage, and the criminal, arguing that it was the absence of decoration that should become the mark of the civilized modern man (Loos [1908] 1998). Similarly, in his discussion of Ripolin brand whitewash, Le Corbusier makes explicit the connection between the absence of decoration, and physical and "inner" cleanliness. Describing whitewash as "extremely moral" ([1925] 1987: 192), he offers a slightly different argument to Loos, suggesting that whitewash, that is an environment of undecorated simplicity, is in fact the endangered expression of authentic cultures, unencumbered by the vulgar trappings of modern life. In linking functional design and its aesthetic to man's physical and moral needs, Le Corbusier articulated a critical position that would influence the design of furniture throughout the twentieth century.

NEW ART AND THE AVANT-GARDE

The first two decades of the twentieth century witnessed the birth of a number of loosely organized progressive arts movements across continental Europe. Although linked internationally by travel and a rapidly evolving print culture dedicated to the arts, these collectives and groupings were often firmly located within national and metropolitan contexts. Each was shaped by its own particular professional, social, and political concerns yet together they shared an ambition to create the new century in a manner distinct from what had gone before. Importantly for furniture design, and design more broadly, these movements sought to question the fundamentals of form and aesthetics in such a way as to reconcile earlier anxieties about industrialization.[2] In doing so, they brought design as a practice distinct from, yet related to, the fine and applied arts, architecture, and the crafts within the fold of modern cultural production.

This is not to suggest, however, that continental Europe, and indeed North America, had not already witnessed something of a modern decorative style in the form of Art Nouveau. Known variously as *jugendstil, modernisme, stile liberty*, and the new art, Art Nouveau was arguably the first mass visual and design culture. Reproduced through paintings, posters, architecture, and furniture, the stylized asymmetric motifs of whiplash curves and languid tendrils announced the start of a new century at the Paris Exposition of 1900. Within this relatively short-lived (it flourished between about 1890 and 1914) and contested new art can be found a number of uneasy factors that artists and designers would wrestle with throughout many of the decades that followed. These included the relationship between high and popular culture, between enduring cultural value and the ephemeral disposability of "fashion," and perhaps most importantly, the role of decoration within a new age.

Whilst it is perhaps best understood aesthetically to be a style that linked the decades just before and after 1900, Art Nouveau nevertheless constituted a broadly coherent set of decorative motifs and visual language that could be applied, perhaps often without discrimination, to any object or surface, be it a chair, a curtain, a button, or a lamppost. In the simplicity and ease of its application Art Nouveau exploited the possibilities of technology, and in consequence gave form to the fashionable commodity "culture" that would, in turn, insist upon its demise.

The Wiener Werkstätte, which was formed in Vienna in 1903 by the architect and designer Josef Hoffman (1870–1956) and the artist and designer Koloman Moser (1868–1918), has been interpreted as a later flowering of Art Nouveau. Hoffman and Moser had been founding members, in 1897, of the Vienna Secession movement, a collection of artists who rejected the historicist conventions of the academy in favor of more progressive, contemporary modes. Under its banner of "To every art its age. To every age its freedom," the artists of the Vienna Secession sought to reformulate the fine arts of painting, sculpture, and music for the modern age.

With the financial backing of local industrialist Fritz Wärndorfer (1868–1939), the establishment of the "Vienna Workshops" brought this agenda to the production and economy of the applied arts. During a thirty-year period the workshops expanded to encompass design and production across a range of applied arts including metalwork, ceramics, glass, leather, bookbinding, graphic arts, and furniture.

The Wiener Werkstätte was largely without political agenda other than to establish a model of viable commercial practice for the applied and decorative arts. Furthermore, it was not especially committed to the artisanal models of the "crafts" that had flourished under the influence of William Morris (1834–96) in Great Britain. These had proffered an ideal founded in opposition to industrial production and sought to establish artisanal craft practices often rooted in traditional, vernacular aesthetics. The Werkstätte, in contrast, pursued a fundamentally modern aesthetic for its work and sought, without compunction, to create contemporary decorative objects for the well-established Viennese middle classes.

Both Hoffman and Moser, its two principal furniture designers, were committed to the immersive vision of *Gesamtkunstwerk*. Roughly translated to mean "total work of art," this conception of the arts as an interrelated "whole" had been central to the philosophy of the Secession movement and provided conceptual and aesthetic connection between the fine and applied arts, architecture, and design. Neither Hoffman nor Moser, however, had any training or background in furniture making and each approached furniture as designers producing work that would be manufactured and realized by others. Whilst this mode of designing differed markedly from many of the decorative art and craft practices of Hoffman and Moser's contemporaries within the *Wiener Werkstätte* (Vienna Workshops), and refuted the post-arts and crafts consensus that dominated British design culture in the first decades of the twentieth century, it typified the ascendancy of the professional architect and designer that would be central to continental Modernism.

This interrelationship of two-dimensional pictorial form and architectonic expression in three dimensions pervaded the concerns of the group of avant-garde painters, designers, and architects that formed around the Dutch painter and critic Theo van Doesburg (1883–1931) and his journal *De Stijl* (The Style) between 1917 and 1931 (Overy 1991). The De Stijl group, which included the painters Piet Mondrian (1872–1944) and Vilmos Huszár (1884–1960), and the architects and designers Gerrit Rietveld (1888–1964), Bart van der Leck (1876–1958), and J.J.P. Oud (1890–1963), was concerned to explore and promote a new art of pure abstraction, which they termed neoplasticism, an art that sought a universalized reduction of form and color. The group's focus upon irregular and asymmetric linear and planar forms, expressed only in primary colors and black and white established a radical vision of abstraction as a highly influential compositional vocabulary of color and form that constituted an explicitly modern language of motifs. It should be noted, however, that the Dutch collective was not alone in this pursuit at this time, and other contemporary avant-garde artistic groups, most notably the Constructivists and Suprematists in Russia, also made the contested relationships between aesthetics and form the focus of their work (Barron and Tuchman 1981: 28–40).

Gerrit Rietveld is the most significant furniture designer associated with De Stijl and created one of the most iconic objects of early modern furniture design, in what has become known as the Red Blue Chair, in 1918. Born in Utrecht, the Netherlands, in 1888, he served an apprenticeship with his father, a joiner, before setting up his own business as a cabinetmaker shortly before joining De Stijl in 1918. Rietveld embraced the new aesthetic language of De Stijl, and his work in both furniture and, subsequently, architecture has often been likened to the rectilinear paintings of his contemporary, Piet Mondrian (Lodder 2006: 30). In his designs, however, the experimental and elemental forms typical of Mondrian's painting were put into pragmatic and purposeful application in the form of cabinets, chairs, tables, and eventually buildings.

Although in the early years of his career Rietveld's designs were developmentally prototypical and iterated through single examples and redesigns, his knowledge and understanding of joinery and cabinetmaking led him to design with a view to mass production (Baroni 1978: 41). Many of his designs, including the Red Blue Chair, were therefore constructed using standard lumber sizes that reduced the need for further work. In this, Reitveld demonstrated a clear understanding of the role that manufacture and possibly even self-assembly might play in making modern furniture widely available, even if in the earlier part of his career this was not in fact possible (45). This was a concern that would later mark his architectural designs for social housing, where the costs of building, prefabrication, and assembly were understood explicitly to be the challenges of the designer.

The Red Blue Chair itself presents what is perhaps one of the most radical and programmatic furniture designs of the modernist canon (Plate 6). It takes the familiar form of the armchair and subjects this to a geometric reduction that results in a construction of lightly interconnected rectilinear elements and planes composed in space. The chair is constructed of three principal forms: the supporting frame, the angled seat, and the reclining backrest, which in the original design were left as plain varnished wood (Wilk 2006a: 31). It was not until 1923, however, that Rietveld made a slightly modified version of this design that became the eponymous painted Red Blue Chair (Lodder 2006: 48).

The decision to paint and varnish this chair is significant for a number of reasons. Firstly, and perhaps most significantly given his training and knowledge of furniture making and joinery, the decision to coat the surfaces of the chair with the shining gloss of paint suggests he believed that the wooden material from which it was made was simply a fact of its construction, not a feature of the design. Secondly, the demarcation of the primary blue seat and primary red backrest from the black painted frame of the chair serves to accentuate the elemental composition of the design. This is further heightened by the primary yellow paint that is used to punctuate the ends of the black-painted timber struts that make up the frame. Finally, the decision to paint this chair some six years after its original conception demonstrates clearly that Rietveld was deeply concerned with the role of aesthetic appearance, perhaps even decoration, in the articulation of the modern three-dimensional form.

"PIONEERING" DESIGNS

The history of design has established the years between the two world wars as the era in which Modernism as a broadly coherent set of ideas concerned to express the rapidly changing contexts of technological and social modernity, came to fruition.

The preeminent institution of this development was the Bauhaus. Formed in Weimar, Germany, in 1919 by the German architect Walter Gropius (1883–1969), the Staatliches Bauhaus has been widely credited with establishing the terms and practices of modern design (Naylor 1985). Translated literally as the "building house," the school's ideological position that placed architecture as the dominant practice within modern design, one to be served by all others, and enshrined as the pinnacle of the school's progressive, evolutionary curriculum reflects the ascendant role of the architect within modernist ideals. In spite of this, the early years of the Bauhaus were characterized by the formalization of different material-based practices such as metal, glass, stone, and wood into workshops in which students specialized. A department dedicated to architecture was not in fact established at the Bauhaus until 1927, following the school's relocation to the industrial town of Dessau in eastern Germany (Naylor 1985: 142). Housed in new purpose-built buildings designed by Gropius and his colleague Hannes Meyer (1889–1954), this move in 1925/6 has been viewed as the point at which the school's emphasis shifted more firmly toward design for industrial production, manufacture, and fabrication.

The years from the mid-1920s are also the period in which Le Corbusier rose from the margins of the Parisian design world to become one of the most influential practitioners of architecture and design throughout Europe and beyond. Le Corbusier had been espousing progressive ideals in art, architecture, and design for some years through his writings such as *Towards a New Architecture* (1923) and *The Decorative Art of Today* (1925). Nonetheless, at the time of presenting the L'Esprit Nouveau (The New Spirit) pavilion, designed in collaboration with the artist Amédée Ozenfant and named after the journal that they had founded, at the International Exposition of Modern Industrial and Decorative Arts in Paris in 1925, Le Corbusier's work was still considered novel yet idiosyncratic in its sparse and minimal presentation (Troy 1991: 192).

The Paris exposition of 1925 is a significant moment in the history of design if only because it demonstrates how far removed the progressive academic discourses of modern design were from the practice of high styles of design that marked this era, particularly for furniture and furnishing. Émile-Jacques Ruhlman (1879–1933), the Parisian designer of luxury furniture and furnishings, was one of the most celebrated figures of the exposition. His Hôtel du Collectionneur (Hotel of the Collector) pavilion typified the glamour of high-style decoration that would later become known as Art Deco (Sparke 2008: 101–3). His furniture designs such as his *Fuseaux* (spindle) cabinet of 1925 often reflected an informed and knowledgeable inspiration from earlier decorative traditions of the eighteenth and nineteenth centuries but were infused with a contemporary aesthetic of modern patterning and marquetry in exotic hardwoods, tortoiseshell, and ivory. This mode of decorative high style, rooted firmly within the tradition of luxury materials and interior decoration, offered a spectacular mode of modern living far removed from the apparent austerity of Le Corbusier's design, and one that gave fashionable shape and form to modernity on both sides of the Atlantic (Greenhalgh 1990a: 71). In this sense, Ruhlman used the traditions of the past to construe decorative motifs for the modern age.

Notwithstanding the global impacts of the Great Depression of 1929, the interwar years were a period of significant growth and professionalization of design in the United States of America. Advances in industrial production, most notably achieved by car manufacturers such as Henry Ford (1863–1947) and subsequently manufacturers of household goods, led to a burgeoning consumer economy that placed design at its core. Because of this, the model of design that emerged in America offered a commercial modernity that sought meaning within the market and modern American consumer practices. This is not to suggest, however, that America did not produce its own progressive designers, the architects Louis Sullivan (1856–1924) and Frank Lloyd Wright (1867–1959) being the most internationally significant, but that the American approach to modern design was one rooted in actual commercial and industrial practice rather than the philosophical polemics that characterized European discourse. Whereas European Modernism was more often than not presented as a fundamental challenge to popular tastes and traditions, the modernity of American design at this time was arguably more willing to look for its meaning in its reception by the consuming American public, a less ideological, more pragmatic model of modernity. In this sense, it could be argued that it provided perhaps the most convincing model of how a modern democracy of living might be achieved through design.

Marcel Breuer (1902–81) was the most accomplished and influential furniture designer of the Bauhaus. Having first been a student in the furniture workshops between 1921 and 1924, Breuer returned to the school upon its relocation to Dessau to run them. Less concerned with the philosophical posturing of many of his colleagues at the Bauhaus, Breuer was intensely concerned with the practical application of his work and the possibilities of manufacture.

The development of Breuer's designs during the middle years of the 1920s reflects the evolving aesthetic language of the Bauhaus. The Child's Chair ti 3a of 1923 is made of wood and plywood, and is oil-painted in red and off-white. In its rigid composition and colored articulation of frame and support, the design suggests the influence of Rietveld's earlier chair, which had been re-presented in Red and Blue that same year. Yet his slatted chair ti 1a, also of 1923, comprises a wooden cantilevered frame with elastic seat and back straps designed to support posture, and indicates an emerging concern with the ergonomic interaction between the body and the chair (Naylor 1985: 106).

It was not until Breuer's Club Armchair of 1925/6, later renamed after his friend and colleague the artist "Wassily" Kandinsky, however, that Breuer began working with the extruded tubular steel that would become the iconic material of modernist furniture design. The chair, made initially of nickel-plated tubular steel and canvas, reimagined the heavily upholstered traditional form as a lightweight minimal construction, influenced by the rational design of the bicycle and tubular steel's potential for mass production (Naylor 1985: 149). The chair comprised a minimal frame of jointed sections across which the strips of canvas, later leather, held the seated body in suspension. In its sleek, almost diagrammatic outline and simple composition of contrasting materials, the Wassily chair represents a point at which the ideals of functionalist Modernism were made explicit in both aesthetic and three-dimensional form (Massey 2011: 69).

It is, nonetheless, the B32 chair (B64 with armrests), later named Cesca and designed in 1928, that remains one of the most ubiquitous objects of the Modern movement. It constitutes perhaps Breuer's most significant contribution to modernist furniture design. Unpatented at the time of its design, the chair is still produced extensively and can be found in almost every kind of interior, high- or low-brow, public or private. Perhaps more than any other chair, Cesca pays homage to the antecedent designs of Thonet (1796–1871). The chair marries the industrial possibilities of chrome-plated tubular steel with the enduring certainty of the bentwood and wicker cane that Thonet had made his own in the previous century. The design comprises a single piece of tubular steel, bent to form a soft geometric cantilever frame. Upon this, the gently curved seat and backrest of bentwood and wicker, and bentwood armrests provide support for the body. The lattice of the wicker canework further accentuates the lightness of the construction and offers the visual permeability that characterizes the chair as a whole (Wilk 2006b: 238). Whilst it might be argued that the Cesca chair lacks the stark and revolutionary impact of the earlier Wassily chair, in its resolved and minimal form, and subtle combination of shinning chrome, varnished wood, and latticed wicker, the design marks the moment of maturity that proved significant for Breuer and for modernist furniture design as a whole.

Eileen Gray (1878–1976) was an important Irish-born designer and architect who worked in Paris throughout the twentieth century. Yet for much of this period, her work and achievement, like that of so many of her female contemporaries, was lost from the canon of modern design. Gray moved to Paris in her early twenties having studied at the Slade School of Art in London. As a young woman she became fascinated with the Japanese art of lacquer work, and she spent many years under the tutelage of Seizo Sugawara (1884–1937) living in Paris (Garner 2006: 11). Although she would go on to design buildings during the later 1920s, Gray came to this from a tradition of decorative arts and commercial interior design, and these influences can be found throughout the apparently modernist designs of her later career.

Eileen Gray designed the E 1027 table for the house of the same name that she designed and built with Jean Badovici (1893–1956) in 1927 at Roquebrune, in the South of France. This simple yet challenging design made of varnished tubular steel and acrylic glass offers an asymmetry unseen in many of the tubular steel furniture designs of this time, and suggests a more aesthetically nuanced model of Modernism than that shown by many of her male contemporaries. Perhaps due to her work and background in the decorative and applied arts,

Gray's work has resisted easy classification, and designers, authors, and curators have too often sought to separate her designs, and particularly aspects of her designs such as furniture, rugs, screens, etc., according to whether they might fit easily within the restricted codes of modernist dogma.

Indeed Gray's work demonstrates a non-compliant aesthetic concern that pushed at the edges of modernist design thinking during the interwar years. For example, the *Fauteuil Transatlantique* (Transat Chair), also designed for the E 1027 House, reconciles the progressive agenda of the Modern movement with the broader decorative tradition of the *assemblier* or *decorater* (interior decorator). Furthermore, other notable designs such as her Bibendum club chair of 1929 with its soft rolled tubes of upholstery sitting in stark contrast to its thin, shining tubular steel frame, or her explicitly utilitarian Folding Hammock Chair of 1938 with its articulated frame and exaggerated rolling form, suggest an approach to Modernism that refused to subjugate the material and aesthetic aspects of design to rigid functionalism. This is a position that Christopher Wilk suggests Theo van Doesburg had in fact taken some years earlier when he proposed that "our chairs, tables, cupboards and other objects for use, those are the (abstract – real) sculptures within our future interiors" (cited in Wilk 2006b: 233). Arguing this was a very rare admission, often denied by Van Doesburg's peers, Wilk asserts, "that architects were very interested in and conscious of the aesthetics of their designs, and that furniture played more than a functional role in the interior" (233).

The aesthetics of materiality was of central concern to the Finnish architect and designer Alvar Aalto (1898–1976). In 1929 Alvar and Aino Aalto (neé Marsio, 1894–1949) won a competition to build a tuberculosis sanitarium in Paimio, Finland. The Paimio armchair 41 (1930) was created during the extended period of design and build that preceded the opening of the sanitarium in 1933. Aalto is widely quoted as having rejected the nickel- and chrome-plated steel used by his many European modernist contemporaries in favor of the birch wood and ply that was indigenous to the country. Aalto chose wood over metal as he felt it more appropriate to the needs and comfort of the many patients for whom the chair was designed, and this marks a significant point in the development of what has come to be understood as a softer form of Modernism that typifies a particularly Scandinavian modern design (Woodham 1997: 56–60).

The design exploited the comparatively low technology processes of steam-bending the birch wood frame, and a continuous roll of plywood to form the seat, back, and headrest (Benton 2006a: 314). Importantly, the chair was required to be strictly hygienic but the absence of upholstery was mitigated by the springiness of the plywood seat that was attached to the frame only at its scrolled ends. The easy availability of the birch wood meant that the chair was cheap to produce and was made widely available beyond the sanitarium for which it was designed, by Artek, the Aaltos' own distribution company.

Paul Greenhalgh has suggested that the years 1929 to 1933 witnessed the end of the "pioneer phase" of Modernism. He has described this as a period of ideas and visions about "how the designed world could transform human consciousness and improve material conditions" (Greenhalgh 1990b: 3). In doing so, Greenhalgh demonstrates the extent to which the nascent design professions were in fact realizing the possibilities of their work. This pioneer phase, he suggested, gave way during the 1930s to an understanding of Modernism better described as the "International Style," the title given to the Museum of Modern Art's (MoMA) showcase celebration of European Modernism in 1932 (1–24). While this more explicitly stylistic model of modern design lacked many of the political and moral purposes that had fueled its creation, it nevertheless established Modernism as the dominant conceptual and philosophical model of architecture, design, and urbanism for the next fifty years.

POSTMODERNISM: AESTHETICS, FUNCTION, FORM

The critical theories of Postmodernism coalesced during the 1970s into a contested and radical paradigm of thinking and practice, and yet what we have come to understand as a postmodern "sensibility" was evident in furniture design many years earlier. Like the preceding ideals of Modernism, the influence of postmodern thinking spanned the fine arts, literature, architecture, and design, and yet in contrast to the hegemonic dogmatism of "International Style" Modernism that typified cultural production by the middle decades of the twentieth century, Postmodernism made culture itself a subject of critical enquiry. Within design, architecture remained at the fore of postmodern theorizing, yet in its attempt to understand and value culture outside the elite prescriptions and judgments of Modernism, the critical challenges and questions that would coalesce into Postmodernism made furniture design a spectacular platform on which ideas and contests about form and function could be played out. Whilst Modernism had built a concept of furniture design rooted in utilitarian function and purpose, Postmodernism made style and aesthetics its raison d'être. However, postmodern acknowledgment that style had a referential purpose in design was not necessarily at odds with utilitarian function, and the opportunity this provided to question and explore the role of function proved to be a liberating force within furniture design, which placed it in the vanguard of critical design thinking (Collins and Papadakis 1989).

At its core, Postmodernism presents a discontent with the singular, universal messages of Modernism although beyond this it accommodated a diverse range of ideas that embodied its commitment to "plurality." For Charles Jencks (1939–2019), the preeminent theorist of postmodern architecture, it was the natural successor to the modernist project, which he famously declared had died with the demolition of the Pruitt Igo social housing estate in St. Louis, USA, in 1972 (Jencks 1977: 9). For Jencks, the Pruitt Igo estate typified the worst excesses of large-scale, impersonal Modernism, and his recognition that the didactic certainties of Modernism, that led to the mass social housing and urban planning which by the 1960s it had made its own, had brought as many problems as it had solved, confirmed to architects and designers during this period, many of whom had been products of modernist education and training, that critical reappraisal was required.

Postmodern design challenged the preeminence of utility and the dogma of form follows function as articulated by the American architect and designer Robert Venturi (1925–2018) in his seminal 1966 publication, *Complexity and Contradiction in Architecture*:

> I am for richness of meaning rather than clarity of meaning; for the implicit function as well as the explicit function. I prefer "both-and" to "either-or", black and white, and sometimes gray, to black or white.
>
> (Venturi [1966] 2002: 16)

Famed for reconfiguring Mies van der Rohe's (1886–1969) famous modernist dictum "less is more" as "less is a bore," Venturi championed a model of design that understood the cultural importance and utility of style, historic reference, and ephemerality. He rejected modernist notions of "universality" of function and form, and in so doing embraced a plurality of popular culture, architecture and design on the understanding that "more is not less" (Venturi [1966] 2002: 16). This rejection of the reductionist tendencies of modern design and its theorizing is at the heart of his polemical argument for Postmodernism. Furthermore, by noting that such modernist luminaries as Le Corbusier and Alvar Aalto rejected simplicity through reduction (18), Venturi offers Postmodernism as a progressive and expansive discourse still rooted to some extent in modernist thinking.

While Modernism had made industrial manufacture the object of its democratizing ambitions, postmodern thinking was forged in a postindustrial world on the threshold of globalization and the digital revolution. Industrial capital and the consumer economy that it had created became the essential context of Postmodernism as expressed by the American critic Frederic Jameson in the dual title of his book *Postmodernism, or, the Cultural Logic of Late Capitalism* (1991). Whilst it is fair to say that in its explicit opposition to modernist dogma, Postmodernism became characterized as anything and everything, Glenn Adamson has usefully described the dual meaning inherent to the concept of being "post" modern. On the one hand, he suggests, "post" is taken to mean "after" Modernism in such as a way as to describe "a distinctive and separate movement" (Adamson 2013: 201). On the other hand, however, he describes a position that makes "post" Modernism "a mere adjunct, like a footnote or epilogue—a postscript" (201). This latter position, one that Adamson notes to be widely held amongst creative practitioners, tends to undermine an understanding of Postmodernism as a radical departure. In light of this, it is particularly interesting to look for Postmodern sensibilities and concerns with style and aesthetics in furniture designs that predate the formalization of Postmodern thinking.

As noted above, by the mid-twentieth century Modernism had achieved international preeminence in design thinking through what Greenhalgh described as the International Style. The dominant influence of modernist thinking was undoubtedly due to the rapid advances in industrial and material technologies during the mid-twentieth century. Yet, as Greenhalgh has noted, the testing of Modernism's central propositions within the industrial contexts it so fetishized made Modernism a stylistic rather than a philosophical position. In this sense, the international proliferation of Modernism in the middle decades of the twentieth century had already rendered it what it had avowedly argued it was not, a style, and as such Modernism was constructed as a series of highly refined motifs of the contemporary age.

MID-CENTURY POSTMODERN

Furniture designs of this period have often been referred to as "mid-century modern" and yet it is clear that many designs, perhaps because they were being created for the burgeoning consumer markets of western Europe and North America, betray many of the characteristics and sensibilities that would be enshrined within the thinking of Postmodernism. Charles (1907–78) and Ray (née Kaiser, 1912–88) Eames were two of the most influential designers of their generation and their work, from the mid-1940s, typifies the way American design absorbed and developed the critical thinking and influence of European Modernism. Married in 1941, having both studied and worked together at the Cranbrook Academy of Art in Michigan, the Eameses established a working partnership that would include furniture design, architecture, graphics, films, photography, and exhibitions (Kirkham 1995).

Their Los Angeles design studio, established initially from the spare room in their apartment, found work during the Second World War, designing and producing molded plywood leg splints for the US Navy. Their experiments with plywood, a material that would define their early furniture designs, demonstrates an innovative commitment to technology and material science. Like their Scandinavian predecessors, the Eameses valued plywood for its low cost and its ability to be industrially formed and mass-produced. Yet, their plywood designs were characterized by an irregular and sculptural organicism of compound curves, and a playful approach to function (Kirkham 1995: 264).

The LCW chair of 1945 and the DCW of the following year are low-seated easy chairs made of molded plywood (Plate 7). The soft form and visually generous proportions contrast with the often-minimalist designs of European Modernism. Unlike Aalto's plywood designs, which drew upon the material to offer a streamlined simplicity of form, these were achieved through a modular design of components formed through compound curves. The earliest design, which was initially produced by Evans Product Company, was displayed as part of an exhibition of "New Furniture designed by Charles Eames" at MoMA, New York, in 1946, where it was seen by George Nelson (1908–86), the newly appointed Director of Design at Herman Miller, the leading US furniture company (Meikle 2005: 142). Nelson struck a deal with Evans Product Company and Herman Miller began marketing the design later that year, thus inaugurating a lifelong partnership between the Eameses and Herman Miller.

Whilst the Eameses' molded plywood chairs use one of the iconic materials of Modernism, the component forms of the designs, tapering legs and gently curved seat and backrest, give them an informal quality of comfort. Importantly, the chairs were designed to be both inexpensive and fashionable, and the Eameses went on to design the individual components of their chairs in different materials and finishes so as to be interchangeable. This suggests that the universality of design that so preoccupied their modernist forebears was certainly not a principal concern of their work. Indeed, far from believing the aesthetic appeal of decoration to be an encumbrance, Charles and Ray Eames positively embraced the aesthetic opportunity of their designs to create objects that through their playful combination of colorful surfaces and materials expressed their contemporaneity (Kirkham 1995: 6–7). Nevertheless, in spite of this evident concern with the aesthetic conception of their furniture, Pat Kirkham has suggested that "at the height of Modernism's hegemony it was difficult to admit simply liking the look of something, especially an object that could be classified as non-industrial, decorative, and trivial" (145).

The Eameses continued to experiment by combining new technologies and organic, sculptural forms, and from 1948 they produced a series of highly influential shell chairs. Initially designed to be made from sheet metal, the DAX Chair of 1948 was the first of their pieces made in fiberglass and consisted of two principal components: a molded fiberglass seat unit, which sat upon a frame of four splayed metal rod legs. The design, which made use of technologies developed by both the military and the car industry, echoed the Organic Armchair that Charles Eames had designed with Eero Saarinen (1910–61) at the Cranbrook Academy in 1940 (Meikle 2005: 140). However, whereas the Organic Armchair comprised a molded plywood seat lightly upholstered with foam and textiles, the use of press-molded fiberglass simplified the manufacturing processes and reduced the costs of the design significantly.

The development of the fiberglass shell chairs, including "La Chaise," a double-skinned, anthropomorphic design, testifies to the Eameses' understanding that technology served design. These ostensibly modernist designs were also made available in different colors and eventually with different legs, and were more redolent of modern and highly fashionable living than dogmatic functionalism. This sensibility remained at the core of Charles and Ray Eames' formulation of modern design. The extent to which their molded plywood and leather Lounge Chair and Ottoman of 1956 has become synonymous with the picture book images of the American Dream show how easily their progressive agenda for design came to embody modern comfortable living. This was not, however, an abstract treatise that treated design as a problem but was rooted in their own experiences of domesticity, taste, and modern living (Kirkham 2009).

The 1950s was also a very significant decade for the revitalization of Italian furniture design. Italian design and architecture construed its own form of Modernism during the interwar years known as Rationalism. Primarily architectural in its focus, Italian Rationalism was distinguished from more explicitly progressive models, such as that of the Bauhaus, by its engagement with Italy's classical traditions. Italy saw significant investment and development of its manufacturing industries in the immediate aftermath of the Second World War as a consequence of the Marshall Plan (Woodham 1997: 124). Much like American industrialization some decades earlier, this was rooted in the motor industry and an emergent market for domestic consumable goods. Importantly, Italy had a long-standing tradition of decorative and applied arts as well as craft manufacture, and the success of postwar Italian design has often been understood to be due in part to the way in which it found a place for these established practices and traditions at the heart of its new industry (Lees-Maffei and Fallen 2013).

This hybridization of old and new can be seen in the work of architect Gio Ponti (1891–1979). Ponti's chair, Superleggera, No. 699 was designed and refined during the period 1951–7 (Sparke 1986a: 185). The chair is made from varnished ash wood and woven cane, and is based upon an everyday traditional, nineteenth-century Italian chair known as a Chiavari chair. The chair's name, which translates into English as "super lightweight," suggests Ponti's preoccupation to maintain the durable, functional quality of the design whilst making it as light as possible. Ponti's chair offers a highly refined and elegant design that brings together traditional artisanal skills and the possibility for large-scale manufacture and production. Indeed, Ponti worked with the craftspeople at the furniture manufacturer Cassina's Brianza factory to exploit the materials properties in the development of his design.

Achille (1918–2002) and Pier Giacomo (1913–68) Castiglioni were two of the most prominent Italian furniture and industrial designers of the 1950s and 1960s. Initially working alongside their brother, Livio (1911–79), the brothers championed what they termed a "common sense" approach to design. This involved interrogating and challenging established thinking about what constituted function, existing material, or technological solutions, and resulted in a series of highly innovative, influential designs, such as the Mezzadro stool (Plate 8). Mezzadro was first presented at the 10th Milan Triennial international exhibition in 1954, although the design underwent subsequent revision until 1957. It was featured as part of a themed display curated by the Castiglioni brothers concerning industrial design within "Art and Production." The display of over one hundred different design objects, alongside design drawings, photographs, and prototypes, sought to elucidate the role and practices of the designer at a time when Italian design was riding high on the strength of a developing industrial economy. It is within this essentially didactic context that the Mezzadro piece must be understood.

The cantilevered stool is composed of a number of commonplace utilitarian pieces: a red lacquered steel tractor seat attached by a wing-nut to a steel strip shock absorber, also from a tractor, which forms a forward-angled upright cantilever and base. This is then stabilized by a rung-like piece of shaped beech wood. As a new design composed from existing utilitarian forms, Mezzadro has been likened to the ready-made objects of Marcel Duchamp (1887–1968). The Castigilonis were clear in their ambition to create a functional and utilitarian object, and aesthetically the design communicates the nature of its assembly and construction in strictly rational terms. Yet, this is not the austere industrial object of purpose, which if taken individually its component parts might suggest, but an elegant composition that playfully construes function within an engaging aesthetic language of its own.

Ettore Sottsass Jr. (1917–2007) was an Italian architect and designer whose work had a profound and iconoclastic impact on the design of furniture during the second half of the twentieth century. He graduated with a degree in architecture from Turin Polytechnic in 1939 but his early career was interrupted immediately by the start of the Second World War. Following a number of years as a prisoner of war, Sottsass returned to Turin and worked alongside his father, also an architect, before moving to Milan, where in 1948 he established his own architectural and design studio. Throughout the early period of his career, Sottsass was heavily involved in the burgeoning design culture that centered on Milan during the early postwar years. He curated exhibitions, wrote for journals and magazines, most notably *Domus*, and produced designs for the stage (Radice 1993).

During the mid-1950s, Sottsass became creative consultant to the Italian furniture company Poltranova and subsequently began working as design consultant to Olivetti, the Italian manufacturer of office equipment and furniture. Sottsass's industrial product designs for Olivetti demonstrate the innovative and playful approach that would later characterize his furniture. His design for electronics in particular, including the award-winning Elea 9003 computer designed in collaboration with Roberto Olivetti (1928–85) and Mario Tchou (1924–61); the electronic Tekne typewriter; and subsequently, the iconic Valentine portable typewriter of 1970, demonstrate a synthesis of design engineering and high style.

In 1966 Sottsass designed Superbox, a tall geometric rectangular cupboard on a plinth-like base. Initially made in small numbers by Poltranova in wood with a red and white laminate striped surface, its totem-like, monolithic quality proved a fundamental challenge to established modes of furniture design. Sottsass continued to reiterate and develop further prototypes of the Superbox during the 1960s and a series of Superbox designs was amongst the most celebrated works at the 1972 exhibition, *Italy: The New Domestic Landscape* at MoMA in New York (Woodham 1997: 194). In their vibrant plastic surfaces, the Superbox designs convey the Pop Art sensibility with which Sottsass was by this point so taken. Yet, the objects offer a radical interrogation of function that would characterize all of Sottsass's subsequent work. They certainly served a function, the storage of objects or clothes, but in these objects this function was offered merely as a preconditional starting point for a design that might offer a sensual engagement far beyond simple purpose (Radice 1993: 120–5). Coupled with the flat, color-blocked patterns that adorned their surfaces, these bold geometric designs offer an early insight into the aesthetic reformulation of the relationship between surface and form that would typify the rest of Sottsass's work.

Pop Art had a significant impact on Italian design during the 1960s and 1970s. Just as the earlier Italian designers of the 1940s and 1950s had looked to America in their formulation of a modern industrial design culture, so too a later generation of architects, artists, and designers found creative influence in the critical debates and ideas that circulated within the preeminent industrial consumer culture of the time. Whilst on the face it, this influence was perhaps most obvious in the brightly colored plastic furniture designs that proliferated during this period, it was the critique of consumer culture at the heart of the Pop movement that had the most lasting and profound effects. Whilst the Italian radical design movements of the 1960s and 1970s sought to challenge the hegemonic consumer and media culture within which they found their practices constrained, they nevertheless celebrated the popular culture, particularly American popular culture that was forcing the reappraisal of the cultural hierarchies so cherished by Modernism. As evident in the work of pop artists such as Richard Hamilton (1922–2011), Andy Warhol (1928–87), and Claes Oldenburg (1929–), objects, particularly domestic objects of design and consumerism, had become fundamental to the terms of this critique.

THE RETURN OF THE AVANT-GARDE

By the late 1970s and 1980s, however, "Pop" aesthetics were deeply engrained within a consumer-driven design culture, and for many leading designers and thinkers Pop had lost much of its critical underpinnings. In Italy, by now firmly established as a leading design and manufacturing nation, a number of groups and collectives, often formed around the design and architectural schools of Milan, Florence, and Venice, sought to work collectively on speculative, propositional work that challenged the hegemonic influence and assumptions of the design and architectural establishment. These groups pursued a radical interdisciplinary vision of a world transformed through design, media, and communication. Alessandro Mendini (1931– 2019) was a journalist, artist, and designer, who as a key member of the radical design group Studio Alchimia, was at the forefront of critical debates in Italian design during the 1970s and 1980s (Woodham 1997: 194–6). Studio Alchimia followed in the wake of a number of groups including Archizoom and Superstudio that formed from the mid-1960s to interrogate the role of architecture, urbanism, and design in the modern world. The brand of radical or "anti-design" that came out of this work was explicitly speculative in its reimagining of the modernist project. Studio Alchimia was more explicitly concerned with furniture design and provided a radical, irreverent forum for a number of established designers including Mendini, Sottsass, Andrea Branzi (1938–), and Michele De Lucchi (1951–). Focusing primarily upon the creation of prototype designs, the group explored the representational character of furniture design and placed this within the interdisciplinary contexts of fine art and media.

Named after the nineteenth-century French author, Poltrona di Proust designed by Alessandro Mendini in 1978 is perhaps the most emphatic statement of Postmodernism in furniture design (Williams 2009: 20). The chair has the striking embellished form of the neo-baroque style of the eighteenth century. This is covered in its entirety by the scaled-up details of a pointillist painting by the Impressionist painter Paul Signac (1863–1935). These deep cultural references, to Proust and Impressionism, embed the chair within an ambiguous frame of meanings, and just as Signac and his fellow Impressionists used painted pixilation to explore the articulation of form, so the seeming immersion of the chair's form within the pattern of the painted surface rejects all consideration of construction and material.

The explicit counterpoint of form and surface, rooted deeply if ambiguously in artistic and cultural associations, was central to the work of the radical design collective Memphis when it launched its first furniture designs at the Milan Furniture Fair in 1981. Led by Sottsass, Memphis comprised a cross-generational group of international designers and critics including Alessandro Mendini, Martine Bedin (1957–), Andrea Branzi, Michele de Lucchi, Hans

Hollein (1934–2014), Arata Isozaki (1931–), and George Sowden (1942–), many of whom had been with the radical anti-design movements in Italy during the 1960s and 1970s. The primary goal of Memphis was to challenge what it perceived to be the hegemonic good taste of Modernism. In many senses this extended the wider project of the anti-design movements of the 1970s. However, Memphis took a largely nonpolitical position and was characterized by Barbara Radice (1943–), Sottsass's biographer and partner, as "anti-ideological because it seeks possibilities, not solutions" (Radice 1985: 141). The furniture designs presented in 1981 were marked by bright, often discordant colors and idiosyncratic forms.

Sottsass presented one of Memphis's most iconic designs, the Carlton Bookcase/Room Divider, at the group's first show in 1981 (Plate 9). Made of wood covered with laminated plastics, the challenge of this piece comes in a number of ways. Its highly decorated and, to the contemporary eye, discordantly colored surface of yellow, green, orange, red, black, and blue was unlike anything seen before. The design, which doubles as a bookcase or shelving unit, spectacularly challenges the perpendicular geometry of furniture by placing its components in non-horizontal or vertical positions. The base of the piece was covered in one of Sottsass's "bacterio" designs, which he had created during the late 1970s. These designs, which would become central to Sottsass's work for Memphis over the coming years, celebrated the superficiality of the shiny laminate surface. In this, the "bacterio" designs worked to blur the form of the object visually in perhaps the most explicit rejection of the Modernist dogma concerning honesty of materiality and form (Rossi 2011: 162).

Memphis championed the importance of "surface," and offered a series of furniture designs that challenged the values and orthodoxies established by modernist thinking. Yet, in hindsight, it is possible to see that the vestiges of Modernism remain in aspects of the most apparently un-modernist work such as Carlton. In its articulation of its individual components through color, its challenging but regular and symmetric geometry, and its flexible and multipurpose function, which is further enabled by its ability to be disassembled and reassembled, this piece offers a critical and aesthetic dialogue with Reitveld's Red Blue Chair about the relationship between form, function, and surface. Importantly, it also realizes the agency of the designer in defining the nature of function, something that Sottsass identified as early as 1954 in relation to the work of Charles Eames, "When Charles Eames designs his chair, he does not design just a chair. He designs a way of sitting down. In other words, he designs a function, not for a function" (cited in Radice 1985: 143).

The Memphis exhibition polarized opinion and left nobody who viewed it ambivalent. It picked up the threads of its predecessor Italian design groups and movements but galvanized these into a resolutely contemporary model of design. Interestingly, however, and much like its apparently reviled predecessor

Modernism, Memphis rejected the notion that it constituted a style, indeed Memphis was described as "a super ideology that one prefers to call an attitude" (Radice 1985: 141). Though this rejection of style seems patently untenable in the face of the designs and drawings produced for the first, and indeed subsequent collections and exhibitions by the group, this does betray continued anxiety about the ways in which style may be used and even discussed in furniture design. Although an aesthetics of superficiality was at the heart of the Memphis group's groundbreaking innovation, style was for the group, nevertheless, a dynamic expression of design, not a resolved, self-referential entity. Notwithstanding this, the radical, discordant aesthetic of Memphis designs had a far-reaching impact on all aspects of design during the 1980s, and has continued to influence radical thinking and innovation in furniture design since.

Droog, a Dutch design collective and company that was established in Amsterdam in 1993 by the art historian and curator Renny Ramakers (1948–) and the designer Gijs Bakker (1942) (Ramakers and Bakker 1998: 9), has often been discussed in relation to the critical discourses of Memphis. Translated from Dutch, the word droog means "dry" and has been used to characterize the often unexpected simplicity and humor of the collective's designs. In much the same way that Italian anti-design movements sought to expand notions of design through challenging the context of its production, Droog's work has been developed through collective exhibitions and events that place design on an inclusively public, cultural platform. Like many of its avant-garde forebears, Droog's design rejects the slick, expensive consumption for which most design is actually realized, and through a focus upon economy, simplicity, and social responsibility the group established an innovative model of furniture design that places issues of design process, aesthetics, and importantly, creative authorship at its core (Ramakers and Bakker 1998).

Knotted Chair was designed by Marcel Wanders (1963–) as part of Droog's Dry Tech I project in 1996. The lightweight design was created by knotting aramid and carbon fiber threads into the basic form of a chair and then impregnating this with epoxy resin to give permanence and rigidity to the design. The chair was subsequently hung in a frame to dry, thus allowing the final fixed form to be shaped under its own weight. In its playful combination of simple hand-knotting and chemical process, the design typifies the inherent contradictions that would become characteristic of Droog's design sensibility, the soft threads of the chair standing rigid to create both the frame and support of the chair (Williams 2006: 99).

The apparently improvised aesthetic of the Knotted Chair typifies a recurrent trope of Droog's work that explores the creative opportunity of found or existing objects. This is most explicitly demonstrated in an influential work that predates the formation of Droog. Tejo Remy's (1960–) "You Can't Lay Down Your Memory" of 1991 is a chest of drawers that comprises a number of differently sized and shaped "found" drawers (Plate 10). Each of these is housed and its function restored by its own individual box, and then all of these are haphazardly "lashed-together" by a large burlap belt (Williams 2006: 32–3). Whilst Remy's work was certainly concerned with issues of sustainability and the recycling of objects and materials, the ambition of this work is to reconstitute those objects and materials entirely to reconceive and challenge notions of function. Designs by Marten Baas (1978–) entitled "Hey, chair, be a bookshelf!" constitute a series of found objects and furniture that are pieced together and reassembled into sculptural forms. In contrast to the "found" aesthetic of Remy's work, Baas's designs are reinforced with polyester and coated with polyurethane, which visually synthetize the familiar but disparate forms into a new and singular, unified piece.

CONCLUSION

The contested relationship between form, function, and aesthetics has been one of the central and dominant discourses of furniture design since 1900, and has been at the forefront of critical thinking and practice throughout this period. Although often seen through the binary interpretations of Modernism and Postmodernism, the relationship between the material fabrication and visual expression of furniture is an inherent one. Modernism and Postmodernism are perhaps less useful for the historic periodization of furniture design than for the critical counterpoint they offer through which to question and explore its ambitions and achievements. Whether designers have sought to make the surface of a design the authentic expression of its materiality, or created objects whose appearances challenge and confound expectations about materiality and function, the relationship between the surface, substance, and style of furniture constitutes a critical node that is deeply rooted within the history and practice of furniture design since 1900.

CHAPTER TWO

Makers, Making, and Materials

ANTONY BUXTON

INTRODUCTION

The making of furniture[1] can be viewed as a process: conception, design, and obtaining and manipulating materials to achieve the desired object. But more than simply process, furniture making is a mode of "practice" that takes place in the wider physical and social context: the practical or social requirement for a piece of furniture; the availability of construction materials and the technology and skills employed to fashion them; and the physical, social, and commercial structures for the conduct of craft and the exchange of its production. Furniture making is thus either an activity or a series of activities (an event), and a form of exchange—the creation of a commodity and its consumption. In the broader perspective we might therefore usefully view furniture production as a particular form of culture, centered in process but largely determined by contingent factors.

There are a number of problems in constructing a representative portrait of furniture production throughout a century: although a virtually universal activity, furniture making has frequently been localized and unrecorded and, in consequence, difficult to analyze. Similarly, as a near universal artifact the volume of furniture production is vast and varied. This account therefore can only hope to present some representative themes. Nonetheless, the twentieth century witnessed significant developments in the nature of furniture production. The growth in domestic markets for furniture reflected increasing disposable income and population growth, and concurrently making largely moved from handcraft to industrial process through the organization of labor, the use of powered machinery and digital technologies, and the scale of enterprise. Design theory also influenced the nature of the product, tending to prioritize functionality over decorative appearance. Although this chapter will focus on domains where these developments have been most marked—Britain, a society early to industrialize production and urbanize on a large scale, and the "Western" world of Europe and North America—it does not ignore developments elsewhere in the world. In addition to marked changes in the culture of furniture production, we will consider continuities of craft production and reaction to industrial methods and materials. A broad survey of furniture production in the opening decades of the twentieth century, therefore, is followed by a discussion of the impact of modernist design theory on materials and modes of production, the later twentieth-century response to modernist functionality, and the late twentieth- and early twenty-first-century impact of new technologies and global scales of production.

FURNITURE MAKING IN THE EARLY TWENTIETH CENTURY

Britain at the start of the twentieth century provides a good context to start this survey. Through much of the nineteenth century it had been at the forefront of industrial development, and was the first society to see a majority shift to urban living. The home became largely divorced, physically and conceptually, from the place of work and home furnishings became a significant part of the newly expanded middle-class identity and ideas about comfort. Increasing wealth, an emphasis on the domestic setting as a statement of social identity, and a rapidly rising population thus created the conditions for large-scale demand for domestic furnishings, fed by promotion in advertising material and a range of journals and advice literature. Decorative style was intrinsically historically sourced; a technical chapter in the December 1895 issue of *The Cabinet Maker and Art Furnisher* (1895: 161–2) instructs the reader on the construction of a late eighteenth-century styled "Sheraton" secretaire, to be constructed out of mahogany—traditionally the timber associated with status—"stained to a deep rich shade" with inlay of satinwood or boxwood. The facing page features "Chats with our Carvers" discussing "Renaissance Detail."

A significant portion of the British furnishing industry was located in the first half of the twentieth century in the East End of London to cater for the increased demand for home furnishings stimulated by the metropolitan department stores and their illustrated catalogs (Agius 1978: 154; Smith and Rogers 2006: 13, 16).[2] An example of a small firm supplying this demand was that of W. and S. Vaughan. By the 1880s the firm was supplying upmarket stores in the West End with furniture in the period "Chippendale," "Adam," and "Old English" styles; sideboards, tables, and cabinets in mahogany and walnut; and upholstered seating, and at the end of the nineteenth century the firm was specializing in the production of folding furniture for the colonial market. A relatively small enterprise, it nevertheless drew materials from across the globe and exported its wares, but its demise in 1897 is typical of the relatively insecure status of many smaller furniture enterprises (Vaughan 1984: 31–49). Furniture was also required for the expanding commercial sector. In 1895, W. Angus & Co. announced the establishment of a new factory in East London to meet the increased demand for their high-quality desks of "selected and well-seasoned timber," in contrast to the "inferior quality of American desks [...] put upon the English market" (*The Cabinet Maker and Art Furnisher* 1895: 164).

The middle-class market therefore demanded furniture in historic styles largely structured of solid wood framework and panels, the traditional mortise and tenon joint often replaced with the drilled dowel joint (Figure 2.1), frequently made of imported hardwood timbers and hand polished with shellac.[3] Many small firms would specialize in a narrow range of products, such as carved or turned components. Much of the timber employed in Britain came from empire sources. A study on British Guiana timbers in 1934 notes the threefold increase in timber consumption in the United Kingdom between 1850 and the First World War, and argues that "Empire requirements of timber [...] should be supplied to the greatest possible extent from sources within the Empire." Purpleheart wood is noted for its similarity to mahogany, and

FIGURE 2.1 Antony Buxton, Traditional mortise and tenon with paneled construction and doweled jointing. Design for commercial "Quaint" furniture by H. Pringuer, *The Cabinet Maker* (1895). Illustration © Antony Buxton.

kubakalli and locust wood also for their good furniture qualities (Case 1934: preface, 37). They were employed by East London makers; thus, although often small in scale, early twentieth-century furniture enterprises were drawing materials from overseas, and selling to both national and international markets. Upholstery was often a distinct trade within its own premises, and upholstered furniture was a large proportion of furniture production and sales, frequently with interior sprung seating.

The apprenticeship system had been largely abandoned during the nineteenth century, apart from some workshops producing quality furniture (Kirkham 1988: 51–3). A parliamentary committee noted:

> There is scarcely a legally bound apprentice in London now at present. Boys go into the shop as errand boys, to sweep up the shavings and run errands for the men, and in a little while as they get bigger and stronger, they get a jack-plane put in their hands, and as they assist the men [...] they pick up a knowledge of the trade.
>
> (*Second Report from the Select Committee of the House of Lords* 1888)

Apart from upholstery nearly all employees in the furniture trade were male, a situation—and prejudice—that largely persisted through the twentieth century (Smith and Rogers 2006: 18). The lack of training in the furniture sector was part of a general concern to foster technical skills in the early years of the twentieth century, addressed in Britain by the establishment of Manual Training Centers by the London County Council (Shoreditch College 1998–2017).

Steam power had been harnessed from the start of the eighteenth century—driving machines from a central power source through rotating shafts and drive belts—to process timber into components (Molesworth 1858).[4] As well as sawing and planing, high-speed machines had been developed to cut mortises and tenons, create moldings and sand wood. But handwork was still extensively employed for the assembly of furniture, staining, polishing, and upholstery. The second revolution in the mechanization of furniture making would be the introduction of electric power; an electric motor attached directly to the machine itself. Early developments took place in the first decade of the twentieth century—a direct-drive bandsaw (employing a flexible continuous steel blade) was developed by the American Crescent Machinery Company in 1901—but its widespread introduction did not occur until the second decade (Hjorth 1937: 14–15). Ultimately electric power would result in portable powered tools such as routers—used to create grooves and moldings—and sanders that could replace much laborious hand work. Wood machine manufacturing enterprises appeared in other industrialized nations, for example, the Otto Martin Maschinenbau firm was established in Germany in 1922. Although working wood with hand tools of sharpened steel blades had always been attended with risk of accident, powered woodworking machinery was amongst the most dangerous to operate. Injury to hands used to be relatively commonplace, and wood dust carried its own hazards. Mid-century studies of industrial health revealed a very high incidence of nasal cancer in woodworkers, especially those working with beech wood (Acheson et al. 1968), and wood dust if uncontrolled also creates a high risk of explosion and fire. Trades unions, such as the National Amalgamated Furnishing Trades Association (NAFTA) formed in 1897 (from the Alliance of Cabinet Makers Associations formed in 1865 to organize labor in London's East End "sweated" shops) sought to establish themselves as the representatives of the furniture worker to improve working conditions as well as remuneration, initially against considerable employer opposition (Reid 1986: 24–5).

Another significant area of English furniture production was located northwest of London in the Chiltern Hills, centered on the town of High Wycombe (Figure 2.2). It competed with the East End of London as the principle center of furniture making in the country from the later nineteenth century. Tapping rich local timber resources for traditional forms of seating, the furniture industry had evolved around specific crafts—the turning of beech legs, shaping (bottoming) of elm seats, and steam-bending of ash back hoops—

FIGURE 2.2 Glenister's factory, High Wycombe, c. 1900. Note the drive shafts and belts for machinery and the furniture components stacked ready for assembly, and young workers. Photograph used with permission of Wycombe Museum, High Wycombe.

producing components that were supplied to "factories" in the town for assembling and finishing, and paid on a piecework basis. A few such independent craftsmen continued into the twentieth century (Cotton 1990: 32–42), but a number of larger enterprises emerged, such as Glenisters and Gommes (Mayes 1960: 121). A hard-fought campaign by NAFTA in High Wycombe during the winter of 1913–14 saw over three thousand workers locked out from thirty-one firms for ninety-one days, but resulted in shorter working hours and better pay, and the establishment of procedures to resolve future disputes by negotiation between employers and the union. To this end a national Joint Industrial Council for the furniture industry was established in 1918 (Reid 1986: 55–67, 85). Elsewhere in the Western world furniture enterprises had industrialized to a greater extent in terms of application of technology, organization of labor, and standardization and marketing of products. By the mid-nineteenth century Michael Thonet in Austria had developed a robust yet light birch wood chair employing steam-bent components, obviating any jointing apart from bolting, a development that also meant the chairs could be dispatched dismantled worldwide (Vegesack, Pauley, and Ellenberg 1996: 23–5). Importantly Thonet's production technology did not require skilled labor, and the emphasis on simple components and client assembly could be seen as the forerunner of present-day flat-pack furniture. Plywood was used for the seats (Pevsner 1939).[5] Hand-woven cane was also employed for seating furniture in the early twentieth century by the Dryad Company of Leicester in England (Ernest Gimson n.d.). In 1917 the American inventor Marshall B. Lloyd developed a substitute for cane consisting of kraft paper twisted around a wire thread, initially highly successful in the United States and after transfer to the English manufacturer Lusty & Sons in 1921, Lusty Lloyd Loom furniture was found internationally in the 1930s in very many public and private settings (Curtis 1997: 7, 18–19, 23).

From the late nineteenth into the early years of the twentieth century Art Nouveau naturalistic forms and themes led to a revival in the decorative technique of marquetry—the combination of variously colored wood veneers to create a pictorial or decorative effect. An important center for the production of furniture decorated in this manner prior to the First World War was the French city of Nancy. The designer and manufacturer Emile Gallé (1846–1904) produced furniture decorated with marquetry designs noted for their botanical detail, executed in rare veneers such as plumwood, rosewood, ebony, pear, holly and citrus on walnut, black locust or birch ground. Despite the highly decorative nature of his designs, however, wherever possible Gallé embraced the use of machinery to facilitate production (Tschudi-Madsen 1967: 50–2; Gallé 2014: 173–89).

In the United States the large potential market and generous indigenous resources of timber encouraged the creation of larger furniture enterprises.

Grand Rapids, Michigan, had been established in the late nineteenth century as the foremost furniture manufacturing center in the country, but was superseded by High Point, North Carolina, in the early twentieth century (Pirc and Vlosky 2010). Both centers accessed local supplies of high-quality hardwoods and employed the expanding railway network to distribute their wares. Workers' interests were represented by the Upholsterers International Union of North America formed in 1892, and the breakaway United Furniture Workers of America in 1937. Concerns similar to those in Britain about the unskilled nature of the workforce stimulated the creation of training programs, modeled on the development of technical education in the 1870s in the German *Realschule* (Editors of Encyclopedia Britannica 2018).

As well as large-scale production to satisfy the commercial and middle-class domestic markets, the early twentieth century saw the continuation of the late nineteenth-century revival in handcrafted furniture. Inspired by the writings of John Ruskin (1819–1900), and the example and ideology of the craftsman William Morris (1834–96), certain makers had returned to a culture that integrated design and making, and largely eschewed the use of machinery as inimical to personal creativity. Furniture making thus became the expression of an anti-industrial ethos rather than focusing on the provision of necessary commodities. In the 1890s London architects Ernest Gimson (1864–1919) and the brothers Ernest Barnsley (1863–1926) and Sidney Barnsley (1865–1926) had established a furniture workshop in the Cotswolds working largely in native solid woods, often referring in their work to local rural crafts. The essence of their designs was a deep respect for the integrity of materials and construction. Gimson and the Barnsleys were largely self-taught, following Ruskin's assertion of learning through personal engagement with the material. (Unlike those in larger factories and sweated shops the maker in the craft shop has to be a generalist, moving from task to task and employing a wide range of skills.) Handcrafted furniture was also made in the Cotswolds by the short-lived Guild of Handicrafts (1888–1907) initiated by Charles Ashbee (1863–1942) (Crawford 2005: 279–97), and by the company of the noted twentieth-century British designer Gordon Russell (1892–1980). Influenced by the anti-mechanical Arts and Crafts ethos as a young man, Russell reputedly struggled to reconcile the introduction of machinery with the integrity of production as his furniture company expanded in the 1920s. He evolved the principle—articulated earlier by Ashbee—that machinery makes a good servant to the maker, but a bad master. As Percy Wells commented on Russell in the *Architects, Journal* in 1926: "[Russell] is not blind to [machinery's] abuses, but he recognizes its right place in saving hand and back breaking labor. He uses machinery but controls it, and his furniture is such as will leave the craftsman scope for individual interest, intelligence and skill, either in the simplest or most elaborate examples" (Myerson 1992: 27–8, 4–7).

Whilst America has broadly embraced the most advanced technology in furniture making there has also been a continuing respect for handwork, such as the much-admired nineteenth-century Shaker furniture. Particularly influenced by the British Arts and Crafts ethos were Gustav Stickley (1858–1942) and Elbert Hubbard (1856–1915). Stickley claimed that the furniture that his Craftsman Workshops produced was both simple and well made, "constructed on primitive lines, planned for comfort, durability and beauty, and expressing the spirit of true democracy" (Stickley [1912, 1915] 1991: 3). The quality of the material was vital: "When I first began to use the severely plain, structural forms, I chose oak as the wood that, above all others, was adapted to massive simplicity of construction" (Stickley 1909: 186). It was also important to understand the material to achieve the best results: "I always try to work with the material rather than force it to my own ends, to retain and emphasize the natural interest of grain, texture and color" (Stickley [1912, 1915] 1991: 3). Hubbard founded the Roycroft Workshops to produce Arts and Crafts furnishings, arguably a more commercial production intended primarily to present the consumer with the spirit of the movement (Searl and Via 1994: 57). The production of Charles Limbert's (1854–1923) company in Grand Rapids, Michigan, employing around two hundred men, was determined by such consumer taste: "the people of today desire their furniture plain [...] severely simple yet graceful and utilitarian" (Limbert 1992: v–vi).[6] The architect and designer Frank Lloyd Wright (1867–1959) decried the "sentimentality of the already over-wrought antique product," "this perversion which Grand Rapids alone yields" and also called for a celebration of the potential of the machine: "Now let us learn from the Machine," which "by its wonderful cutting, shaping, smoothing, and repetitive capacity, has made it possible to so use it without waste that the poor as well as the rich may enjoy to-day beautiful surface treatments of clean, strong forms" (Wright 1901). In the west of England, a highly successful company, Shapland and Petter, saw no contradiction in applying the most advanced technology in the production of furniture with an Arts and Crafts character, to make it more affordable. The founder Henry Shapland (1823–1909) had invested in the most advanced American machinery at his works in Barnstaple, Devon, as well as in dust extraction—the previous works had been destroyed by fire—and electric light. The coastal location facilitated the importation of timbers from Scandinavia, South America, South Africa, and North America, meaning such diverse timbers as oak, chestnut, ash, walnut, cherry, poplar, mulberry, birch, and rosewood could be employed (Bennett 2005: 14, 76).

The Arts and Crafts furniture makers may have produced beautiful articles, but they largely failed to enhance the lives of ordinary people in the manner they desired. As Charles Ashbee commented: "We have made of a great social movement, a narrow and tiresome aristocracy working with great skill for the very rich" (1938: 201). The satisfaction was for the maker, and for their small, enlightened, and affluent clientele. Nonetheless, this movement had a disproportionate influence on the emerging system of British technical education. Associated personally with the Cotswold's makers, William Lethaby (1857–1931) was instrumental in the creation of the London County Council Central School of Arts and Crafts in 1896 serving as first joint principal, and as first professor of design at the Royal College of Art. Lethaby's emphasis in furniture design was on the emulation of the best, practical qualities of rural joinery. Other Arts and Crafts makers also played a prominent role in British technical education, such as Sidney Barnsley's son Edward (1900–87) at Loughborough College.

THE MODERNIST IMPACT ON FURNITURE MAKING

In the early part of the twentieth century the emphasis in furniture making was on traditional forms and materials, with the assistance of mechanization to speed up the processing (sawing and molding) of timber—and the use of labor-saving techniques for the jointing of structures. After the First World War through to mid-century, however, attempts were made to align furniture making more closely with industrial design, to make the rationale behind its structure and materials primarily ergonomic function, thereby making sound furnishing more affordable and accessible. These efforts were all part of the design philosophy broadly referred to as Modernism. This changed perception of what constituted "good" furniture ultimately had a profound influence on the culture of making. Increasingly, furniture design and manufacture led a shift in consumer taste away from the derivative decoration associated with social status concerns, toward Le Corbusier's "post bourgeois" modernity (Frampton 2001: 161).

Perhaps ironically these developments can in part be seen to have grown from the anti-mechanical Arts and Crafts movement. In *Das Englische Haus* (The English House) of 1904–5 the German writer Hermann Muthesius (1861–1927) expressed his admiration for the integrity of traditional structures and materials found in British Arts and Crafts houses and furniture. But whilst Josef Hoffmann (1870–1956) of the Vienna Secession movement aimed to bring together the talents of creative artist and craftsman, he also sought efficient manufacturing solutions for the furniture he designed in the early years of the century, creating chairs with bentwood frames and perforated plywood seats and backs, the joints both decorated and reinforced with turned wooden spheres. Richard Riemerschmid (1868–1957), a member of the Deutcher Werkbund (German Association of Craftsmen), rationalized the design of furniture by imitating the functionality of the machine (*machinenstil*) and standardizing the components (*typenmöbel*) where possible. In other words, he pursued the application of common sense, or *sachlichkeit*, rather than an emotional approach to design (Pevsner [1936] 2005: 32–5). The Bauhaus, established under the direction of the architect Walter Gropius (1883–1969) in 1919 in the town of Weimar, Germany, was highly influential both in the application of Modern design theory to industrial production and in its dissemination of a model for technical education. Gropius wrote

> The furniture section of the Bauhaus has a double aim, through experimental work in its carpentry and joinery sections to arrive at clear solutions to the problems that are at the base of various furniture types, working out types which make advanced production possible, [and] the training of pupils who are by their artistic and technical competence are in a position to exercise a sound and progressive influence on the furniture industry.
>
> (Gleiniger 2000: 325–6)

At first Gropius attempted a fusion of artistic inspiration with craftsmanship, but by 1921 he embraced a design approach developed by Marcel Breuer (1902–81) that was more applicable to industrial production (Seckendorf 2000: 404).

Breuer was initially influenced by the furniture designs of the Dutchman Gerrit Rietveld (1888–1964) of the "De Stijl" movement in Holland. Under the direction of Theo van Doesburg (1883–1931), De Stijl adopted a design emphasis on geometric grids and forms, underscored by contrasting painted finishes. As a result, Rietveld's designs for seating and storage furniture consisted of simple frameworks in wood or metal and flat planes. To meet egalitarian principles, versatile and affordable materials such as fiberboard and triplex were employed, as was the concept of customer furniture self-assembly (Simon Thomas 2008: 99–101). Breuer's simple framed slat chair TI1a (1924) with wooden frame and horsehair seat imitates this approach (Seckendorf 2000: 404–5). In the mid-1920s Breuer then progressed to the use of a continuous bent and welded frame of polished tubular steel in chair design with fabric seats to realize "architectonic" design principles—furniture designed with the same spatial and structural logic as buildings. A specialist company, Standard Möbel of Berlin, was established for the production of a range of Bauhaus metal and glass furniture (Gleiniger 2000: 325–6). This was furniture making as engineering, a far cry from wood-based production. In Britain, Practical Equipment Limited was established in 1932 to produce similar lines of tubular steel furniture, combined with solid wood boards and upholstered seats, largely for commercial and institutional settings (Grace's Guide 2020).

In France, the architect Le Corbusier (1887–1965) was also creating designs for seating that employed tubular steel framing. Perhaps as importantly, in his writings he was articulating the modernist shift of perspective from individual pieces of furniture with distinct conceptual associations to furniture regarded generically as "equipment" for the functional aspects of living. In his 1925 book,

Decorative Art of Today, Le Corbusier analyzes furniture as ergonomic *types*, and his installation for the 1929 Paris Autumn Salon (*Salon d'Automne*) was significantly entitled "Equipment for the Home" (Le Corbusier 1925: 69–79; Rüegg 2012: 119–21). Le Corbusier and his furniture collaborators Charlotte Perriand (1903–99) and Pierre Jeanneret (1896–1967) were members of the Union of Modern Artists (UAM), founded in 1929 to pioneer industrial series production to make beautiful and useful objects available to all. Other UAM members included René Herbst (1891–1982), who also explored the use of metal tubing in combination with glass in his furniture. Despite his moniker "man of steel," Herbst nevertheless retained many wooden elements (Duncan 1992: 100). The highly innovative furniture designer and fabricator in metal Jean Prouvé (1901–84), who established a workshop as ironworker and manufacturer in Nancy in the early 1920s, was also a member. Prouvé viewed the machine as an instrument of craftsmanship, and design as an industrial form of art with social responsibility. Having explored other materials, he found his inspiration in sheet steel, and the manner in which it could be manipulated—bent and welded—into structures for furniture combined with solid and laminated wood sheet (Pfeffer-Lévy, Darbois, and Fields 1998: 27–31).

Designers working in the style described as Art Deco adopted the simple volumetric forms of Modernism, but opted for highly decorated surfaces and innovative finishes. Jacques Emile Ruhlmann (1879–1933) employed exotic veneers such as amboyna inset with ivory, Michel Dufet (1888–1985) snakeskin, André Groult (1884–1966) sharkskin, Jean-Michel Frank (1895–1941) plaited straw, and Le Corbusier upholstered in ponyskin (Duncan 1992). Oriental lacquer with eggshell embellishment enjoyed a vogue, adopted by Jean Dunand (1877–1942) and Eileen Gray (1878–1976), who learnt her skill in Paris from a Japanese tutor, Seizo Sugawara (1884–1937) (Starr 2013: 43–6).

Alongside the introduction of innovative materials—steel and glass—perhaps the most significant and enduring development of the second quarter of the century was that of a new and highly versatile way of creating structures in wood: lamination (Figure 2.3). The gluing together of thin layers of wood was not new. It had been used since the eighteenth century (with the grain running at right angles to that on the adjacent layer) to create stable flat components and subsequently achieved mass application as plywood. Wide-scale production of plywood commenced in the mid-nineteenth century with steam-powered saws, and later rotary slicing, facilitating the production of thin slices of wood. In the early twentieth century plywood was commonly employed as a cheaper, stable, and lighter substitute for parts of carcass furniture that were not visible—backs, drawer bottoms, and tops lipped with solid wood—and in utilitarian furniture such as public seating (Edwards 1994: 11; Kirkham 1995: 201–2). But it had not been used significantly as the principal element of furniture structure. The use of lamination for this purpose can largely be credited to the architect and

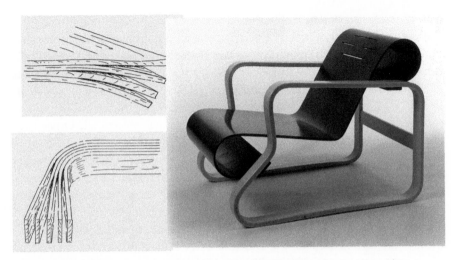

FIGURE 2.3 Antony Buxton, Plywood (top) and lamination construction. Alvar
Aalto's Armchair 41, "Paimio Chair," 1932. Photograph courtesy of Auk Archive/
Alamy Stock Photo.

designer Alvar Aalto (1898–1976) in Finland. The choice of wood for functional
design, rather than steel, can be seen as part of broader Scandinavian values,
respecting natural materials and sound craftsmanship and the harmonious social
environment that they create. Seeking foremost to express functionality, Aalto
nevertheless criticized "steel and chromium surfaces" as "not satisfactory from
the human point of view" (Aalto 1978: 77). He experimented in the creation of
curved structures in wood similar to those possible in tubular steel, not by steam
bending, but by running saw cuts into the solid wood to increase its pliability,
and form a curve that was then made permanent with glue (Fleig 1975: 200–1).
The development of casein (milk protein) cements, more powerful and enduring
than traditional animal glues, were an essential part of this technique.[7] It was
therefore possible to use a natural and traditional material, whilst overcoming
the structural complexity inherent in traditional wood jointing techniques.
Wood lamination was presented as aesthetically pleasing as well as functional.
The Finnish Artek company was formed to manufacture furniture designed
by Aalto, and does so to the present day (Pearson 1978: 141–4). In Britain,
similar laminating techniques were explored by Gerald Summers of the Makers
of Simple Furniture Company to mold a viable chair from one sheet of ply, and
Marcel Breuer (fleeing Nazi persecution in 1933) also designed molded ply chairs
and tables for the British Isokon company similar to those of Aalto (Kirkham
1995: 204–7). These developments in lamination were largely restricted to
forming curves in two dimensions only. Given the fibrous, tensile nature of
wood, achieving a shape molded in three dimensions presented significant

challenges. This problem was tackled by Eero Saarinen (1910–61) and Charles Eames (1907–78) in their prize-winning entry in the New York Museum of Modern Art's "Organic Design in Home Furnishings" competition in 1940, achieving a complete laminated seat shell set on wooden legs (207). As opposed to the multicomponent *machinenstil* design analogy, Eames and Saarinen's "organic" approach attempted to integrate all elements of the structure into one continuous form. Eames's laminated wooden chairs initially combined seat and leg forms, but subsequently returned to a seat shell on separate legs of wood or more commonly steel. He subsequently experimented with plastic materials that could be molded into the seat shell, initially polyester plastic reinforced with fiberglass, one of the advanced materials developed for the military during the Second World War and released for civilian use by 1950 (233–4). Such "plastic" materials could also be infused with pigmentation, simply and durably creating a vibrant range of color. In the early 1950s Charles and his partner Ray Eames (née Kaiser, 1912–88) also saw the potential in molded steel mesh for seat shell forms attached to steel rod legs or leg structures, as with the previous versions (210, 240). And in the late 1950s the Eameses employed cast aluminum components—principally legs—in combination with laminated seat shells in their luxurious reclining seating, finished in rosewood or walnut veneer with deep leather cushions (210, 240). The Eames design was promoted by its manufacturer, the Herman Miller Company of Michigan, as "the most advanced furniture being produced in the world today" (221, 223). This same company produced the Marshmallow Sofa designed by George Nelson (1908–86) in 1958. Upholstery had always been a highly labor-intensive form of seat making, and Nelson experimented with cheaper standardized round foam cushions in bright fabric, vinyl, or leather to cover the frame. Modular storage units with wood or metal panels were also developed by Eames. These units had overall standard dimensions for combination but could vary in function and internal design. This type of case structure became commonplace in the postwar period. In Britain, the "G Plan" system by the Gomme Company of High Wycombe became particularly successful, growing in part out of the experience of producing standardized Utility furniture during the Second World War. The need for simple furniture in war time had presented Gordon Russell, one of the directors of the scheme, with a way of introducing modernist design to a conservative British public (Myerson 1992: 83). To harmonize furniture with homogenous postwar building projects, efforts were made to standardize the size of units, one such scheme being promoted by the Hille Company in Britain (Edwards 1994: 98–100).

Furniture making had thus during the second quarter of the twentieth century diversified widely into industrial materials and processes, reflecting a modernist emphasis on functionality and affordability. Synthetic wood finishing compounds had also been developed and the finishing of furniture—staining and spraying—

had become mechanized. Staining of wood enables different timber species and board materials used in one item to be blended together with a uniform color. Stain is also often required for replicas of historic furniture. Traditional natural pigments had largely been replaced by synthetic aniline stains (derived from coal tar from the mid-nineteenth century) and natural oils, varnishes, lacquers, and waxes by nitro-cellulose finishes developed for use on early automobiles. Spray technology—the application of atomized stain or lacquer—was developed for industrial use (from its medical atomizer origins) by the American DeVilbiss company and was widely adopted in the second quarter of the twentieth century (Grace's Guide 2017).[8] Spray finishing also permits the addition of pigmentation to the finishing lacquer. Subsequent developments have added a range of alternative synthetic finishes for furniture, many now of water-based acrylic latex (Pattou and Vaughn 1944: 121–4; Edwards 1994: 84–7).[9]

Another highly significant mid-century development in materials and production techniques was the introduction of plastic: organic polymers derived from petrochemicals. After the Second World War an innovative culture of furniture design and production emerged in northern Italy, stimulated by the international Milan furniture exhibitions established in the early 1960s. Injection molding techniques—the forcing of heated polymer into a mold—were employed for the creation of one-piece plastic furniture (Figure 2.4) that featured at these exhibitions. An early example was the S-shaped "Panton" chair designed by Verner Panton (1926–98) in 1960 and manufactured by the Vitra company for Herman Miller from 1968. Initial versions were made of polyester strengthened with fiberglass, later substituted with high-resilience polyurethane foam. The Panton chair demonstrates the way in which bright pigmentation can enhance plastic forms. Other examples from the 1960s are

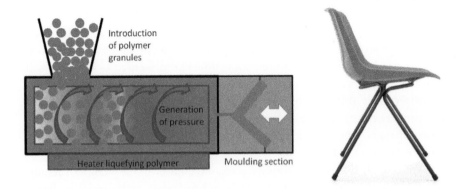

FIGURE 2.4 Antony Buxton, Simplified diagram of the injection-molding process. Robin Day, Polyside stacking chair, 1963. Photograph © Hille (https://www.hille.co.uk/).

Marco Zanuso (1916–2001) and Richard Sapper's (1932–2015) children's stacking chair K1340 (later K4999) manufactured by Kartell from 1964; and Vico Magistretti's (1920–2006) *Stadio* table and *Selene* chairs from the same period. The British designer Robin Day's (1923–2000) *Polyside* stacking chair (1963) with injection-molded polypropylene seat and steel rod legs for the manufacturer S. Hille and Company has sold in its millions around the world. Injection-molded plastics seemed to be the obvious material of choice for furniture in the 1960s—durable, flexible, and cheap—until the OPEC (Organization of Petroleum Exporting Countries) oil embargo quadrupled the price of oil in 1973. Nevertheless, it remains an important furniture material, not only for structures but also for furniture fixtures and fittings. The 1950s also saw the emergence of another phenomenon that had an impact on furniture design, consumption, and making: "Pop" culture, with its emphasis on youthful qualities of sensory enjoyment, affordability, and disposability. Iconic forms appeared, such as the bright red lip-shaped "Marilyn" sofa of cold expanded polyurethane and elasticized fabric cover designed by Studio 65 in 1972. Informal socializing and individualism were epitomized by Eero Aarnio's (1932–) *Ball Chair* of 1963/5 and the fiberglass chair of 1968. Fluorescent colors sprayed on fiberglass and plastic were complemented by shiny white surfaces. The adoption of manufactured board composed of wood chip bonded in formaldehyde resin—particle or "chip-board"—which could be faced with wood veneer, paper printed in imitation of wood, or a durable melamine resin sheet facilitated the efficient manufacture of components for self-assembly. This "ready-to-assemble" (RTA) furniture, also known as knock-down (KD) or flat-pack furniture (a concept credited to the American Erie J. Sauder in 1951), included such examples as Max Clendinning's (1924–) "slot-together" *Maxima* chair of 1966 assembled from standard flat components, and Donald Maxwell's (1937–) *Cube Kit furniture* of 1976, which consisted of white boards to create various items of storage and table furniture.[10] The new informality encouraged moveable and impermanent furniture forms, such as inflatable PVC (polyvinyl chloride) chairs (De Pas, D'Urbino, and Lomazzi design for Zanotta in 1976), and the *Sacco* "bean bag" seat, a fabric bag filled with polystyrene beads, of 1968/9.

Furniture was also designed in cheaper materials to be disposable; for example, Willie Landels's (1928–) *Throw Away* series of upholstered expanded polyurethane foam sofas and chairs designed for Zanotta in the 1960s, or Gaetano Pesce's (1939–) *Up* series (for C&B Italia in 1969), informal seating in nylon-jersey covered polyurethane foam sold vacuum packed. The ultimate in disposable furniture was the paper chair, made of polyurethane-coated laminated paper with a printed pattern, such as the "Chair Thing" designed by Peter Murdoch (1940–) in 1964 for International Paper Inc. Modernist design thus stimulated through the mid-twentieth century a significant rethinking of traditional assumptions about furniture. For example, it could be made of a number of industrial and artificial materials—metals, glass, plastics, and paper—and wood processed into new forms. In addition, the emphasis was now on form and function, and not on decorative embellishment. As a result, much furniture making took place in a factory employing synthesized materials, rather than a workshop using solid timber.

POSTMODERNISM AND FURNITURE MAKING

Despite such new possibilities in materials and processes in furniture making, traditionally styled pieces continued to constitute a significant part of the market, particularly in the later twentieth century. Embracing the "post-modern" critique of the functionalist assumptions underpinning modernist design, a number of designers and makers sought forms and materials that deliberately restored cultural associations. This approach was employed with flair and humor by the Memphis design group in northern Italy in the 1980s, creating apparently illogical asymmetrical forms and employing a wide range of materials, from bright pastel shades of "Pop" patterned melamine and fabrics to rare wood veneer, frequently on the same piece (Sparke 1988: 214). Other designers utilized disused industrial materials as components in their work. For example, Ron Arad (1951–) reused the Rover car seat for his *Rover Chair* of 1981, Tom Dixon (1959–) employed catering ladles and pans to construct his *Bull Chair* (*c.* 1986), and the *bricolage* of the French *artiste-artisan* Andre Dubreil (1951–)[11] employed a range of metal components to create pieces evoking the French baroque style. Also creating unexpected associations, Philippe Starck (1949–) has used injection-molded transparent polycarbonate for his *Louis Ghost* chair (2002), based on a late eighteenth-century form.

In the 1970s, furthermore, there was a small but significant resurgence of the Arts and Crafts ethos in "designer-maker" furniture: individual pieces produced by small workshops employing a mixture of powered machinery and handwork. Throughout the twentieth century a small number of craft workshops had continued to operate in Britain, such as those of Edward Barnsley, son of the Cotswolds' maker Sidney Barnsley, and his apprentice Alan Peters (1933–2009). The most vocal advocate of this type of craftwork has been John Makepeace (1939–), who at Parnham House in Dorset in 1976 created a college for fine furniture making. Early in his career Makepeace realized that for the small workshop, denied the economies of large-scale production, to attempt to imitate modernist design was illogical. Instead such production should, as with the Arts and Crafts predecessors of the late nineteenth century, emphasize its individual and handcrafted character. According to Makepeace, then, "designer-makers" should regard themselves primarily as artists and unapologetically charge accordingly for their work

(Myerson 1995: 95–103). In the United States, Wendell Castle (1932–) was a prominent figure in the Arts and Crafts revival, creating intensely sculptural forms (Taragin 1989). George Nakashima (1905–90) drew on his Japanese heritage to explore the natural qualities of wood, often leaving elements of the tree form and natural "defects"—cracks and knots—within his furniture (Nakashima 2012). Similarly, the British designer-maker Philip Koomen (1953–) has celebrated the variable character of locally sourced timber (Koomen 2004) (Plate 11). Vocational colleges, such as the National School of Furniture in England, continue to provide training in this niche, and magazines such as the American *Fine Woodworking* magazine have also helped to foster a serious amateur furniture making community.

Concerns for the environment in the later twentieth century have impacted the culture of furniture making with respect to its primary natural raw material, timber. The view of the world as one integrated ecosystem, and the accelerating exploitation and destruction of forests for timber—particularly those in tropical latitudes—has implications for the global climate system and biodiversity (Lovelock 1995: xiv). Localized and small-scale engagement with the natural environment combined with a celebration of traditional craft has found expression in Green Woodworking. At Gudrun Leitz's (1953–) educational center established in the early 1990s, for example, and set in natural woodland in the west of England, timber is worked "green" straight from the trees with hand tools. The limited and controlled extraction of timber—"thinning"—allows for continual regeneration of the woodland. Similarly, Hooke Park Forest, now run by the British Architectural Association, seeks to develop innovative ways of sustainably employing timber in buildings and interiors (Architectural Association n.d.). It was such considerations that directed the designer David Colwell (1944–) toward abundant and fast-growing ash as an ideal material for a range of steam-bent ash chairs with modern lines (Colwell n.d.).

Environmental groups such as Friends of the Earth International (FoEI) have campaigned for the limitation and control of logging, particularly in the area of greatest biodiversity, the tropics. This is where the largest reserves of natural rainforest still exist and also a part of the world with a rapidly expanding population. The sourcing of timber has thus become an ethical, economic, and political issue, both in Western markets and globally, with the rapid development of global consumption (Ajani 2011). With varying success, global regulations have been instituted (United Nations Agenda 21, 1992) and FoEI have attempted to shame timber importers in the developed world that trade in timber felled outside these controls (Matthews 2001). The Forest Stewardship Council (FSC) established in 1993, an international, nongovernmental organization, has created a trading logo to certify timber that has been correctly sourced (Forest Stewardship Council n.d.). The European Union, moreover, has adopted its own Timber Regulation ("BM TRADA Highlights Plywood Testing Findings" 2015), and in the United Kingdom a trade body, the Timber Trades Federation, has instituted a Responsible Purchasing Policy (RPP) to guide members and reassure consumers. It has, however, also been argued that the majority of the timber felling in the tropics is due to population pressure, and that sustainable extraction of timber could maintain forests while simultaneously raising local standards of living (Panayotou and Ashton 1992; Burgess 1993).

Whilst the argument will continue on the ethical qualities of timber as a furniture material—as environmentally destructive or as sustainable resource—another solution lies in manufactured wood. This broad technology takes natural fibrous material and bonds it into a substitute for natural wood. Earlier examples of plywood and chip- or particle board have been mentioned above. A twentieth-century form (from the 1960s) is medium density fiberboard (MDF), which is a commonplace, stable component for flat surfaces and case structures, and when veneered can give the appearance of authentic wood (Edwards 1994: 21). It can also be faced with the very durable melamine resin sheet (Editors of Encyclopedia Britannica 2013). Its introduction has stimulated new technologies of construction. Other fibrous cellulosic materials such as straw and bamboo can be used to make successful timber substitutes as well. Concern has grown, however, over "off-gassing": the gradual seepage of toxic elements, such as the formaldehyde used in the manufacture of particle board, into the environment after manufacture (Gilbert et al. 2008). Similarly, awareness of the highly toxic volatile solvents in synthetic lacquers has led to the development and widespread adoption of acrylic based finishes carried in water. At the same time, the hazardous conditions of furniture production in the past, with regard to physical injury and dust inhalation, have been substantially improved due to tighter health and safety regulations, better guarded machines, and more effective means of dust extraction.

FURNITURE MAKING IN A HIGH-TECH AND GLOBAL CULTURE

The late twentieth and early twenty-first centuries have seen new and significant influences on the culture of furniture making. The development of computer technology has made possible the integration of design and manufacturing and potentially removed much furniture making from direct human intervention. Global systems of manufacturing and marketing have led to the establishment of commercial enterprises employing highly sophisticated technology to produce furniture in large volumes, with economies of scale previously unimagined. Concurrent with these technological and commercial developments, an increasingly urbanized global population with an appetite for domestic comfort, receptive to a worldwide media, has resulted in a significant degree of homogeneity of taste in consumption.

The computer, as in other walks of life, has had a transformative impact on furniture manufacture, its many ordering capabilities referred to generically as computer-aided manufacturing (CAM). The design process can be carried out on the computer using a CAD (computer-aided design) software package, which can communicate dimensions directly to the control systems within programmable machines, a facility described as computer numerical control (CNC) (West and Sinclair 1991). Such machines can, for example, largely autonomously and with great accuracy mill components from a sheet of particle board (Figure 2.5). A range of processes are made possible by a variety of tooling, and lasers can also be employed in place of physical cutting. The insertion of material into machines can be fully or semi-automated, minimizing manual involvement. Specialist manufacturers of such machinery cater for a global market, and the cost of sophisticated factories favors the creation of larger enterprises specializing in products catering for the largest possible market. The prime example of the development of global furniture enterprise is the Swedish company IKEA, which has risen to a preeminent position with currently over 350 large retail outlets in forty-six countries, as well as online marketing. Its success is based on attractively designed, affordable furniture,

FIGURE 2.5 CNC furniture production. Photograph © Elma Verhouden/Wikimedia Commons.

and the correct environmental image. Design and production is tightly controlled and integrated. The KD construction of many items both reduces cost and makes them suitable for online sales (Jonsson and Foss 2011). The market penetration of IKEA has helped to change tastes and consuming habits, and thus impacts the whole culture of furniture making. But much furniture is still made in smaller enterprises, the British furniture trade employing 115,000 people within 8,116 companies according to 2013 government statistics (British Furniture Confederation n.d.). Global developments in consumer taste and manufacturing processes can also influence furniture making in the developing world. For example, the Itex Company in Nigeria has grown from its establishment in 1996 to one of the foremost indigenous furniture enterprises in the country and in West Africa. Meeting the appetites of the growing West African middle class it has adopted the international connotations of modern Italian styling, increasingly employing the most sophisticated machinery, and where possible making use of local timbers (Itex Furniture n.d.).

In an increasingly globalized economy, however, possibilities still exist for small furniture enterprises, making bespoke items or furniture designed specifically for individual built contexts. The gradual lowering of the cost of CNC means that smaller enterprises will be able to employ digital technology for innovative and specialist production, and, working in collaboration, potentially compete in larger markets; a process described as "post-industrial" or "neo-craft" production (Kautonen 1996; Steffen and Gros 2003). Three-dimensional printing, by which a wide range of materials can be extruded (printed) to create the digitally directed form, as applied to furniture making is at present still in an exploratory phase, although it seems probable that its importance will increase (Rifkin 2012). As the cost of the process diminishes this also promises to be a versatile technology that can be applied at a small, specialist level. "Craft" will continue to be exercised, but "virtually" on a computer rather with hand tools.

CONCLUSION

Since the beginning of the twentieth century the culture of furniture making, particularly in the Western world, has undergone a marked transformation. The modern factory employing computer directed machinery and, subject to labor representation and working safeguards, is a far cry from the London East End "sweating shop." The act of furniture making is dependent on demand for the product, on commercial conditions, and on technologies and skills. Over the century consumer taste has changed in line with social and economic developments, with the result that historical and decorative styling has increasingly been replaced with simple functional forms. Timbers sourced from around the world have been complemented by innovative materials and processes—those adopted by modernists in metals, laminated wood, and plastics—helping to meet new requirements of domestic convenience. The use of artificial boards such as MDF for self-assembly furniture has led to highly mechanized modes of volume production: component manufacturing rather than furniture craft. The making process has been fundamentally altered by the adoption of electric power in the workshop and by the application of the computer. However, despite the creation of large technically sophisticated industrial enterprises mass-producing furniture for international markets, there is continuing potential for furniture making on a small scale, responsive to local preferences and requirements, employing many of the benefits of developed technologies and materials, but retaining some individual and crafted elements. As an object that is so intimately connected with human life, its conduct and affections, the sentiments associated with "craft"—the nature of the materials and the actions of the human hand—will continue to be associated with furniture.

CHAPTER THREE

Types and Uses

MARJAN GROOT

CULTURE, TYPES, USES, TYPOLOGY, AND HISTORIOGRAPHY

This chapter discusses types and uses of furniture in a cultural history of furniture in the twentieth century. It will address different cultural contexts and attend to designers' debates about ideal types and type-lessness distinctive to the twentieth century. A "cultural history" implies more than just a design history (Figure 3.2 and Plate 14), examining furniture in relation to meaning and use function in a broad range of contexts. Furniture types document cultures of punishment (Figure 3.1) and class relations as well as leisure activities, such as sport and music (Plate 12), or less common uses devised by homeless people, for example (Plate 16). The classic survey study *World Furniture* from 1965, compiled by an international team of experts under the editorship of Helena Hayward and covering antiquity until the 1960s, included furniture beyond Europe and America—briefly examining the Far and Middle East and "Primitive furniture" in African countries; a cultural history in today's ever faster globalizing world should certainly include furniture types and uses evocative of socio-geographical encounters between cultures (Plates 13 and 15). Virtually all cultures share some of the main furniture types: chairs, tables, beds, and chests. They may, however, vary in use and symbolic meaning.

The word type—stemming from the Latin *typus*—has two broad meanings. One meaning refers to a symbol for something. The other meaning is that it refers to a form, structure, or character defining a particular group or class of objects and forming a smaller division of a larger set, potentially expressing ideal properties. Western culture has become familiar with this second meaning of the word type through classifications, or categories analogous to the taxonomies deployed in nineteenth-century natural history. Such typologies were then also applied to other phenomena, furniture being among them.

Furniture types are classified in many different ways, but use is the foremost criteria. The word "use" refers to employing things for a particular end to support specific needs and actions. Uses have formed types and subtypes of furniture for specific goals. While the main type-categories distinguish between sitting, eating, working, relaxing, sleeping, and mobility, refined subtypes in all of these categories can reference a very particular use, for example, by a person, in a specific geographical region, or of a distinctive material. Different types and uses also mix. A twentieth-century "director's chair," for example, has become a common name for a foldable chair with textile seating and back used by film directors because it is very light and mobile while working on a film set. However, the form and folding principle as such had already been in use for ages and, later, as military campaign chairs on battlefields. Hence, while in general types are designed to facilitate actions in everyday life, particular types may also be used in other ways and be not only practical but also importantly ceremonial.

While trade catalogs of English furniture and upholstery firms in the second half of the eighteenth century already categorized their designs as furniture types, typologies have also provided the core structural principle of taxonomy in composing furniture histories in conjunction with dictionaries or national surveys. Important nineteenth-century works were compiled by architects and connoisseur-scholars, such as the *Dictionnaire* (1871) by Eugène Emmanuel Viollet-le-Duc (1814–79), which covered French medieval and Renaissance furniture with "only" three hundred entries. *Dictionnaire de l'ameublement* (1887–9, 3 volumes plus 1 plate volume) by Henri Havard (1838–1921) offered detailed descriptions of more than six thousand different furniture types in France, locating them in written sources from the Middle Ages until the end of the nineteenth century and across Europe. According to Havard, the developing historical sciences of humanities since the 1830s brought about interest in art, industry, costumes, and furniture as well, especially by "erudites." Furniture was thought to reflect important developments in human civilization (Havard 1887–9: vol. 2).

Notwithstanding their descriptive, encyclopedic, and antiquarian approaches, old reference works such as Havard's dictionary remain valuable sources for detailed facts on most furniture types in today's age of Wikipedia. More recent overviews are of a relatively more modest size. In *A Short Dictionary of Furniture*, first published in 1951 and revised and enlarged in 1969, the prolific mid-century British author on furniture and design history John Gloag (1896–1981) described the development of furniture types, makers, materials, methods of construction, and styles in Britain and the United States, including lists of type-names and terms of chairs and chests for the period 1100 to 1950 (1969: 785–813, 196–8, 213). The 1,225-page French inventory, *Le mobilier domestique: Vocabulaire typologique* by Nicole de Reyniès, published in 1987, reevaluated Havard's work, including the word typology in its title and offering illustrations of 4,428 furniture types from the Middle Ages to the beginning of the twentieth century arranged according to use.

The evolution of basic furniture types into ever more subtypes within a main type resonates with a sociology of status signifying hierarchies of aristocratic and bourgeois identities. In combination with materials and production, subtypes distinguish between ranks, between more and less sophisticated people, between rich and poor. A bureau for a company director is different from a table-desk used by a lower employee: the director's bureau may be made of precious timbers with a leather writing surface and have multiple drawers and lockers to signify power, authority, and secrecy, all connected with the etymology of the word "bureau," which, as Havard explains, itself actually was derived from a particular cloth (Havard 1887–9: 1:467–8). The French "bureau ministre" still indicates the superior status of this separate type-form. Such a bourgeois and traditional nature of historical furniture types was challenged in the early twentieth century by modernist designers through their choice of materials, such as tubular steel, and through limitations in the number of types. However, within this relatively small sector of metal tubular furniture designed between 1927 and 1940—chairs, "chaise longues," writing desks, heaters—no less than 2,100 chairs have been documented as a separate category by Otakar Máčel in *2100 Metal Tubular Chairs: A Typology* (2006). This classification reinforced the avant-garde status of such furniture by constructing new elaborate typologies. The same can be said about the nineteenth- and twentieth-century designers' chairs compiled in *1000 Chairs* by Charlotte and Peter Fiell (2012), chairs which first constitute the development toward Modernism and later the dispersal away from it. By contrast, Ray Hemachandra and John Grew Sheridan's *500 Cabinets: A Showcase of Design and Craftsmanship* (2010) focuses on the cabinet as type by offering examples of outstanding contemporary design and artisan manufacturing, for example by British master-craftsman John Makepeace (1939–).

The reference works by Havard, Gloag, and De Reyniès show how subtypes evolved and refined from the Middle Ages to the end of the nineteenth century. In his classic work *Mechanization Takes Command*, first published in 1948, the critic and historian Sigfried Giedion (1888–1968) related this differentiation to the creation of intimate surroundings (Giedion 1948: 293–325). However, subtypes may not change basic types and use function essentially. In the twentieth century, computer tables as subtypes of tables, for example, were not designed until the home computer came into households around 1990, but their form kept referencing tables or table-desks for writing, working, and studying regardless of developments in the types of computer (Atkinson 2010: 136–82). For almost twenty to thirty years, computer tables had a clear use function, but they became unnecessary when portable laptops and tablets replaced them. Likewise, the box, chest, and cabinet once served as containers of devices for playing music, be they simple or sophisticated. The importance of music as a cultural entertainment led Thomas Edison (1847–1931), among others, to produce phonograph furniture-types destined for home use. Other types were small decorated melody-playing cigarette boxes, big symphonic or philharmonic orchestra organs for outdoor fairs, or electrical pianos for dance halls and private use. Musical furniture remained popular while the mechanisms themselves, already existing in earlier centuries, continued to develop. Adaptation to accommodate novel technologies brought about the Wurlitzer music box known as the "Multi Selector Phonograph" of the 1940s and the record players of the 1950s (Science Museum Group n.d.). Many of these fixed musical furniture types and their use would become obsolete with the developments of electronic and digital devices after the late 1970s, such as those developed by the Japanese brand Roland, and of mobile consumer devices such as the Walkman and "boombox." These new forms then also importantly forged new cultural uses as no other type of fixed musical furniture could: the Walkman became *the* tool for the popular health culture of jogging, while the boombox stimulated many new dance forms from the 1980s onward, notably hip-hop, house, and in particular break-dance out on the street (Plate 12). With names such as "ghetto blaster" or "Brixton briefcase," the boombox referenced its popularity among youth and minorities subcultures and became an outlet for societal critique in usually poor neighborhoods in cities (Kerb 2004; Howsyourdad 2006).

Technological advancement during the nineteenth and twentieth century also refined furniture to be more responsive to people with restricted movement. Such furniture types extend back to invalid chairs (or *chaises de commodité*, Havard 1887–9: 1:648–9) that had already been designed in the mid-sixteenth century for elite rulers such as the Emperor Charles V (1500–58), to give him relief from his sickbed during the final months of his life in the Monastery of Yuste in Spanish Extremadura. Developed for general resting, in the twentieth century these chairs acquired electronic controls for moving up and down, and extending headrests, footrests, and armrests. Similar mechanisms facilitate patients' well-being and comfort in our hospital beds today. Still, while the technical means have continued to develop, along with ergonomic comfort, it seems that most types of adjustable furniture and their uses in Western culture have changed very little in essence.

Having defined the nature of types, introduced the role of historiography, and indicated the importance of technology with regard to types and uses, this chapter will now consider everyday uses of furniture types in a social context as documented through written and spoken language. Then it will address types as form-experiments in the canon of Western furniture design between 1900 and 1980, culminating in new uses in the twenty-first century. The reasoning for this threefold structure is motivated by the uses of furniture. Novels and documentary photography demonstrate how furniture types function in daily life, revealing sociocultural conditions and practical circumstances. Types that principally express designers' form experiments, by contrast, have gained a symbolic role in the guiding and formation of a design canon. Manifesto statements, often illustrated with visual representations, articulate symbolic roles expressed within tangible pieces of furniture. Because form and innovation frequently constitute the primary criteria for designers who wish to show their particular vision through furniture types, the canon either isolates the types from everyday use or presents us with an idealized view of use in an orchestrated design setting. But it also envisions the challenge of type-lessness.

LANGUAGE, TYPE, AND FORM

Linguistic wordplay provides revealing insights into the cultural history of the uses and symbolic meanings of many types of furniture across different cultures. A "chair," "table," "bed," "closet," or "cupboard" evokes other activities as figures of speech. Some expressions are old yet still in use and some reflect new customs in twentieth-century culture. For example, being "the chair" is a sociocultural demarcation of high rank for the leader or head of some body, unit, or organization (Havard 1887–9: 1:627; Brewer 1970; *OED Online* 2021a). The expression originates from a real chair that marked the place of the most important person; lower-ranked people sat on stools, stood, or sat on the ground. Chairs with a higher back and armrests indicated a higher status. This ranking continues today. As head of the family, a woman or man may be sitting at the head of the dining table on a bigger chair with armrests; at a board meeting, the person leading it may be sitting at the head or in the middle of the table in a larger chair to mark her or him out; and queens and kings still sit on thrones, particularly on ceremonial occasions.

An informal American understanding of the term "the chair" subverts this hierarchy when it means the electric chair used for the death penalty. The electric chair was developed after scientific disputes during the so-called War on Currents between Thomas Edison and George Westinghouse (1846–1914), and the first use of electricity in execution was in 1890 (Rejali 2009: 125–9). The electric chair experienced its heyday between the early 1920s and the late 1960s. Many of these chairs later fueled the morbid imagination through nicknames, such as "Old Sparky" (Figure 3.1), a nomenclature that appears to have derived from the sparks flying around the heads of the convicts during their

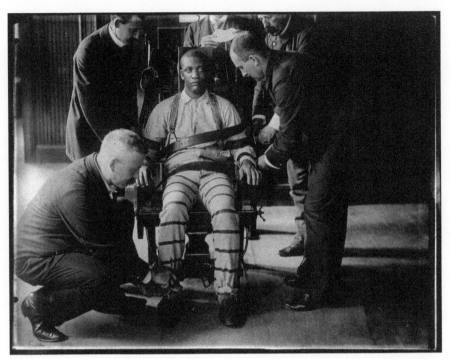

FIGURE 3.1 A man being strapped into the electric chair at Sing Sing prison, *c.* 1900. Photograph by William M. Vander Weyde (American, 1871–1929). Courtesy of George Eastman House Collection, Acc. no. 1974:0056:0386.

execution. "Old Sparky" soon became a generic name for electric chairs as well as acquiring sinister association with a particular example in Sing Sing prison in Ossining, New York, which was reported to have executed 614 prisoners between 1924 and 1964. Less infamous electric chairs were "Old Smokey" (New Jersey) and "Yellow Mama" (Alabama), the latter used since 1927 after being built by a British inmate and painted yellow with highway-line paint (*OED Online* 2021c). Despite the debate surrounding the use of these chairs from a humanitarian point of view, they have become iconic through display in the realms of crime and punishment and in high culture, with many examples now in prison museums as well as in art galleries when they are represented in paintings of Pop artist Andy Warhol.

The positioning of people, and the forms and uses of chairs and tables can also, however, indicate equal status. People spend many working hours in meetings or a conference where a "round-table discussion" gives a sense of speaking without one person taking the role of leader. A table, furthermore, indicates that there is some work to do and the round form denotes the democratic nature of the meeting and work, which is done collaboratively with all participants capable of being looked in the eye. Using a circular form frees participants from a hierarchical order. Likewise, a round dining table transforms the sharing of a meal into a truly communal gathering.

The bed can express inactive as well as active uses. Thus, many idioms reference the notion of sleep, rest, or quiet, yet "sleeping with someone" or "going to bed with someone" is an active sexual encounter that turns the bed into a place of excitement. Closets and cabinets, furthermore, through both their type and form connote the hiding of immaterial thoughts or acts. When dealing with unpleasant experiences from the past, for instance, having suppressed these for some time, we have a "skeleton in the closet." The closet hides away and makes invisible; the skeleton points to something awful and psychologically disturbing. This meaning of the phrase "a skeleton in the closet" had been used in earlier centuries as well (Ayto 2009), but in more recent parlance the closet can also involve a desire no longer to hide lesbianism and homosexuality: to "come out of the closet" or to be "coming out." In this context, in use since the 1960s, the hiding is both a personal and a societal issue, homosexuality still being seen as a threat to "normal" family life. However, this expression seems to have originated in the early twentieth century, when it was taken from the concept of the "coming out" of young upper-class women at a party where they were first formally presented to society (their début) after reaching an adult age or becoming eligible for marriage (*OED Online* 2021b).

Cultures, Classes, and Societies

While wordplay invoking furniture may vary in meaning across different languages, there are also many similarities. Likewise, the significance of the practical and ceremonial functions and uses of furniture in daily life resonates across cultures, periods, and styles. These connections are exemplified in fictional writing. In northern India, for example, the protagonist Laila of the 1961 novel *Sunlight on a Broken Column* by Attia Hosain (1913–98) observes how types of furniture are so much intertwined with people's lives that they creep into their bones determining posture, physique, and appearance from the day they are born. Knowing that peasants used to sit on the ground, not on chairs, and that they wore clothes of cotton, not silk, Laila witnesses how the contrasting backgrounds of guests are apparent in their arrival at an official festive party. Thus, Mrs. Agarwal, who grew up in the culture of humble peasants, "looked uncomfortable in silks and shoes and sitting on chairs even after years of prosperity. Imagination clothed her more suitably in cotton, seating her on the ground, barefooted, in a traditional kitchen" (Hosain [1961] 1988: 183). As Laila notices, very few people can escape the cultural habits of using particular types of furniture associated with their class in the way they walk, sit, stand, or work; a mingling of the social and biological that Pierre Bourdieu (1930–2002) has called the people's "habitus" (Bourdieu [1984] 2010). Strict social class distinctions also determine daily living in Laila's own wealthy and esteemed Muslim family. Domestic realms for women (called *zenana*) and men are separated, while types and uses of furniture show how "native" and "British" quarters coexist for a long time. When eating in the room of Laila's Aunt Abida, they are seated around a table cloth spread on a sofa or long bench called a *takht*. The *takht* could also function as a bed and as a seat connoting authority like a throne (Hosain [1961] 1988: 36). While Hosain's story tells us about enormous social and economic changes during the westernization of India between the 1900s and 1950s, when the subcontinent faces divisions between old and new generations, the traditional and the westernized, and between Muslims and Hindus, it also shows that these changes do not instantly affect existing customs and furniture types. The uses of pieces of furniture reflect daily human occupations as well as traditions, and functions and conventions that determine form and type.

Of course, the intended practical function of a piece of furniture can always be denied by using it in contrasting ways that we like or need instead. We have probably all, for instance, chosen a table or chair to stand on when we wanted to change a light bulb, hang a picture on the wall, or clean something. Beds, in addition, are very often used for sitting as well as sleeping. In Hosain's novel, for example, sitting together on the string bed creates a caring intimacy between the family's faithful woman servant Hakiman Bua and the girl Laila: "She [...] unrolled a thin striped carpet over the bare strings of her bed, and said again, 'Come and sit down'" (Hosain [1961] 1988: 39). Thus typologies can extend across geographical and cultural borders, expressing understanding with cultures other than one's own. Economic status can also transform how types are utilized, with less wealthy people needing to use their few pieces of furniture in multifunctional ways, as indeed the string bed of the servant Hakiman Bua plays many roles in the humble room in which she lives.

Political conflicts could also pose limitations on available furniture types. In Britain, and on the European continent, this was the situation after the two world wars. When the British government built houses during and after the First World War as "Homes fit for heroes," furniture for such houses was designed by Percy A. Wells (1867–1956) and promoted in exhibitions by the Design and Industries Association (DIA), founded in 1915. It was published in Wells's book *Furniture for Small Houses: A Book of Designs for Inexpensive Furniture with New Methods of Construction and Decoration* (1920). Besides being rational, economic, hygienic, and austere, hence altogether fit for purpose, there were small varieties within each one of the seven suggested furniture types, such as "Dressers and sideboards"; this indicated the furniture trade and craft as target group rather than consumers (Evans 2006). During the Second World War, the British Utility Furniture Scheme was devised as a government rationing program to meet the basic needs of many people when a lack of raw materials and disturbed manufacturing processes restricted consumption. The scheme, which lasted until 1952, was formulated by an expert committee of designers including the Arts and Crafts-trained furniture maker Gordon Russell (1892–1980) and the author of *A Dictionary of Furniture*, John Gloag.

Furniture may not only serve a practical purpose or be "used" symbolically to indicate status, it may also fulfill a psychological need as a tangible trace of memories. In *La pensée sauvage* (1962), the anthropologist Claude Lévi-Strauss (1908–2009) proposes that through archives, objects, and furniture we bring forth the contradiction of a lost past and a present in which it survives (Lévi-Strauss 1962: 321; De Reyniès 1987: XIII). Such temporal discrepancies have been explored by many novelists, such as the French Symbolist writer Marcel Proust (1871–1922) at the beginning of the twentieth century. In his *À la recherche du temps perdu* (In Search of Lost Time), the preservation of old family furniture features as a hyperbolic memorializing of generations and times past. As Proust's housekeeper Céleste Albaret (1891–1984) recalled in 1973, some rooms in the large and high apartment were packed with old wooden furniture from Proust's parents, which they had in turn inherited from his mother's uncle. There was a chandelier and candelabras which were never used; the writer worked in his bed beside a little table lamp with a silk shade. Céleste's memoirs documented the lamp and bed in a function that went beyond the use associated with their typology (Albaret 1973: 74–7).

CHALLENGING TYPES: THE WESTERN EUROPEAN MODERNIST DESIGN DISCOURSE, 1900–25

Having paid attention to furniture types and uses in a general cultural-societal context we will now examine how professional Western designers and architects in the twentieth century have taken up two challenges in intervening with types and uses as these are commonly understood. Is there such a thing as type-less furniture? Is it possible for furniture *not* to be perceived as furniture?

Designers' involvement with furniture types and programs initially responded to the poor conditions in urban working-class housing. A century of industrialization, population growth, and migration from the countryside to the cities had created an urgent need for more and better houses. While the issue had existed since the early 1800s at least, it was in 1901 that Benjamin Seebohm Rowntree (1871–1954) denounced the living conditions of the poor classes in Britain in his book *Poverty: A Study of Town Life*. The infrastructure needed to assure sanitation and clean water for each household was a governmental responsibility. Designers, however, felt stimulated to focus on design solutions for minimal dwellings and utilitarian furniture for the working and middle classes. This focus was particularly strong from around 1905 onward in

Germany, with furniture programs conceived in the Vereinigten Werkstätten für Kunst im Handwerk (United Workshops for Art in Craft) in Munich and the Dresdener Werkstätten für Handwerkskunst (Dresden Workshops for Craftsmanship), both founded in 1898. The designers Bruno Paul (1874–1968), Richard Riemerschmid (1868–1957), Bernhard Pankok (1872–1943), and Peter Behrens (1868–1940) were the leaders of this movement and together they also formed the Deutsche Werkbund (German Work Federation) (Günther 1982: 36; Nerdinger 1982: 16–20; Bloom Hiesinger 1988: 14–18, 94). The workshops wanted to realize William Morris's (1834–96) idealistic goal to design a sound yet artistic range of crafts affordable to a large number of people, while in terms of design they greatly admired the work of their contemporaries, notably architect-designer Mackay Hugh Baillie Scott (1865–1945) and his fellow Scotsman Charles Rennie Mackintosh (1868–1928). Another rhetorical aim, therefore, was to educate the taste of consumers by offering an alternative to historical styles of commercial furniture production.

Modernist design discourse developing shortly after 1900 importantly stimulated a rethinking of types when designers and architects began to question the notion of type, while at the same time adding flexibility to the uses of furniture. In 1908, Bruno Paul coined the term *Typenmöbel* (Type furniture) for a modular system or *Baukastensystem* (Building system), produced by the Berlin workshop of the United Workshops for Art in Craft.[1] Two years earlier, the *Maschinenmöbel* (machine-made furniture) of good design and quality for a relatively low price by his colleague Riemerschmid had established the principle. Having begun their careers designing *Jugendstil* reform furniture in the late 1890s, their *Maschinenmöbel* advocated the change toward more austere and pragmatic designs by means of "good form, good materials, and machine manufacturing" (Günther 1982: 38). In general, *Maschinenmöbel* and *Typenmöbel* reduced the number of furniture types for more efficient production techniques. In the designers' view, their "mobile way of life, nomadic in apartment buildings" demanded furniture of a relatively small size that was easy to assemble and to extend (Popp 1916: 6). Chairs, tables, and beds were designed as basic forms while the chest as a type was formed by modular units. Paul called it "type furniture for city and country." "Types" also referred to ensembles of furniture for a limited range of "types" of interiors, categorized as I to III. Set I, for instance, intended for laborers, was the most basic and cheapest type: a range consisting of furniture for a living room, kitchen, and bedroom. Acknowledging the influence of America and England, the system had standard measures and forms for wooden panels, drawers, side panels, and compartments, which could then become "furniture cells" (*Möbelzelle*; Popp 1916: 3–6, 31, 34–6). Nonetheless, some of Paul's *Typenmöbel*, allowing for variation in, for example, types of sideboard or clothing chests, were not always that simple in design.

In the course of the twentieth century the principle of assembled furniture with changing and flexible types, especially sideboards, dressers, and chests, was taken up by many firms and designers and in many price categories. These then featured in museum-organized home exhibitions that displayed the work of upcoming designers, as in the oft-cited Design for Home Furnishings exhibition at the Museum of Modern Art, New York, in 1940. The principle finally achieved almost universal success through its mass manufacturing by the Swedish furniture firm IKEA (Mårtenson 1981; Kristofferson and Jewson 2014). Although not invented in the twentieth century, furniture to be assembled by personal preferences of consumers clearly became one of this century's principal developments, whether for living room, bedroom, or kitchen. It did not really lead to completely new types; rather, it merged the functional and the symbolic by being practical as well as signifying rational and systematic flexibility of truly modern living.

These designers of the 1900s, however, did not extend their idealistic programs for modern furniture to theorize about the spatial effect of dwellings. This was done slightly later by the functionalist avant-garde. The most famous example of such an early flexible space for living is the Rietveld Schröder house in the Netherlands, dating from 1924 (Figure 3.2). Mrs. Schröder-Schräder (1889–1985), the widow

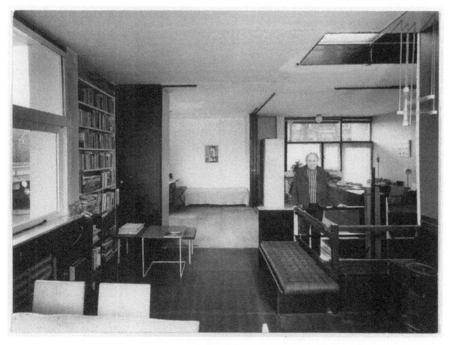

FIGURE 3.2 First-floor living room of the Rietveld Schröder house with Mrs. Schröder-Schräder, Utrecht, the Netherlands, 1924. Photograph © DACS 2020. Centraal Museum Utrecht/Pictoright Amsterdam.

of the lawyer Fritz Schröder (1878–1919), commissioned the furniture designer and maker Gerrit Rietveld (1888–1964) to design a new house for her and her three young children. In collaboration, they created a type-less living space in the house by suggesting different and flexible functional spaces through colors—red, white, blue, yellow, gray, and black—and floor plan alone. The family area on the first floor became one free-flowing space with color indicating the different use functions, offering the possibility to turn this space into separate rooms—living room, bedrooms—by pulling out side panels, which were hidden during the day.

To ensure this reconceptualization of space, Rietveld designed the furniture as well. This included only a few detached pieces, one being a sofa-bed. All of these formed "color sculptures," which matched the colored planes of space (Plate 6). Beds and tables were fixed to the wall and could be pulled up when not in use. Cupboards were incorporated into the walls. This was not, as such, a new solution but was now designed to allow the space to act freely upon the beholder. To not spoil the experience of the environment, possessions ("stuff") were denied visual presence. Contemporary photographs, however, show that this was difficult to respect at all times: we can see lamps and books, dishes in the kitchen waiting to be washed, flowers placed in a vase, and a television with a toy airplane resting on it. Obviously quite an effort was required to live in such modernist aesthetic environments.

Interestingly, these modernist designs facilitate new flexible uses of space but perpetuate traditional typologies of furniture. Between 1919 and 1923 Rietveld designed a children's chair, an "easy chair," and a dresser for different clients (Kuper and Reitsma 2012). Type-less and flexible space, then, appears easier to visualize and to realize than type-less furnishing, unless the identity of furniture is denied, becoming a form of sculpture. Theo van Doesburg (1883–1931), the most outspoken artist-designer of the circle of Dutch creative personalities known as De Stijl after their eponymous journal, argued that furniture as "abstract-real" sculpture would define the interior space (Doesburg 1919). Referencing Rietveld's first pieces, the chair was an:

> unintentional, yet relentless processing of open spaces, involving the contrast: necessity, sitting, chair. Material limitation opposing rich, undisguised and permanent expression of open spaces. Chair. Mute eloquence as of a machine.
>
> (Doesburg 1920: 46)

Machines and "sitting on air"

Van Doesburg's reference to the chair as "a machine"—a term which was actually coined when describing the reclining chair Model 670, designed by Austrian architect Josef Hoffmann (1870–1956) in 1905 (see Plate 2), as a *Sitzmaschine* (sitting machine)—was envisioned a few years later in the medium of steel. Modernist designers not only wanted the spatial effect of an interior to be harmonized and not intruded upon by many different types of furniture, but also embraced simplification by reducing the number of types to serve basic, "ideal" actions in modern life (Wilk 2006a: 225–48). For a brief period, steel became the prime material for these postwar *Typenmöbel*. For Hungarian-born Marcel Breuer (1902–81), the steel chair mirrored the evolution of the needs and actions of human beings. In the emerging international context of the Bauhaus school in Germany, then still located in Weimar, Breuer designed his first so-called African Chair in 1921 (Plate 13). Made of wood and woven textile upholstery by Gunta Stölzl, it functioned as a cultural-evolutionary type-statement in the development from a past, signified by this non-Western "primitive" throne-form, to "Western civilized present." Breuer's real goal, however, was to attain the logical evolution from the "primitive, emotional" wooden African throne-chair to the tubular metal frame of the cantilever chair, finally to arrive at an *elastischen Luftsäule* (elastic air column), an invisible "floating" chair to "sit on air." This not-yet-realized final phase of the "air-column" was visualized in a 1926 Bauhaus filmstrip-narrative of a woman in sitting posture without support (Breuer 1926). Due to the persistent modernist narrative promoting minimal line, form, color, and modern materials, Breuer's African Chair was recovered and reevaluated in the Bauhaus collection in Berlin as late as 2004 (Bauhaus Online n.d.).

Fellow avant-garde functionalist designers came up with similar plans to limit the number of furniture types. The Swiss-French architect Charles-Édouard Jeanneret, known as Le Corbusier (1887–1965), presented a Pavillon de L'Esprit Nouveau (Pavilion of the New Spirit) at the exhibition of modern decorative and industrial arts held in Paris in 1925 as "a dwelling type realized exclusively industrially, systematically using standardized elements" with built-in cabinets and closets. In *The Decorative Art of Today* Le Corbusier argued for "need-types," "functions-types," and "furniture-types," plain standardized furniture for universal human tasks which operated as extensions of our bodies (Le Corbusier 1925: 3, 67–79). His declaration in the Purist journal *L'Esprit Nouveau* (The New Spirit) implied that it sufficed to furnish a house with a desk chair for working, be it an existing industrial, nineteenth-century design; a chair with slightly reclining back for sitting comfortably; and a "chaise longue" for resting (Eliel et al. 2001: 51–2, 110–11). The latter two types were of steel and codesigned by Le Corbusier and Charlotte Perriand (1903–99), and the "chaise longue" in particular has become iconic through a photograph of Perriand relaxing in it, with her legs seductively exposed (McLeod 2003: 36–63, image on 49).

The brothers Heinz Rasch (1902–96) and Bodo Rasch (1903–95) from Stuttgart illustrated their categorization of furniture types according to essential human activities in daily life with a photograph of a man working while sitting "on air" without any furniture to support him, similar to Breuer's concept of an "air column." A woman photographed for a brochure on household articles (Rasch and Rasch 1928) demonstrated two basic postures. Tables supported the active posture of working or eating, and resting implied two types: one for reclined sitting and one for lying down (*Brüder Rasch* 1981: 108). The Rasch brothers also specified types for particular activities, such as a work chair and a radio chair, the latter indicating their sensitivity to the consumption of the radio as a modern medium of communication. Discussing the skeleton structure of houses, and referencing paper room dividers of the Japanese dwelling house, they also celebrated flexibility in living, arguing that changes in mores take place in the family dwelling which "must, therefore [...] be variable" (124). Their drawings for an *Einfamilienreihenhaus* (one-family dwellings) envisioned in Stuttgart indicated quite small proportions: ninety-six square meters on two floors of six meters wide and eight meters deep each, and stimulated the design of flexible furniture for multiple uses and to stack away (68–71). They actually designed a number of folding and collapsible chairs and armchairs, as well as a desk with suspended drawers, which could be dismantled to become a table. They advocated machine-made manufacturing of furniture, writing that "All development means improvement. The improvement of the chair concerns its solidity, lightness, comfort and cheapness. Handicraft has reached its limits." In this statement, weight had a particular fascination: bent plywood furniture by Peter Behrens (1868–1940) at the Werkbund exhibition of 1927 in Stuttgart weighed two kilograms for a three millimeter thickness of plywood and a writing desk with drawers weighed twenty kilograms (*Brüder Rasch* 1981: 9, 14, 17–19, 24–9, quote on 122).

However, all varieties of Modernism could not and would not break with types: claiming to be revolutionary in terms of form, material, and to a certain extent also in terms of perception of space, they limited but did not escape actual basic types of furniture and their common uses.

ESCAPING AND DECONSTRUCTING TYPES IN DESIGN DISCOURSE, 1930–70

Biotechnique as metaphor

Functionalist Modernism was rivaled for "type-lessness" in the interwar years by Surrealist alternatives to *Typenmöbel*, such as the furniture sculptures developed from 1924 by Austrian-born architect Frederick Kiesler (1890–1965). Working toward a more theatrical concept, Kiesler envisioned an *Endless House*, which would dissolve the boundaries between different disciplines, combining theatre and stage sets, designs for gallery interiors, furniture designs, poetry, painting, and sculpture. His house-model sculptures of the early 1930s, such as the *Nucleus House* and a one-family *Space House*, led to the *Endless House* as a small fertile cell. He theorized these environments through the concept of "Correalism" where "the physical, mental, social, mystical, and magical energy of man" unite (Kiesler 1949). In his "Correalist manifesto or the united states of sculptural art" of 1947, Kiesler equated living with being with oneself and the dwelling with a living organism, a spatial and spiritual continuum evoking to the human embryo. Presenting his ideal space in the context of Peggy Guggenheim's (1898–1979) Art of This Century gallery in New York in 1942, he included a Correalist chair with "coordinates of the forces which bring forth the new object and its functions" (Kiesler 1949). The "chair" had a wavy form for four different functions expressed through different colors: a sitting function in blue; a pedestal for sculpture in green; a double-sided easel for paintings in yellow; and a series of benches in gray-yellow.[2] In 1959, the model for *Endless House* opposed Le Corbusier's functionalist house as a "machine for living."

While generating type-lessness, the metaphor for living organisms and wombs, as well as for the irregular and dark spaces of grottos in relation to houses for living, was important for the Surrealists. In a description of *Goût* (Taste) in 1933, Tristan Tzara (1896–1963) compared this basic house form to a protective "motherly" space, dwellings of peoples before Western "civilization," and prenatal comfort (Vidler 1996: 164). Such metaphors oppose the active everyday life spent eating and working at tables and sitting on chairs.

Type-lessness and escape spaces

Surrealist organicism of the late 1920s and 1930s inspired experimentations in 1960s furnishing. Thus, we can discern the tracks of two conceptual lines of thought in the twentieth century regarding types of furniture: on the one hand a Romantic-Symbolist-Surrealist mode, stretching toward Postmodernism, and on the other, an ever-present functionalist-rationalist mode. Both strands deployed futuristic rhetoric and can be called modern but there is a difference between functionality and play, and how they respond to cultural progress. This complex referentiality among design cultures is embodied in the *House of the Future* of the British designer duo Alison Smithson (née Gill, 1928–93) and Peter Smithson (1923–2003). Designed in 1956 for the Ideal Home Exhibition in London (Jackson 1998: 104; Heuvel and Risselda 2004), the House suggests an optimism at odds with the evolving Cold War period's "anxious existentialism" as expressed in the "This is Tomorrow" show held at the Whitechapel Art Gallery in 1956 and reflected upon by J.G. Ballard in his dark science-fiction novels (Colombino 2012). Although the *House of the Future* was conceptualized as an innovative organic capsule, nonetheless it perpetuated basic modernist furniture types: chairs for sitting, a reclining chair, a standard lamp, and a "dialogue table," which could sink into the floor. Besides audiovisual technology and form, the novelty of the house appears to reside mainly in its deployment of plastic materials for the structure and furnishings.

In the early 1960s, architecture and design opened up the fixed form by continuing the principle of linked modular compartments or "cells," which were ideally type-less through a fusion of space and furniture. Important examples were conceived by the Danish designer Verner Panton (1926–98) and the British collective Archigram, with Peter Cook (1936–) designing a *Plug-In City* in 1963–4. Both Panton and Archigram were also among the earliest to design inflatable furniture that in terms of function resembled the relaxing chair. A transparent *Cushicle* of 1966 by Michael Webb (1937–) for Archigram recalls the personalized enclosure of the Surrealists' womb-like environment albeit in un-Surrealist transparency and with technological devices (Plate 23). The *Cushicle* as type did not show any physical activities by the inhabitants, and as such was more or less repeated around the year 2000, for example in a retro follow-up called *Instant ego*, a foldaway hood to unzip and form a capsule with inside projections of "cyberspace landscape" by three young designers working as PO.D in Paris (Smith and Topham 2002: 110–11). The opaque membrane of this prototype "cockpit" dwelling, *Instant ego*, a form of architecture-on-demand, showed the electronic wires as veins under a skin, connecting twenty-first-century inhabitants to a virtual reality.

Other 1960s designers envisioned an entire inflatable cylindrical home with blown-up furniture, as did Vietnamese-born and French-educated engineer-designer Quasar Khanh (1934–). His *Structures Gonflables* (inflatable structures) were installed at the Musée d'art moderne-Musée des arts décoratifs in Paris in March 1968 along with other exhibits by the group UTOPIE (*Catalogue de l'exposition structures gonflables* 1968). Making one literally sit, or sleep, on air, inflatable furniture seems to follow up on the functionalists' ideal of "sitting on air" attempted in tubular steel. It only really became possible, however, through the innovative material of plastic. Blown-up plastic furniture denies fixedness of form because it suggests temporality (it is not always inflated) and, as a material, can potentially be shaped into many different forms. As linguist and cultural philosopher Roland Barthes (1915–80) wrote in 1957, plastic, which does not exist as natural substance, embodies the myth of infinite transformation (Barthes 1957: 171–3). And yet, designs such as the *Structures Gonflables* do not transform basic use-types. While achieving an ephemeral quality through thin plastic membranes, fixedness of type is only denied when the furniture is not inflated. In consumer markets inflatables have become popular for leisure furniture, such as waterbeds and chairs, and children's play cushions and seats, types that do not demand permanent use.

Danish designer Verner Panton's *Phantasy Landscape* of 1966, however, truly enacts the merging of living space with furniture through one form with multiple functions. Nonetheless, photographs of the fantastic and dreamlike landscape use suggest gendered disconnection from everyday working life. Two physically inactive women lounge about, seemingly watching a screen presenting another woman sitting just like them. A man in the distance appears to be working at a small table-desk, the only item to remind one of a fixed furniture type. The *Phantasy Landscape* was originally installed as a room design on a pleasure boat by the chemical company Bayer AG at the "Visiona" exhibitions in 1968 and 1970 in Cologne and is perhaps best used as a relaxation module, its function primarily suggesting resting and sleeping rather than working (Plate 14). Indeed, entering the *Phantasy Landscape* oneself—an option that happens quite seldom—one becomes immersed in a sense of play. As such it denies function as the core of real life (Bourdieu [1984] 2010: 172). Newness through form involved informal and relaxed postures of youth and popular culture to no longer submit to the "type" language of bourgeois culture. In this way it did stimulate changes in seating postures with bench compositions for lounging in popular living landscapes during the 1970s (Holschbach 1995). However, by denying everyday working life it also remains in the symbolic realm of the design world, its form becoming associative of a womb fantasy. Referring to a landscape and not a house, its title extends Kiesler's concept of the endlessness of module compartments enlarging the form by repetition. The round, arguably organic form of this landscape-space is realized through the use of rubber.

The sculpture-furniture *Phantasy Landscape* was exhibited with changing colored lights to further enhance the fantasy aura of the installation, making an overwhelming experience of intense blue and red form units. Similar color effects supporting avant-garde psychedelics heightened musical performances of British rock band Pink Floyd, who, on their studio album *Atom Heart Mother* (1970) included a composition with sounds of their producer enjoying his breakfast: "Alan's Psychedelic Breakfast" (Powell et al. 2017). This tonal spatiality seemed to offer parallel experiences to a psychedelic trip, which Aldous Huxley (1894–1963) described over a decade earlier in *The Doors of Perception* of 1954, suggesting a revision of the everyday cultural order after the Second World War. While Huxley's earlier technological dystopia *Brave New World* of 1932 satirized rational modernist-functionalist utopian visions in service of political totalitarianism, in *The Doors* the British author addressed the limitations of rational human perception through symbolic intellectual language systems. Intoxication by the drug mescaline made him experience the differences in perception between looking and reading, and between design and literature. The sensual intensity of color, form, and space through objects brought a new insight into the very Nature of Things: four bamboo chair legs in the middle of a room incited Huxley to reclaim Gertrude Stein: "A rose is a rose is a rose. But these chair legs were chair legs were St. Michael and all angels" (Huxley 1954: 20–2, 23).

Verner Panton explored the unit principle further in the 1969 *Pantower*, which allowed for a variety of seating postures in the vertically aligned units that were meant to save space, in this way symbolically addressing solutions for densely populated future cities. Other designers also came up with contemporary solutions that promoted flexibility while denying fixed separate types. These include Italian designer Joe Colombo (1914–78) with his *Tube Chair* for Flexform (1969), where "tube" references the functionalist tubular steel but is in fact referring to foam-coated plastic PVC tubes clipped together to allow various seating configurations, stored one inside the other as one tube. The 1960s designers also kept exploring the sculptural form, as exemplified by the *Chair* that Jane Dillon (1943–) designed for her degree at the London Royal College of Art in 1968 (Jackson 1998: 180). The powerful metaphor of biotechnique, which associates furniture and dwellings with living and natural bodies and processes, continued to inspire many designs as well, as with the Japanese Metabolist group who, around 1968, focused on biological cycles of growth and decay for buildings as well as organisms. While biological metaphors remain powerful for imagining house types, they remain equally problematic for furniture types. Yet, many forms from the 1990s keep referencing and favoring capsule house types where no furniture seems needed, as in the publication *Extreme Houses*, where an *Embryologic House* of 1999 by Greg Lynn (1964–) would be customized for individual clients and designed and produced using computer numerically controlled (CNC) machines (Hensel and Menges 2006: 92; Lynn 1999; Smith and Topham 2002).

Postmodernism, types, and culture 1980–2015

Writing on design as well as museum displays increasingly framed the chair as the ultimate personal design challenge for designers and architects, turning the tubular chair into an icon of the Modern movement (Mundt 1998; Máčel 2006). The chair as a type became a statement of the designers' and architects' personality—and that was male, first and foremost. As a form of small architecture, the chair did so through novelty in material, technology, and form but not as type. Designer chairs were presented as a historical "genealogy of species" by companies such as the Swiss Vitra and Italian Cassina, producing miniatures as collectors' items next to reeditions of vintage pieces (Vitra 2021). The popularity of the designer's chair fuels a specialist jargon: there is a Rietveld chair or Marcel Breuer's tubular-steel and leather "Wassily chair," discussed in more detail in Chapter 1, "Design and Motifs."

In the discourse of canonical design these chairs have become the "weapons" by which design principles are fought out between functionalists and anti-functionalists. In contrast to the intellectual and abstract modernists, anti-functionalists liked to reference popular culture, for instance through playful sofa-forms that evoked movie stars and sportsmen. The Surrealist painter Salvador Dalí (1904–89) designed a satin sofa in the form of red or pink lips in 1937, named after the lips of the sexy 1930s American movie star Mae West

(1893–1980). A pink variation was commissioned by the wealthy British poet and artistic socialite Edward James (1907–84), who turned Monkton House, part of his inherited West Dean estate, into a Surrealist environment in collaboration with Dalí, other Surrealists, and the British decorator Syrie Maugham (1879–1955) (Wood 2007). Nearly half a century later in 1983, the Austrian architect-designer Hans Hollein (1934–2014) and the Italian firm Poltronova came up with a postmodern reference to the "Mae West Lips Sofa" by honoring Marilyn Monroe (1926–62), another "buxom blonde model-turned-actress," who by then had become the sexiest woman of twentieth-century popular culture (History 2009). Hollein's sofa was inspired by Marilyn's white skirt blowing up high and exposing her legs as she stands over a subway grate on the New York City set in the film *The Seven Year Itch* of 1954, directed by Billy Wilder (1906–2002). This sensationalist anti-bourgeois dress scene contributed to the discord in Marilyn's tumultuous liaison with baseball player Joe DiMaggio (1914–99) between January and October 1954. Joe's standing as a legendary American figure had already been celebrated in 1970 with the creation of a sofa-bed-chair in the form of a giant leather baseball glove or "Joe seat" by Italian designers Jonathan de Pas (1932–91), Donato D'Urbino (1934–), and Paolo Lomazzi (1939–). Being a very elegant player who embodied the American dream of fame and fortune, DiMaggio was behind much of the mid-century success of the New York Yankees as a center fielder; Joseph Durso recalled in a *New York Times* obituary how DiMaggio's "56-game hitting streak in 1941 made him an instant and indelible American folk hero" (Durso 1999).

Challenging the sofa-type as form and playing with its reputation as both a seductive and bourgeois type of furniture, these first postmodernist designers overcame its ordinary domesticity. The regular sofa-type, however, lived on as daybed for other consumers. In today's China, for example, middle-class living has adapted the sofa as a desirable Western furniture piece. For particular consumers in the neo-capitalist Chinese culture, the sofa indicates the changes in fashions when exploring the house as a personal dwelling in a busy working life and makes for a new class distinction after the class-less society of China's communist past within which Chinese culture is reevaluated (Zhixian 2008: 103).

After the visionary experiments of the 1960s, Postmodernism was explicitly framed as a design movement in the 1980s, firstly by Italian designers. The ideology of Western functionalist Modernism was overturned by reevaluating decoration, ornament, historical forms, and local cultures. Postmodern designers played with common furniture forms without challenging them as types and uses, but the international working climate of design collectives sometimes led to cultural clashes and hybrid types, as with Masanori Umeda's (1941–) "dwelling" *Boxring*. Working with the rebellious Milan-based Memphis group of Ettore Sottsass (1917–2007) reclaiming the powerful traditions of Italy as a nation of design (Sparke 1988) (Plate 9 and Figure 4.4), Japanese designers were among the first to participate in the international postmodern design world. *Boxring*, presented in the first Memphis collection of 1981, was conceived as a square podium of *tatami* floor matting with cushions for sitting, creating the nucleus of one small space without furniture connected to traditional Japanese family rooms and suggestive of a tea-ceremony setting. But, and like other type-less designs, *Boxring* purposely questioned these traditional resonances, adding a confrontational element alluding to Japanese wrestling and boxing on a marked-off mat. It extended the perception of the Japanese-designed interior as an aesthetic depersonalized place so admired from a modernist perspective by Western designers, into a place where generations and cultures may be in conflict as well. In the 1950s, such atomic age confrontations between East (Japan) and West (North America) were famously staged in films by the director Yasujiro Ozu (1903–63), whose celebrated *Tokyo monogatari* (Tokyo Story) of 1953 takes place in traditional Japanese interiors with very few pieces of furniture, which, after use, are always stacked away. As Charles Terry wrote in *Contemporary Japanese Houses* in 1964, "the house had few furnishings because people sat and slept on cushions or mattresses spread on the tatami. These were stored in closets and brought forth as needed" (Seike and Terry 1964: 9).

From the 1870s onward, Japanese houses and interiors were admired as well as idealized by Western designers who favored visible construction and, since 1920s, emphasized modernist spatial emptiness (Taut [1937] 1958; Seike and Terry 1964; Hayward 1965: 283; Hours et al. 2014). Real traditional Japanese interiors, however, were not only empty but also deployed subtle lighting effects generating the excitement of barely perceived objects, rather than the harsh visibility afforded by daylight and electric light bulbs. Such spaces were, in their own way, the antipode of the glass façades of Western modernist housing. In 1933, at a time when Japanese culture was becoming ever more westernized, the novelist Junchirō Tanizaki (1886–1965) criticized the Western "failure to comprehend the mystery of shadows" in their admiration for the simplicity of Japanese rooms (Tanizaki [1933] 2001: 29). Tanizaki admits that the necessities of modern life such as heating, electric lights, sanitation, and air-conditioning do not fit with the traditional Japanese house (5). They spoil the poetics of the space, and "the purist may rack his brains over the placement of a single telephone, hiding it behind the staircase or in a corner of the hallway." While considering the outdoor toilet as the most aesthetic of all elements of Japanese architecture, "a place of spiritual repose" (9), he finds that a flush toilet surrounded by white walls destroys "good taste and the beauties of nature." In practice Japanese homes did use several types of furniture— though these were mainly tables and low chests allowing mobility of furnishing (Hayward 1965: 280; Seike and Terry 1964). Western-inspired bungalows in Japan from the 1960s mixed Japanese emptiness, traditional cushions for seating on the floor, low tables with a Western Arts and Crafts feeling, and the glass window walls championed by Modernism that broke with previous values of darkness (Plate 15). Meanwhile, Japan's core values of simplicity, emptiness, and design of small houses have inspired and fascinated European design until today; in spring 2017, the exhibition "The Japanese House after 1945" at the Barbican in London testified to this.

Metaphors rethinking the old and new, modernity and tradition, as embodied by designer furniture such as *Boxring*, remain present on the cusp of the twentieth-first century, a time that has been defined as "super-modernity" (Augé [1995] 2008). With growing interconnectedness through mobility of traffic and the internet society, flexible placeless, and modular type-less living gains new relevance. American designer Andrea Zittel (1965–) explores traditional mobile living in *A–Z escape vehicles* (1996) inspired by "lowbrow" caravan-houses and in modular flexible spaces called *A–Z cellular compartment units* (2001; Morsiani and Smith 2005; Zittel n.d.). Her strikingly simplified design *Interior* invokes carpets as the agents of movement from place to place by picturing the designer sitting on a floor carpet within which purely visual straight lines demarcate furniture. A rectangular shape, two white plates, and "place squares" express a table and seats, while a second carpet serves as a wall where lines evoke windows. As with nomads, who expressed their identities and life stories through colorful patterns in the weaving and knotting of carpets, *Interior* affords protection from an outside world. Its minimalist super-modern design metaphorically generates mental well-being associated with spiritual meditation while it simultaneaously proposes a shield from conflicts resonant with the role of carpets as essential types of furniture in politically and religiously conflicting zones with people on the move. Considering this theme in his essay "Carpets" the Brazilian-Austrian philosopher Vilém Flusser (1920–91) pessimistically positions carpets as hiders of truth: "Carpets are hung on walls so as to conceal cracks in the wall." From the perspective of the 1980s, he argues this topos was "not the worst way of describing the situation of culture today" (Flusser 1999: 95–8).

Real life in visual documentation

I would like to end this chapter by addressing the sociocultural contexts of furniture evidenced in twentieth-century social and documentary photography. Furniture types associated with colonization figure in photographs of plantation house verandas in the Caribbean, for example: the ease of a rocking chair and "tropical" cane seating demonstrating the power relations and raw materials of the region. During the economic crisis of the 1930s, Walker Evans (1903–75) photographed the furniture of Alabama tenant farmers for James Agee's (1909–55) book *Let Us Now Praise Famous Men*, contextualizing an austere metal bed in a bare wooden space as timeless while embodying a life of poverty (Carter 2015: 70–1).

Social documentary photography also provides evidence of the failure of ideals of the modernist city, where furniture types that once signified a futuristic utopia take on new lives amidst dystopian underworlds. In the Ukrainian city of Kharkov in the late 1990s, which interwar western European functionalist architects and designers once considered a model of progressive new architecture and lifestyles, Boris Mikhailov (1938–) photographed the homeless adapting old tables and chairs to multiple forms of use (Mikhailov 1999). Similar conditions and reconstructions of type and use are witnessed in "Landscapes for the Homeless people" in Los Angeles (1988–92) by Anthony Hernandez (1947–), or in British communities and towns by Martin Parr (1952–). The photographs by Mikhael Subotzky (1981–) and Patrick Waterhouse (1981–) observe the 54-story Ponte City apartment tower of Johannesburg in South Africa built in 1971 for immigrants and newcomers before it became a prime symbol of urban decay (Vladislavic 2014). More recently, the huge sociocultural, economic, and demographic changes in China's ever-developing megacities are visible in the furnishing of stable homes as well, and one of the interiors in the series "Shanghai living" of 2004–5 by photographer Hu Yang (1959–) pictured a small bedroom-dwelling with one bed (Zhixian 2008: 125–6). Meanwhile, homeless people everywhere create open-air urban living rooms under bridges, sitting or resting on street furniture in parks, along the roads, and in shopping malls, finding shelter in subway or underground spaces. Continuous production in present-day consumerist societies makes furniture seldom wear out or lose its function altogether. Furniture discarded by previous owners to suit new fashion and aesthetic refurbishment is reused (Plate 16).

These photographs represent random types and uses of furniture in the daily lives of millions far from the consumerism of designer furniture yet creating a sense of place and home that all humans share. Nonetheless, such fugitive furnishing can acquire an aesthetic look when it is decontextualized, for example, in the catalog of the China Design Now exhibition held in the Victoria and Albert Museum in London in 2008.

CONCLUSION

This chapter positioned types and uses of furniture in the twentieth century as serving multiple practical and symbolic purposes across cultures and societal classes. In this cultural history, "type-lessness" is problematic, perhaps because it defies not only functions but also social categorization. A Google search for "typeless furniture" gains no real hits, proposing instead "timeless furniture" and images of designers' classics that have become iconic. And yet, there is a sense of the type-less in twentieth-century furniture. Designer furniture, though it has a practical justification, does just as much to shape the symbolic realm of canonical design discourses as it does to reflect trends in popular culture, collective and personal psychological drives, and fashions. The sculptural quality of furniture pieces remained a clear goal for architects and designers throughout the century, alongside successful commercial furniture types such as assembled modular units attending to daily practical functions. Recent digital technologies facilitate ever more mobile living and working with computer software even making furniture types responsive to moods, for example, by changing color; nonetheless, most people still live in houses in which tables, chairs, and beds as long-established furniture types determine their everyday living as well. Perhaps the fearful observations of debatable fascist tendencies in 1935 made by newspaper editor Doremus Jessup in the novel *It Can't Happen Here* by Sinclair Lewis can both alarm as well as soothe us today:

> It seemed to him unidealistically probable, for all the "contemporary furniture" of the 1930s, that most people would continue, at least for a few hundred years, to sit in chairs, eat from dishes upon tables, read books [...] sleep in beds [...] and in general spend twenty or twenty-two hours a day much as they had spent them in 1930, or 1630.
>
> (Lewis 1935: 112)

ACKNOWLEDGMENT

I would like to thank Claire O'Mahony for her suggestions regarding this chapter.

CHAPTER FOUR

The Domestic Setting

PENNY SPARKE

In the nineteenth century, the idea of domesticity, which had become highly visible two centuries earlier in the Netherlands, was reinforced by the phenomenon historians call "The Separation of the Spheres" (Rybczynski 1986; Wolff 1990). This referred to the way in which, when men left the home to work outside in the commercial sphere, middle-class women were left behind with a role as guardians of the home. Above all their role was to ensure that the home acted as a refuge, that it conferred the appropriate social standing upon their families, and that it adhered to the requirements of fashionable taste (Sparke 1995). Strongly linked to ideas about class and gender, therefore, the home and its furnishings had a specific set of roles to perform. Above all, they (and the female homemaker) were responsible for resolving the inherent tensions that existed between, on the one hand, the home's commitment to continuity and the past and, on the other, its part in taking society forward into the modern world.

By 1900, therefore, the cultural demands on furniture destined for the home environment went beyond fulfilling the necessary stylistic requirements. They were much more deeply rooted, linked to the heart of the challenge of the twentieth century, which was to offset the negative social and cultural effects of industrialization and urbanization while taking advantage of the many technological and aesthetic possibilities that they offered. Various strategies were developed to enable furniture to meet that challenge. While some addressed the need to maintain levels of tradition in the home, others aimed to respond to modernity, while still others (probably the largest category) sought to develop a compromise between the two, a kind of hybridity, to attempt to resolve the tensions between them.

TRADITION

The requirement of the modern home to perform the role of a refuge from the outside world, had, and continues to have, huge implications for the furniture that is placed within it (Rybczynski 1986). "Home" is essentially an emotional abstraction, linked to ideas about security and place and proximity to loved ones (Cieraad 1999). It also, however, extends to material cultural artifacts—furniture included—that can, like human beings, be "familiar" and "loved," and which become representations of domesticity's more abstract meanings. Furniture can provide a level of security through memory and association, and it can also offer different levels of comfort, both psychological and physical (Logan 2001). The expectation of furniture items in the home to provide a feeling of continuity with the past has manifested itself in a variety of ways over the last hundred or so years.

The inclusion of antique, reproduction, or historically inspired pieces of furniture in the home has existed throughout the entire period under consideration (Harris 2007) (Plate 17). From late nineteenth-century historicism, to the interwar Georgian revival, to the reintroduction of wing-backed chairs and tapered-leg tables in the 1950s, to the fashion for chintz and the English Country House Style (Girouard 1978) that emerged in the 1970s with its Windsor chairs and pine dressers, and which can still be found in many homes today, the desire to embrace the past through one's choice of furniture has been a constant theme.

For the most part, this compulsion has manifested itself in the inclusion of furniture items from the preindustrial era. In the United Kingdom Georgian and Regency pieces have been strongly favored—whether original or reproduced—although items from other periods and in a variety of styles and types have also been present in many homes. Recently, the need to embrace history in this way has been extended to the revival, not only of furniture pieces from the preindustrial era, but also of styles that emerged after 1900. The 1960s, for instance, saw a renewed interest in turn-of-the-century Art Nouveau and the Art Deco movement of the 1930s while, more recently, the fashion for "mid-century modern" pieces—whether the furniture designs of the Americans Charles Eames (1907–88), Eero Saarinen (1910–61), and Harry Bertoia (1915–78); or of the Scandinavians Hans Wegner (1914–2007) and Arne Jacobsen (1902–71); or the British designers Robin Day (1915–2010) and Lucienne Day (née Conradi, 1917–2010), and Ernest Race (1913–64)—has been widespread, showing the importance of domestic furniture's role in maintaining the past in the present (Guffey 2006).

In turn, the interest in furniture from the past has stimulated a number of supply routes, among them the antiques trade and the secondhand market (Harris 2007). Today, online opportunities for buying secondhand furniture, such as eBay, also exist, as do car boot sales and specialist trade fairs.

The presence of comfort in the home is firmly linked to its role as a refuge from the onslaught of the present. As well as being provided psychologically by an investment in the past, which brings with it the familiarity of the tried and tested and the reassurance of memory and nostalgia, comfort is provided by furniture in the way in which it offers our bodies rest and respite in a physical sense. No other furniture object offers this more than the sofa (or the couch or settee as it has been called at different times in the years in question).

Through its links with the notions of stability, security, and comfort, the sofa has had a key place in the domestic setting since 1900. Coming into its own in the seventeenth century as a key status symbol, it established a place for itself in the homes of the wealthy, quickly becoming synonymous with the idea of aristocratic leisure (Edwards and Treve 2006). In spite of being an overt signifier of luxury it did not, however, provide much physical comfort at that time. Indeed, the minimal upholstery and rigid high backs and arms of early settees, or double armchairs as they really were, would undoubtedly have confined their sitters to a strictly upright position. Gradually deeper upholstery was used to provide an enhanced level of comfort. This was especially the case in France where the modern sofa as we now know it came into being (Auslander 1998).

With the advent of tea-drinking as an important social ritual, enabling people to engage more intensely with their immediate seated neighbors and have more intimate conversations with them, the eighteenth century saw an increase in the popularity of the sofa in well-to-do homes. It extended an invitation to rest and relaxation, offering its sitters, or loungers, a plethora of soft, stuffed cushions and an expanse of well-padded forms on which to spread their reclining bodies.

By the time the sofa had reached the British and American middle-class home in the middle years of the nineteenth-century domesticity had become intertwined with the separation of the spheres that required the home to be a haven. In that context comfort was manifested both visually and materially. It was embedded in the softness of the multiple and diverse fabrics that covered the hard surfaces in the parlor—those of the mantelpiece and the numerous side tables among them—as well as in the deep upholstery of its sofas and armchairs (Grier 1997). Draping fabric across surfaces softened them both visually and to the touch. In that context the sofa played a very key role, offering Victorians a moment of repose from the ever-increasing demands of life in the public arena. That level of comfort depended upon forms that were neither fixed nor rigid but which responded rather to the impact of the body. Technologically, that was made possible by new forms of upholstery, especially the utilization of steel springs, which introduced elasticity and bounce into the Victorian sofa. Buttoning also became widespread.

MODERNITY

Industrialization and urbanization heralded the era of modernity. There were numerous cultural responses to that complex new condition, including from the world of furniture design. For people who sought to distinguish themselves by embracing innovation, twentieth-century domestic furniture was also a marker of social aspiration and change. The Art Nouveau movement in architecture and design at the turn of the century, for example, offered complete sets of furniture that instantly marked their owners as willing to grasp the future and risk, positioning themselves as part of an adventurous aesthetic avant-garde (Greenhalgh 2000). This was also the first time that the idea of the *Gesamtkunstwerk*, the sense of domestic furniture appearing as a unified whole, rather than being a set of disparate elements, came to the fore (Figure 6.1).

Art Nouveau and Jugendstil architects led the way in the creation of their own homes. When he decided to create a complete home for himself in the Brussels suburb of Uccle, Henry van de Velde (1863–1957), for example, looked to Britain and to William Morris (1834–96) for inspiration. The exterior of Bloemenwerf, the house he created for his family, owed much to Arts and Crafts neo-vernacular designs, and inside the walls of his villa, van de Velde and the members of his family created a set of spaces, the structure, furniture, and furnishings of which were conceived and designed as a *Gesamtkunstwerk*. The set of chairs around his dining table featured softly curved backs that flowed into their gently curving legs. Even the flowing forms of his wife's dress, designed by van de Velde from Morris fabric, were echoed in the interior spaces she inhabited. The architect described his constructions and decorations as organisms, a metaphor that helped him explain the way in which he conceived of the exterior and the interior as a single entity (Greenhalgh 2000).

The dramatic cultural shift that resulted in furniture becoming aligned with the architecture that housed it, rather than as previously with the psychological and physical needs of the home's inhabitants, led directly to the architectural and design Modern movement of the 1920s and 1930s. It was driven by architects who sought furniture equivalents of the highly rational buildings they envisaged as prototypes for simple, inexpensive mass housing. Influenced less by ideas about comfort and continuity, and more by the contemporary forces of mechanization and standardization, they sought material solutions to the "problems" of living at home, to the activities, that is, of sitting, eating, sleeping, and resting, among others. The pendulum swing that took place at that time engendered a whole new language of domestic furniture items, which the modernists chose to describe as pieces of equipment rather than of decorative art. They also put a new emphasis on built-in furniture, an extension of the architectural structure itself (Benton 2006a).

In sharp contrast to the Victorian items that had represented physical comfort, however, modernist furniture designs of the 1920s, with their dramatic combination of chromium-plated tubular steel and black leather, which emerged as a reaction to what was seen as the previous century's love of comfort, clutter, and bulkiness, expressed a reluctance to embrace domesticity. Indeed, the designs in question could be used in both dwellings (the functional term used by the modernists to replace the more emotional concept of "home") and offices (Benton 2006a). Architectural space rather than furniture mass became the ideal and open-framed chairs were developed to avoid obscuring the defining characteristics of interior spaces, whether of dwellings or work environments.

Where the sofa was concerned the rigidity of the seventeenth-century seat returned and sofas disappeared from view for the most part. Only a few modernist multiple-seaters emerged, among them a three-seater version of Le Corbusier's (1887–1965) famous LC2 armchair of 1928, designed some years later (Rüegg 2014). Generally, however, Modernism favored the single chair and sacrificed overt comfort in favor of spatial clarity.

Recognizing the inevitability of the need for material objects in their otherwise abstract, spatial settings a number of modernist architects, Le Corbusier among them, also chose to complement their built-in furniture with "freestanding" furnishings, sometimes mass-produced items bought "off the shelf" and sometimes objects made to their own designs over which they could maintain a high level of control. The contemporary materials utilized in many of their designs—tubular steel, glass, and plywood, among them—determined a particular aesthetic that quickly came to characterize modernist furniture. One of the items of furniture equipment that Le Corbusier introduced into several of his interiors was not designed by him but fell, rather, into the category of the "ready-made." The leather "club" armchair, which first made an appearance in his 1925 Pavillon de L'Esprit Nouveau, had its origins in the élite male social club and provided a very particular alternative to feminine domesticity.

From 1925 the Bauhaus-trained architect and designer, Marcel Breuer (1902–81), had understood the potential of tubular steel, a material that he had encountered through his bicycle, to transform the bulky club armchair, of which Le Corbusier was so fond, into a skeletal version of that same design. With its open tubular steel frame Breuer's armchair could provide the same utilitarian function as a traditional armchair without blocking the spatial continuity of the room that contained it. He was dissatisfied with his first version: "It is," he wrote, "my most extreme work, both in its outward appearance and in the use of materials; it is the least artistic, the most logical, the least 'cosy' and the most mechanical" (Wilk 1981: 38). He went on, however, to develop it through several stages until it was finally resolved to his satisfaction. In contrast to Le Corbusier's idea of using "off the shelf" items, Breuer's approach was to design his own mass-produced furniture pieces to enhance and reinforce the spatiality of his interiors and their standardized nature. It was a strategy that was subsequently emulated by several other modernist and neo-modernist architects, from Mies van der Rohe (1886–1969) to Norman Foster (1935–).

Once again comfort was facilitated by technological breakthroughs but in the 1950s it was foam rubber that transformed the profile of the sofa rather than horse hair or steel springs. Nowhere was that more in evidence than in Italy where several designs, including Osvaldo Borsani's (1911–85) famous P40 design, were available both as a lounge chair and as a sofa. With its splayed metal legs and organically shaped arms, Marco Zanuso's (1916–2001) "Lady" design was also realized as both a single and as a double sitting object (Sparke 1988). The lightness of foam rubber meant that elegance and comfort could be easily combined.

The legacy of interwar Modernism resurfaced in the 1960s (Figure 4.1). The new plastics offered novel possibilities and there was a strong sense of optimism in the future. The 1950s and 1960s witnessed the democratization of the concept of lifestyle. What had once been the prerogative of a few was now

FIGURE 4.1 Living Room 1965 in The Geffrye Museum, London. Photograph courtesy of The Geffrye, Museum of the Home, London.

available to many. Being "modern" meant inhabiting domestic spaces in which the modern lifestyle—meeting, talking, reading, relaxing, and eating—could be experienced. Modern sofas helped make that possible.

The interest in the forward-looking impact of new technologies subsided somewhat in the 1970s as the Western industrialized world was challenged by the oil crisis, but by the 1980s the simple aesthetic of Modernism could be seen again in the world of domestic furniture. This time, however, it was style- rather than ideology-led. A new minimalist style became popular in the domestic setting and furniture responded to the trend, reducing its forms and colors in response to the widespread demand for simplicity. Designer culture came to the fore, aligned closely with the concept of lifestyle, which for the youth of the era, meant urban loft living and high-tech furniture. Designers, such as the Israeli Ron Arad (1951–), offered iconic designs—such as his Rover seat chair—which conformed to the new ideal. The designer chair took on another level of meaning in that context, performing the role of a potent symbol for a new generation for whom the concept of design was synonymous with a modern, aspirational lifestyle. In the twenty-first century that style-rich, ultra-modern domestic ideal has faded from view a little and furniture has lost some of its cultural capital. Arguably it has been replaced by a new belief system that positions itself positively vis-à-vis the future just as Modernism had done over half a century earlier. The so-called green movement in design, motivated by a desire to enhance material sustainability, has had its influence on furniture in the domestic setting. The result is less about aesthetics, however, than about sourcing objects and materials, recycling and repurposing, a throw-back in some ways to the advice offered to homemakers back in the 1950s.

HYBRIDITY

Modernism engendered a new domestic aesthetic that, visually at least, stood in direct contrast to the heavier period, reproduction, overtly comfortable furniture that it had reacted against. On one level, that dramatic shift meant that, by the middle years of the century, domestic furniture fell into two different categories, namely, traditional or modern. However, there was, of course, a middle ground that, arguably, defined the vast majority of furniture items produced in the twentieth century, especially in the area of furniture designed for the mass market.

Many twentieth-century furniture items for domestic consumption tried to position themselves somewhere in between the extremes of cultural conservatism and radicalism. The popular 1930s three-piece suite, for example, which comprised comprising a sofa and two matching armchairs, and which quickly became a familiar appendage of the suburban sitting room (no longer the parlor), swung the pendulum back in the direction of bulk and comfort and brought with it a new model of domesticity that made a nod to the past. However, it also paid lip service to the idea of the modern world, mostly through the simplified forms and abstract patterns used on the upholstery fabrics.

Alongside the neo-modern pieces of this period the need to have one foot in the past and the other in the future continued into the era between the end of the Second World War and the early 1970s. Ambiguity was created by the coexistence of the pull of tradition and the push of modernity. Nowhere was that more apparent than in attitudes to that powerful domestic symbol—the sofa. The compromise that emerged was a new and extremely subtle concept of modern comfort that was simultaneously backward and forward looking. A strong desire to maintain a level of comfort—which perpetuated the Victorian domestic ideal—was accompanied by an acknowledgment of the importance of modern life and the role of design in taking people into a future, rational world dominated by progressive technology. Indeed, the notion of comfort itself was arguably transformed in those years, from one that was associated with physical immersion to one that was more cerebral and intellectual. It was a new mood, a new attitude, a new way of thinking.

The postwar modern living room built on the developments of the interwar years. It continued to reject the Victorian parlor's love of clutter, replacing it with a light interior aesthetic that favored, once again, sofas raised up on legs and slim upholstery, which combined elegance with comfort. An added component was an alignment with the world of contemporary abstract sculpture that confirmed for postwar sofas a place in the world of modernity. The idea of the Regency sofa with its tight upholstery and slim legs was also frequently invoked as a rationale for elegant, light forms but it was often combined with an element of Victorian comfort. A winged two-seater of the 1950s, designed by Ernest Race (1913–64), for example, combined short splayed wooden legs with a buttoned, upholstered back (Conway 1982). Writers in texts about modern interiors of the 1940s and 1950s frequently described what they saw as a search for a modern equivalent to Victorian comfort but without the bulk. It was even possible to mix an antique Regency sofa with modern armchairs, so similar were their proportions.

The ambivalent sensibility that characterized the search for a modern definition of comfort in the years after 1945 emerged within a number of national modern design movements simultaneously, and was epitomized in a number of iconic sofa designs that became models for mass emulation. In Denmark, for example, Borge Mogensen's (1914–72) famous "Spokeback" sofa (designed in 1945 but not manufactured until 1963) brought tradition in touch with modernity. Its high sides and back contained its sitters as if they were located in a small room. It was almost a piece of mini-architecture, evoking a sense of a modern, comfortable lifestyle that eschewed luxury and Victorian heaviness.

Demonstrating a similar respect for the architectural space that enveloped human beings, but also keen to provide a level of modern comfort that did not depend on the reworking of traditions, the idea of the modular sofa emerged in the United States in the 1950s and quickly took off as a solution to the need to provide modern comfort in spaces both within and beyond the home (Quinn 2004). George Nelson (1908–86), among others, offered an example in 1956. The British designer Robin Day's design for modular seating, produced by Hille, furthermore, found a place in the new University of Sussex campus opened in the early 1960s, bringing domesticity out of the home. Showing no traces of historical styling this simple, minimal design was sufficiently upholstered, nonetheless, to provide the level of comfort required in that setting (Jackson 2001).

By the 1960s the modern sofa had made a long journey. While in the examples provided by Day and others it had succeeded in moving completely away from its origins and achieving an unprecedented level of simplicity and modern comfort, the second half of that decade witnessed a shift away from the obsession with the "modern" to a new zeitgeist that embraced a reassessment of history. Britain's Terence Conran (1931–) was among several designers to respond to that challenge returning as he did to the traditional buttoned and quilted "Chesterfield" model, first created in the eighteenth century. He retailed it through his Habitat store (Phillips 1984). A simple reworking of its conventional profile transformed it overnight into a modern object that was not out of place in a contemporary setting.

From the 1960s up to the present the sofa has retained its role in our lives as a marker of stability, relaxation, and comfort. Today it comes in a number of guises—modern and traditional as well as somewhere in between. Technologically it utilizes a wide range of upholstery techniques and materials and it fits into the enormous range of possible styles—from country cottage to high tech—that characterizes our contemporary interiors, both domestic and non-domestic. While our pastimes have expanded from the social activity of tea-drinking to include watching DVDs together as well as the more private tasks of working on laptops and iPads, and whether we sit alone on them or with others, the physical and psychological security, the relaxation and the comfort we require of our sofas has remained in place.

Hybridity was evident much more widely as well. Although the impetus to design furniture items for the modern world remained in place after 1945, the extreme rationalism of the prewar years was tempered considerably. The work of the Americans Charles and Ray Eames (née Kaiser, 1912–88) represented that modified approach. Working in the areas of architecture, interiors, furniture design, exhibitions, and film they both looked back to earlier Modernism and yet, at the same time, anticipated the postmodern manifestations of the late century (Drexler 1973). The era of postmodernity that they anticipated was one that, in the words of Robert Venturi (1925–), favored "complexity and contradiction" over "simplicity and clarity" ([1966] 2002: 7)

Working through the middle years of the century the Eameses had the advantage of being able to see where the ideals underpinning architectural and design Modernism had not been met. They looked to a future that was less preoccupied with technology and more firmly committed to a modern material world inspired as much by history and culture as it was by the machine. Nowhere was this more evident than in their designs for furniture. From a background in architecture, Charles Eames ventured into furniture design as a form of experimentation through which to test new materials and production techniques, and to discover innovative forms that would lead to fresh ways of living. Eames set out to find new solutions to an old problem, that of sitting. In 1941 he and Eero Saarinen were awarded first prize in the Organic Furniture competition organized by New York's Museum of Modern Art. Eliot Noyes (1910–77), the energy behind the competition, had offered the challenge. "A new way of living is developing," he explained, "[which] requires a fresh approach to the design problems and a new expression" (Drexler 1973: 22). It was significant that Charles chose to collaborate with a Scandinavian designer who had absorbed his culture's valiant efforts to maintain links with tradition while embracing modernity. The organically shaped, molded plywood shells he developed with Saarinen were among the most significant technological breakthroughs to have an impact on designed artifacts in the twentieth century and the chairs, screens, and coffee tables he created throughout the 1940s have subsequently become "design classics."

The Eameses continued to pursue the formal challenges of new technologies in their furniture designs of the late 1940s and 1950s. Their 1946 molded plywood chairs with metal rod legs, for example, exploited new methods of bonding metal to wood with the addition of rubber pads, while Charles's 1949 fiberglass chair was well ahead of his time (Plate 7). It was, as Edgar Kauffmann Jr. (1910–89) explained in his *Introductions to Modern Design*, the "first one-piece plastic chair to feature the natural surface of its material, variegated and satiny." The storage cabinets of interchangeable parts of 1950, Kauffmann explained, were "the first [...] to forsake traditional furniture construction" (1950: 27). Perhaps nowhere was the idea of the modern lifestyle better expressed in a single designed artifact, however, than in the Eameses' famous rosewood lounge chair of 1956, a compromise between modern style and comfort.

One area of hybridity, therefore, was exhibited in the decision made by numerous designers to embrace new forms but to realize them in traditional materials. The result was a softer version of modernist furniture that was favored in Scandinavia and in Britain. While Alvar Aalto (1898–1976), Bruno Matthson (1907–88), and others took that route in the former location, in the latter the designer Gerald Summers (1899–1967) added his contribution with a set of pieces that included a bent plywood armchair manufactured in 1939/40 by his company, Makers of Simple Furniture Ltd. (Deese 1992).

Summers's design used a single sheet of birch plywood, consisting of thirteen layers of thin veneers, out of which all the constructive elements were formed. Firstly, the veneers were cut into shape. Next, cuts were made to separate the back legs and armrests from the chair's body. The veneers were brushed with glue and held in a mold for eight hours to bend the legs and armrests in different directions. Finally, the front legs were cut and formed. The entire procedure required neither the use of heat nor steam and involved a minimal amount of labor. With its organic shape Summers's lounge chair was comfortable, even without cushions, and with its smooth surface and lack of metal connectors, it also fulfilled the ideal of hygienic furniture. According to Summers's widow, the model was conceived for use in the tropics, which is quite possible as, unlike other plywood models by other contemporary designers, Summers's lounge chair proved stable when it was exposed to heat and humidity for several weeks during an environmental stress test.

The model's unusual shape was probably inspired by Alvar Aalto's furniture (Figure 8.1), especially the chair models that were created for the Paimio Sanatorium in Finland and which were shown in London in 1933. Summers may have either seen Aalto's furniture on that occasion or he might have been introduced to the Finnish designer's work by the founder of Isokon Furniture, Jack Pritchard (1899–1992), who had visited Aalto and the production sites of his furniture in Finland.

Many other hybrid styles appeared throughout the century, from Art Deco to Postmodernism. Another form of hybridity was a mixture not of styles but of types. To gain acceptance there was a tendency, in the 1930s, for new machines destined for the domestic setting—radios, for example—to mimic furniture items. The process of what has been called "furniturization," demonstrated the symbolic supremacy of furniture at that time and the power it had to make homemakers feel comfortable. By the end of the twentieth century that trend had ceased, however, and household technologies came to look more and more machine-like and no longer needed to be disguised as furniture to be able to enter the domestic arena.

BEYOND STYLE

In spite of the fact that, on one level, most twentieth-century domestic furniture items fit into one of three cultural categories—traditional, modern, or hybrid—it was their contextual settings, that is, the encompassing spaces and associated artifacts and accessories, which gave them their deep meanings beyond the styles in which they presented themselves.

One way of understanding furniture is to look at the way it is arranged and the social behaviors reflected by, and indeed often driven by, those arrangements. The example of a fairly ordinary late nineteenth-century parlor in Manchester depicts what looks, at first sight, like a set of furniture items arranged rather randomly. Closer inspection shows, however, that there is little that is random in that setting. Rather, the female figure reading in the background is positioned near what little light is available from the window. She sits alone in a single chair, comfortable with her own interiority, while the other chairs are all located near to little side tables, complete with potted plants, offering family members and visitors a chance for social interaction.

While, stylistically, that enclosed, dark interior could not be more different from that of modernist architect Ludwig Mies Van der Rohe's light, open plan interior in his Villa Tugendhat in Brno of 1930, interestingly one can observe a similar strategy in the arrangement of the furniture items within it (Figure 4.2). The full impact of open planning becomes visible on the villa's middle floor, which features an 80 by 55 foot open space. With the exception of the kitchen and the staff living quarters situated at its west end, the floor consists of a single living open space. This is an area for family conversations, for dining, for entertainment or family leisure time, and for social interaction. The furniture is

FIGURE 4.2 Mies van der Rohe, Chairs in the Villa Tugendhat, Brno, 1930. Photograph courtesy of Wikimedia Commons.

also positioned to support the activities that take place in that space. The main furniture groupings include a round reception table with four tubular steel-framed Brno chairs at the entrance to the living space; three Barcelona chairs and ottomans (1929) and three Tugendhat chairs (1930) arranged around a Tugendhat coffee table (1930) and positioned next to a Moroccan onyx screen in the main living area; a dining area with an expandable rosewood table and Brno chairs (1930) together with an enormous semicircular Makassar ebony screen; a library area with a pigskin-covered sofa (1930) and three tubular-steel framed Brno chairs (1930) arranged around a bridge table; and a rear living area with a large desk and two cantilevered chairs with armrests. A single metal-framed chaise longue (1931), upholstered in red fabric, is also present. Facing outwards, and accompanied by a small side table, it offers an opportunity for private contemplation, or for a quiet read, similar to that being enjoyed by the woman in the Victorian parlor (Lange 2006).

While the furniture items in the Villa could not be more modern and progressive, and those in the Manchester parlor are of mixed historical styles, both rooms contain furniture items that encourage (possibly even determine) the activities that take place in them. This basic role for domestic furniture remains true up to the present day, although with the advent of the new technologies in the home, the nature of some of the activities that take place in it has changed. This comparison indicates that, if one puts the questions of styles and materials to one side and focuses on the lives that are being lived in furnished houses, there is a level of continuity, rather than disruption and change, in the role of domestic furniture of the period in question.

IDEALISM

Both because of its links with social aspiration and the ideal of comfort, whether psychological or physical, furniture destined for the domestic setting is always aspiring toward an unrealizable goal. Throughout the twentieth century a number of aids were provided to consumers of furniture and homemakers to help them (to attempt to) translate the ideal into the real. They included advice books, articles in specialist magazines and journals, exhibitions, displays in museums and department stores, and radio and television programs.

Advice literature relating to domestic furniture covered a spectrum from how to make it, to how to arrange it tastefully, to how to take care of it (Figure 4.3). The first was included in a body of literature, aimed at male readers, which provided amateurs with the means of making simple furniture items. A 1910 American book titled *Home Decoration*, written by Professor Charles F. Warner, whose aim was to help people create a model home, made it very clear that he was talking to men. "It is taken for granted," he wrote, "that the interested reader is familiar with the use of the common hand tools for woodworking or

FIGURE 4.3 Victorian Drawing Room in The Geffrye Museum, London. Photograph courtesy of The Geffrye, Museum of the Home, London.

that he can, with some assistance, perhaps, easily command their use" (Warner 1910: 130). In another section, he took his reader through all the rooms of the house, telling which furniture items would best be placed there. He suggested the addition of two Morris chairs in the hall to provide "solid comfort," for example, reflecting the preference at that time in the United States for solid wooden furniture, described as "Mission" because it had an ascetic look to it (50).

Nearly four decades later, W.P. Matthew's *The Practical Home Handyman: A Comprehensive Guide to Constructional and Repair Work About the House* of 1946, for example, offered tips on the construction of bookcases built into a recess, as well as a two-tier open bookcase and occasional and card tables. As Matthew explained, "a folding or collapsible table which can be used for card-playing, or an occasional side-table for tea in the garden, can be made with reasonably small expenditure in material and effort" (1946: 52). The same author also advised his readers on how to repair upholstery, as well as telling them how to remove water stains from a tabletop.

By far the largest number of domestic furniture advice books, however, related to the importance of the expression of taste in the home. For the most part they were directed at women. The art critic John Ruskin had observed a gendered division of labor in the home in the nineteenth century, implying that women's domestic activities came naturally to them and therefore did not attain the status of "art," which required the kind of creative skills that were accredited to men (Ruskin [1865] 1949: 86).

Domestic advice literature aimed at a wide audience emerged in the second half of the nineteenth century and continued as a distinct genre at least until the 1950s when it was joined by television, which along with specialist magazines, gradually took center stage in this context. By the early twenty-first century the internet could be added to the list. The nineteenth century, however, provided the templates for the kinds of advice that would continue to be given well into the twentieth century. The year 1868, for example, saw the publication in England of Charles Eastlake's (1836–1906) *Hints on Household Taste, in Furniture, Upholstery and Other Details* (1869), which offered a model for subsequent home decoration and furnishing advice books. Much has been written about the misogynistic tone of Eastlake's text, and there can be little doubt that he blamed women for what he, like many others, saw as their weakness for fashionable goods, their commitment to amateur "fancy-work," and their gullibility in the presence of persuasive salesmen, which lowered the taste standards in the British interior. He advocated the use of dados and friezes, of a sideboard in which to display old china vases, and decorative and furnishing features that all came to characterize the aesthetic interior of the 1870s and 1880s. *Hints on Household Taste* went into multiple editions on both sides of the Atlantic.

Between 1870 and 1890 vast numbers of such books were published. Some of the most notable publications of the 1870s included five titles in the "Art at Home" series, published by Macmillan and Company between 1876 and 1883; Mrs. Haweis's (1848–98) *The Art of Beauty* (published in the *St. Paul's Magazine* in 1876 but later in book form); and H.J. Cooper's *The Art of Furnishing in Rational and Aesthetic Principles* of 1876. The 1880s, the decade in which the aesthetic interior was at its most popular, saw even more decorating advice books make an appearance. As the twentieth century progressed furnishing advice books addressed ever wider audiences as increasing numbers of people were able to purchase furniture and engage in the activity of expressing their taste in the homes both through their choice of items and the ways in which they integrated them into their interior settings.

SUBVERSION

For the most part, twentieth-century furniture supported the social and cultural status quo, reflecting mainstream values. Although the modernists had attempted to use architecture and design as agents in a program of social and political change, such were the forces of the market that their work quickly became style-driven and fashion-led. By the mid-1960s in Britain a reaction against the tenets of architectural and design Modernism was beginning to be felt and it was becoming clear that, in spite of furniture's traditional function as a symbol of domestic stability, it was beginning to be perceived once again as a potential agent for social and cultural change. A new generation of designers—including Max Clendinning (1924–), Jon Bannenberg (1929–2002), Peter Murdoch (1940–), William Plunkett (1928–2013), Bernard Holdaway (1934–2009), Nicholas Frewing, and the team of Jean Schofield and John Wright—embraced the novel concepts of "knock-down," "inflate," and "throwaway" furniture and spawned such lasting classics as Clendinning's "Maxima" range for Hille—a set of self-assembly, flat-pack chairs with frames made from lacquered plywood—and a side chair for Liberty's, which featured a painted plywood frame; Murdoch's so-called paper chair for Perspective Designs, which in reality was made out of robust cardboard strengthened with resin (a spotted version appeared in 1964 followed by one with a more complex pattern four years later); and Holdaway's "Tom-o-Tom" range for Hull Traders, designed in 1965 (Greenberg 1999).

Made of compressed cardboard, chipboard, and polyurethane paint, the "Tom-o-Tom" dining chair was part of a range of furniture pieces—including, by 1969, an armchair, table, lamps, bins, stools, and children's toys—most of which were designed around a set of circular forms, in particular, cylinders, discs, and spheres. The pieces were all created to be part of a furniture family that was envisaged to grow over time and was intended for use in a number of locations, among them private homes, schools, hotels, and waiting areas. Conceived in the middle of the 1960s Holdaway was influenced by the new, flexible lifestyle of the youthful adherents of the Pop revolution in taste and style. He sought to create a collection of furniture pieces that would make that flexibility a lived reality. To that end the pieces could be grouped together in a number of different ways to encourage a variety of living behaviors. They became familiar appendages in a diversity of spaces in which young people lived out the tenets of the Pop lifestyle, which encouraged change and ephemerality.

To be accessible to young consumers living on modest incomes the "Tom-o-Tom" pieces were also designed to be as low-cost as possible. The main strategy for keeping their cost low was Holdaway's decision to use cheap materials. Chipboard was employed where the greatest strength was needed, namely, for the seats of chairs and the tops of tables. The pieces were finished in brightly colored polyurethane paint, which was sprayed on to their surfaces. It provided a robust and durable finish that acted as a counterpoint to the cheap and ephemeral nature of the structural materials. The form of this chair, with its high back and round seat and trunk, demonstrates a simplicity that was important to its basic manufacturing process. It also helped mark a break with the conventional dining chair form with its square seat and four legs.

Designs that challenged conventional lifestyles were also created in Scandinavia in the late 1950s and 1960s. Danish designer Nanna Ditzel (1923–

2005), for example, notable for being a woman in the male-dominated world of industrial design, from the mid-1940s onward created—with her husband Jorgen (until his premature death in 1961) and subsequently on her own— numerous iconic design objects that helped to put Denmark on the map as a country renowned for its production of innovative accessories—furniture, interior design, ceramics, textiles, and jewelry, in particular—for the modern age. Perhaps no single piece the couple designed expressed this more imaginatively than their 1959 wicker egg chair, which, suspended on a chain from the ceiling, was frequently featured—complete with a cross-legged model—in the pages of fashion and modern interior magazines, suggesting a new liberated lifestyle, free from earth-bound anxieties, which was embraced by an idealistic generation of young stylish people in the 1960s.

Another attempt to exploit the radical potential of furniture was made in Italy in the late 1960s when groups such as Superstudio and Archizoom set out to break away from the stylistic dominance of late Modernism and the power of the manufacturing industry, and align furniture with ideas about social and political change. They were inspired by the non-mainstream work of the veteran Italian designer Ettore Sottsass (1917–2007), who had been challenging furniture conventions since the 1950s and who went on, in 1981, to launch Memphis, a furniture collective whose work was a deliberate provocation, an act of defiance, an attempt to blow away the cobwebs and wake people up (Sparke 1982) (Figure 4.4).

Memphis was not a bolt out of the blue but rather the result of a sustained program of design radicalism that Sottsass had initiated back in the 1950s when he had first sought to find ways out of what he saw as the "bourgeois" cul-de-sac of modern design. Questioning the formulaic, "form follows function," all-white, geometric school of design, linked to interwar architectural Modernism, he looked, instead, to the worlds of contemporary abstract art, vernacular culture, and a little later, the exoticism and spirituality of the ancient cultures of the East and the energy of Western contemporary popular culture manifested in music and fashion. Like the modernists, and ironically also like William Morris before them, Sottsass was an idealist. By the time he came to form Memphis he had refined his ideas. As he explained, "By dint of walking among the area of the uncertain (due to a certain mistrust), by dint of conversing with metaphor and Utopia (to understand something more) and by keeping out of the way (certainly due to an innate calmness), we now find we have gained some experience" (Sparke 1982: 42).

In the late 1970s, emerging from a period during which he had almost stopped producing objects, Sottsass decided to join with a group of his younger friends and colleagues, as well as with a handful of more established collaborators in various parts of the world, to make a dramatic statement that would challenge what had become the very predictable world of design linked to visual elegance and social

FIGURE 4.4 "Casablanca" by Ettore Sottsass 1981 – Memphis Milano Collection Sideboard in plastic laminate with internal shelves W. 151, D. 39, H. 221 cm. Photo Credit Aldo Ballo. Courtesy Memphis, Milano.

status. He turned the conventional rules on their head and proposed a design approach that, like some of the earlier Pop designs, valued image over object, surface over form, and short-term impact over sustained meaning. He found his model of communication in the world of contemporary media and developed an approach to design that prioritized the values of the fashion system over that of architectural Modernism. The objects presented by Memphis paralleled the "couture" models shown at mannequin parades that were immediately replicated through the mass media and disseminated to audiences across the world. Aping this system the Memphis designers ensured that their work was quickly visible worldwide. It didn't matter that the "prototypes" were crudely made, nor that the bookcases didn't hold many books. More important was the fact that they generated images that could be emulated and spread across the globe.

This is not to say that Memphis *became* the mass media. True to his craft Sottsass's cupboards did have doors and door handles and the lights of the Italian designer Michele de Lucchi (1951–) did provide illumination. The fact that Memphis became immediately fashionable, its patterns appearing on carrier bags and dresses, which was par for the course, however, evidence that Sottsass had taken control of the media. Like all fashion, however, it was hard to sustain the level of impact and Memphis finally had to come to an end, aware that its program had been fulfilled.

HOME FROM HOME

It has become clear through this chapter that twentieth-century domestic furniture did not always stay in the home. Indeed, by the end of the nineteenth century it could already be found in a number of different locations, from hotels to restaurants to railway carriages, anywhere in fact where it was necessary to make people feel at home when they were actually outside it, engaged in a range of activities such as work and travel (Plate 25).

Motivated by their suspicions about domesticity, the modernists reinforced the permeability between private and public spheres by designing furniture items that were equally "at home" in both. This was reinforced by their choice of industrial materials. One of Charles and Ray Eames's great achievements was, also, to consolidate Modernism's desire to eradicate the difference between "public" and "private" interiors such that there was an increasing level of interchangeability between them. The new modern interior aesthetic they created combined lightness with comfort and came to define a wide variety of environments. Whether in the private areas of the home or in the more public spaces of airports or receptions areas it signified a new relationship with modernity and a new modern identity for those who inhabited them.

By the end of the twentieth century the concept of the home office had emerged, bringing work of a non-domestic nature into the home and further eroding the separation of the spheres.

The *Nomos* furniture system was designed by Sir Norman Foster between 1982 and 1986 to be equally at home in the domestic sphere and in the office (Jenkins 2005) (Figure 4.5). It was developed over a period of years in response to the designer's own requirement, in his own architectural office, for

FIGURE 4.5 Norman Foster, Tecno Nomos table, 1987. Photograph © Tecno/Foster + Partners.

a multipurpose system that would accommodate all his needs. The "high-tech" architect of such innovative structures as the Willis, Faber and Dumas building in Ipswich (1971–5), and later the Hong Kong and Shanghai Bank in Hong Kong (1979–86), wanted to create a flexible and adjustable family of tables, desks, and working surfaces that could be used for a wide variety of functions, whether in the work place or the home, and he set out to develop one in the early 1980s. An early version was used in the Renault Distribution Centre, designed by the Foster office and opened in 1982. The project soon came to the notice of the Italian furniture manufacturer Tecno SpA, best known for its highly mechanized furniture designs by Osvaldo Borsani, and the Foster office and the Italian firm took it forward together from that point onward.

The result, launched in 1986, was a family of multipurpose tables based on a tubular chromium-plated metal frame, which has been likened to a lunar landing unit and a grasshopper, and a glass top (laminated tops were also available). Important aesthetic features of the design include the round feet, with their protective coverings, that bring the splayed legs neatly to the floor; and the metal engineered structure, once again with protective rubber pads at the meeting point with the glass, that supports the table surface, which most importantly, is visible through it. The table is available in a number of formats—rectangular, round, or ovoid among them—and can be used on its own as a simple dining table or desk in the home, or in an office setting, rendered more complex by being formulated in multiple configurations and adding a spinal column that conceals cables. In whatever form it appears *Nomos* is characterized by its elegance and lightness and its compatibility with modern interior spaces of all kinds. It confirmed Foster's wish to push technology and engineering structures to their limits while also creating timeless forms. Over the years, new variations on the original theme, and numerous accessories, have been developed.

CONCLUSION

This chapter has shown that the evolution of domestic furniture took place, throughout the twentieth century, within a social and cultural context, sometimes following change and at other times initiating it. To the changes already outlined could be added the loss of servants, the scientization of the home, and the democratization of home entertaining along with the emergence of the "housewife-hostess," all of which transformed the way in which the domestic setting functioned and required new furniture types and spatial configurations. As we continue to refine and define what we mean by "home," however, a concept that, with the advent of mobile technologies, is more flexible and open-ended than ever before, the furniture that will be needed to complete it, will, inevitably, change as well.

CHAPTER FIVE

The Public Setting

HELENA CHANCE

INTRODUCTION

When has the proximity of two, otherwise unexceptional, park benches been more charged with meaning than in this collision of transgressive and conservative cultures in a public park? The narrow void between the benches, a well-intentioned tactic by the city authorities to encourage social interaction in a public place perhaps, becomes the metaphorical, as well as physical, gulf that separates the fearless transvestites from their cautious neighbors (Figure 5.1).

FIGURE 5.1 Transvestites on a park bench in Tompkins Square Park, New York City. Photograph courtesy of Andrew Holbrooke/Corbis/Getty Images.

Furniture in public settings physically and symbolically marks the ambiguous and often uncomfortable ways by which we negotiate public space with strangers.

It is commonly said that tall buildings have come to define the modern city. Arguably, though, the way we have furnished our urban landscapes, including streetscapes, parks, playgrounds, shopping malls, museums, hospitals, and transport hubs, tells us as much about the changing experiences of urban and suburban living, the impact of political and economic changes, patterns of work, consumption and leisure, and new technologies and materials, as our buildings do. In rural and seaside settings, too, a furnishing of the landscape includes seating, picnic tables, litter bins, and signage; and at motorway service stations, national parks, theme parks, and beaches, these signal our consumption of heritage, sports, and other leisure pursuits, as do the transport means by which we reach those sites. Streets, squares, landscapes, and public buildings are furnished ostensibly for a "common good," but that very notion is arguably inappropriate within modern cities of multiple identities and needs.

As globalization and new technologies have connected the developed and much of the developing world, giving us greater mobility, more people can enjoy a larger variety of public spaces than ever before. But what do we mean by "public" and how have the concepts of "public" and "public setting" changed in the twentieth and twenty-first centuries? How we define public and private space changes over time and depends on cultural differences. Most rural land is privately owned, but in some countries such as the United Kingdom, legislation gives us the right to roam freely across private land along designated footpaths. National parks were originally appointed as areas of protected land, but our elected representatives no longer exempt parts of them from private sale. Before the emergence of local government in the later nineteenth century, urban space was privately owned, but as the public sector advanced, more streets, parks, squares, and public buildings, such as libraries, town halls, museums, and hospitals, came under the control of central and local government. After the Second World War, essential services including transport and telecommunications also became part of the "public realm," but in some Western countries, notably the United States and Britain, "civic space" gradually eroded as public services were privatized and urban land was sold off to private companies.[1] Today, much urban and suburban space, including shopping malls, railway stations, squares, and increasingly streets, is managed and controlled by the private sector, or by both public and private interests. For this discussion, therefore, the public setting is defined as any place intended for use by the public and where everyone has a right of access, with or without payment. In terms of function, some spaces mentioned, such as churches, schools, and universities, are more "private" than others; and many spaces designed for public use, for instance, parks, streets, and squares, are used by individuals and groups for private business or socializing or by the homeless or dispossessed for their private dwelling.

The scope for "public setting" is therefore immense as well as antithetical and not all typologies or places can be included, but this discussion underlines how furniture designed and placed for public use reflects changing notions of "publicness" by those who manage public spaces and design for them. Examples show how and why furniture, for comfort and rest; traveling or working; leisure, shopping, and socializing; or for political expression, enables "living" and "performing" in public spaces. For reasons of brevity, discussions of "street furniture," defined as any apparatus that furnishes streets, squares, and parks, including bollards, street lamps, and waste bins, will be largely limited to benches, chairs, and tables. Surfaces like walls, steps, and plinths will be included because people have always used them as furniture, whether legitimately or not.

The approach here is indebted to authors from the fields of philosophy, sociology, geography, anthropology, and design who have considered the ways in which the physical and social spheres in which we live shape our lives and our behaviors. The work of French philosopher and sociologist Henri Lefebvre, born as the century opened in 1901 and who died nine decades later in 1991, provides a framework for the discussion. Lefebvre shows us how the changing spatial forms and perspectives in everyday life within capitalist societies, which he defines as "conceived space," "lived space," and "perceived space," produce social relations, and how the interrelationships between space, people, and objects in space relate to the whole (Lefebvre 1991: 38–41). Based on these triads, the discussion develops chronologically and telescopically. The first section takes "space" as a focus, borrowing from Lefebvre's concept of "conceived space," or that which is envisaged and realized by architects and urban planners. The discussion will consider the cardinal structures that shaped the design and furnishing of public space in the first half of the twentieth century in the context of social and technological change, focusing on how furniture design contributed to changing expressions of civic and national identity and power in public places. The second section, "place," examines "lived space" in the period from the 1960s to the 1980s when theories of place and place-making contributed to a new paradigm of "living well" in space and a greater understanding of how furniture defines and gives function and meaning to places. In the third section, "body," examples of furniture designed for public space in the past twenty-five years will be discussed, illustrating Lefebvre's concept of "perceived space" or space as a product of social action. Lefebvre has suggested that despite the structures of power which dominate space, such as governments, the police, planners, or architects, the possibility remains for individuals or groups to assert their power as autonomous citizens and to resist dominant ideologies. Designers in the twenty-first century, in challenging orthodox definitions of design and function, have interrogated the way our bodies interact with objects in space, not only to give us more autonomy in the ways we use and respond to furniture, but also to express rights of self-determination in public spaces.

SPACE: POWER AND IDENTITY

In the first half of the twentieth century, diverse but interconnected reforming movements, originating in the nineteenth century, shaped the design and placing of furniture in public places in North America and Europe. While designs conceived by architects, designers, and urban planners differed spatially and stylistically, reformers were united in calling for more beautiful, orderly, dignified, and respectable public spaces as towns and cities—now with better sanitation and cleaner and brighter streets—expanded. The Civic Art and City Beautiful movements, for example, championed by landscape architect and planner Thomas Mawson (1861–1933) in the United Kingdom and journalist and planning theorist Charles Mulford Robinson (1869–1917) in the United States, promoted classical architectural styles, wide ceremonial boulevards, and parks and gardens as sites for public life, to connote power and order and promote civic pride. Mawson's design for the new public gardens at Southport in the northwest of England, with landscaping, planting, and seating integrated with classical detail and symmetry, is emblematic of civic authority and beneficence (Mawson 1911: 332–4). For much of the twentieth century, and even today in Britain, we see the legacy of these ideals in town squares and parks where prim seating amidst council carpet bedding physically and symbolically regulates public space (Figure 5.2).[2]

FIGURE 5.2 Station Square, Harrogate, 1940s. Postcard from the collection of Helena Chance.

City Beautiful design reforms at the turn of the nineteenth century inspired the new benches for Central Park in New York, which replaced the original crafted wooden rustic benches of Frederick Law Olmsted's (1822–1903) *rus in urbe* picturesque.[3] The new benches, installed along the Mall between 1890 and 1901, were manufactured in wrought iron because cast iron was considered too "common." Like military massing along the Mall, the elegant hooped-iron arms symbolized civic pride and order while they invited the crowds of promenaders to act upon the stage of the modern city (Cooper Hewitt Museum 1994). Popular literature of the period reveals that park benches represented both opportunity and anxiety for men and women, providing the potential for exciting or sometimes inappropriate encounters with strangers. Sleeping on public benches was associated with homelessness or unemployment (Humphrey 1911; Chapman 1922) and so in Central Park, the location of benches, in open spaces, were designed with circular arms for single occupancy, making lying down impossible, or other "improper" behavior difficult. Little has changed for in the twenty-first century many public seats constructed in cold, perforated metal or mesh have dividing arms making barriers to intimacy or sleeping (Figure 5.3).

Charles Mulford Robinson, with his progressive approach to social space, promoted high-quality public places and street furniture for poor urban areas, and picnic furniture for rural areas to facilitate the enjoyment of leisure time (Mulford Robinson 1904: 262–75, 322). He also called for less formality in the streetscape in imitation of his ideal found in the promenading and café culture of European cities such as Paris and Barcelona. In Paris, he suggested,

6069—The Mall, Central Park, New York.

FIGURE 5.3 Benches lining the Mall, Central Park, New York, from a souvenir postcard, *c*. 1895. Postcard from the collection of Helena Chance.

the moveable chairs available for hire created "open air salons of the street" with "their constant movement and gaiety" although he warned that they should be "appropriate" in their coloring and kept in good repair (214–17). However, attempts in the early 1900s by the authorities in New York to introduce European-style flexible seating into parks for a nickel a time met with stiff resistance. Many New Yorkers, less bound than Europeans by centuries of traditions and social hierarchies, were furious. They turned out "en masse" in Central Park in the summer of 1901 to protest by occupying the chairs without payment or by boycotting them altogether. "The Hired Chair Outrage" as the incident became known met with success, for the authorities revoked the chair license and celebrations followed with fireworks, speeches, and songs. By no means all New Yorkers, however, were opposed to the new seating arrangements. In a letter to the *New York Times*, one reader supported the chair policy because "self-respecting" people could choose not to sit next to "unclean, often drunken, and generally foul-mouthed loafers" on park benches (Rosenzweig and Blackmar 1992: 382–4).

In Europe, a similar desire among the social elite for a separate urban space could be seen at the Parc Güell in Barcelona, designed by architect Antoni Gaudi (1852–1926) and built from 1910 as part of an exclusive housing development. Gaudi's distinctive avant-garde style expressed Catalan national identity and appealed to a patrician group distinguishing itself through architecture and design. The "Banc de Trencadis," a serpentine, mosaicked seat curving around the terrace atop Sala Hipostila in the park, provided space for residents to see and be seen. All citizens eventually enjoyed its celebrated comfort when the park opened to the public in 1926. Popular legend has it that Gaudi asked a workman to plant his naked buttocks in the wet plaster to mold the perfect shape, while the ingenious bumps and drain holes along the back of the seat, which allow for rapid drying, testify to Gaudi's attention to the human body's needs. How many times do we seek in vain for a dry seat after a spell of rain?

In common with exterior public spaces, the interiors of public buildings were furnished not only to enable public life but also to induce a sense of civic responsibility and national pride. George Post (1837–1913), the architect chosen to design and furnish the capitol building in Madison, Wisconsin, is likely to have been selected for his skill in eclectic borrowings from dominant European and North American cultural and political ideals. Trained in Paris, Post used classical language for the building to reflect the pride of the city authorities and its citizens, thus symbolically linking them to the supreme political and social influence of ancient Greece and Rome. Inside the building, however, the furniture denotes power through its articulation of both the universal values of classical iconography and reforming Arts and Crafts and Art Nouveau elements, thereby reflecting a modern, democratic America (Viegut Al Shihabi 2013). The building's interior expresses a cosmopolitanism that was entirely appropriate for a nation rapidly taking the leading role on the Western industrial stage.

In mainland Europe, architects and designers found alternatives to the historicist Beaux Arts and vernacular Arts and Crafts approaches by producing some radical and innovative solutions to expressing national identity and modernity.[4] Architect Otto Wagner (1841–1918), whose work is regarded as formative in the advent of modern architecture, designed and furnished the Imperial-Royal Post Office Savings Bank, built in Vienna from 1906. He avoided references to classical architectural language, instead employing reforming Secessionist principles and functionalist pragmatism, and using, for example, aluminum throughout as a signifier of modernity. The cuboid brown-stained bent beech stools for customers in the main counter hall echoed the shape and transparency of the glass vaulted roof and counterbalanced the aluminum-clad and riveted pillars that supported it. The building symbolized the modernizing project of the imperial city, meeting the needs of citizens participating in public life and commerce.

SPACE: LEISURE, TRAVEL, AND HEALTH

In the first half of the twentieth century, new technologies, population growth, and changes in work and leisure were catalysts to a greater range and variety of public spaces, and accelerated demands for furniture with economies of scale and materials (Relf 1987: 82–3). Luxury as well as essential travel in ships and trains precipitated commissions and furniture was also required for theaters, restaurants, factories, schools, hospitals, playgrounds, and offices springing up in expanding towns and cities. A social revolution in sports and leisure required economical seating that prioritized function over style—stadium, music hall, and by the 1920s, cinema seating. The success of the Morris Furniture Group, founded in Glasgow, Scotland, in 1884, illustrates these trends, for the company supplied furnishings for ocean liners built on the River Clyde in 1904, then began to manufacture office furniture in 1910 and supplied cinema seats in 1920 (Morris Contract Furniture n.d.).

Modernist architecture and furniture design and new materials emerging in the 1920s with their revolutionary approaches to space and form became expressive of the modern age of public health and the power of social democracy. Public and private clients building health and community centers, or transport hubs, commissioned architects of the Modern movement who aimed for synthesis and dominion of space, in other words the *Gesamtkunstwerk* or total work of art. Avant-garde furniture worked interdependently with functionalist architecture in creating a healthy new openness, spareness, and transparency of space, the furniture, as Peter Conrad has suggested, "perched on the floor like birds alighting briefly on a branch" with the heavier historicist-style pieces "put[ting] down roots like a tree" (1999: 291). Bright, open public buildings furnished with variations on tubular steel and glass, or with light, slender, and flowing wooden forms, heralded a utopian future of healthy, socially engaged, and upwardly mobile citizens. In the Netherlands, for example, designer W.H. Gispin (1890–1981) supplied tubular steel, chrome, and glass furniture for the departure hall of the Holland-America Shipping Line in Rotterdam in the late 1920s, in the spirit of Marcel Breuer (1902–81) and his followers at the new Bauhaus in Dessau, Germany. Fritz August Breuhaus (1883–1960), designing chairs for the ill-fated Hindenburg airship in the 1930s, also used a tubular structure in aluminum, still a new material for furniture, to make them necessarily light. He upholstered the chairs in yellow leather for a luxurious elegance to appeal to the social elite traveling in this new, but short-lived, mode of transport.

The Finnish architects Aino Aalto (née Marsio, 1894–1949) and Alvar Aalto (1898–1976), who designed the building, fittings, and furniture for the Paimio public sanatorium, completed in 1933, were also influenced by Marcel Breuer's tubular steel furniture, which the Aaltos had bought for their home in Turku. Alvar designed chairs for the sanatorium dining hall, but his masterpiece was the graceful Paimio sunbed to which sheepskin sleeping bags could be attached for winter sunbathing (Worpole 2000: 49–57). Partly modeled on Paimio, and in a drive by local authorities to curb tuberculosis, public health facilities sprang up across Europe in the 1930s, including the Finsbury Health Centre (1938) in London, where light wood Aalto-designed armchairs and stools furnished the lucent spaces. The versatility, flexibility, and relative cheapness of Aalto's furniture contributed to its popularity for both domestic and contract use. The company Finmar Ltd., founded to market Aalto's furniture in the United Kingdom, was successful in selling significant quantities for both private and civic buildings designed by Modern movement architects such as Serge Chermayeff (1900–96), Eric Mendelsohn (1887–1953), and David Pleydell Bouverie (1911–94). The restaurant at Chermayeff's De La Warr Pavilion, a community center in Bexhill-on-Sea on the south coast of England, contained about fifty of Aalto's "Verandah" chairs (K. Davies 1998). The use of warm wood for furniture and interior fitments as a foil to the colder concrete, glass, and steel was a design device pioneered by Aalto and borrowed by many architects working in the 1950s and 1960s (Plate 18).

While the production of furniture for health centers, schools, universities, and new leisure industries remained high on the agenda between the wars, the phenomenon of motor traffic presented new challenges to towns and cities. Municipalities took control of furnishing the "mechanical street" with a diverse range of street furniture supplied by engineering companies, with the result that by the 1930s, the urban landscape in many towns and cities appeared cluttered and chaotic. According to Frank Pick (1878–1941), who directed the transformation of London Transport and its infrastructure in the 1930s, an "absence of design" was the cause of the "untidy" streets (1934: 102). Pick's choice of architect Charles Holden (1875–1960) and others to design the seating and upholstery in London's stations, buses, and trains, combining modern forms with traditional systems of comfort, perhaps testifies to his approach. Urban reformer Lewis Mumford (1895–1990) agreed with Pick's endorsement of professional designers in his 1938 book *The Culture of Cities*. Designers, he advised, should work with public authorities to enable coordinated planning schemes for the public good. Like earlier urban reformers, Mumford does not discuss the design details of street furniture although for him, high-quality public spaces, parks, gardens, and civic institutions reflected a healthy social democracy.

There appears to have been little innovation in furniture design for outdoor space between the wars but there are some notable exceptions. Hans Coray's (1906–91) "Landi" chair designed for the Schweizerische Landesausstellung (Swiss National Exhibition) held in Zurich in 1939, used the metaphors and materials of the machine age to symbolize national pride and modernity, much like the new chairs made for Central Park at the turn of the century. Coray chose the "Swiss metal" aluminum, one of Switzerland's most important exports, and borrowed his perforated design from the aviation industry to express and reflect a modern public with more freedom of mobility. The chair weighed only three kilograms, making it light and flexible enough to move around, and allowing the fair's visitors to redefine the space according to their preferences (Vitra Design Museum n.d.). British designer Ernest Race (1913–64) was to borrow Coray's idea of lightweight and maneuverable chairs for public exhibitions when he designed his "Antelope" chair for the 1951 Festival of Britain in London. Race's chair was made of steel and plywood to a more conservative design, perhaps aimed at a British public less receptive to the functional Modernism of mainland Europe.

SPACE AND THE INTERNATIONAL STYLE

For the three decades following the end of the Second World War, urban renewal schemes sponsored by national and local governments and increasingly by private developers transformed the nature of the public realm and made it more visible. However, as comfortable public spaces they were constantly challenged by the demands of traffic and also by the increasing heights of buildings surrounding plazas unsympathetic to human scale and the creation of pleasant public space. Lefebvre is one of many who wondered how, despite the Bauhaus ideologies of improving social space, we ended up with "the worldwide, homogenous and monotonous architecture of the state whether capitalist or socialist" (1991: 126).

Modernist ideologies dominated urban planning and reconstruction from the 1950s to the 1970s. Local authorities and private developers alike rejected pedestrian-friendly streets in favor of pedestrianized precincts, plazas intersected by busy highways, and high-density, high-rise housing, at best, overlooking a public garden or playground. Architect Gordon Cullen (1914–94) blamed poor-quality urban design on the large scale and speed of modern development (1967: 13). Denise Scott Brown (1931–) has argued that architects in Europe and America taking control of urban design as they would the design of a building for a single client, compounded the problem by losing the variety that a design team could achieve (1990: 21). But as American sociologist William H. Whyte (1917–99) argued in his 1988 film *The Social Life of Small Spaces*, some modernist spaces designed by one architect with a singular vision became highly successful public spaces. Significantly, though, the seating was not street furniture, but architecture. A review of illustrations in architectural magazines of the 1960s reveals that most architects did not include street furniture in their plans, for the task of furnishing streets was normally delegated to subcontractors and technical teams. To retain control over the space and those using it, architects would integrate seating into the architectural structure. Perhaps one of the most imaginative examples can be found at the Barbican arts and housing complex in London, designed and built between 1955 and 1982 by architects Chamberlin, Powell, and Bon, where there is brick seating in circular sunken gardens for residents and visitors.

Whyte's film explains that city authorities in New York had given floor space bonuses to developers building skyscrapers since the early twentieth century, on the condition that they included a plaza in the scheme. According to Whyte, many developers created dreary empty spaces, but the Seagram Building and Plaza designed in the 1950s by the émigré Mies van der Rohe (1886–1969) is an exception. The design unites building and landscape seamlessly, retains a neoclassical simplicity, and provides ample places to sit in a variety of configurations without separate seating to interrupt the space. Taking time out from the office, crowds of New Yorkers come to the Plaza to eat lunch or to socialize on the granite and marble ledges that bound the fountain and on the steps. Other examples of well "furnished" modernist public spaces shown in Whyte's film were those that made possible people's favorite activity in public space, watching other people, and which gave the public both private and social space.

As Mies was reinventing the furnishing of public space in the 1950s, poor quality in the design of public spaces and furnishings persisted, according to journalist Ada Louise Huxtable (1921–2013), who complained of a "visual anarchy" of historicist design (1959: 107) (Figure 5.4). Modern styles of street furniture were being promoted by the early 1950s ("Outdoor Seats: A Competition for Manufacturers" 1953: 30–2), but providing new, well-designed seating in precincts, parks, and playgrounds did not mean they were comfortable or appealing places in which to "dwell." Blocks of flats built in the postwar reconstruction of the Lijnbaan in Rotterdam, which surrounded

FIGURE 5.4 Modernism in the form of excessive street furniture assaults the streetscape of the country town idyll. Cartoon by Louis Hellman published as the frontispiece to the Council for Industrial Design's *Street Furniture Design Index* (1972/3). Photograph courtesy of the Design Council Archive, University of Brighton Design Archives. www.designcouncil.org.uk

a sunken public garden, were expressions of civic responsibility and social democracy. However, a photograph of the site suggests low-budget planting with regimented benches standing to attention in response to the monotonous, unrelenting environment. The modern benches, designed to complement an angular and rational International Style, were typical for new developments in this period.

Lewis Mumford's recommendation in 1945 that urban design would be improved by collaboration between government and designers became official policy in the period of reconstruction and new development after the Second World War. The *Street Furniture* directories published between 1963 and 1983 by the state-funded British Council of Industrial Design (CoID, founded in 1944 and renamed the Design Council in 1972) and by the American Public Works Association from 1976, present a snapshot of design for streets in this period shaped by government policy to promote "good" modern design as a "physical expression to the new social, political and cultural agenda" (Herring 2014: 2). The CoID called for a coordinated, rational approach to the design and siting of furniture to meet the needs of new-build or conservation areas and promoted a range of furniture based on modern variations of traditional forms, mostly using steel or precast concrete frames and wooden supports and backs, with PVC and plastic seating appearing in the 6th edition (1974–5). However, the new designs were not always popular with the public who resented the imposition of functionalist forms on the streetscape (Herring 2014: 4). The CoID directories presented pedestrianized streets in Munich and Copenhagen as models of good urban design, with their mixture of seating around planters and fountains and scatterings of movable chairs, although the recommended British arrangements in the directories never quite reached the spirit of the northern European examples. Perhaps the most accomplished design appears in the 1979 CoID directory. A bench forming part of a series of coordinated street furniture designed for the new town of Milton Keynes in the late 1960s could be ordered either in perforated steel or wood. Unlike the other benches in the catalogs, this one has grace and personality and its lightness of fluency of design looks to the future.

Language used in both the British and American street furniture directories, including "streetscape," "a sense of place," and "placemaking" marks a turning point, discernible from the 1960s, as designers and architects began to consider people's emotional needs in public places, instead of being preoccupied with civic pride and imposing a planning and architectural tour de force. The American directory of 1979 also heralded the new Public Art movement, which attempted, through collaboration with communities, to improve the "aesthetic and educational" value of public space contributing to more variety in the public realm.

PLACE-ATTACHMENT AND THE PUBLIC DOMAIN

"The public domain is the theatre of an urban culture. It is where citizenship is enacted, it is the glue that can bind an urban society" (Rogers 1997: 153).

Architect Richard Rogers (1933–) in his 1995 BBC Reith Lectures on the past, present, and future of cities, popularized a debate that had been active for at least the previous forty years—how to make cities more humane and "livable." While his polemic was fueled by a pressing need in the 1990s for sustainable approaches to architecture and urban infrastructure, his theory of a "humanist city" had its roots in mid-twentieth-century doctrines seeking alternative approaches to Modernism. The public and private sectors had come under attack for overly rationalized, univalent planning and design, which critics argued, eschewed human needs, increased stress and crime, and did not stand the test of time (Jacobs 1961; Newman 1973). Advocates of Postmodernism and its planning equivalent, urban design, argued that built space should be designed for comfort and enjoyment taking into account contexts of place and culture to reflect a pluralist society (Turner 1996: 7).

Postmodernism had "deeply confused and multiple personalities" (Relf 1987: 229) that this discussion will not attempt to unravel, but it will consider the ways in which furniture design for public places responded to theories of "place-making" to make "good" and more "livable" spaces, where social, cultural, and aesthetic hierarchies were dismantled to create inclusive spaces that prioritized "lived space" or "dwelling" over monumentality, wealth, and power (Lefebvre 2000: 190–5). Cultural geographers were among those from a number of disciplines writing in the 1960s and 1970s who argued that "good places" are those to which we become emotionally attached through connections to our histories and cultural symbols. American geographer Yi-Fu Tuan (1930–) argued that objects play a central role in place-attachment, giving us a sense of security (Tuan 1977: 187). Designers attempted to create a sense of place through furniture design and location by considering people's physical and emotional needs and preferences in public spaces or by building cultural symbolism into their designs for emotional impact. The very diversity of human needs means that no design solution will ever suit everyone and, as public space became increasingly privatized, commodified, and gentrified in the second half of the twentieth century, many public places came to express not social inclusion, but exclusion.

In the 1960s and 1970s, the concept of "urban design" brought together architects, landscape architects, planners, and engineers in a common aim to improve the quality of urban spaces. One of those was British architect Gordon Cullen (1914–94), whose book *Townscape*, first published in 1961, motivated the movement of that name. Cullen advised that well-designed and situated furniture could connect people emotionally and give them possession of spaces, and he included some furniture design "doodles" in the book to inspire designers to be more observant of the "English" climate (2002: 16, 162–3). Cullen's designs for sheltered seating and a fanciful swivel-tilt Perspex and aluminum chair that turned according to the wind direction, look quaint today, but the concept, which considered optimal spatial conditions for human comfort, was prescient.

The Swiss-born architect Willy Bruegger (1945–) meanwhile, who designed fixed seating and tables for the new Robson Square in Vancouver, Canada, came up with an ingenious way to create a comfortable yet flexible environment for office workers and visitors. Architectural firm Arthur Erickson (1924–2009) and landscape architect Cornelia Oberlander (1921–) designed the square, combining new buildings and landscaping to create an accessible public place of varied levels on a human scale that echoed the wide spaces of the ocean city. Breugger, working closely with Oberlander, responded to the modernist, but not monolithic, environment by designing concrete (of the same mix used for the buildings) and Canadian cedar wood furniture echoing both the soft and hard elements of their surroundings (Herrington 2013). As Bruegger recalls: "We hoped that, office workers on a sunny day, would enjoy their lunch break outside, so I added a little bit of encouragement through design." To enable occupants of the seats to choose their orientation and to make a convenient surface for eating lunch, the backs of some benches are turned to ninety degrees, giving a table surface in an innovative, constructivist form. (Today, these tables might also be ideal for laptops.) Bruegger acknowledges the influence of Austrian-born architect Christopher Alexander (1936–) on his designs, who had suggested in his book *A Pattern Language: Towns, Buildings, Construction*, published in 1977, that ancient patterns of building and design, such as the placing of seats under a tree to face the view, provided the best models for human needs (Breugger, email correspondence with the author, April 30, 2015). In Robson Square, the furniture pays attention to people's psychological needs, revealing perhaps the influence of another esteemed theoretician writing in the 1970s, Jay Appleton (1919–2015), whose persuasive "prospect and refuge theory" (1975) described the conditions by which we feel secure in certain environments.

The concrete benches in Robson Square were not popular with some (Breugger, email correspondence with the author, April 30, 2015) and, in fact, research conducted in 1978 at the Federal Building Plaza in Seattle, Washington, found that wooden benches were overwhelmingly preferred for seating, followed by steps and planters (Cooper Marcus and Francis 1998: 41).[5] In the 1970s and 1980s, observational studies of people using public spaces addressed shortcomings in the type, design, materials, and orientation for public seating in preventing people's enjoyment of places (Gehl 1971; *The Social Life of Small Urban Spaces* 1988). Movable chairs and tables of the type recommended in the early twentieth century by Mulford Robinson were overwhelmingly the most popular types of seating for everyone in public places, but only if they were free to use. In his studies of people using public space in the 1980s, William Whyte noticed that people constantly rearranged the chairs in New York City's Paley Park (opened in 1967), allowing them to take control of the space to suit their needs (*The Social Life of Small Urban Spaces* 1988). Originally designed by Harry Bertoia (1915–78) for Knoll International in 1951, the chairs are unmistakably modern, but their popularity could also be connected with cultural symbolism, for their design recalls the public life ideal of nineteenth-century Paris, seen for example in Edouard Manet's (1832–83) painting of *Music in the Tuileries Gardens* of 1862 (National Gallery, London, NG3260). It could be significant that, by the late 1990s, no chairs in either New York's Paley or Greenacre (another successful small park with movable chairs) parks had ever been stolen, which might suggest successful place-making through design, although it is also likely to be related to the nighttime closures of the parks (Cooper Marcus and Francis 1998: 43). It will be interesting to see if a similar policy for placing "bistro chairs" in the streets and squares of London's new King's Cross development in 2014 proves as successful.

PLACE, CONTEXTS, AND CULTURE

The location and orientation of furniture in public spaces can contribute to a sense of place, but as the seating in Robson Square in Vancouver and Paley Park in New York illustrate, place-making through furniture design also comes from cultural symbolism responding to the contexts of place and the cultures of those using them. Practices and methods of context-making through the furnishing of public space in the 1970s and 1980s supported not only the civic responsibilities but also the commercial interests of those managing the spaces.

Postmodernist pastiche became a favored style of design for the burgeoning commercial spaces eager for visual and emotional stimulation to capture consumer attention. Inspired by commercial "pleasure-zones" such as Disneyland (1954–5) or Las Vegas with their nostalgic and fantastical imagery, designers pilfered from the past, or from forms and symbols from popular culture, drawing the public into a witty and playful theatrical performance. Hans Hollein's (1934–2014) furnishing for the Austrian Travel Agency office in Vienna, 1976–8 (demolished 1987), momentarily transported the expectant traveler into the exotic lands of their dreams. Seated on stools in a chess-board of "Wonderland" options, customers found themselves in a fantasy of brass palm trees, a golden pavilion, and chrome columns as a prelude to their hoped-for journeys (Plate 19). It is no coincidence that in the postmodern age, some of the most popular public places are commercial theme and pleasure parks and large shopping malls where architecture and design connects the public to a utopian past and present of storybook narrative, fueling a desire to consume. One of the most popular tourist destinations in the UK today is Bicester Village, which opened in 1995. The shopping village is a pastiche mix of small Cotswold town and "main-street USA," with "traditional" street furniture suggestive of a civic ideal of small-town life, a controlled space of commodified authenticity. The nostalgic past of innocence and safety sits incongruously alongside the globalized homogeneity of the shops and cafés.

Place-making through retrofitting, using reproduction furniture, became common in urban conservation areas, historic districts, living history centers, and national parks, as the postwar conservation and "heritage" movement intensified in the 1970s (Samuel 2012: 68–75). In Britain the Victorian Society, founded in 1958, fueled nostalgia for the civic values of nineteenth-century streetscapes. Developers installed "traditional" furniture styles of the type rejected by the Council for Industrial Design in the 1950s and 1960s ("Outdoor Seats: A Competition for Manufacturers" 1953). Curlicued cast iron and wooden benches sporting civic liveries, or litterbins in black and gold, connected the public to benevolent civic responsibility. Retro and reproduction styles continue to be popular today, although some local authorities are notoriously arbitrary and indiscriminate in their specifications for street furniture, driven perhaps by expediency. On the esplanade of Criccieth, a seaside town in North Wales, the plastic liveried litter bins, hybrids of Victoriana and Art Deco, sit uncomfortably beside "brutalist" benches, their end frames in textured concrete, the latter a legacy of the Design Council's recommendations for street furniture in the 1970s.

Designs that eschew pastiche or nostalgia but use subtle symbols and metaphors tend to survive the vagaries of fashion and enjoy a more permanent presence. Ron Carter's (1926–2013) bench designed for London's Victoria and Albert Museum café in 1985, contributed to a strong sense of place and permanence to reflect the museum's responsibility to educate and entertain the public in comfort. The elegant wooden structure is appropriate for an innovative museum of design and decorative arts, for the design acknowledges the work of Scottish architect and designer Charles Rennie Mackintosh (1868–1928), but it is not a pastiche. Designers commissioned to reinterpret our industrial past in contemporary contexts have also connected people to the past while avoiding pastiche and nostalgia (Plate 20). Designer Rodney Kinsman (1943–) presented a more oblique but effective reference to the industrial past in his designs for beam-mounted seating for airports and other transport systems. The steel braces of his "Trax" seats, designed for British Rail in 1989, recall the architectural structure of Victorian railway stations, while the upward-projecting seats, perched on light pedestals, place waiting passengers in the present, anticipating the journey to come (Jackson 2013: 205).

PLACES, PUBLIC AND PRIVATE

In the postwar period, discussions about design for public spaces began to focus on how to create comfortable places to which people would feel culturally and emotionally connected. Furniture designed for interior spaces remained diverse and often original in an increasingly competitive global market, although in the 1980s, innovation was more visible in the private, luxury, leisure marketplace, where playful bespoke objects gave spaces such as restaurants and boutique hotels a competitive edge. With some exceptions,[6] furniture designed for outside space remained relatively conservative until the late 1980s. Advancing gentrification in deteriorating urban neighborhoods bred historicist designs, and the need to economize in times of recession suppressed innovation. Critics complained that public spaces remained bland, as monolithic architecture and unimaginative urban design persisted and the privatization and commercialization of space created a new kind of homogeneity (Drabble 1991: 37; M. Davies 1998).

Commercial public spaces such as shopping malls and theme parks are designed to attract people with spending-power while the disappearance of spaces such as libraries, parks, and playgrounds, as well as legislation to exclude "the other" from public places, marginalizes and disempowers the poor. Those, like some youth and the homeless, who do not conform to normative behaviors, are now barred in some places from their preferred uses of space by intensive management and increasing surveillance (Carmona, de Magalhães, and Hammond 2008: 41; Doherty et al. 2008: 292). In 1997, for example, more than seventy cities in the United States had either banned or restricted begging, sleeping, and "other homeless activities" in public places and some authorities were considering making voluntary donations to beggars illegal (Minton 2006: 11). Design for public seating now more frequently excludes the "dispossessed" or those who need to sleep or wish to skateboard, with bumps, ridges or arms incorporated into seating, or benches installed that can only be leant but not sat on, to deter lingering or "dwelling." A more insidious method by some developers, in what is now known as "hostile architecture," is to install spikes at ground level to prevent occupation.

To counter trends for homogenous, hostile space and accusations of banality, exclusivity, and conservatism in urban design and furnishing, designers and their clients, from the state, private, or voluntary sectors, began to produce some more imaginative design for public places from the 1990s. By confronting archetypal forms and functions of furniture, designers empowered citizens to become cocreators in the making of a more pluralistic, animated, and inclusive public realm.

BODY, OBJECT, AND MEMORY

A shift in the critical intensity of questioning about the social role of objects in defining and expressing our identities, actions, and emotions has contributed to the wave of innovation in the late twentieth and early twenty-first centuries. Guided by anthropological, social, art, and design theory, designers are changing the way we interact and engage emotionally with objects in a mutual performance. This is not an entirely new idea: from William Morris (1834–96) to David Pye (1914–93) and beyond, designers have emphasized the roles of the senses and aesthetic pleasure when creating and encountering "good" design. Anthropological studies of objects such as *The Meaning of Things* (Csikszentmihalyi and Rochberg-Halton 1981) and design studies based on post-structuralist theory have also deepened an understanding of the ways in which objects become the texts through which we express ourselves and anchor our personal and social lives. As Stuart Hall (1932–2014) argued, "Things 'in themselves' rarely if ever have any one single, fixed and unchanging meaning [...]. It is by our use of things, and what we say, think and feel about them— how we represent them—that we give *them a meaning*" (1997: 3).

Some of the most interesting furniture designs today construct layers of meaning through the ways in which the human body interacts with the furniture object in a reciprocal performance. In *The Production of Space*, Henri Lefebvre reminds us that our experience of social space proceeds from the body. Our senses, from smell to sight, provide us with different "layers" of connection with space: "the passive body (the senses) and the active body (labor) converge in space" (Lefebvre 1991: 405). Lefebvre's ideas were a catalyst to a new area of research and practice—studies of the "art of living" in which the life of each individual became a work of art. These included the activities of the Situationists (Guy Debord, their main activist, was a pupil of Lefebvre's) whose artistic avant-garde interventions in urban spaces in the 1950s and 1960s opened up new possibilities for the role of the individual with non-conformist approaches to the design of space and objects. Lefebvre's and the Situationists' legacy for furniture is one of the body as performer in space where objects are no longer just the props, but they become works of art in themselves through their engagement with the body, resisting "normal" social rituals in public space and affirming the rights of citizens to occupy space for their own needs.

The school chair, for example, had not evolved since the 1950s and 1960s when children had to sit still and straight. So in 2008, designers Edward Barber (1969–) and Jay Osgerby (1969–) began to think about the less formal ways of interaction in the modern classroom. They watched the restless bodies of children at work in schools and found a solution to the chair that contravened years of conventional behavior. Their light plastic "Tip Ton" chair designed for Swiss furniture manufacturer Vitra (named after the innovative Tipton School in the West Midlands) has a forward tilt action that responds to the sitter's movements and encourages better posture and easier communication. The Tip Ton had the potential to ease more flexible ways of working, but at a cost of more than £200 apiece, Vitra had to abandon their utopianist project to improve school furnishings and they now market the chair for homes and offices.

The cost of Tip Ton chairs might have discouraged further attempts to find alternative seating-types for school children, but designers looking for ways to improve the comfort and quality of life for older people and for diverse ethnic groups in public places have found some affordable and original ways to unite body and furniture in public places according to social need. In 2014, the Royal Institute of British Architects (RIBA) initiated the "Streetscape Challenge," a competition to reconsider seating for the elderly in Grainger Town, Newcastle-upon-Tyne. The company Medical Architecture proposed adding "warm to the touch" plastic and wood composite backs and arms to the existing cold granite seating, and specified seating of different heights with signage of greater legibility. The city of Newcastle upon Tyne already has a reputation for innovative urban design that takes into account diverse social and cultural groups, funded by private companies with interests in improvements. As part of the same initiative to improve and provide new outside public spaces in the city, Newcastle City Council and the business district improvement company NE1 identified places in the city center for new "pocket parks" to benefit local communities, including the inhabitants of the city's China Town. Local residents, many of them elderly, can borrow chess and checkers sets from the nearby supermarket and enjoy a game on the sustainable hardwood playing tables that come with slate chessboard inserts. This example of "inclusive design"[7] focuses on the needs of the Chinese community, although another initiative by NE1, to install ping-pong tables across the city in the summer of 2015 to bring new "performers" and activities into the public realm, holds more risk. What could be fun for one group or individual might be a nuisance to another.

The idea of animating public space with objects has a long history, but the public art movement that emerged in the 1970s made contemporary art more visible in the exterior public realm. Today "art" furniture, or furniture/art hybrids, with which the public can interact are increasingly appearing in public places, an idea that perhaps originated with the furniture sculptures of Constantin Brancusi (1876–1957) at Târgu Jiu in Romania, made in the 1930s, or the American artist Scott Burton's (1939–89) responses to Brancusi's furniture made in the late 1970s and 1980s. The various seats designed for the "High Line" in New York, a disused elevated railway converted by private, public, and voluntary interests into a highly popular linear park by James Corner, Elizabeth Diller (1954–), Riccardo Scofidio (1935–), Charles

Renfro (1964–), and Piet Oudolf (1944–), are composites of furniture, kinetic sculpture, and objects for play. The High Line that covers thirty blocks and 2.4 kilometers of the city, both subverts and reinforces the "meanings" and memories of the place by the ways that mnemonic objects are re-presented, some as temporary art objects, and others as permanent furnishings. The High Line's family of benches, some with back supports, others arranged for conversation, recall the original rails as they "peel up" from the deck to affirm the walking route ahead. Along the line, walkers can rest at the Diller Von-Furstenberg sundeck, where they may roll the wheeled loungers along the track into different configurations depending on their preferences for socializing or solitary rest.

The public art movement has also supported projects where public seating becomes a canvas for art, or a medium for literary expression. In 2014, for instance, the National Literary Trust in the UK and public art agency Wild in Art installed fifty benches across London illustrated with stories linked to the city, from John Wyndham's (1903–69) *The Day of the Triffids* of 1951 and George Orwell's (1903–50) *1984* of 1949 to Michael Bond's (1926–2017) *Paddington Bear* of 1958 and Julia Donaldson's (1948–) *The Gruffalo* of 1991, connecting Londoners and visitors to the city's literary past. In the countryside, too, benches combining the visual, material, and literary arts have delivered intellectual enjoyment, metaphor, and public memory. Furniture designer-maker Angus Ross (1963–) and poet John Wedgwood Clarke (1969–) placed six benches at viewpoint sites along the Yorkshire Wolds Way in 2011 in an interpretation of the classic commemorative bench. The steam-bent flowing oak wood responds to the importance of water in shaping the gentle curves of the hills and sustaining the settlements there, and the words speak about the people, past and present, who have shaped the cultural landscape (Angus Ross 2015). These kinds of public art and furniture projects increasingly deliver opportunities for furniture designers to distinguish new public spaces with sculptural work that is both conceptual and functional.

BODY, PERFORMANCE, AND RESISTANCE

The benches on the High Line and London's literary benches have given us alternative forms of public seating, but the human body interacts with them in relatively conventional ways. Even the user of a Tip Ton chair, while sitting more informally, will remain upright with feet on the ground. A more distinctive type of public seating confronts us with taboos, such as lying down and being in close intimacy with or, more contentiously, touching strangers. Designers and artists invite the body to lounge in informal configurations or explore the structures physically, such Danish artist Jeppe Hein's "Modified Social Benches" designed for the "Please Touch the Art" exhibition in Brooklyn Bridge Park, New York, in 2015. These objects dismantle boundaries between the public and the private and between the body and the object as they unite in a mutual performance.

Argentinian designer Diana Cabeza's (1954–) concept of *Nidos Urbanos* (Urban Nests) presented in 2005 was inspired by research in the margins or "non-places" of Buenos Aires where the homeless build shelters from discarded materials. Cabeza observed how the private world is created in a public space, and her "nests," reminiscent of Gaston Bachelard's (1884–1962) metaphor for security in his book *The Poetics of Space* (1964), gave nurture and connection to the natural environment (Muzi 2010: 99–100). In Germany, designer Konstantin Grcic (1965–) responded critically to the function of accepted furniture typologies in creating his "Landen" bench (2007). More like the Apollo Lunar Module than furniture, the adventurous are impelled to explore the structure with their bodies and up to eight people can sit together in this "social hub." Similarly, British designer Peter Newman's (1969–) "Skystation" 2005, a "dimpled chromium droplet," draws heads together for relaxed conversation or mutual enjoyment of the sky. "Future City," the urban design company that manages the project, plans to install one hundred Skystations across Britain and around the world, to bring informal and spontaneous human interaction to public spaces and to reinforce the bonds of shared identities and emotions (Future City 2014). Just as furniture for older people is becoming more inclusive, so the social needs of young people, some of whom prefer to use public spaces for play and sports such as skateboarding and parcours, are being partially addressed.

These examples of public seating illustrate strategies of resistance to social norms and archetypes, but design activism takes a more political approach, resisting dominant political and social ideologies. Henri Lefebvre argued for the potential for all citizens to resist hegemonic power in public spaces: "The political power that holds sway over 'men', though it dominates the space occupied by its 'subjects', does not control the causes and reasons that intersect within that space, each of which acts by and for itself" (1991: 413). The "right to the city movement" inspired by Lefebvre and seen in the activities of the Situationists and other groups in the 1960s, has been "rekindled" in the social forum movement of today (Hoskyns 2014: 84) and is expressed in recent attempts to transform urban spaces. In 2013, for example, the "Parlons Banc" (Let's Talk bench) project by Collectif Cochenko in Paris, a group committed to "social urban design," began to draw attention to the negative effects of the increasing privatization and homogenization of public space, and to the role of public seating in expressing a civic consciousness (Collectif Cochenko n.d.). With support from the City of Paris and by codesigning and building with a local homeless charity and social center, the Collectif installed a temporary wooden bench with planters in La Place de la Rue de Buisson Saint Louis, provoking a debate about how local residents wished to use their public spaces. The wooden bench, a deliberate departure from "artful" aesthetics, expresses personal and collective autonomy, encouraging informal social interaction and close engagement with nature for the youth who helped with the planting (Plate 21). Encouraged by the way the project initiated dialogue between community groups, councilors, and city engineers, and highlighted the multiple ways in which a single space can be used, the Collectif trialed some alternative street furniture models in the autumn of 2015, including "nomadic" and "for hire" types.

CONCLUSION

Collectif Cochenko's bench project highlights the opportunities for designers wishing to engage community participation in furnishing public space in the twenty-first century. However, this approach will always have limitations, for the very diversity of "publics" today means that no solution will ever please everyone.

Through the first half of the twentieth century, "the public" was regarded as a homogenous whole and people using public spaces treated more as passive audiences for whom design would control and educate. At the same time, furniture assisted people's participation in social democratic space and provided a threshold between public and private. Throughout the second half of the twentieth century, planners and designers gained a better understanding of the ways in which furniture animated the "theatre of public space" for a heterogeneous public. Furniture became props that gave definition and individual and collective agency to spaces and places, and alternative types and configurations of furniture were designed to assist "habitation" of space. However, in the second half of the twentieth century, furniture in public places increasingly served a desire to consume rather than to "inhabit" space for socializing, solitary reflection, or dwelling. Lefebvre's utopian "right to the city" argument, where all citizens should play a part in the production of public space, was increasingly assaulted through privatization. As the commodification and gentrification of urban and suburban space advances, activists, the dispossessed, and bohemians are excluded, or exclude themselves, moving to the margins of the city, or to private places away from the public gaze. As designer Diana Cabeza has suggested, furniture in the "edgelands" or "non-places" of the public realm comes from the objects and the materials that are rejected by others (Muzi 2010: 100).

In the later twentieth century and into the twenty-first, some furniture design for public space is arguably becoming more socially and culturally inclusive. Private companies and developers and public authorities are funding new types of furniture to serve a more heterogeneous and pluralist society. Concepts of codesign and inclusive design, and a greater understanding of the emotional, experiential, sustainable, and performative possibilities for designed artifacts, have placed people center stage as collaborators in shaping public space. In too many public places, however, furniture remains banal, uncomfortable, or poorly placed and does not accommodate those with special needs. Those planning public spaces have also been slow to embrace the ways that digital technologies are changing patterns of work and leisure. Improvements are on their way, for prototypes of responsive street furniture for disabled people, such as sensors in seating and "talking" signage, were being tested, for example, in London in 2015 (Howarth 2015). Convenient resting places for work in "the third space"[8] of today's mobile society are now appearing among seating or as stand-alone workstations at some airports (a new furniture type for public space), although tables with power sockets are still hard to find on many trains.

At the time of writing this chapter, an exhibition at the Victoria and Albert Museum in London highlighted the centrality of design and architecture in defining and redefining public spaces, drawing attention to the politics of public space as privatization encroaches on our rights of access and engagement with spaces. As the state gives up more space to private enterprise and people's role in shaping public space is challenged in the austerity of the early twenty-first century, we need to educate young designers interested in furnishing public space to confront social norms and conformist perspectives and to embrace new technologies creatively.

ACKNOWLEDGMENTS

The author would like to thank Stephen Ward, Professor of Planning History, Oxford Brookes University, Professor Jake Kaner, Associate Dean of Research, Nottingham Trent University, and Ellie Herring, Lecturer in Design History and Theory, The Glasgow School of Art, for their advice.

CHAPTER SIX

Exhibition and Display

CLAIRE I.R. O'MAHONY

INTRODUCTION

Display is a performative act. The dynamic networks of objects, makers, and consumers that forge furniture's cultural history are orchestrated into narrative by the sensory experience of an exhibition, shop display, or an "app." Scenography, audiences, and their interaction frame the social rituals of furnishing the home, café, office, etc., projecting fantasy as realizable. Various modern spectacles demonstrate continuity and rupture with the past as well as prototyping future selves and societies. The phenomenon of the international exposition remained a core site of exchange from the Universal Exposition held in 1900 in Paris to the 2016 International Furniture Fair Singapore. The agency of organization for such events has arguably shifted ever further from the hands of designers or governmental jurisdiction to the extended role of commerce as a mediator of professional and national interests. The role of museums as educators, arbiters, and promoters of furnishing taste and commerce through exhibitions, publications, and merchandising remains powerful. These institutions' choice of which designers, makers, period styles, and types of furniture to honor, acquire, or commission is indicative and productive of social mores and fashion as well as their potential subversion or appropriation. Temporary displays of purchasable furniture alongside museum objects in auction houses, department stores, and airports reveal the permeability of boundaries between elite culture and mass consumption. Enticing simulacra of these material displays reside within the covers of "mail order" catalogs, the advertising pages of magazines, and the virtual showrooms of the movie set, television screen, and website.

In attempting to grapple with the plenitude of provocative forms of display in the modern age, this analysis focuses upon three themes within display as core manifestations of the cultural history of furniture: temporality and place in international exhibitions; the politics of "soft power" in furnishing model dwellings; and embodied experience in furniture display.

TEMPORALITY AND PLACE IN INTERNATIONAL EXHIBITIONS

In a review of an 1896 exhibition of industrial goods in Berlin, the sociologist Georg Simmel (1858–1918) recognized the potential alienating and opiating effect of contrasting sensations and didactic narratives experienced on a visit to an international exhibition:

> Modern man's one-sided and monotonous role in the division of labor will be compensated for by consumption and enjoyment through the growing presence of heterogeneous impressions, and the ever-faster and more colorful change of excitements. [...] Nowhere else is such a richness of different impressions brought together so that overall there seems to be an outward unity, whereas underneath a vigorous interaction produces mutual contrasts, intensification and lack of relatedness.
>
> (Simmel [1896] 2010: 284, translation by Sam Whimster)

The project of an international exhibition has fundamental contradictions at its heart. The representation of so many nations in close quarters presents tensions between the "contrasts" and "outward unity" of cultures. Through centenary and decennial retrospectives of art and design as well as fictive peasant or colonial villages where costumed craftspeople dramatized artisanal traditions as if aloof from the passage of time, these expositions afforded opportunities to travel through time and place (Simmel [1896] 2010; Burton 1983; Peer 1998; Filipová 2015). The physical experience of visiting a world's fair vacillated between a sense of magisterial control and neurasthenia; the illusory acquisition of encyclopedic knowledge soon disintegrated before the sheer multitude of objects and sites magically brought together in a fairy city that vanished at the summer season's close. Guidebooks, maps, instructive panels and signage complemented by smiling attendants naturalized the narrative authority projected by the fairy city's displays. Overstimulation induced acquiescence, quietening any internal dissent with the identities asserted by every feature observed as we stroll.

André Maurois relished the visual spectacle of "glimps[ing] at the same time, the towers of Angkor, the thatched roofs of Togo, the red Kasbahs of West Africa." Nonetheless, he closed his eyes to synthesize the temporal multivalency of the 1931 Paris International Colonial exposition into supratemporal sonority: "A gramophone sings; an airplane roars. Very far away the tom-tom of a Negro [*sic*] summons up the most ancient rhythms. I love to find in this enclosure of Vincennes the Melody of the World, and its History" (Maurois 1931 cited in Morton 2000: 5). The furnishing of the 1931 exposition's "Salon of Africa," an office created for Colonial Minister Paul Renaud (1878–1966), used these contrasts of time and space to legitimate France's colonial project.[1] The juxtaposition of indigenous materials and "high style" modern profiles in the furniture and décor embody and naturalize the forced exchange and hierarchies of colonial resources for metropolitan finesse. Émile-Jacques Ruhlmann (1879–1933) orchestrated an extraordinary counterpoint of light and dark, curves and angles in his ensemble (Plate 22). The contemporary critic Marcel Zahar (1898–1989) characterized the luxurious club arm chairs as a "mastodon variety." Their elliptical bodies in russet Moroccan leather with white piping rest on solid square ebony feet able to support the minister's weighty guests with a "restful corpulence [...] an air of well-being" (Zahar 1931 cited in Brunhammer 2002: 134). The color notes of the minister's desk in Macassar ebony, silvered bronze, "galuchat" (shark skin), and ivory resonate with echoes of the black and gold palette of the Napoleonic Empire style. The simplified geometry of its silhouette suggests the contours of carved African sleeping stools and the masks avidly collected by modernist artists (Plate 13). The colored marble in the oval floor design and the curved surrounding murals by Louis Bouquet (1885–1952) represent timeless intellectual and artistic dialogues with France's colonies. Powerful, naked sub-Saharan African muses tower over Apollo seated with his lyre, whilst veiled figures bespeak the scientific and Islamic traditions of Arab North Africa. This exhibition of furniture embodied the fantasies, fears, and force of the colonial project, normalizing these narratives, literally imbedding them in the interior furnishing.

Visitors to international exhibitions required intrepid navigational skills in their search to find examples of furniture. Physical and intellectual agility was needed to negotiate the contrasts of natural wonders and industrial achievements, high art and popular amusements. Many exhibitors despaired of gaining attention or recognition amidst these cacophonous events. Patrick Geddes (1854–1932) bemoaned the challenge facing the critic and visitor hoping to assess the 1900 Paris Universal Exposition:

No man has been able actually to see [...] this vast, indeed too vast, labyrinth of labyrinths, this enormous multitude of collections, this museum of museums. How can one briefly give an idea of what needs shelves of volumes for its mere catalogue?

(1900: 655)

This distracting multiplicity of focal points led Siegfried Bing (1838–1905), director of the Parisian gallery-shop "L'Art Nouveau," to construct a special pavilion for his enterprise with installations of integrated model rooms in which to sleep, entertain, or work. Bing's strategy had been embraced by many collective artistic societies and design workshops who hired or collaborated with public gallery spaces to host temporary exhibitions on a more human scale. In contradistinction to the melee of the Crystal Palace Great Exhibition of 1851, for example, the Arts and Crafts Exhibition Society helped to define the public understanding of craftwork through installations at the New Gallery in London between 1888 and 1910 (Hart 2010). The success of the first Secessionist exhibition in Vienna meant the group had the funds to commission its own gleaming "house of art," the Secession Building, from Josef Maria Olbrich (1867–1908) in 1898 (Koppensteiner 2003). Alongside poster, Japanese print, and international painting exhibitions, the group's dynamic display program included a number of installations of craft and furnishing that were also transmitted by means of their illustrated journal *Ver Sacrum* throughout the Austrian-Hungarian Empire and a global community of subscribers (Naylor 2000). Founded in 1903, the Weiner Werkstätte (Vienna Workshops), a cooperative company forged by design-focused members of the Secession, also recognized the efficacy of such periodic special displays in attracting furnishing commissions from a circle of aesthetically discerning affluent clients, reaching its apogee in the famous Stoclet Villa in Brussels (1905–11). The firm also launched a network of boutiques, first in Vienna and then beyond in Berlin and London before the First World War, even opening a store on 5th Avenue in New York in 1922, which operated until the firm's liquidation in 1932 (Noever 2006). Themed showroom exhibitions such as "The Laid Table" and "Garden Art" invited consumers to imagine their furnishings and domestic wares in use. These commercial displays gained prestige by association through the workshop's participation in exhibitions at the Austrian Museum of Art and Industry, in Austrian pavilions at international expositions and with sympathetic design associations in other countries such as the Deutscher Werkbund in 1914 in Cologne. Design collectives, their temporary exhibitions and artistic journals were important disseminators of local and transnational currents in modern furniture design.

The decision to position furniture displays in these multiple intersecting orbits of the international exposition, the museum, and the market generated productive dialogues amongst designers as well as ensuring maximum exposure to potential buyers and critics. Like Bing, Herman Muthesius (1861–1927) provided a vital conduit. In 1902 Karl Schmidt (1873–1948), president of the Dresdener Werkstätten für Handwerkskunst (Dresden Handicraft Workshops) financed and gained agreement from the municipal authorities to hold an exhibition of Heirat und Hausrat (Marriage and Household Goods) in Dresden's exhibition palace. Muthesius ensured that Schmidt was part of a group of German designers who visited Glasgow in 1903, facilitating an encounter with Charles Rennie Mackintosh (1868–1928) and his wife Margaret MacDonald Mackintosh (1864–1933), which prompted a commission for them to design a bedroom for the exhibition. Although the Dresden Handicraft Workshop displays focused principally upon their own membership, giving pride of place to Richard Riemerschmid (1868–1957) who created ten rooms, the event showcased a number of international exhibitors including the Mackintoshes, Olbrich, and Mackay Hugh Baillie Scott (1865–1945). The Mackintoshes' white bedroom ensemble was composed of elegant high-backed chairs and fitted cabinets with a discrete square motif, which was echoed in Margaret MacDonald Mackintosh's embroidered panels (Figure 6.1). A review in *Innendekoration* by the critic Beuttinger echoed the discontent voiced by Simmel and Geddes proposing the psychological effect of the furnishings as restorative amidst these pressures of modernity: "Mackintosh's bedroom with its light colors and unadorned furniture gives a thoroughly calming effect like an antidote for our hectic, nerve-shattering times," concluding "[Mackintosh] does not seek motifs and does not wish to appear deliberately modern. He is Mackintosh and is always new" (Beuttinger 1904: 166). The tensions between expressing cosmopolitan modernity and providing a retreat from its destabilizing variety reside at the heart of exhibition display. A new hybrid format, the international design exposition, offered a welcome clarity of aim yet still functioned on a world stage.

The contrasting advantages of the intimate focus of artistic society exhibitions and the global ambitions of the world's fairs prompted Turin to boast stewardship of a new exhibition format in 1902: the First International Exhibition of Modern Decorative Art. This exhibition strategy would recur periodically throughout the twentieth century, perhaps most famously in Paris in 1925 and 1937. Unlike the five nineteenth-century world's fairs in Paris, these projects reflected a determination to reassert the French capital's cultural preeminence by adopting the sharper focus on modern design pioneered in Turin. Nationalist anxieties generated by the success of an installation of Munich furniture shown at the Salon d'Automne of 1910 prompted rival French factions to unite in support of the ambition to host a Paris design exhibition (Troy 1991; Gronberg 1998). Their reasoning varied. Professional bodies such as the Société des artistes décorateurs founded in 1901 argued for the merits of a chauvinistic celebration of France's luxury traditions. The leading Ministry of Education official and design critic Roger Marx (1859–1913) championed the moral and social reform the display could promulgate, educating a wider public in aesthetics by infusing everyday life with well-designed objects (Dell 1999). Although the project was formally commenced under the auspices of

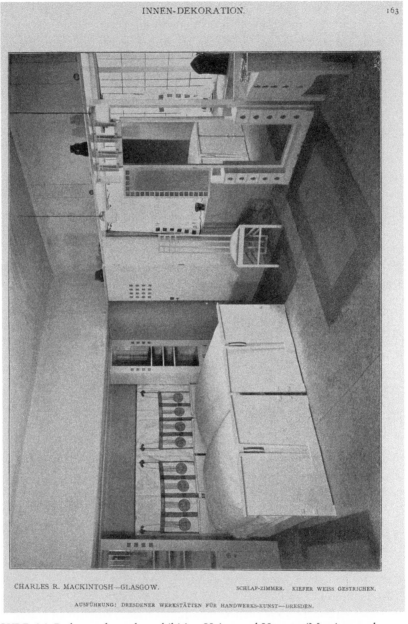

FIGURE 6.1 Bedroom from the exhibition Heirat und Hausrat (Marriage and Household Goods), organized by the Dresdener Werkstätten für Handwerkskunst (Dresden Handicraft Workshops), 1903, designed by Charles Rennie Mackintosh and Margaret MacDonald Mackintosh. Illustrated in E. Beuttinger, "Ausstellung der Dresdener Werkstätten für Handwerkskunst," *Innendekoration*, 15 (1904): 163. Photograph courtesy of the Heidelberg University Library.

a ministerial commission appointed by the Chamber of Deputies in 1912, the centrifugal forces that would culminate in the outbreak of the First World War and the financial insecurities that ensued after the cessation of hostilities meant this exposition was delayed until 1925.

The nomenclature of these new specialist design exhibitions is evocative of the shifting debates about where furniture was deemed to reside on a spectrum of cultural production from high art to mass production. Whereas the Turin exhibition signaled a comfort with aligning modernity with "decorative art" without hesitation, the titles of the two Paris exhibitions underlined a growing perception that modernity required decoration and artistry be associated with industry. The 1925 project was an "international exposition of decorative and modern industrial arts" whilst the 1937 display was "dedicated to art and technology in modern life." The jury's entry requirements in 1925 were that all exhibits had to express "modern inspiration and real originality." The eclecticism of objects that were deemed to meet these criteria revealed the volatility of the principles and practices of modern design (Smith 1927).

Modernity was one amongst many rival, intersecting preoccupations in furniture displays. Within the 1925 Paris Exposition, pride of place was still given to the national manufactures of Gobelins and Beauvais in the Ministry of War (Salon de la Guerre) installation positioned opposite the great hall in the Grand Palais, the ceremonial heart of the exposition (Lazaj and Ythier 2012). This interior exemplified many Janus-like dualities: modernity and tradition, state patronage and private elegance, commemoration and commodification (Figure 6.2). Robert Bonfils (1886–1971), who designed one of the exhibition's four famous posters with a youthful woman and antelope, had been approached in 1919 by the official intermediary of the Gobelins for a commission to design furnishings for a receiving room in the Ministry of War. This ensemble was installed in 1925 to create the effect of a model room, including a carpet, also designed by Bonfils, and a large tapestry *The Departure of the Americans* from a cartoon by Gustave Louis Jaulmes (1873–1959). The shape and ornament of the furniture mingled historicism and contemporaneity. The furniture frames inset with laurel and braid carving in gilded wood were executed by the École Boulle, both evoking and simplifying the enclosed, upholstered silhouette of the "bergère" chair form of the Louis XVI epoch.[2] Bonfils's upholstery pattern designs also resonated with the historical leitmotif of the seasons with floral swags and damascene background for which the Gobelins was renowned. However, the vibrant palette, graphic drawing style, and especially the mechanized modernity of the martial scenes represented ensured that these pieces met the exhibition's requirements for modernity and originality. *Infantry* is personified by a soldier standing watch over a plough in the snow, a scene resonant with a biblical text: "They shall beat their swords into ploughshares" (Isiah 2:4). The timelessness of this setting and the olive branch entwined around the bayonet of his rifle is made startlingly contemporary by the inclusion of recognizable attributes of the First World War French infantryman, popularly known as a "poilu": the Adrian helmet and "horizon blue" uniform adopted in 1915. *Aviation* and *Navy* include a biplane in flight and a gray dreadnought battleship firing guns at sea as the focal point of the chair back designs. The scale of the central *Artillery* sofa affords the most elaborate composition; it witnessed the latest military technology and strategy. The subtle camouflage devised by the "Chameleon" artist corps (O'Mahony 2010) blends the canon into the surrounding autumn foliage whilst white arcs shudder out from the woven surface embodying the discharge of the gun instigated by the helmeted figure in the middle ground. Traditional furnishing forms made this commemorative ensemble grand and timeless, yet the contemporaneity and dynamism of its representations of modern warfare infused the interior with an unexpected modernity.

FIGURE 6.2 Upholstered tapestry furniture (Artillery "canapé"; Aviation and Infantry "bergères") in the Salon de la Guerre, displayed in the Grand Palais at the Exposition Internationale des arts décoratifs et industriels, 1922–6, wool and silk, seven threads to a centimeter; sculpted and gilded carved frame; upholstery tapestries designed by Robert Bonfils; weaving by Manufacture nationale de tapisserie des Gobelins; and carving and gilding by the École Boulle Paris. Photograph © Ministère de la Culture – Médiathèque du Patrimoine, Dist. RMN-Grand Palais / image Médiathèque du Patrimoine.

The juxtaposition of nostalgia and modernity was not just a feature of the Paris 1925 Exposition; exhibitions within Anglo-Saxon cultural traditions, especially in America, the United Kingdom, and its empire, also manifested ambivalent attitudes to historicist and futuristic furnishing. The declarative emphasis within the narratives of 1930s exhibitions upon science and corporations as the future saviors of Great Depression America was typified in the furnishing of the model homes created for the Century of Progress Exhibition held in 1933 in Chicago. Nonetheless, the nostalgic allure of period furnishing, especially reproductions of the Colonial and Federal eras, also remained a constant within model home displays in San Diego in 1935, in Dallas in 1936, in San Francisco in 1939, rising to a crescendo in the 1939 New York World's Fair (Wilson 2010: 142). From the inauguration of its first display in 1908, the large-scale Daily Mail Ideal Home Exhibitions held in the vast space of London's Olympia juxtaposed remarkably eclectic stylistic modes. These annual events were devised by Wareham Smith, who managed the newspaper's advertising, assisted by Frederick Moir Bussy, who ran the Special Publicity Department (Ryan 1997). Bussy recognized that hosting exhibitions would prime a profitable advertising and promotions income stream for the newspaper, introducing private consumers into the closed dialogue between building supply firms and the architects who secured most of their trade. The successful gambit of the Ideal Home displays resided in targeting attention exclusively upon the domestic sphere and especially its female consumers by displaying fully realized examples of homes with furnishings, appliances, and a garden. Similar initiatives such as the Salon des Arts Ménagers in France (1923–76) encouraged women to embrace new technologies, enhancing the hygiene and efficiency of the modern home, especially in the kitchen (Rudolph 2015: 87–116). For the 1920 Ideal Home Exhibition, the Design and Industries Association collaborated with a focus group of housewives to award prizes for the best labor-saving designs as well as for a "Chamber of Horrors" to avoid. In 1930 the "House that Jill Built" competition gave a married woman reader of the paper the opportunity to have her ideal home designed by an architect to her specifications with a budget of £1,500. The displays encouraged taste and technology in all its forms and through prizes and surveys, invited women to participate actively in imagining as well as consuming the model home.

The furniture chosen to create the reality of these "ideal homes" suggests that the newspaper and designers recognized the merits of attending to both historicist and modern taste. Amidst the jubilation of the Festival of Britain, the Women's Institute commissioned the architect Lionel Brett (1913–2004) to construct a model home for the 1951 Ideal Home Exhibition. The brief was to make a house that responded to the results of a 1942 questionnaire of their membership about their best and worst experiences of domestic design. Norah Glover (1923–) recognized the reality that most domestic postwar homes embraced a complex variety of furnishing in her design. In the Festival of Britain simultaneously on display on the Southbank, the white heat of technology informed the multipurpose space of a living room designed by Lucienne Day (née Conradi, 1917–2010) and Robin Day (1915–2010) and the latest scientific advances of crystallography inspired the upholstery, carpets, and wallpaper of the Festival's Regatta Restaurant (Wise 1951; Jackson 2008). By contrast, in Glover's Women's Institute home new acquisitions of rationed Utility scheme furniture cohabited with older pieces and inherited heirlooms, interconnected by "make do and mend" feminine crafts of quilts and rag rugs throughout (Ryan 1997). This blend of contemporaneity and nostalgia satisfied the multiple tastes sought within the Ideal Home exhibitions. From its earliest days, evocations of comforting continuity such as a highlight of 1910, "The Tudor Village," were interspersed with attention grabbing modernity. Shown in the 1913 Art Furniture section, Omega workshop furnishings secured the copy-selling scandal of the "Post-Impressionist" exhibitions of 1911–12 for the fledgling Daily Mail Ideal Home Exhibition project. As a 1913 review in *The Bystander* warned, the gestural color applied to an Omega bed might not suit most Ideal Home exhibition visitors being "the sort of decoration that brings healthy sleep to the tired Futurist, but we fear that to us, the uninitiated, it rather suggests a nightmare!" (Reed 2004: 128).

Furnishing display cultures also envisioned life in the future. The Daily Mail Ideal Home Exhibition commissioned its first "House of the Future" in 1928, a home from "the year 2000" designed by Stephen Rowland Pierce (1896–1966) and R.A. Duncan (Figure 6.3). *Popular Mechanics* published three illustrations of the house and garden in golden section and emphasized the modernity of new materials: pivoting windows in "Vitaglass"; walls in "a hornlike substance [...] with camouflage designs," which housed all wiring and temperature control piping. Alongside new technologies ("built in radio [...] television set and [...] tele-newspaper") futuristic furnishing's most salient features were adaptability and mobility. "Pneumatic armchairs, with enormous inflated cushions can be deflated and folded up into a small space when not needed." Levers within a tripartite dining room table meant it could be "completely set, even to the centerpiece of flowers in the kitchen and then wheeled into the dining room passing through a standard-width door" ("Home, Sweet Home of the Future" 1928: 923–7). The most famous "House of the Future" was designed by Alison Smithson (née Gill, 1928–93) and Peter Smithson (1923–2003) for the 1956 Ideal Home Exhibition. In this atomic age home poised between metaphors of cloud-cave-car-clothing, a volatile future-past effect was expressed in the technological and organic hybridity of its "Pogo," "Egg," and "Petal" chairs manufactured by Thermoplastics Ltd. (Colomina 2004). However, the temporality of this futuristic model home was duplicitous. The architectural wall frames were a handmade fiction in plywood; only the furniture was realized in the futuristic media of polyester resins and Perspex. Furthermore,

PLATE 1 Model of the villa Arpel film set and props of *Mon Oncle* (Dir. Jacques Tati (1907–82), 1958). Recreated at the 2014 Venice Biennale. Photograph courtesy of Wikimedia Commons.

PLATE 2 Josef Hoffmann (1870–1956), "Sitzmaschine" (Machine for sitting), 1904. Photograph courtesy of DeAgostini/DEA/AL PAGANI/Getty Images.

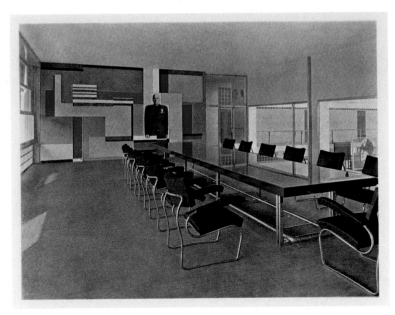

PLATE 3 Furnishings designed by Giuseppe Terragni (1904–43) for the director's conference room, Casa del Fascio, Como, 1932–6, from Giuseppe Terragni, "La costruzione della Casa del Fascio di Como," *Quadrante*, 35 (6) (1936): 19. Photograph Collection Centre Canadien d'Architecture/Canadian Centre for Architecture, Montréal.

PLATE 4 Egøn Möller-Nielsen, (1915–59) "Ägget" (egg) playground sculpture on the Tessin Estate, Stockholm, Sweden, 1955. Photograph courtesy of Wikimedia Commons.

PLATE 5 Billiard room in Villa la Sapinière, Evian, © 2015. Photograph reproduced by kind permission of Franck Paubel.

PLATE 6 Gerrit Rietveld (1888–1964), "Red and Blue" Chair, *c.* 1918, wood, painted, 86.5 × 66 × 83.8 centimeters; Seat height: 13' (33 cm). Gift of Philip Johnson. 487.1953. New York, Museum of Modern Art (MoMA). © 2016. Photograph courtesy of the Museum of Modern Art, New York/Scala, Florence.

PLATE 7 Charles Eames (1907–78), Side Chair, Model DCW, 1946, molded and bent birch plywood and rubber shockmounts, 174.9 × 48.3 × 54.6 centimeters. Gift of the manufacturer. New York, Museum of Modern Art (MoMA), Acc. num. 70.1946 © 2016. Photograph courtesy of the Museum of Modern Art, New York/Scala, Florence.

PLATE 8 Achille Castiglioni (1918–2002), "Mezzadro" stool, 1959 (Zanotta, S.p.A., Italy), tractor seat, steel and beech, 51.4 × 49.5 × 51.4 centimeters. Gift of the manufacturer. New York, Museum of Modern Art (MoMA), Acc. num. SC7. © 1972. Photograph courtesy of the Museum of Modern Art, New York/Scala, Florence.

PLATE 9 Ettore Sottsass (1917–2007), "Carlton" Bookcase/Room Divider, 1981 (Sottsass for Memphis), plastic foil. © 2016. Photograph courtesy of DeAgostini Picture Library / Scala, Florence.

PLATE 10 Tejo Remy (b.1960), "You Can't Lay Down Your Memory," chest of drawers, designed and manufactured 1991, metal, paper, plastic, burlap, contact paper, and paint, 141 × 134.6 × 50.8 centimeters. Frederieke Taylor Purchase Fund. New York, Museum of Modern Art (MoMA), Acc. no. 432.1996. © 2016. Photograph courtesy of the Museum of Modern Art, New York/Scala, Florence.

PLATE 11 Philip Koomen (b.1953–) "Pondlife" Bench (2003) using sweet chestnut thinnings from a local wood. Photograph by kind permission of Philip Koomen.

PLATE 12 A break dancer performing with a boombox on the street and group of young people watching him, 2016. Photograph courtesy of Wikimedia Commons.

PLATE 13 Marcel Breuer (1902–81) and Gunta Stölzl (1897–1983). "African" Chair, 1921/4. Photograph courtesy of VG Bild-Kunst Bonn (für Gunta Stölzl); Bauhaus-Archiv / Fotostudio Bartsch, Karen Bartsch.

PLATE 14 Verner Panton (1926–1998) "Oresund - Visiona II" at the Danish Design Centre, 1970, wood, rubber, wool. Photo Credit: Atlantide Phototravel/Getty Images.

PLATE 15 Kazumasa Yamashita (b.1937–), Living room in a so-called A-house in Karuizawa, Nagano. Chairs and cushions by Katsuhiko Shiraishi, c. 1962. Photograph from Kiyosi Seike and Charles S. Terry, *Contemporary Japanese Houses*, vol. 1 (Tokyo: Kodansha, 1964), 195.

PLATE 16 A "living room" on the street under a bridge, furnished with a bench, chair, and plant, January 2014. Photograph courtesy of Marjan Groot.

PLATE 17 Regency sofa in John Cavanagh (1914–2003) studio, 1957. Photograph © John French / Victoria and Albert Museum, London.

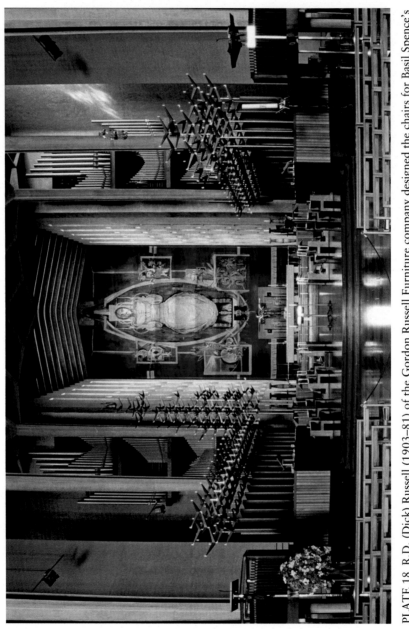

PLATE 18 R.D. (Dick) Russell (1903–81) of the Gordon Russell Furniture company designed the chairs for Basil Spence's modernist Coventry Cathedral (1955–62), in 1961. Their color adds warmth to the interior. Photograph courtesy of Andrew Holt/ Getty Images.

PLATE 19 Furnishing for the Austrian Travel Agency office in Vienna, 1976–8. Archiv Hans Hollein (1934–2014). Photograph courtesy of Private Archive Hollein.

PLATE 20 Kathryn Sumroy, "Timber Stack," 2013. Award-winning designer/maker Kathryn Sumroy designed her bench in collaboration with local school children in response to the history of the canal in Chelmsford, UK, particularly in relation to timber transport. Commissioned by Taylor Wimpey, Chelmsford City Council and the public artist/producer Zoe Chamberlain. Reproduced by kind permission of Kathryn Sumroy and Buckinghamshire New University. Photograph by Enrico Garofalo.

PLATE 21 Collectif Cochenko, "Parlons Banc" (Let's Talk bench) project, 2012, pine, La Place de la Rue de Buisson Saint Louis, Paris. Photograph courtesy of Philippe Calia pour Collectif Cochenko.

PLATE 22 Minister of Africa Office designed by Emile-Jacques Ruhlmann (1879–1933), Raymond Subes (1891–1970), Louis Bouquet (1885–1952). Moroccan leather, sharkskin, Macassar ebony, ivory, animal tusks, silver, silvered bronze, spun brass for the 1931 Colonial exhibition and housed in the Palais de la Porte Dorée, Paris. Photograph © RMN-Grand Palais / Jean-Gilles Berizzi, © ADAGP, Paris and DACS, London 2016.

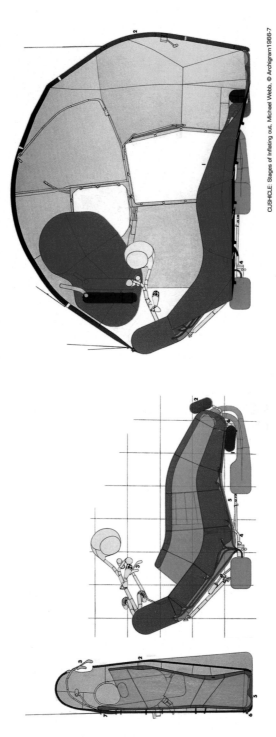

CUSHICLE: Stages of Inflating out, Michael Webb, © Archigram 1966-7

PLATE 23 "Cushicle": Stages of inflating out; Suit: unopened; Combined Suit and Chassis: opening out; Total Cushicle: fully opened, opened out, and in use, designed by Michael Webb © Archigram 1966–7. Image supplied by The Archigram Archives 2016 through Shelley Power Literary Agency Ltd.

PLATE 24 Sir Edwin Lutyens (1869–1944), Oak safe cabinet, 1903–1904. Photograph courtesy of the Victoria and Albert Museum, London.

PLATE 25 Seating in the French Brasier automobile of 1906. Image from the collection of Gregory Votolato.

PLATE 26 Jurgen Bey (b. 1965–), "Ear" Chair, 2001. Photograph by Roel van Tour, Pim Top and Mathijs Labadie. Courtesy of Studio Makkink and Bey BV.

PLATE 27 Marc Newson (b. 1963–), "Skybed" Qantas, 2003. Photograph courtesy of Marc Newson.

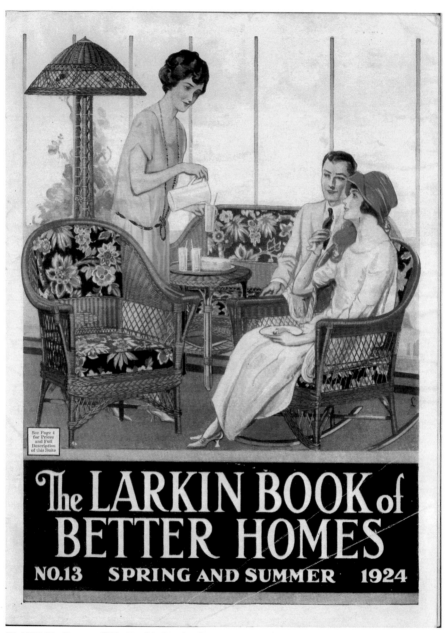

The LARKIN BOOK of
BETTER HOMES
NO.13   SPRING AND SUMMER   1924

PLATE 28 Cover of *The Larkin Book of Better Homes* (1924). Photograph courtesy of the Collection of Mike Jackson, FAIA.

BEDROOM

Bedroom furniture shown in one of the most popular G-Plan colour combinations – lilac and white. **206** *Bedside-table*, **1871** magnificent *dressing-table* and **1040** roomy four-foot wardrobe. **908B6** *double-bedhead* (see inset) with swivel frames to receive two divans. These will then swing apart for easy cleaning and bedmaking. **885** *dressing stool* and **403** *chair*

PLATE 29 *Guide to the G-Plan*, 1962 catalog. Photograph courtesy of the High Wycombe Furniture Archive, Buckinghamshire New University.

PLATE 30 Martin Crane's dilapidated recliner on the set of the television sitcom *Frasier* 1993–2004 Grub Street productions Art Direction by Roy Christopher (1936–2021). Photograph courtesy of Paul Drinkwater/NBCU Photo Bank/NBCUniversal/Getty Images.

PLATE 31 Pages from Swedish furniture designer IKEA's old catalogs, hung in a contemporary modern art museum in Stockholm on June 18, 2009. Photograph courtesy of OLIVIER MORIN/AFP/Getty Images.

ONS IN RADIO AND TELEVISION

Tonight, a soldier in the South Pacific speaks to a mother in Illinois. A farmer in New England settles down to war news from London. A band plays, and three thousand miles away a boy and a girl dance. A bank president, an actor, a Texas ranger talk through the still night air.

The miracle of the electron!

Tonight, air raid wardens gather in fire houses and police stations. In a television studio, instructors warn of incendiary bombs, describe fire-fighting techniques. Thirty thousand air raid wardens thus completed training courses in New York City—the first instance of mass education by television—through receivers in 81 precinct police stations.

The miracle of the electron!

It is almost half a century now since Marconi proved to an astonished world that messages could be transmitted without wires. Today, electronic transmitting tubes flash the music and pageantry of the world through space at the rate of 186,000 miles a second. From microphone and electron oscillator, through which course millions of free electrons, radio waves ripple out over city, forest, and sea.

There is no part of earth where radio cannot now reach. In the electronic tomorrow, sound and sight will travel the air waves. You will relax at home in your armchair, and watch a ball game, a stage show in full and glorious color. You will see a red robin sing as you hear it, wander with explorer through greening wilderness, follow with your eyes a plane soaring over the Andes. This is not far in the distant future. General Electric research is building for a day when your home will be a window on the world.

17

for Radio Lange, 1931. BHA, Invent. No. 4216. Photograph courtesy Berlin.

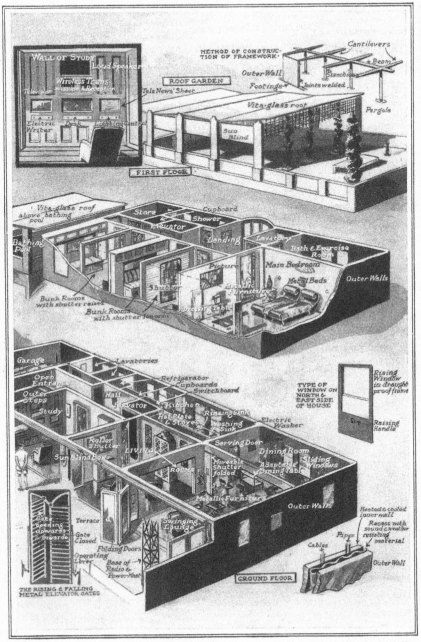

924 POPULAR MECHANICS

© The Illustrated London News

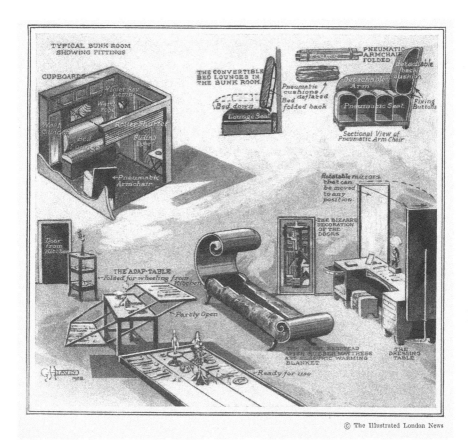

FIGURE 6.3a, 6.3b, 6.3c Illustrations from *Popular Mechanics* (June 1928) of the House of the Future installation in the Daily Mail Ideal Home Exhibition of 1928. Photographs from the collection of Claire I.R. O'Mahony.

the Smithsons' vision of "1980" sat within that year's Ideal Home theme of "An Englishman and His Castle." The chivalric scenography of brightly painted fifteenth-century knights on rearing steeds in an honor guard on a "moss-green" carpet with a castellated backcloth designed by Maxwell Haylett likened avid "demobbed" consumers to crusaders:

A colorful medieval world of jousting knights and tented fields reminiscent of the romantic pages of Scott [...] Nor is the theme as illogical as it may seem. With the end of a troubled era [...] the old drawbridge could give way to something nearer to the modern conception of a front door. Unheard of luxuries like carpets and Byzantine fabrics, imported for the first time by the Crusaders heralded a new age of comfort.

(Sheridan 1951: 132)

These multiple temporalities afforded connections both with the distant past and the troubled recent present to help visitors imagine their ideal home in a brighter future.

Alongside international exhibitions, museums, and private galleries, and commerce also promoted model rooms to foster a range of design idioms suitable to the furnishing needs and aspirations of fluctuating contemporary social structures. The reception in North America of the luxurious furnishing that had been the hallmark of the Paris 1925 exhibition demonstrates the complex intersections between public institutions and the marketplace in educating and prompting the consumption of furniture.[3] The following year, North American consumers were introduced to the lavish "moderne" style of furnishing through touring displays composed from the Paris exposition in department stores such as Bloomingdales in New York and branches of Eaton's department store in Toronto and Montreal (Wright 1997: 3–34). The desire to promote North American variations on this daring style also underpinned the formation of the American Designer's Gallery on West 57th Street in New York in 1928–9 (Friedman 2007).[4] The model room created a space through which the visitor could imagine how to furnish their own reality, favoring past, present, or future as suited their needs and desires.

Model room furniture displays provide new variations on the theme of the well-established if contested, principally museological phenomena of the period and typological room (Porter and MacDonald 1990). As Jeremy Aynsley's tripartite taxonomy of the curatorial conventions of the modern period room suggests (reconstitutions in museums, preservation in situ, and "imaginary spaces"; Aynsley 2006: 9–10), the furniture of a model-room display misleads as much as it captures or authenticates period or contemporary attitudes. Emulating the archetypal room installations of national museums and even often transplanting whole interiors from stately homes, displays such as the Daily Mail Ideal Home exhibitions regularly included reconstructions of historic and futuristic interiors of various guises. Installations from the 1920s such as "The Nursery of the Nations" and "Old Kitchens of the Nations," or the Smithsons' 1956 "House of the Future" immersed the visitor once again in the spatial and temporal dislocations that had unnerved Simmel and Geddes at the dawn of the century: the delectation of such transnational, transhistorical, typological confections proposed a heady mixture of the unique and the everyday dramatizing "imagined communities," pasts and futures (Anderson 1983). The 1922 Ideal Home Exhibition included an "authentic" Lanarkshire miner's cottage, a transplanted, temporary display of an actual building and its inhabitants, redolent with the stereotyping and power dynamics of the displays of Indigenous, colonial peoples previously discussed. No doubt conceiving this well-intentioned project as a prompt to conscience, Lord Northcliffe (1865–1922) also recognized that it risked instilling a complacent affirmation of the nostalgic idyll of the rustic cottage which he had hoped it would problematize. The bed shared by the whole family in this single-room space readily became a picturesque cottage object rather than a testament to the urgent need for housing reform:

> The Miner's Cottage looks of course, very comfortable indeed. It has electric light, which is rare in miner's cottages. It is a beautiful dry place and in many mining villages it rains nearly every day. There is no indication that there are no sanitary arrangements and the casual looker goes there and says "How delightful."
>
> (Ryan 1997: 45)

Historicist or futuristic, exhibitions revealed the lengths and limits to which furniture responded to the reconfigurations of domesticity engendered by financial crisis, war damage, and rival economic ideologies.

DISPLAYING THE "SOFT POWER" OF FURNITURE

Museums and spaces of commodified purchase often cooperated in the twentieth century to articulate powerful "narratives" about individuality, the ideals and realities of modern dwelling, national identity, and political ideology through furnishing taste (Bhaba 1990: 1–9). Joseph Nye Jr. has termed cultural forms of persuasion within economic and political diplomacy as "soft power": "the ability to affect others to obtain the outcome one wants through attraction rather than coercion, or payment [...] soft power was essential in winning the cold war" (2005: 94). Throughout the twentieth century, the promoting of "good design" also promulgated particular societal formations from the British middle-class respectability of the Daily Mail Ideal Home exhibitions to the socialist utopias proposed in model collective apartments constructed in exhibitions held in interwar Stuttgart and Cold War Moscow. The impact of these installations was widely disseminated through print and cinematic journalism. Collaborations between powerful institutions such as the Museum of Modern Art in New York (hereafter MoMA), metropolitan department stores, and government agencies proselytized political hegemony under the aegis of the improvement of public taste. Such projects had their roots in the aesthetic pedagogy of nineteenth-century design reform movements, which facilitated the formation of national design museums and professional training. Important precedents include the 1852 *Gallery of False Principles of Design* display curated by Henry Cole (1808–82) and Richard Redgrave (1804–88) for the inauguration of the Museum of Ornament at Marlborough House in London, which has been recreated in the museum's current incarnation, the V&A Museum.[5] Popularly known as the "Chamber of Horrors," this display

critiqued the mass-produced, highly ornamented design that had dominated
the Great Exhibition in the Crystal Palace the year before (Yasuko 2004;
Frayling 2010). Whereas most didactic displays principally targeted consumers
purchasing furniture for a middle-class family house, social housing exhibitions
and national pavilions in periods of postwar reconstruction also purported to
engage with the furnishing solutions required by the conditions of the displaced
or lower-income echelons (Bullock 2002; Wilk 2006a; Cupers 2014).

Model dwelling displays proposed new ways of life in their furnishing.
The loss of life and devastation of the built environment enacted by both the
world wars created cycles of pressure and opportunity, which precipitated new
forms of furnishing for affordable housing. The societal shift whereby "surplus
women" could no longer aspire to the expectations of marital homemaking
focused attention on the requirements for the limited space of bed-sitting rooms
and collective flat dwellings. This transience and constraint was coupled with
a positive vision of a modern life of healthy sport, free-flowing air, space, and
light encouraging minimal, adaptable forms of furniture. These transformations
took on particular acuity in Soviet installations, which conceptualized a new
communal life, as in the reading room designed by Alexandr Rodchenko (1891–
1956) for the Lenin workers' club exhibited in the USSR Pavilion designed by
Konstantin Stepanovich Melnikov (1890–1974) at the Paris 1925 Exposition
(Kiaer 2005). As a letter from Rodchenko to his wife Vavara Stepanova (1894–
1958) proposed, the modesty of plain wood and the universalizing effect of the
geometric abstracted contours of his chairs and multipurpose tables bespoke
a much deeper message about the ways in which furniture might become
"comrades" in the designing of a new social order:

> Objects in our hands should also be equal, also be comrades, and not black,
> gloomy slaves like they have been here [...]. Objects will be understood, will
> become people's friends and comrades, and people will begin to know how
> to laugh and enjoy and converse with things.
>
> (translated in Garnwell 2015: 191–2)

The industrial processes brought about by the innovations and demand required
by war, be it materials such as tubular steel or the techniques of serial mass
production, encouraged new forms of furniture design. Favored in both elegant
villas and social housing, this multipurposed, lightweight moveable furniture
embodied rival political and economic models as well as changing private mores
of the proposed model inhabitant(s). The critical reception of twentieth-century
exhibitions of "modernist" furniture reveals deeply contradictory and opposed
ideological constructs around individual and collective dwelling being ascribed
to modern furniture. These projections of identity and geopolitical "soft power"
would continue to reverberate in the furnishing shown across retail showrooms,

state-funded displays, and museums during the tidal social transformations of the world wars, the Depression, and the Cold War.

Model displays could embody intangible theory and as yet unrealized experience. Designers, curators, and retailers recognized the usefulness of the temporary exhibition in exploring the reactions of potential consumers to prototypes and samples, fostering their desires and aspirations. The allure of meticulously planned showroom installations designed by Gilbert Rohde (1894–1944) for Herman Miller Inc. during America's 1930s Great Depression (Ross 2004; Obniski 2007) or the famous Britain Can Make It Exhibition of 1946 provided windows onto desirable objects, which allowed the spectator to project the pleasures of future consumption and plenitude in times of constraint (Sparke 1986c; Macguire and Woodham 1997). Ephemeral displays also often provided a transition from designers' abstract principles expressed in print to the material and experiential dissemination of their project to a public and patrons. In the Netherlands, the rival positions of the journals *De Stijl* and *Wendingen* (Turnings) were tested out in designs for a café shown in a 1919 applied art exhibition at the Haagsche Kunstring (The Hague Art Ring) as well as the celebrated display of three model houses at Léonce Rosenberg's (1879–1947) Galerie de l'Effort Moderne in Paris in 1923 (Troy 1983). The cover design of the journal *L'Esprit Nouveau*, founded by Amedée Ozenfant (1886–1966) and Charles Jeanneret (Le Corbusier, 1887–1965), was used as the entrance motif of their pavilion at the 1925 Paris Exposition declaring a threshold between theory and practice. In their glass industry display in the Die Wohnung (Dwelling) exhibition staged in Stuttgart in 1927, Lily Reich (1885–1947) and Mies van de Rohe (1886–1969) demonstrated how the stark simplicity of a glass and metal transparent house could be humanized by the textural upholstery of chairs in chamois and cowhide and naturalizing rosewood tables (Colomina 1998: 133–4).

Model displays not only embodied theoretical principles but also offered insights into the ever-changing interpretation and status of particular furniture designs and their makers. Three interwar exhibitions of Bauhaus furniture in Weimar in 1923, in Paris in 1930, and in New York in 1938, testify to the historiography of the critical understanding of this influential design school. When the Thuringian Legislative Assembly challenged the Bauhaus to prove the success of the school's pedagogic program, Walter Gropius (1883–1969) and his colleagues recognized the efficacy of staging an exhibition, a new manifesto in three dimensions replacing the Expressionist cathedral woodcut by Lyonel Feininger (1871–1956) from the school's 1919 foundation. The 1923 *Haus am Horn* (House on Horn Street) model house envisioned an airy, rational space minimally furnished with geometric wooden frame chairs designed by Marcel Breuer positioned on an abstract woven carpet design by Martha Erps (later Breuer, 1902–77) (Forgács 2012). The inventive wooden cabinets painted in bright colors designed by Alma Siedhoff-Buscher (1899–1944) also provided infinite variations of use from seating and play purposes to the storage of her innovative children's toys. However, although these storage units were purchased by Nikolaus Pevsner (1902–83) in his early career as a curator, they rarely gained a mention in histories of the Bauhaus until the twenty-first century (Kinchin and O'Connor 2012: 77–8). The primacy of metal furniture design, more evocative of a modernist teleology of industrial aesthetics and production, would overshadow the importance of upholstery, wooden furniture, and women designers at the Bauhaus. The critical reception of Bauhaus furniture in interwar exhibitions reveals the multiple narratives ascribed to the school. A review decrying the 1923 Weimar exhibition's "attempt to return to the primitive art forms of inferior races" (Forgács 2012: 81) demonstrates the persistence of the craft methods and Dada-Expressionist ethos of the foundational period of the school. Bauhaus furnishings were later exhibited abroad in 1930 under the aegis of the Werkbund at the Salon of the Société des artistes décorateurs in Paris. Many French critics expressed anxiety that the display demonstrated a worrying recurrence of German industrial dominance. Pierre Lavedan, in a review in *L'Architecture*, feared that faceless Bolshevism was reflected in the glittering surfaces of tubular furniture: "No doubt as in Soviet Russia, the State has liberated [children] from the yoke of family life [...] in M. Gropius' house, the poor little things will not even have anything to break, when everything is in steel" (Lavedan 1930 cited in Overy 2004: 349). The apotheosis of the MoMA Bauhaus 1919–28 exhibition of 1938 curated by Alfred H. Barr Jnr. (1902–81) migrated modernist furnishing away from the troubled aesthetic and politics of interwar Europe to an American landscape of machine age formalism. Persuading an American purchasing public that the adoption of simple modern forms signified discerning taste would become a refrain in debates amongst designers, museum curators, journalists, and retailers in the contested economic landscapes of both the Great Depression and the Cold War boom.

The "soft power" of exhibitions extended the sphere of the art museum into collaborations with the marketplace, industry, and government diplomacy, which recognized furniture as a useful ideological vehicle. In 1938 John McAndrew (1904–78), the first of the rising stars of the Departments of Architecture and Industrial Design at New York's MoMA, instigated an annual series of displays of *Useful Objects* and curated the first Alvar Aalto (1898–1976) exhibition of Architecture and Furniture at the museum (Riley and Eigen 1995; Winton 2004). In 1940 whilst Europe once more descended into world war, Elliot Noyes (1910–77) championed the solutions of modernist furniture designers from Europe and North and South America through a design competition. The winning entry by Eliel Saarinen (1910–61) and Charles Eames (1907–78) and other admired runners-up were exhibited in the 1941 Organic Design in Home Furnishing exhibition. The Low-cost Furniture Design competition and ensuing exhibition of 1948 not only brought Robin Day (1915–2010) to the attention of an American public but also the dissemination of the exhibited products would exemplify the adaptation of the military industrial complex to peace time in the postwar period (Plate 7). The scion of a Pittsburgh business dynasty who had started his professional life in the family firm's furnishing and merchandising departments, Edward Kauffmann Jr. (1910–89) became director of the museum's Architecture and Industrial Design Department in 1949. He devised ambitious projects wedding new design with market dissemination. Three exhibitions a year between 1950 and 1955 were devoted to "Good Design," a collaboration with the powerful retailers Merchandise Mart. In these displays of hundreds of currently purchasable designs, an orange and white tag designed by Morton Goldsholl (1911–95) indicated MoMA approval. Two displays were held at the Chicago retailer before culminating in a Christmas exhibition at MoMA in New York. These displays created circuits of affirmation between elite museums and retailers to promote new furnishing idioms in the hope of supplanting the allure of historicist forms with a mass-market purchasing public.

As scholars of nineteenth- and twentieth-century advice literature have persuasively demonstrated, the proselytizing of particular furniture styles and types could motivate purchases in subtle ways (Ferry 2003; Lees-Maffei 2014). Historical period styles might attract the consumer desirous of an aura of inherited status whilst the latest vogue might express the discernment of future period taste. Nonetheless attempts to chart such volatile associations reveals that ascribing causality between didactic narratives and consumption is misleading. Postwar exhibitions indicate that particular materials, shapes, and functions of furniture design expressed fluid significances. In the model homes created by Belgian organizations for the 1958 Brussels Exposition, the state-funding of "social furniture" instigated by 1956 Belgian legislation prompted unstable interpretations ranging from modernist middle-class taste to the benevolent utopianism of social housing, revealing "fragmented national debates on domestic living" (Floré and De Kooning 2003: 337). The critical reactions to the display of furniture in the modern period demonstrate the mutability of the cultural history of these objects. Sociological analyses of contemporary globalized branding indicate the ongoing mobility of furnishing's associations and their communication despite corporate strategies of consolidation: "Just because a brand is about one place does not mean that the channels are constructed and transmitted locally [...] brand channels are rooted in global circuits that are constantly reworked and renewed" (Power and Jansson 2011: 150). The "soft power" of display is useful but volatile. The impact of Kauffmann Jr.'s support of the Danish furniture designer Finn Juhl (1912–89), not least in a 1948 *Interiors* article, might be argued to have assured his United Nations commission to furnish the Trustee Council Chamber in the New York headquarters (Hansen 2006: 467). However, such acclaim should not occlude the polyphony of formulations of cultural identity proposed in exhibitions of Scandinavian furniture of the 1950s. The narrative of what characterized Danish modern furniture adopted distinctive cadences across the many nations in which it was exhibited.

Since the 1930s, exhibitions within Denmark had constructed an attractive narrative that reconciled rival strategies of scientific modernity with traditional craft, which could readily be tuned to position Scandinavia as a useful intermediary amidst Cold War tensions. A nexus of designers from pedagogic institutions, most canonically Kaare Klint (1888–1954), head of the furniture school of the Royal Academy of Denmark, and cooperative networks of architects and furniture craftsmen such as the Cabinetmakers Guild Furniture exhibitions, which had attracted acclaim since 1927, dominated the understanding of Danish furniture in the twentieth century. The rhetoric promulgated through exhibition catalogs and press reviews branded Danish furniture very effectively as honest, well designed, handcrafted, and democratic. This vision was disseminated beyond the Nordic context through exhibitions such as Scandinavia at Table organized by the Council for Industrial Design or Heal's 1951 Scandinavian Design for Living in Britain, displays at several Milan Triennale exhibitions as well as the Formes Scandinaves exhibition held in 1958 at the Musée des Arts Décoratifs, Paris. These encouragements to a wider European appreciation of Nordic furniture were also attractive to an American consumer public that had been educated by MoMA curators and represented an influential market eagerly sought by the governments, industries, and tourist agencies of Scandinavian countries. This encounter was facilitated by the Design in Scandinavia exhibition, which toured two Canadian and twenty-two American cities between 1954–7, showing over 700 design objects to over 650,000 people, and triggering ancillary displays and pedagogic projects in department stores and schools in each hosting city (Brooklyn Museum Archives 1954). Bringing together design from four nations (Denmark, Finland, Norway, Sweden), the exhibition attracted glowing reviews and led to the formation of the Scandinavian Design Cavalcade in 1955, which aligned the promotion of tourism with a season of late summer design exhibitions. As late as 1960, MoMA would mount another touring exhibition, the Arts of Denmark: From Viking to Modern, under Kauffmann's aegis at MoMA visiting Chicago, San Francisco, and other regional cities.

The encouragement of Scandinavian design as a manifestation of international relations moved seamlessly between powerful cultural institutions into the spaces of purchase. Frederick Lunning (1881–1965), who owned the New York branch of George Nelson Inc., founded the biennial Lunning Prize for Scandinavian designers under the age of thirty-six in December 1951. In addition to $5,000 and the chance to study abroad, an exhibition of the winner's work was held in the 5th Avenue store (Woodham 2005). Debates within Federal Trade Commission and Danish Foreign Office journals about protecting the nomenclature and core characteristics of "Danish Modern" demonstrate the role of government. The contributions of industrial producers in forging the "Danish Modern" exhibition narrative had largely been neglected until recent scholarship (Davies 2000; Hansen 2006). These influential exhibitions orchestrated by wholesale retailers, such as FDB-Møbler, Finmar, and Den Permanente, established in the interwar period for collectives, including the Cabinetmakers' Guild and the Danish Society of Arts, meant industry and business also shaped this branding narrative. By the 1960s Den Permanente's displays facilitated 75 percent of its annual sales to international clients, especially in the United States and as far afield as Japan; just one of many industrial firms whose mass-produced examples disseminated the reputation and encouraged the consumption of Danish furniture most widely.

As the editor Lazette van Houten recognized in a 1954 review in *Arts and Architecture*, this cultural advocacy in America of Danish Modern furniture design spoke to the aspirations of the postwar youthful intelligentsia:

> Young men and women [felt] drawn to the work of particular designers. They ask[ed] for them by name, taking a purely aesthetic pleasure in a silhouette, a construction detail, a recognizable form. These were middle-class young, the kids who recognize[d] a Gauguin or Matisse when they [saw] one but who could never hope to own an original. They [could], however, own [...] chairs and tables originating in the workshops of craftsmen artists.
>
> (cited in Hansen 2006: 474)

However, these young urban American consumers purchased much more than just an elegant chair when they brought home a "Hornback" design by Hans Wegner (1914–2007). Advertised in the pages of *House Beautiful*, on display at both MoMA and as a commodity purchasable in the showrooms of George Jensen Inc. on 5th Avenue, this chair furnished 1950s consumers with the status of an aesthetic elite intimated by van Houten and theorized by Pierre Bourdieu (1930–2002) as manifestations of "distinction." It also was a diplomatic tool within Cold War rivalries. The ideological positioning of the Scandinavian democracies meant these designs exemplified the political alliances being mapped onto the contrasting aesthetics and lifestyles of the superpowers. A 1953 editorial titled "The Threat to the Next America" by Elizabeth Gordon (1906–2000), editor of *House Beautiful*, a leading monthly American magazine founded in 1896, exemplified one of the starkest articulations of how home furnishing operated as a key materiel of the Marshall Plan:

> Two ways of life stretch before us. One leads to the richness of variety, to comfort and beauty. The other, the one we want fully to expose to you retreats to poverty and unlivability. Worst of all it contains the threat of

cultural dictatorship [...]. If we can be sold on accepting dictators in matters of taste and how our homes are to be ordered, our minds are certainly well prepared to accept dictators in other departments of life [...] this well-developed movement has social implications because it affects the heart of our society—the home.

(Castillo 2010: 112–13)

Resonant with the stark polarities that would crystalize in the Nixon-Khrushchev "kitchen debate" at the American National Exhibition in 1959 (Haddow 1997; Reid 2008; Oldenziel and Zachman 2009), modern furnishing was appropriated as a manifestation of rival expressions of "soft power" throughout the twentieth century. Displays articulated multiple, contrasting ideological models of the modern age proposing the material experience of narratives of nationhood, which belied "its conceptual indeterminacy, its wavering between vocabularies" (Bhaba 1990: 1).

EPILOGUE: FURNISHING THE SENSES

In 1934 the trade journal *The Furnishing World* published a slim volume of advice for a nascent profession: the "display man." R.A. Caradoc offers seven chapters on the "technical side of window display," advising on the importance of planning, harmony, color, etc. The remaining half of his volume attends to the "ideas side." Various stratagems may entice potential customers to visit a shop window "each week, as regularly [...] as they go to the cinema." Useful tropes include a taxonomy of display types (one product, one brand, topical, model room, and price); seasonal variety ("ideas for every month"); and triggers of "curiosity" such as the narrative devices of a window within a window, mannequins or cut out figures, or recreations of the most recent film because "cinema is the college of the masses." The final chapter counsels the display man always to test the success or failure of the window by "listening to window-gazer's conversation and tabulating results" both for one's own business and those of competitors. A successful furniture window display offers both "realism" and imagination: "Remember you are presenting a natural picture, and that you want the window gazer to imagine that he or she is the human element in it. You want them to visualize a similar scene in their gardens or homes" (Caradoc 1934: 59). The accompanying photographic illustration contrasts Heal's window of traditional "tavern" furniture with the latest tubular furniture designs provided by W. Rowntree and Sons Ltd., Scarborough, to a fashionable local bar (Figure 6.4). Rowntree's vignette is populated with mannequins representing stylish feminine clientele attended by waitress dummies proposing the complex interrelationships between sight and the other senses through which display engages our imagination.

FIGURE 6.4 Photographs of furniture window displays in Sheffield, *c.* 1934.
Illustrated in R.L. Caradoc, *Sales-increasing Window Display Schemes for Furnishers*
(1934: 80). Photograph courtesy of the Bodleian Libraries, University of Oxford.

Caradoc's counsel that the window display should invite the gazer to imagine entering the space, and tacitly thereby the narrative fictions it represents, suggests an embodied spectatorship theorized by phenomenological philosophy. Maurice Merleau-Ponty (1908–61) conceptualizes a multisensory experience of beholding:

> The form of objects [...] stands in a certain relation to their specific nature, and appeals to all our senses as well as sight. The form of a fold in linen or cotton shows us the resilience or dryness of the fiber, the coldness or warmth of the material [...]. One sees the weight of the block of cast iron which sinks in the sand, the fluidity of water and the viscosity of syrup. In the same way, I hear the hardness and unevenness of cobbles in the rattle of a carriage and we speak appropriately of a "soft", "dull" or "sharp" sound.
>
> ([1945] 1962: 229–30)

The cultural history of furniture displays should wrestle with the challenge of recuperating this evanescent, embodied sensation at the heart of the experience of exhibition, recapturing the vertigo experienced by the critics Simmel and Geddes amidst the cacophony of the world fair, the imaginative immersion striven for by the installations of furniture by Bing, Ruhlmann, MoMA, and Caradoc.

Furnishing shown at Montreal's Expo '67 offers an evocative epilogue to this chapter's consideration of temporality; "soft power" and experiential display (Figure 6.5). "Talking chairs," made of plywood, molded polystyrene foam, and aluminum, upholstered in orange and green, designed by Grant Featherston (1922–95) and Mary Featherston (née Curry, 1943–) and manufactured by Aristoc Industries were the lynchpin of the Australian display. James Maccormick, principal architect of the Australian Pavilion, collaborated with Robin Boyd (1919–71) on the interior and landscape design[6] to conceive of it as "a place of relaxation and extreme comfort, a quiet haven of tranquility" (Maccormick cited in Barnes, Hall, and Jackson 2009: 85). Temporal narratives and displacements were afforded both by visual juxtapositions of aboriginal bark paintings, contemporary Australian abstract art, futuristic technology structures, as well as by interactions with the pavilion's twenty-eight smiling hostesses and the sound recordings disseminated in each of the 240 "talking chairs" (wired to an underfloor state-of-the-art sound system manufactured by Rola). The spatial affect of the staged spontaneity of the chairs' positioning within the fluid expanse of the pavilion invited the phenomenological experience evoked by Merleau-Ponty. The "talking chairs" spoke of diverse Australian national narratives amidst Canada's internal transnational dialogues and the universalizing thematic of the Montreal Expo: "Man and his World" (Expo '67 1967). This multilinguistic experience was signaled through coloristic visual

FIGURE 6.5 Talking chairs in the Australian Pavilion at Montreal's Expo '67, 1967, molded rigid polystyrene shell, polyurethane foam, elastic webbing, polyurethane foam, upholstery fabric, speakers in headrest, designed by Grant and Mary Featherston. Manufactured by Danish Delux and Aristoc Industries Melbourne. Photograph courtesy of the National Archives of Australia AA102/206 45.

sensation: an orange or green seating cushion in the chair alerted the potential sitter to the choice of French or English listening experiences. The activation of each chair's sound system was tactile and corporeal: the weight of a body seating itself in each chair acted as a play button for three-minute recordings of great Australians audible from the headrest. A review in the *Montreal Star* captures how this furnishing display typifies the performance of cultural history, these chairs "talk, but it is a subdued message, a very soft sell, with just a wistful note of down-under accent. One [...] watches the kangaroos at play" (cited in Barnes, Hall, and Jackson 2009: 92). The "talking chairs" embodied individual sensation, modern design, collective memories of nation, and nascent narratives of globalized technology. Simmel and Geddes experienced neurasthenia amidst the cacophonous array of narratives proposed in the world's fairs around 1900. Maurois deployed sensory constraint closing his eyes to hear the "melody of the world" at the 1931 Colonial Exhibition. This Australian furnishing display articulated the distinctive "soft power" of modern transnational encounters, engaging all the senses to connect "Man and His World" by sitting on a chair.

CHAPTER SEVEN

Furniture and Architecture

GREGORY VOTOLATO

INTRODUCTION: THE CARAPACE

When Michel Foucault (1926–84) wrote, "I believe that the anxiety of our era has to do fundamentally with space," he was pointing out the essential difference between what he called "protected places and open places." He pointed out that, "one might attempt to describe these different sites by looking for the set of relations by which a given site can be defined" and that "one could describe, via the cluster of relations that allows them to be defined" those sites of safety and relaxation, of physical protection, of emotional security, or simply of privacy that protect from intrusion into one's solitude or concentration (Foucault 1984: n.p.). Furniture of various kinds, sited in many types of structure, used for multiple purposes in diverse locations or moving through space, can provide such opportunities for definition. Before pursuing his famous study of heterotopias (places and spaces that function in non-hegemonic conditions), Foucault cites the influence of philosopher Gaston Bachelard on our understanding of how the space of the imagination intersects with the real spaces of everyday life, such as those of work and leisure, of escape and refuge. It is such spaces within the realm of furniture, and particularly its protective nature in relation to its function and significance, which I aim to examine here.

The growing interdisciplinarity of design history over the past forty years has facilitated or even demanded the study of subjects previously discussed independently, such as furniture and architecture. Here, I will consider them as intimately connected fields alongside apparel and engineering. Furthermore, I will take them beyond the architecture of buildings to include furniture designed for transport vehicles and vessels, following the Swiss architect Le Corbusier, who cited autos, aircraft and ocean liners as models for a new architecture in the 1920s. (Le Corbusier 1927). While the modern definition of furniture retains the stand-alone object—sofa, wardrobe, cabinet—modern architecture has, to a considerable extent, absorbed furniture since the middle of the nineteenth century through its emphasis on built-in furniture and modularity. Meanwhile, that broadening concept of what constitutes furniture has expanded into providing shelter and catering to the popular desire for personal space within an increasingly crowded world.

Bachelard employs the analogy of the mollusk's shell to discuss structures that give human beings both physical and emotional security and cites the potential of storms to demonstrate that duality defining any shelter. While the robustness of that structure keeps out the ferocity of nature and enables its occupants to appreciate the beauty, drama, and thrill of the storm. This idea of the protected interior, in relation to the dangerous enormity of the outside, is an inescapable element of daily life at sea. And the qualities of the ship's cabin, with its fitted furniture of bunk beds and storage cabinets, gives that experience its structure and form.

A young seaman, who traveled during the early twentieth century through many violent storms in an area of infamously turbulent seas in the southern hemisphere between 40 and 50 degrees latitude, which is known as the Roaring Forties, described the sailor's wooden berth, the mattress built up at the outer edge by anything that could be easily found, coiled rope, clothing, or canvas, to restrain the recumbent body. "We fit down into a V between the mattress and the sidewalls and can't be rolled out. Even at that, we frequently have to brace ourselves against the upright stanchions to stay in" (Dew 2006: 62–3). That idea, of furniture keeping either its user or its contents "in," is one of the central challenges for designers, particularly in the broad field of transportation on land, sea, and in the air.

American transcendentalist philosopher Henry David Thoreau extolled the virtues of such a close fit between homes and their occupants, as he said, "whose shells they are" ([1849] 1980: 37). Similarly, Bachelard (1994: 38–46) compared the nooks or corners where we enjoy curling up in our homes to a snail in its shell. Thoreau ([1849] 1980: 93) described his hut by Walden Pond as "a sort of crystallization" around him, and when the winter storm raged over the pond outside, he sat behind the securely closed door and enjoyed its protection. And those elements of the house, its door, roof, and glazed windows, all have their equivalents in a variety of furniture types, the traditional Victorian china cupboard, the sturdy 1940s Wilson Shelter Table, or the Ball Chair designed by Eero Aarnio (1932–) in 1963.

The hybridity of common furniture types is a theme of Bachelard's discourse on drawers, chests, and wardrobes, in which he suggests that the secret life of even the most utilitarian objects has to do with the securing of our dreams or most personal pleasures. The common office filing cabinet standing passively in the corner of a film noir detective's office becomes an agent of intimacy when a bottle of whiskey is pulled from its bottom drawer. Bachelard quotes Arthur Rimbaud's 1870 poem "New year's gifts for orphans (Les étrennes des orphelins)" to reveal the sense of promise in a locked wardrobe. "The wardrobe had no keys [...] Many a time we dreamed of the mysteries lying dormant between its wooden flanks and we thought we heard, deep in the gaping lock [...] a vague and joyful murmur" (Bachelard 1964: 80). Thus, the locked wardrobe is the repository of hope, of family lore, of an intimacy only truly open to the key holder, but a source of fantasy for others, as we will see in the work of British furniture maker David Linley (1961–). That wardrobe may contain seldom-used household linen, but it also holds securely a provision of mythology extending from speculations on the craftsmen who built the cabinet, to the bodies that have lain upon the linen, or about the thoughts of the person who folded it and arranged it on the shelves.

ARCHITECTURE AND FURNITURE

Analogies with architecture are fundamental to the multi-coding of the furniture I shall discuss, with scale as the main differentiating feature. Like buildings, certain furniture types contain our bodies, but at a more intimate scale, wrapping us, supporting us as well as representing us, particularly if we are thinking of domestic furniture selected, assembled, or even designed and made by oneself. At the most basic level, storage furniture contains and protects our possessions, yet in our modern materialist culture, the chest or its relations may also represent what Bachelard calls a "philosophy of having." It is a site of acquisition and, depending on its particular function or type, it tells of certain kinds of acquisitiveness.

The knowledge of libraries is contained on shelves of varying dimension. The large shallow drawers of a plan chest may hold the precious architectural drawings of Charles Rennie Mackintosh (1868–1928) or Edwin Lutyens (1869–1944), just as an atmospherically controlled art storage warehouse will protect the upholstery of antique chairs and sofas or the delicate silks of long-dead kings and queens. In this sense the clean, dry cupboard, cabinet, or chest is a miniaturization of the warehouse, a repository for our possessions typically locked away and perhaps protected by security cameras or intruder alarms. Both those buildings and that furniture represent wisdom, information, or the wealth of individuals, governments, or companies and reveal through their design the care we take of their contents.

Structural features link the hammock and tent, both lightweight tensile structures, both employing in their construction a minimal framework and a textile membrane, for support in the former and for enclosure in the latter. Both are light, easily demountable, and transportable. Yet they also share other less obvious qualities. In colder climates hammocks and tents appear mainly in the warmer summer months for recreational purposes and the two equally suggest seasonal leisure and relaxation. Hammocks and smaller tents encourage a recumbent physical posture. They are places to sleep and to dream. On a hot afternoon, napping in the shade of a tree, suspended above the ground, and swaying gently in a canvas hammock can be one of life's laziest pleasures. The double hammock, like the two-person tent, is a place of physical and emotional intimacy. Yet for armies on the move tents and hammocks both signify rapid response, flexibility, and practical solutions to the need for shelter and comfort in extreme situations.

In the book, *Mechanization Takes Command* (1948), Sigfried Giedion's (1888–1968) discourse on Carpaccio's painting of *St. Jerome in His Study* (Scuola degli Schiavonni, Venice, *c.* 1605) presents the structured space in which the saint works as an archetype of the modern office, well planned and equipped with a fold-away writing table and a pivoting chair, each on its own wooden plinth, demonstrating early mechanization in the workplace. Another painting of the same subject, Antonello da Messina's depiction of *St. Jerome in His Study* (National Gallery London, 1460–75), shows the saint working in a compact, planned construction of cabinetry designed specifically to suit the need of a scholar for a degree of self-containment within a larger communal space, in this case that of the church and monastery. The emphasis here is on the study as an independent structure within a complex, open-plan, double-height space.

Giedion's analysis of the Carpaccio contributed to his thesis about the influence of mechanization on the historical improvement of physical comfort through the use of hinges, pivots, and movable planes in late medieval furniture differentiated into types, such as the chest, chair, and desk. But in Messina's depiction, the saint's study is conceived and constructed as an integrated and freestanding enclosure of cabinetry, raised on a single dais and partially screened by wooden bookshelves, separating it from the cold stonework of the large medieval building in which it is situated and effectively creating there a separate personal space. In this example the distinction between furniture and architecture is held in delicate balance due to the approximation of an architectural scale in the timber structure of Jerome's study, which is even more familiar to twenty-first-century eyes than it could have been to Giedion, writing in the 1940s. With our experience of system furniture for offices, the comparatively recent notion of the office cubicle, and the sorts of structures incorporating a raised sleeping area, storage, or bathrooms inserted to domesticate former commercial or industrial "loft buildings," Saint Jerome's study becomes more easily comprehensible.

At this point I will turn briefly to a further analogy that arises in the exploration of furniture as a carapace, and that is its relation to clothing. Adrian Forty wrote about the long tradition of scholarship invoking the interlinked histories of dress and architecture in his lecture *Of Cars, Clothes and Carpets: Design Metaphors in Architectural Thought* (1989), citing the comments of theorists ranging from Vitruvius (*c.* 80–15 BCE) to Eugène Viollet-le-Duc (1814–79), John Ruskin (1819–1900), Reyner Banham (1922–88), and Giedion on the lessons for architecture found in the study of dress and products. Although Forty's essay addressed debates of the 1980s between modernists and postmodernists regarding the propriety of symbolism and disguise in relation to style, it also resonates with issues of what I will call protective coloration or camouflage in those objects that keep us safe in our sense of self, our cars, clothes, and the carpets on which our sofas sit.

Today, when minimalism has become a leading factor influencing popular taste, if our design choices are colored in harmonic tones of gray, we may consider ourselves safe in those choices, safe particularly from the scorn of potential critics. This phenomenon is perhaps most noteworthy in relation to interior design, fashion, and automobiles, all notably shorn of color since the millennium, particularly in Britain, where black has become the fashionable choice for clothes and cars among taste tribes ranging from Goths to minimalists. It is ironic that late twentieth-century postmodernist designers' overthrow of conventional taste standards and their promotion of stylistic plurality, often involving extraordinarily vivid color combinations and knowingly kitsch patterns, were largely trumped by the conservatism and anxiety of manufacturers and consumers with regard to color. For standard production cars, black exterior paintwork is currently as common as in the days of Henry Ford and gray or black is nearly universal for upholstery and other interior surfaces. With regard to domestic interior design, the gray sofa in a white space has become an unassailable defense against accusations of bad taste. In contemporary design the defensive condition of chromophobia has grown out of insecurity among the fashion-conscious, a condition aggravated by the postmodernist demolition of traditional taste standards.

In the highly regulated sphere of military apparel, whereas the uniform is an essential classifying device, often modified for the purpose of camouflage, protective armor historically has signified high rank and exceptional fighting skill, communicated by refined craftsmanship and ornamentation. Yet its primary function was always to protect the wearer from physical injury, either in battle or in sport such as jousting. Armor was refined slowly over centuries, alongside the fortress, citadel, or castle, all symbols of resolve, physical defense against invasion and obstacles to social and political upheaval. Their appearance expresses the most robust construction technology at each period in history. Today, when armies rely more than ever on speed and mobility rather than solidity as primary defensive measures, the highest transport and communication technologies are employed to protect combatants against threats ranging from bullets and burns to visual detection. But armor continues to play its part.

Research conducted during the two world wars found that among airmen, the greatest percentage of casualties resulted from low-velocity missiles, primarily shrapnel, eventually prompting the first scientific design and mass production of "flak suits," the effectiveness of which led to more sophisticated types of body armor for air crews to protect them while moving, often at low speed and low altitude within the fragile fuselage of a helicopter (Dunstan 1984: 10–12). The flak jacket developed along with the metal helmet and, most important here, the armored pilot's seat as twentieth-century descendants of the medieval knight's shield, helmet, and suit of armor.

The architecture of the armored train, tank, and ironclad ship took on some of the qualities of the fort, bunker, and pillbox as war became increasingly mechanized in the age of steam power and internal combustion engines. In those early vehicles of modern warfare, the carapace remained a hard shell, like those found in nature. However, with the advent of the aircraft, which required the lightest possible external skin to perform its primary function, efficient flight when fully laden with people, cargo, and armaments, the protection of pilots and crew devolved to the chairs in which they sat during flight and to their protective clothing, the two often used together in experimental, ad hoc combinations. In effect, their chairs became part of their body armor, strengthening that age-old relationship between furniture and dress. Within the thin-skinned architecture of the aircraft fuselage, the pilot's flak jacket and armor-plated chair became her or his main line of defense in the air.

For civilians, protection from bad weather conditions, from visual recognition, or from social intrusion has always been obtainable from the lightest of membranes, umbrellas or the daily broadsheet newspaper, or wearable integument, such as a hoodie or the hijab. Alternatively, such membranes may be inhabited, like a hammock or a tipi. If in common mythology the turtle can travel on foot with its house on its back, can modern man do the same? And can that portable house also be conceived as a hybrid of clothing, architecture, and furniture? British designer and theorist Michael Webb (1937–), a founding member of Archigram, a group of conceptual architects working together in the 1960s, published two memorable designs that employ such a fusion.

Webb's *Cushicle* and *Suitaloon* of 1964 and 1967 (Plate 23), which have remained influential to subsequent generations of architects, were ideas for wearable structures described by Webb as clothing for living in. Inspired in part by the model of the astronaut's space suit, they were formed of a lightweight metal skeleton, equipped with heating, and a helmet containing a communication system. The *Cushicle's* inflatable skin, a textile bubble, provided the protective barrier against the elements and a degree of privacy sufficient for use within an urban or public environment. The devices were designed to be worn like a suit with a backpack. And with the addition of clip-on accessories they could carry supplies of water and food.

The *Suitaloon* added more of the functions of furniture, most significantly an expandable cushion taking the form of a chaise longue on which the wearer could recline when the bubble was inflated. This commanding element, a chair, which distinguishes *Suitaloon* from other "products," is the crucial link between its fragile architectural identity and its function as clothing. Thus, highly technological apparel could contain the elements of a home for an independent traveler, a nomad (Cook 1999: 63, 80). And its integration of structure and contents expands the notion, central to modern domestic architecture, of built-in furniture.

PROPERTY

In more conventional homes the role of furniture in the protection of personal property is an ever-present concern, particularly in affluent parts of the world and in this age of expanding consumption. Recalling Bachelard's "philosophy of having," those pieces of furniture that conceal our valuables by resembling something ordinary also hide the elements that physically secure them, including elaborate locks or fireproofing. Such is the case of a deceptively innocent-appearing oak cabinet in the Victoria and Albert Museum in London designed by the architect Edwin Lutyens and made in 1903–1904 for the home of a wealthy British stockbroker, adventurer, and sportsman Herbert Johnson (1856–1949) (Plate 24). Designed in the style of a seventeenth-century Dutch cabinet, the robust forms of its base are the only visible clue to the actual content of the chest, a modern steel fireproof safe, requiring chunky timber legs and extra metal structure in the base to support its weight.

For the expanding needs of office workers in the late 1800s the roll-top desk provided maximum efficiency and security of paperwork. Particularly popular in smaller offices where confidentiality of information was especially important, these patented marvels of organization were commonly used by lawyers, doctors, and accountants as well as businessmen. Franz Kafka (1883–1924) described their amenities which included:

> a hundred compartments of varying sizes in its top part, and the President of the Union himself would have been able to find a fitting place for each of his files, but there was also a regulator on the side, and you could, with a turning of the crank, achieve a variety of rearrangements and new fittings suited to your pleasures and demands. Thin partitions on the side sank lazily and formed a new floor picking itself up or a ceiling rising with

new compartments; even after one turning, the top part had a completely
changed display, and everything moved according to how you turned the
crank, either slowly or unreasonably fast.

(Kafka 1938: 46)

In addition to the security offered by such a dizzying multiplicity of spaces in
the desk, the whole thing was lockable under a tambour made of timber slats
joined together to roll up and down through parallel slots in the desk's raised
sides, forming a perfect carapace for genuine protection of information. Such
a desk was the kind of product developed, patented, and produced in large
numbers by the Wooten Company, whose "Cabinet Office Secretary" matches
Kafka's description and can be seen as an ancestor of the modern office work
station.

If the Lutyens cabinet hid the owner's valuables, the safe it contained protected
those valuables from the omnipresent threat of fire. And so the furnishings of
twentieth-century offices also employed metal in their construction to guard
ever-expanding volumes of paperwork from the effects of fires, including
smoke and water damage, if not actual incineration. Elaborate wooden office
furniture was recognized as highly combustible, particularly when cigar
smoking was nearly universal among the managerial class. This realization led
to the foundation of companies such as the Metal Office Furniture Company
in Grand Rapids, Michigan, the predecessor of Steelcase, incorporated in 1912
to produce fireproof metal office furniture. Their first products were filing
cabinets and safes, but metal waste baskets were perhaps their most successful
deterrents to fire, particularly useful in hotel rooms where many lethal fires
started in cardboard or wicker waste baskets (Servas and Olsen 1987: 4–11).

In the domestic sphere the symbolism of safety has been provided by
furniture in a variety of ways influenced by changing fashions in architecture,
interior design, and product styling. Since the beginning of mass consumption
of manufactured goods, new products have typically employed familiar imagery
borrowed from earlier times to impart to prospective users or consumers a sense
of safety, particularly when very real danger was present in the use of the object
type. If early steamships were furnished to resemble stately homes or hotels
in period styles to reassure justifiably nervous passengers, the early makers of
electric lamps, which could easily transmit an electrical shock to the unwary
user, styled their products to resemble antique classical urns, eighteenth-century
French "torchères," or turned candlesticks. With the arrival of television in
the 1950s, as that unfamiliar technology settled into position magically as
the centerpiece of the world's living rooms, it was disguised in similar ways,
taking more grandiose forms when housed in large cabinets together with
multiband radios and phonographs, all of its technology hidden away behind
hinged wooden doors in various historical styles. Even when the television was

more fully embraced and modernist furniture had become widely popular, the electronic components of the receiving equipment remained concealed within contemporary-style cabinetry, often with a Scandinavian flavor. Finally, when authentic timber cabinetry was abandoned, the television's metal or plastic shell continued to be finished with wood-grain effects linking the machine with both timber construction and nature.

In the postmodernist period, some designer-craftsmen perpetuated the notion of cabinetry as a secretive and mysterious element within the home. Evoking Rimbaud's and Kafka's speculations about the secrets hidden within the locked or disguised compartments of chests and wardrobes, the British furniture maker David Linley created a series of writing desks conceived as detailed models of well-known historic buildings including the Russian Imperial Pavlovsk Palace near Saint Petersburg and the grandiose Monte Carlo Casino in Monaco by the architect Charles Garnier (1825–98). Linley's work is characterized by novelty, exquisite craftsmanship, and narrative content for its appeal, and it shares its luxurious essence with the work of his teacher John Makepeace. Along with his characteristic choice of grand buildings as subjects, a Linley signature motif is the inclusion in his works of secret drawers, even employed in his bespoke kitchen cabinets, typically included to introduce an element of mystery and wit. The location and operation of those hidden drawers or compartments are known only to the client to enhance an intimate relation between owner and object, a fundamental ambition of much contemporary craft.

At the opposite end of the aesthetic spectrum, the signature built-in cabinetry used by minimalist architect John Pawson (1949–) in his interiors is intended to disappear within the spare elegance of his spaces. The Zen-inspired emptiness of his buildings requires occupants to consider carefully every object, utilitarian or ornamental, placed within the space as if it were on exhibition in the setting of a modern art gallery. As many of Pawson's clients have been art collectors or gallerists, it is unsurprising that their decisions are informed by a sophisticated understanding of contemporary art and display methods. Extensive storage is therefore the key to the maintenance of purity within the living space. The configuration of the interiors of his cupboards may vary depending on what is to be stored within them, but their doors are always the same, simple panels of smoothly finished medium-density fiberboard (MDF) typically extending from floor to ceiling and shorn of any visible hardware. All that can be seen is the shut lines separating one identical door from the next. Therefore, it is the very blankness of the surface of these cupboard doors and the speculation about what may lie behind them that makes them so intriguing. At the same time, they create a defense against the intrusion of material goods into the serenity of a nearly empty habitation. A sense of absolute calm is protected from the chaos of consumption and from Bachelard's "philosophy of having."

SAFETY

In the history of furniture, there are to be found many instances in which users have adapted or employed furniture ad hoc as shelter. One of the most extreme and desperate of such episodes occurred in the mid-twentieth century with the advent of aerial bombardment and its sustained uses against a civilian population in the London Blitz by the German Luftwaffe in 1940–1 and again by unmanned rockets toward the end of the Second World War. Although these were not the first air raids, their scale and duration provoked a determined reaction among the British people, the Ministry of Defence, and the furniture industry to obtain some degree of protection, particularly for people in their homes during a bombing raid. Houses themselves provided cellars and under-stairs refuges that were effective mainly against the effects of shrapnel such as flying shards of glass or smaller bits of falling plaster. But for more serious damage and for people living in flats, without access to Anderson Shelters, corrugated iron structures half-buried in the earth most commonly in private gardens, an alternative was the Morrison Shelter (Figure 7.1).

This was an indoor steel-topped table shelter, popularly named after the Minister of Home Security, Herbert Morrison (1888–1965). It was designed by the eminent Bristol University Professor John Baker (1901–85), a structural

FIGURE 7.1 J. Baker, "Morrison" table shelter, *c.* 1941. Imperial War Museum, Q(HS) 99. Photograph © Imperial War Museum, London.

engineer and expert in metallurgy who applied his Plasticity Theory to the design in timber and steel of a domestic shelter, which was produced in kit form by many manufacturers and distributed to less well-off families free of charge. Designed to be slept in at night and used at other times for meals or games, the shelter occupied the floor space of a double bed and was slightly higher than an average dining table. It came in knockdown form for home assembly with over 350 parts. Its main elements were a steel top, heavy timber subframe, and wire mesh sides, one of which was hinged for access. The brilliance of its design was its exploitation of the failure characteristics of the sheet steel, operating in this design somewhat like the crumple-zones of a car, as the plasticity of the steel allowed it to absorb impact without failing completely. The Morrison Shelter could not withstand a direct bomb hit but was capable of surviving the collapse of a typical two-story house. Over 600,000 were built and distributed during 1940–1 and again in 1943 in preparation for the V2 attacks on southern England (Margolin 2015: 852). At the same time Winston Churchill (1874–1965) endorsed an alternative shelter bed design and a prototype was made and displayed at Heal's furniture showroom in London. This was a single bed with an arched tubular steel frame and a matching arched steel lid, which was hinged and could be lowered over the occupant(s) in the event of attack. After consideration, the Baker design was adopted for its greater capacity and strength.

The human instinct to employ furniture for shelter took other novel forms during the Blitz. As British schools rarely have basements to shelter in, the standard apparatus of the classroom was sometimes considered better than nothing to protect children from sudden daytime air raids. Nursery school teachers in the heavily targeted East End of London, for example, would tuck their small pupils onto the shelves of wooden clothes cupboards for protection from shrapnel in the event of a bomb exploding nearby.

In the Cold War climate of hostility and paranoia between the nuclear-armed West and the Soviet Union during the 1950s, the threat of sudden atomic bombardment was never far from the minds of European and American citizens, who built basement and garden nuclear fallout shelters, fully furnished, stocked with canned goods and water. Meanwhile, schools drilled their students in precautionary measures devised by government agencies. The American civil defense film, *Duck and Cover*, was made in 1951 to be shown to pupils as part of a public awareness campaign about how to react during a sudden nuclear attack. The film advised children to follow their teacher's command by diving beneath their school desks, to crouch there and cover their heads with their hands as a deterrent. *Duck and Cover* was aired to generations of school children until 1991 when the Cold War finally ended. In all that time the unlikeliness that a tiny wooden or steel school desk could serve as an effective shelter in the event of nuclear attack was lost on Cold War generations, yet the sense of emotional security represented by that very personal item of public furniture was significant in reassuring children that they were not completely at the mercy of fate.

I will return here to the subject of special-purpose military furniture within the architecture of the aircraft fuselage. Following pioneering initiatives in First World War aviation, by the outbreak of the Second World War an aviator's chair could provide the single most effective means of protection against injury or death from flak. Seats such as those fitted to the Consolidated B-24 Liberator bomber for pilot, copilot, and waist gunner featured armored backs, which were spade-shaped to protect the occupant's head and trunk. Some versions also provided an armor plate under the seat to intercept ground fire. Other models employed tall backs that curved around the sides of the occupant as in a traditional wing chair to give a degree of lateral protection. Seating within the Sperry Retractable Ball Turrets installed in American and Allied military aircraft including the B-17, B-24, and designer Isaac Laddon's PBY Catalina flying boat, protected the gunner, according to the Air Crewman's Gunnery Manual, with an armor steel plate that "forms the bottom of the seat and extends up to the hinge of the door, protecting the gunner's trunk in battle position."

To address the circumstances of more recent warfare, in the 1980s the United States Army Aviation Branch commissioned the firm Ordtech Military Industries (OMI) to develop a new armored pilot seat fabricated from a lightweight composite material to provide helicopter pilots with enhanced protection against an increasingly common threat from small caliber ground fire when flying low at slow speed. The resulting carbon fiber composite seat with leather cushions on an adjustable steel frame included a five-point harness to protect the aviator against crash injuries as well as ballistics. In terms of ergonomics, the seat was tailored for individuals between 5 percent to 95 percent "physique distribution," meaning that it is nearly a one-size-fits-all protective chair. Yet it was also designed to accommodate crew wearing a bulky survival jacket, one-man dinghy, and night vision equipment. The seat was tested and used on Bell and Puma helicopters as well as the giant C-130 Hercules transport plane. Such aviation chairs are not styled for beauty, but their purposeful appearance lends those cockpits appropriate gravitas.

In the event of a military aircraft suffering catastrophic mechanical or structural failure, it would be the pilot chair that offers the best chance of survival, through escape. High-technology furniture such as the Martin-Baker Mk 16 ejection seat, designed for the Eurofighter Typhoon aircraft, introduced in 2003, contains an oxygen supply, communication system, and like the Ordtech seat, accommodates a wide range of pilot sizes and weights. It is also compatible with wearable equipment such as chemical and biological protection suits, the descendants of simple flak jackets.

Company founder, Sir James Martin (1893–1981), a British aircraft and component manufacturer, began in the mid-1930s to experiment with ejection seats for military planes, an interest that developed further while he was manufacturing armored seats for Spitfires during the Second World War, and particularly after the death of Martin's partner, test pilot Valentine Baker (1888–1942) during a test flight of the company's MB3 aircraft. This event affected Martin such that pilot safety became his primary concern and led him to reorganize his company as a specialist ejection seat manufacturer.

Martin-Baker became pioneers in this highly specialized and technical field of chair design and manufacturing. Martin established the principle of using an explosive charge to deploy an ejection seat in advance of even the progressive German and Swedish manufacturers who produced similar designs in the late 1930s. Following the development of jet fighters such as the Gloucester Meteor, Martin-Baker also led research into the effects of g-forces on the human body as a result of ejection during flight. They gradually increased the capabilities of the ejector seat to operate effectively at low altitudes and very slow speeds. Ultimately, their ejection seat was proved effective at zero-speed and zero-altitude, establishing its usefulness even in the event of mishaps on the ground.

Whereas Martin's company belonged properly to the aviation industry rather than the furniture industry, traditional chair makers and other firms specializing in timber products were recruited to the defense effort in a variety of ways during the Second World War. One project that generated a true modernization of spirit within that conservative field of manufacturing, steeped in craft techniques, was the production of the fast and capable all-plywood Mosquito aircraft, many components of which were made in the English furniture-producing town of High Wycombe, outside of London.

Whereas pilot seats may have limited interest or benefits for the general population, the ordinary car seat has evolved to protect the entire motoring public from a variety of threats. In the early days of the automobile one of the most dangerous accidents for drivers and passengers alike was that of being thrown from the car. Among the first women to achieve success in motorsports, Dorothy Levitt (1882–1922), was also a pundit promoting motoring to women in Britain. In her booklet published in 1909, *The Woman and the Car: A chatty little handbook for all women who motor or who want to motor*, she wrote, "the hardest thing is to keep in the car [...]. It is far harder work to sit in the car than to ride a galloping horse over the jumps in a steeplechase" (quoted in Wosk 2001: 137–40).

At that early moment in the history of the automobile, open cars typically accommodated passengers in individual bucket seats, shaped like contemporaneous tub chairs found commonly in well-furnished homes and executive offices. When mounted upon the car, their purposes were twofold, to link the appearance of the car with the safety, stability, and luxury of home and also to wrap around each occupant helping to hold them on board; while their upholstery conformed to domestic types, deeply tufted and buttoned in leather to resist the elements, it was their shape that kept the sitter in place (Plate 25).

Bucket seats were by the 1920s generally replaced by bench seats, particularly in North America and France, to increase the passenger capacity of closed family cars. Between the wars, the industrial designer Walter Dorwin Teague (1883–1960) wrote, "Automobile manufacturers have made, in the past few years, a greater contribution to the art of comfortable seating than chair builders in all preceding history" (Teague 1940: 62–3). Yet it would be decades before they made a similar contribution to protecting their passengers in ever-faster cars.

With the debut in the late 1950s of so-called personal cars, a new vehicle segment influenced by sports car and racing car design, the bucket seat came back into fashion everywhere. Its shape and equipment then evolved along with new safety legislation to incorporate seatbelts and increasingly tall headrests added to avert whiplash injuries. Motorized or manually operated mechanisms controlling height, rake, and horizontal position further tailored the driver's experience, enhancing control, and therefore safety, as well as comfort and style. By 1998 Biomechanics Corporation of America's "intelligent" car seats housed a computer in the squab (seat back) to control the contour of the chair's entire surface, automatically custom-fitted to any occupant with personalized lumbar, thigh, and back support to keep drivers alert. Such electronic enhancements were followed by the introduction of sensors that could detect the driver falling asleep at the wheel, a common cause of accidents.

While comfort and styling were the great commercial motives for improving seat design in cars, safety began to occupy center stage with a spike in accident statistics as car use increased in the developed world during the 1950s. In the United States, crash testing using dummies disclosed that the cause of most injuries was lack of passenger restraint. These findings resulted in the design and construction of the Cornell-Liberty Safety Car, conceived by the engineer Frank J. Crandell to promote so-called passive safety. The car's six bucket seats featured inertia-reel shoulder belts and integrated head restraints to reduce whiplash. The driver occupied the center of the front row, with passenger seats set slightly back to the right and left, so as not to obstruct side views, while in the back row the central chair faced the rear, demonstrating that the orientation of seats was as important to safety as their shape or construction.

Meanwhile in Europe, Mercedes, Volvo, and certain other manufacturers prioritized safety in the interior design of their production cars, focusing attention on the seat by introducing such devices as the modern airbag, used first in 1981 in combination with three-point shoulder belts, pretensioned to reduce the risk of injury from the airbag itself. Daimler-Benz continued as a leader of safety innovation. In the design of seats for their Smart city car, sheet steel shells, like those used for pilots' chairs, were used to enhance the security of the driver and passenger particularly in the event that the short cabin space should be penetrated from behind in a crash.

Similarly, in many police cars, the squab of the driver's seat is armored to prevent knife attack on officers sitting in front by detainees in the rear seat, which itself is lowered to inhibit prisoners from attempting any kind of assault. Many police cars and cruisers are factory equipped with Police Package equipment including "24-hour duty" seats with reinforced frames, anti-sag springs, and washable vinyl upholstery in a neutral overall interior design scheme tailored to subdue agitated prisoners and to protect officers from aggressive behavior.

PRIVACY

If Foucault's idea that the anxiety of modern life, particularly in a metropolis, is related fundamentally to our control over the space we inhabit, certain furniture types have been devised to ameliorate that free-floating discomfort brought on by feelings of exposure or by a simple lack of privacy. Yet some examples have gone further by combining that sense of privacy with features designed to achieve a feeling of control over the surrounding space while also making the user more physically comfortable. Various forms of wing chair do this to some extent and the traditional Porter's Hall Chair is a prime example. This type of chair dates back to late medieval times, when the front door to a great house or a public building would be attended constantly by a servant, who would sit for long periods in a draughty place waiting to receive callers. It was developed in the nineteenth century for use in the poorly heated lobbies of hotels and clubs.

The design of the Porter's Chair emulates the egg or mollusk's shell by wrapping around the sitter at the sides and curving up and over the head, creating a partial enclosure anticipating modernist designs such as Eero Aarnio's Ball Chair. As it evolved, heavily tufted upholstery was added over the wrap-around timber frame helping to trap body heat or the warmth from a nearby fireplace for the comfort of the user. Later versions also included innovations such as open or glazed portholes in the chair's sides at eye level to increase the porter's effectiveness as a guardian of the door and as a hidden eye, able to keep track of all movements within the reception hall without being seen doing so. In the twentieth century similar chairs, made in wicker or other woven materials, became popular as beach and porch chairs for seaside homes, providing partial privacy, protection from sea breezes, and an opportunity to glimpse nearby comings and goings without appearing inquisitive. Thus, the chair gave its user control over her or his comfort as well as a sense of security while inconspicuously observing the local scene.

A similar sense of the chair behaving like a room within a room was created with the Ear Chair (2001) by contemporary Dutch furniture designer Jurgen Bey (1965–) (Plate 26). Designed originally for the large reception space in the headquarters of a company that required quiet, contemplative places for individuals to work alone or in small groups but where chance encounters were seen to stimulate creativity, this range of multipurpose chairs was distinguished by its large ears, descendants of seventeenth-century chair "wings," available with right or left ears in various lengths. The chair's integral writing surface also contributed to the performance and the strong visual identity of the design, which communicates its potential to provide a private workspace or to be arranged in a cluster to create an intimate sheltered meeting place. The spatial character of the Ear Chair was also enhanced by its thick upholstery, which was not only comfortable but added to a muted acoustic that allowed the chair to function like a telephone booth, keeping the sitter's conversations inside and ambient noise out. Its chic styling and the practical advantages of this design conform with ideas about the evolving nature of workplaces in the digital age, when hot-desking and mobile communication devices have liberated many people from the traditional office, while also creating a need for more casual, flexible, and relaxing places to work, alone or in company but still requiring a semblance of privacy and disincentives to unwanted intrusion.

Like the images of Saint Jerome's study, as discussed by Giedion, the Ear Chair represents a celebration of brain work, acknowledging and dramatizing a type of concentration that can tolerate a degree of ambient activity and sound but is intolerant of disruptive intrusion into the flow of personal thoughts. Such a theory underpinned the development in the 1950s and 1960s of the German design group Quickborner's concept of the office landscape (*Burolandschaf*), which developed the use of furniture and screening to create a sense of privacy within the open floor plans of typical modern office buildings while rejecting the monotonously rigid effects of Taylorism on the offices of the first half of the century. Office landscape used standard contract furniture arranged in organic, irregular patterns with potted plants and curving screens providing a semblance of visual privacy and a slight reduction in ambient noise, in other words protection from distraction, while encouraging more informal interaction among workers.

The reality, however, was less than ideal as the available conventional furniture, metal desks, filing cabinets, and swivel chairs proved ineffective in protecting office workers from distraction and interruption. The result was a shift to office environments of high-walled workstations and of systems furniture such as Herman Miller's Action Office, introduced in 1964 as a kit of parts designed by George Nelson (1908–86) and Robert Probst (1921–2000) with consulting psychologists and anthropologists. Such systems of contract furniture were intended to extend the flexibility and efficiency of the office landscape while providing additional defense against distraction and a semblance of privacy. To achieve that, their designers developed customizable elements of storage, screening, and seating that could be configured in many different combinations.

At their most basic level, such permeable workspaces are the direct descendants of Saint Jerome's study. Yet the ideas on which Action Office was based, when employed by less able and more cost-conscious firms than Herman

Miller, produced the familiar Taylorist nightmare of repetitive office cubicles parodied in the Kafkaesque comedy film *Playtime* of 1967, directed by Jacques Tati (1907–82). Since classical times, tables and chairs have been arranged to celebrate the ritual of dining, but the conditions of modern life provoked a particular dramatization of that ritual in the late nineteenth and early twentieth centuries, reflecting the social upheavals of the period. The Glaswegian architect Charles Rennie Mackintosh employed the formula of high-backed rectilinear dining chairs drawing a semi-enclosure around a dining table to emphasize its centrality as a social focus in the genteel but avant-garde Willow Tea Room opened in 1903 by Miss Catherine Cranston (1849–1934). Rather than crudely blocking out distractions or confining the diners within their group, the effect instead was to focus their attention upon one another and upon the delights of tea and pastry, lunch, or dinner on their table, set within the splendor of the larger surrounding space. Such a snug semi-enclosure for a group of women, dining out together, suggested the height of propriety for this emerging form of social activity, which reflected the growing emancipation of women enjoying the new opportunity to dine out together without the accompaniment of men.

At the same historical moment, in the suburbs of Chicago the architect Frank Lloyd Wright (1867–1959) applied a similar formula to the dining room furniture in his Prairie Houses, so-called because their long, low profiles echoed the horizon line of the flat Midwestern prairie landscape. Wright's Frederick Robie House of 1908–11, perhaps the greatest of that series of buildings, demonstrates the use of furniture as a symbolic and practical defense of family unity expressed through the formal ritual of dining together, albeit at just the moment when both Wright and Robie were facing marital breakdown.

That dining room employs the familiar Arts and Crafts amenity of a built-in sideboard, but extends the idea of integrating architecture and furniture to the room's lighting and, significantly, to the table, which is like an icon of the house itself. Although freestanding, its blocky structure appears as a logical outgrowth of the building, with integrated lamps surmounting the pillars that support the tabletop. The chairs that surround it resemble those of the Mackintosh tearooms but with an even more austere geometry, their straight high backs emphasizing that sense of mutual attention among the diners, uniting the family group. Here, the metaphor of safety, in the sense of family security, takes a highly stylized form.

The psychological aspect of seating patterns is well known and frequently studied. In particular, face-to-face seating, once very common in vehicles, has been almost universally rejected in public transportation design partly because it is deemed uneconomic in vehicles considered to be mass transporters, such as today's city buses and trains. Uninterrupted rows of forward-facing paired seats flanking an aisle are more economical in coaches and aircraft while longitudinal bench type seats along the carriage walls allow considerably more space for standing passengers aboard underground trains and city buses.

In the age of the lone traveler equipped with a smart phone or tablet, those devices may have more effect than a vehicle's seating layout as psychological defense against the intrusive behavior of other passengers. Yet there are exceptions to such a view as demonstrated by the design of London's New Routemaster buses, which offer travelers a relatively high proportion of seats to standing space and provide some face-to-face seating arrangements for the enjoyment of parties of up to four traveling together. Such seating opportunities reflect that same focus on a small group, which excludes the surrounding community, as does the dining furniture by Wright and Mackintosh or Jurgen Bey's Ear Chairs, discussed above.

For longer distance trips and overnight passages, various kinds of enclosure have filled that gray area between furniture and the internal space of a vehicle or vessel to lend the traveler security and the illusion of privacy. Among the oldest examples are found in ship's cabins, where fitted bunks, storage compartments of various sorts, commodes, and so on are constructed as part of the fabric of the ship and as such reflect the vessel's solidity. Whether they are built of wood or metal, it is reassuring that the bunk in which you sleep and the drawers where you keep your possessions are sturdy and will not move with the pitch and yaw of the ship. In Bachelard's view storms demonstrate the strength of any shelter, as the robustness of that structure enables its occupants to appreciate from a position of safety the drama and excitement of the weather. A protected interior in relation to the forbidding enormity of what lies outside is the most inescapable fact of any ship at sea.

The distinction between the typically narrow berth, built into an ordinary ship's cabin, and the spacious beds of first-class staterooms aboard the great ocean liners of the past was described by Evelyn Waugh (1903–66), narrating the experience of passengers aboard a storm-tossed *Queen Mary* in the novel *Brideshead Revisited*. His central character, trying to sleep in the large bed of a palatial suite muses:

> In a narrow bunk, on a hard mattress, there might have been rest, but here the beds were broad and buoyant; I collected what cushions I could find and tried to wedge myself firm, but through the night I turned with each swing and twist of the ship—she was rolling now as well as pitching—and my head rang with the creek and thud which now succeeded the hum of fine weather.
>
> (Waugh [1945] 1973: 228)

Such an experience departs from the conventional wisdom that the domestic familiarity of a real bed would be superior in its psychological reassurance than the typical nautical berth in the conditions of a storm. Yet in most cases during the age of ocean shuttle services, when ships were the only means of going abroad, the use of furniture types and styles typical of mansions or hotels was considered by shipping lines and their interior designers to offer patrons the greatest sense of security when sailing into bad weather, a bulwark against their darkest fears.

Some of the more ingenious concepts in furniture designed for transport vehicles were the convertible types devised for trains during the age of steam, adjustable travel chairs, fold-away sleeping berths, and roomettes, which were compartments transformable from sitting rooms in the daytime to bedrooms at night. Giedion was enraptured by the mechanics of comfort in nineteenth-century patent furniture that inspired the cabinetmaker turned railroad entrepreneur George Mortimer Pullman (1831–97) to develop a string of important innovations for his passenger cars beginning in the 1860s and continuing through the second half of the century. His innovations and those patented by other train builders of his time relied on earlier developments such as collapsible and portable military camp furniture and the curtained fold-away sleeping berths of early canal boats, which democratized transport amenities that in the past had been available only to royalty. Most significantly here, Pullman's achievement demonstrated a modern approach to architecture and furniture design in which both aspects are conceived in relation to one another from the start of a process leading, ultimately, to a complete and unified environment. This is demonstrated clearly by the congruence of architecture and built-in furniture in Frank Lloyd Wright's Prairie and Usonian Houses.

In addition to the physical comfort of having one's daytime travel chair converted into a full-length flat bed for overnight journeys, the retreat offered by the Pullman sleeping car's curtained berths was a precious opportunity to find some solitude amidst the hundreds of passengers occupying the confined linear space of the railroad car. The American travel writer Richard Ingraham described in 1835 the similar escape he was provided, within the large open cabin of an early Mississippi Riverboat, by his private sleeping berth, "where I could draw the rich crimsoned curtains around me, and with a book or pen pass the time somewhat removed from the bustle, and undisturbed by the constant passing of the restless passengers" (Tryon 1961: 182). Such a personal space provided by simple curtaining allowed travelers to retreat from the shipboard community behind the simplest of physical barriers, one that would also become commonplace in the Pullman sleeping car and European "wagon-lit" until the rise of the automobile and the airliner.

Along with transportable military furniture and the convertible sleeping accommodations of canal boats, commercial patent furniture of the nineteenth century also employed inventions, such as specialized hinges and latches, that enhanced individual privacy, the Holy Grail for travelers as the age of mass transportation dawned. Swiveling and reclining barber and dentist chairs with movable foot plates, adjustable headrests, and hydraulic lift and recline mechanisms were developed and refined in parallel with the transport chairs of the Pullman era, and innovations in each furniture type contributed to the development of the others, consequently affecting the nature of long-distance overland travel, first for more affluent travelers but soon also for the masses.

That cycle began again with the advent of commercial aviation, with the pioneering generation of long-distance passenger aircraft adopting first-class Pullman-style service and furnishings for its wealthy passengers. Beginning service in 1947, the Boeing Stratocruiser was among the first airliners with real transoceanic capability and a fully pressurized cabin allowing the plane to fly comfortably above the weather. Its elaborate convertible furniture, central to Walter Dorwin Teague's interior design strategy for this premium double-deck airliner, closely followed the design of Pullman sleeping cars. Its upper berths hinged down from the ceiling while the backs of the day chairs below folded flat to form the lower berths, both of which were then curtained off for complete visual privacy.

With the replacement of such dinosaurs as the propeller-driven Stratocruiser by jet airliners in the 1950s, and with the rapid subsequent development of low-cost flying, the expectation of privacy in the air receded but did not disappear entirely. Whereas the economy traveler was offered no semblance of separation from the hundreds of other passengers in the tubular space of the jetliner cabin, first-class and business travelers were typically provided some defense against unwanted intimacy with fellow passengers by the design of their travel chairs. Although the Pullman-style sleeper berth no longer suited the harsh economic realities of space distribution even for the highest fare-payers, the sleeper pod emerged as a new form of premium furniture aboard commercial aircraft.

Typically, British agency Tangerine Design's Club World Sleeper Pod, introduced by British Airways in 2000, offered a distinctive alternative to the curtained sleeping berth to provide the privacy expected by overnight passengers in upper-class travel. In a similar vein series of Skybed sleeper seats designed by Marc Newson (1963–) for Qantas Business class, introduced in 2003, were distinguished by a hard, external shell like that of an Eames lounge chair (Plate 27). Within that carapace, the seat back contained panels that unfolded to form a flatbed for overnight flights, leaving the shell to cocoon the head and upper body of its recumbent occupant and to provide maximum privacy when combined with a foldaway screening panel between beds.

An even more significant feature of this and other similar travel seats introduced since the millennium were their multichannel entertainment systems and a power outlet to charge the traveler's own laptop, phone, or tablet. Most important, however, was the integrated seatback video screen combined with headphones to block ambient sound. This powerful new focus of attention, offering the traveler entry into a virtual world, now provides the greatest psychological escape from the communal transport interior, substantially reducing the need for physical barriers between individuals.

Within the premium sections of the latest airliners, various ingenious forms of storage compartment, including shoe cupboards, lockable cubbyholes for documents, niches for pens or eyeglasses, and drinks holders also contribute to the passenger's sense of occupation and organization. These latter features are the elements that customize the seat, providing security by making it feel like home for the duration of the flight while genuinely protecting the essential paraphernalia of travel, passports, tickets, medicines, and so on. Yet while storage solutions may help to create the semblance of genuine personal space, it is the virtual world created by the video screen and headphones, now available in even many of the least expensive economy seats, that provides the most highly valued protection for today's traveler.

CONCLUSION

The carapace provided by any item of furniture can take many forms, either embedded in the design of that object or projected onto it by poetic inspiration. In some cases both may be present, but they can range from the substantial and clear articulation of shape, material, ornament, or other visible characteristics to conjuring a sense of emptiness. Their composition can include highly technological manifestations of the need for physical security or the subtlest barriers against foreign encroachment into personal space or the disturbance of a delicate thought process or an emotional state. These behaviors of furniture are often carefully cultivated responses by their designers or makers to indisputable needs, but they are also products of imaginative play, of the psychological need for a sanctuary, which may be vacant, inhabited, observed, real, or imagined. Any item of furniture can become a cipher for our dreams of security, our love nest, or our bulwark against despair, humiliation, sadness, or discomfort of any sort, our shelter in a storm.

CHAPTER EIGHT

Visual Representations

CLIVE EDWARDS

Visual representations of twentieth-century furniture in advertising, sales catalogs, and other visual devices provide core evidence of the "cultural history" of furniture. This chapter not only examines the role of visual cultures of consumption in formulating taste, markets, and identities through the persuasion of advertising, graphic design, and commercial photography but also through theatrical/filmic use, televisual commercials, and websites. This methodology allows for historical analysis through the lens of visual culture. To some extent it also provides a corrective to the emphasis on many "designer" furniture objects that have made up much of the popular history of twentieth-century furniture.

WHAT IS VISUAL REPRESENTATION/CULTURE?

2D and then 3D

The visual culture of twentieth-century furniture covers multiple forms including, though not limited to, print, TV, film, digital media, photography, and the products themselves. The role of visual culture as a shared practice for the representation of meanings of such matters as taste, identity, lifestyle, etc. makes this a vital tool for analysis. Visual representations exist as the images themselves but they are also part of a set of processes and practices—the ways in which we define ourselves. Through a range of approaches including compositional analysis, content analysis, psychoanalysis, semiology, and anthropology as well as discussion of the "viewing apparatus technologies," the critical encounters with imagery in this chapter will allow a historical analysis of twentieth-century furniture's visual culture to develop.

Images play a central role in the formation of values and beliefs, including the perception of gender, sexuality, ethnicity, race, and class. Visual culture studies visual matter and their cultural contexts to understand the meaning of the imagery and to identify a culture's visual meaning systems, which are conveyed in and through images. This involves an analysis of the context of the image's production and dissemination, and how contexts alter meanings. In addition, the reception of images is always affected by nonvisual elements including ideologies, texts, beliefs, prior experience, and the viewer's visual proficiency. Our responses to the visual are therefore already acculturated by our learning and value systems. For example, our choices as to which images we find appealing often reflect ourselves (identity), what we take as normal, and our reactions to others' choices.

There are three levels of looking at images: the image itself, what is physically or graphically there; the viewers, how do people see and perceive the images; and the context, how cultural, historical, and institutional considerations change the meaning from one country or time to another (Hall, Morley, and Chen 1996).

CODES AND SYMBOLS

Within the analysis of visual representations the role of codes and symbols or semiotics has become hugely important. Visual culture is used to encode identities in several ways, including the personal, the national, the ethnic, the sexual, and the membership of subgroups and cultures. Images are therefore expressions of cultural meaning, in that the rhetoric of the image goes beyond the objects denoted to reveal a complex web of cultural connotations. The photographic image normalizes and naturalizes cultural meanings, concealing their constructed nature from us. According to Kostelnick and Roberts (2011: 85–104), these processes can be defined as: the arrangement that reveals the structure; the emphasis on certain parts of the image; clarity to assist decoding; the conciseness of the image; its tone or attitude; and the ethos of trust it offers. These six points are useful for analyzing images.

ADVERTISING

The scholar of visual culture Nicholas Mirzoeff argues that the ability to "absorb and interpret visual information is the basis of industrial society" and is of primary importance in the "information age" (1999: 5). One of the key features of twentieth-century visual culture has been advertising and its relationship with people. Advertisements are commercial sales messages, as well as aspirational social/cultural messages. Therefore, advertising creates structures of meaning or metaphors where goods are not valued for themselves but are based on constructed social values and transferals of meaning. In wider terms images sell, entertain, teach, and provoke ideas, emotions, and memories. Media and visual works carry quantities of visual information so that we can read these images to understand the culture of twentieth-century furniture.

An example of the process is this brief analysis of the American Lane Company's (Altavista, VA, 1912–2001) hope or dowry chest range. Originally developed in 1920s America, early advertisements in journals such as the *Saturday Evening Post* emphasized the cleanliness and protective virtues of the cedar wood used. By 1926 advertisements particularly highlighted the dangers of moths through using an enlarged illustration of a moth pupa. These issues reflected the concerns of the time. By 1929 the company was advertising the chests with images of women in rooms with a chest and a strapline such as "What fine gifts for her"; establishing the model of a man giving a woman a gift of a "hope" or "bottom drawer" chest. In 1939 they returned to the image of the moth, described as Public Enemy No. 1; no doubt a reference to the famous FBI most wanted list. During the Second World War the imagery changed again with a depiction of a soldier on active duty, with thought bubbles illustrating his sweetheart and her dreams of a hope chest. After the war the endorsement by screen stars such as Shirley Temple (1928–2014) and, later, Miss America shows a sea change in the publicity for furniture that would become very popular across the industry. However, the graphics still reflected a taste for sickly-sweet imagery of hearts and ribbons. By 1955 a contemporary look was shown in advertisements with a graphic style that reflected another change—this time to Modernism. By 1964 the depiction was again completely renewed with advertisements in teen magazines such as *Ingenue*, and by the 1970s stylish photography and smart models (along with catchy text), played to a completely new audience in magazines including *Playboy*. The same product is encoded in a variety of ways that express the changes in visual cultures over a period of fifty years.

VISUAL CULTURE AND FURNITURE

Twentieth-century furniture is no different from that of other periods in that furniture acts as a function, sign, ritual, control, identity marker/market, as well as being part of taste formation. In any event, the context remains an important consideration in how these work. The way furniture "looks" is based on perceptions, not on manufacturer or design. People furnish with an image in mind, a particular style that reflects their identity and lifestyle. Twentieth-century furniture is defined by developments in aesthetic education, displays, and the role of tastemakers, along with the increased role of symbolic goods with cultural capital embedded in them. The following sections look at the history of both "high-style" and popular twentieth-century furniture through the lens of visual representations, codes, and symbols, and the rhetoric of the image. For the historian and scholar, the sheer range of outputs related to visual culture can be overwhelming so we have to take snapshots to identify trends.

1900–19: EARLY TWENTIETH CENTURY

By the beginning of the twentieth century, consumers were well versed in the visual culture of furniture. The previous century had already begun to introduce the ever-growing furnishing public to the influence of visual culture in relation to furniture through illustrated books, magazines, and advertising. In addition, retail stores were ever-more conscious of the sales appeal of spaces that offered opportunities for the visualization of interiors and products, rather than simple displays of lined-up goods.

Advertising by 1900 was an established business system with agencies, brands, and an infrastructure to support itself. It also recognized that the use of images could help manipulate the viewer and be suggestive of ideas and emotions. For many furniture buyers, the lure of historical styles was important and reproduction furniture was the mainstay of the industry at this time. The visual and material culture of "old" furniture designs reflected revivalism, an evocation of the past and an interest in antiques, all of which relate to concepts of cultural capital and perceived status. For example, in 1899 the Colonial Furniture Company of Grand Rapids, Michigan, advertised "Colonial Furniture" by mail. The black-and-white image showed a couple in eighteenth-century dress admiring a table of dubious heritage with the tag line "It's colonial." The image supported by the text reinforced American ideals of nostalgia and history initially fueled by the 1876 Centennial exhibition. A year later the London furnishing firm Oetzmann & Co. (1848–c. 1947) were advertising a carved "antique" coat rail styled with Tudor detailing and a seemingly incongruous straw boater hat hanging on a peg. The hat linked the object to contemporary use and helped decode the image. Even in the (then) newest of media, film, the Vitagraph motion picture company of America noted, in 1909, that for historical accuracy and detail, furniture used in the film *The Life of Napoleon* was from a loan exhibition of reproductions of Napoleonic furniture made in France for the furniture department of Frederick Loese & Co. of Brooklyn, New York (Uricchio and Pearson 1993).

Whilst the reproduction styles ranging from the sixteenth to the late eighteenth century remained most commercial, other more contemporary styles were evident in advertising. For example, the American Arts and Crafts group, the Roycrofters, advertised their wares as "The Antithesis of Chippendale," illustrating the advertisement with a simple "Morris" adjustable easy chair and a solid round pedestal table. The images supported the moralizing text representing a tone and ethos that was in opposition to fashionable reproduction styles.

The Arts and Crafts approach was particularly evident in illustrated publications where watercolored images, as opposed to photographs or black-and-white drawings, were widely evident. The Swedish painter and designer Carl Larsson (1853–1919) in his book *Ett Hem* (Our Home) (1899) promoted a version of the Arts and Crafts that was widely published at the time through his attractive colored drawings of his own interiors. In contrast, Casimir Hermann Baer's (1870–1942) *Farbige Raumkunst* (Color in Room Decoration) (1911) was full of colored drawings of furniture and rooms by architects including Josef Hoffman (1870–1956) in the Secession style as well as northern European designs by Herman Gesellius (1874–1916), Armas Lindgren (1874–1929), and Eliel Saarinen (1873–1950).

Retail catalogs also convey something of the visual culture of the times. Morris and Co.'s *Specimens of Furniture and Interior Decoration* (*c.* 1912) has sepia photographs of recognizable Arts and Crafts pieces along with reproductions of Georgian and even Tudor styles. In the United States, meanwhile, line drawings of Mission and Arts and Crafts furniture were identified as plates (as found in superior artistic publications) on each page of the catalog of Walter S. Mackay and Co. of Oakland, California, titled *Quaint Furniture: Carpets, Furniture, Draperies* (*c.* 1910).

In contrast to these often rather austere images of "honest" and "truthful" furniture, the contemporaneous Art Nouveau style offered a startling alternative (Figure 6.1). Engaging with the emotions and the excitement of something new, slightly unfamiliar illustrations like the competition entry drawing by Charles Rennie Mackintosh (1868–1928) of a proposed "House for an Art Lover" produced in 1901, and published in the *Zeitschrift für Innendekoration* (Magazine for Interior Decoration) reflected this style. A little earlier, in volumes 11–13 for 1897–8, *The Studio* magazine showed photographs of works by Art Nouveau designers at the Paris Salon and also contained a long article on the Glasgow school with images of, among other things, Mackintosh furniture and interior designs. Although Mackintosh furniture and interiors were an acquired, expensive, and esoteric taste, the commercial versions of it were well shown in the catalog of British retailer Waring and Gillow. Here a cover (*c.* 1905) sports two panels of Mackintosh-inspired roses with sinuous curves flanking modern women in Liberty style dresses. Companies often showed variations of artistic or quaint furniture in their catalogs. This was surely an example of the trickle-down effect of visual culture.

1920S: MODERNITY AND HISTORICISM

The high-profile visual impact of Modernism on furniture has, to some extent, eclipsed what was happening in the vastly larger and more representative homes of the majority. Here individuality and expression of identity were more important than social progressiveness. The evidence of "standardized" furnishing estimates, provided by department stores or furniture retailers to customers, clearly shows how retailers thought people expected particular rooms to look. Whether it was "Modern," "Traditional," "Art Deco," and so on, they could all be manipulated to suit a price bracket or style change for a particular retailer or manufacturer's range.

For example, the 1925 advertisement by the American Walnut Manufacturers Association (AWMA) titled "The Pride You Take in Ancestral American Walnut Furniture" demonstrates the continuing taste for the Colonial style in the United States. It shows a photograph of a woman in typical 1920s dress resting on the arm of a Chippendale-derived chair with a ghostly drawn eighteenth-century figure (probably George Washington) on the other side of the chair, against a backdrop of a walnut tabletop, which is hanging like a painting. The image clearly depicts concepts of heritage and both personal and national identity. By contrast, another advertisement by the AWMA in the same year showed a photograph of a traditional style set of furnishings in the dining room of the Beverly Hills home of the film stars Douglas Fairbanks (1883–1939) and Mary Pickford Fairbanks (1892–1969). Here the image was not selling the actual goods but rather the idea that buying walnut furniture would link the consumer to the glamorous world of Hollywood, yet not sacrifice the Colonial image. In this way a dual coding was evident.

The continuing play on the value of past skills and crafts was also seen in an advertisement for the Associated Furniture Manufacturers of Grand Rapids published in *House and Garden* in 1924. Here under the title "In Grand Rapids as in Damascus" a venerable bearded craftsman working with a sword is shown overlaid with an image of a similarly bearded woodworker with a hammer in hand. The inference (also explained in the text) was that of the practice of skilled craft traditions in Grand Rapids, but also makes an assumption that the reader will understand the link with damascene metal work and the symbolic appeal of craftsmanship across cultures and generations.

In England similar strategies occurred in the market for old-style furniture whether antique or new reproductions. In 1926, the London retailers Gill and Reigate, "By appointment to HM the King," advertised the company name but not any particular models. The image featured a large paneled sixteenth-century room with a Tudor table and Jacobean chairs: a clear link with Britain's heritage and the Royal family.

Department stores and large-scale retailers often used multiple images, crammed into advertisements without context, as collages that were cheap and simple to produce. In the *Larkin Book of Better Homes* (1924) (Plate 28), by the eponymous credit mail-order firm, a color front cover of a stylish woman serving drinks to a fashionable couple relaxing in a wicker suite sets the aspirational tone. Commercial reality soon follows on the subsequent pages, with sepia images for living room furniture sets; black and white for individual pieces, as well as bedroom and dining room ensembles; and color images for accessories and carpet and linoleum. The emphasis was still on colonial-derived designs for cabinetwork and three-piece suites, but the visuals were simple, concise, and unchallenging, with price being the main issue.

For those who wanted to be modern during this period, Art Deco was a natural choice, as it offered an alternative to the historic derivatives but did not engage with particular ideologies. The publication of images of furniture and interiors in superb color plates in works such as *Intérieurs en Couleurs* (Interiors in Color) (1926) and in magazines such as *La Vie Parisienne* (published weekly between 1863 and 1915) where fashion plates used Art Deco styled furniture, was matched by retail showrooms that dressed their spaces in the new styles and produced sumptuously illustrated catalogs. The French *Décoration Intérieure Moderne* (Modern Interior Decoration) (*c.* 1925), a retail catalog with 128 pages on yellow paper with warm-toned sepia photographs of various room settings and individual pieces in high Art Deco style, exemplified the modernity through the arrangement and contexts of the furniture displayed.

For many consumers, however, film was the visual medium that displayed Art Deco at its best and most extravagant. Numerous examples from musicals to murder mysteries show this. One of the first films to abandon painted backdrops was the *Single Standard* (1929) for which Cedric Gibbons (1893–1960) created a vast space with numerous vertical emphases and references to modern art for the grand salon used by Greta Garbo's (1905–90) character. A similar effect was created in *The Kiss* (1929) where the sets, especially the bedroom, reflected contemporary hedonistic French taste in a soundless black-and-white film. Moviegoers took ideas from these designs into their own homes.

Whereas this popular culture was relatively easy to decode a certain amount of cultural capital was required for more "difficult" images. For example, the front cover image of the book *Der Stuhl* (The Chair) (Rasch and Rasch 1928) shows a male figure apparently seated, but actually without any support. The image emphasizes the author's interest in ergonomics but does require some perception to decode this. On the other hand, the equally modernist *Der Stuhl* poster (1935) by Artur Bofinger (1909–) with its minimal negative outline of a chair form was created to advertise a furniture exhibition at the Kunstgewerbemuseum in Zurich, Switzerland. The flat areas of shape and color have a contemporary art feel but are concise enough to explain the concept. Both these make reference to the fashionable gestalt concept of reification, whereby a partial visual image is completed by the mind. A third example is an illustrated catalog, *Möbel Der Staatlichen Bauhochschule Weimar* (Furniture by the Bauhaus Weimar) (1925), by Erich Dieckmann (1896–1944) that is full of "Typenmobel," a modernist concept of simple, unadorned, and easily produced furniture. Here the image, content, and typography all represented the concept of modernity developed by the Bauhaus.

1930S: MODERNITY AND THE MODERNE

By now the reader should be aware that the cultural history of furniture has many branches and is not a linear development defined by iconic images and texts. For example, in the 1930s, furniture was designed in a variety of styles including Art Deco, the Moderne, neo-baroque, Surrealism, Eclecticism, Streamlining, and the International style as well as versions of a wide choice of historic styles and adaptations. This varied range of traditional and modern designs coexisted in most countries, as individuals made their particular taste and identity choices. Nevertheless, fashion could be important.

At this time a revitalized but still eclectic design scene, for example, demonstrated the nature of American visual culture in furnishings. In 1932–3, the New York Museum of Modern Art opened an exhibition *The International Style* that showcased modernism. Around the same time, the restored eighteenth-century Colonial Williamsburg site opened, where, since 1936, the foundation has offered reproductions, adaptations, and interpretations of seventeenth- to early nineteenth-century antiques from its collection. Furthermore, the 1933 *Century of Progress* exhibition in Chicago became a setting for the display of Art Deco and Streamlined products.

Modernity, nontheless, was a key theme of the 1930s. Whether it was American or European, commercial or esoteric, being modern was the thing. This was of course as varied in furniture as much as in any other category of designed objects. In 1931 the American Heywood Wakefield Company (1897–) advertised photographic sets of a lounge and dining room designed by Gilbert Rohde (1894–1944), whose portrait was also displayed, along with a brief biography of the designer. His Contemporary Range was an interesting hybrid of modernist forms and Art Deco detailing with the added sign of the image of the designer, giving trust and reassurance. In 1934 the London department store Harrods promoted "The Modern Note" in furniture. They advertised Australian silkwood cabinets with a collage of images, which illustrated the textual content. Clearly inspired by Art Deco, but with exotic timbers used, the illustrations included a lounge table and a cocktail cabinet/bookcase reflecting the higher social status of the store's customers.

It is not surprising that modernist furniture would often be advertised using contemporary graphic design. Two examples demonstrate how this could be seen as challengingly creative and not straightforward to decode. The Swiss Wohnbedarf AG's (founded 1931) catalog *Das Neue Holzmobel Aalto* (New Wooden Furniture by Aalto) (1933) bore a cover image of abstract sheets of plywood "roll" and the outlines of an Alvar Aalto (1898–1976) armchair side frame (Figure 8.1). Inside there were simple black-and-white images of Aalto's ply furniture, its dimensions and prices. The second example is *Die Federnde Aluminium Mobel* (Springy Aluminum Furniture) (1934), being a manufacturer's

FIGURE 8.1 Cover of *Das Neue Holzmobel Aalto* (1933). Photograph courtesy of the Canadian Centre for Architecture, Montreal.

catalog with an image of Marcel Breuer's slatted aluminum chaise longue that was superimposed with a drawn outline of a feminine figure recumbent upon it. Although easier to decode, it still had a tone of elitism in its sophistication.

A fascinating sidelight on the reach of Modernism in the visual and material is the issue of doll's house furniture as part of children's visual culture. An example advertised in a 1936 issue of *Meccano Magazine* advertised Dinky Toy doll's house furniture with "every model based on a typical example of modern design."

While the modernists were emphasizing aspects of their approach to identity and lifestyle, another visual connection was sometimes made that appeared to make a connection between craftsmen and consumers. This made an apparent link between the traditional bespoke high end of the trade and the average consumer, and continued right through the century. Two examples demonstrate this. An advertisement in *Punch* magazine of 1935 for the high-end London design-based Heal's store shows a customer and cabinetmaker in conversation about a commission, clearly making the consumer visualize themselves in the same situation as if they had shopped at the store. Two years later, the large-scale American Kroehler Company (*c.* 1902–78) produced an advertisement showing a photograph of a craftsman at work on upholstery and a seamstress sewing, and crucially a third image of a customer sitting on the finished sofa with accompanying text extolling the craft skills embedded in the product. The inference was that both companies produced bespoke products.

In 1930 around eighty million Americans attended cinemas weekly (65 percent of the population) so it was evidently a great source of visual inspiration, especially in terms of lifestyle and identify formation (Pautz 2002). The 1933 film *Dinner at Eight*, featuring Jean Harlow (1911–37), for example, gave Depression-era audiences a taste of extravagance in the amazing Art Deco interiors that emphasized angles, glossy reflective surfaces, and streamlined Moderne furnishing designs, including such items as Harlow's dressing room with a fringed vanity and stool. An example of the retailers' acknowledgment of the social changes was their response to moviegoing. One publication, devoted to visual merchandising or window dressing, noted that the filmgoers of 1934,

> see fine Tudor dining halls, luxurious bedrooms, handsome bachelor apartments, typical American labour saving kitchens and the newest ideas in flat furnishing [...]. When they return to their own homes, they unconsciously make comparisons. Women in particular have a predilection for this, and very often the comparison throws up the furnishings of their own homes in a very unfavourable light.
>
> (Caradoc 1934: 79)

The author suggested that shop windows could be dressed to tie-in with the movies: "In this way, the film-goer, when she does her shopping the following day, can be shown how she can furnish her home in the same delightful film-like way, but at a price that can be compassed by her limited means" (Caradoc 1934: 79).

Aping women's magazines of the period, some businesses developed the film theme and produced catalogs that presented the "homes of the stars" with the furniture being part of the photo studio set up. The British Times Furnishing Co.'s *Good Furnishings* booklet was set out like a woman's magazine, with Hollywood stars such as Cary Grant (1904–86), Randolph Scott (1898–1987), and Ida Lupino (1918–95) featured in room settings. The magazine/catalog included a short fiction story, beauty tips, and knitting patterns, which were intermingled with images of Times furniture and interiors, budgets, furnishing tips, and plugs for the company's Furnishing Advisory Bureau (Veasey *c*. 1935).

1940–50: WARTIME AND CELEBRITIES

During this period of immense change the growth of a market for modern and contemporary furniture began, although a taste for tradition remained uppermost. An American Grand Rapids Furniture Makers' Guild advertisement of the 1940s shows a line drawing, illustrating a housewife with a baby in a high chair, in a room furnished with reproduction Federal American style cabinets that again stressed the heritage and workmanship inherent in the products of the city. An unusual image used in a 1940s Stickley Furniture advertisement presents an elegant woman dressed in an exotic gown, in a vaguely Renaissance portrait mode, with the strapline "Tables *too* have personality." The image clearly portrays the idea that this "graceful" product complemented "the charm of the owner."

The ideas of authenticity and heritage were explored in an American publication titled *Your Home and Drexel Furniture* (Drexel Furniture Ltd., 1903–). This 1939 promotional booklet showed room settings and listings of images of individual pieces derived from a variety of eighteenth-century models. However, a most revealing set of photographs at the end of the booklet was entitled "How the twentieth century brings you the eighteenth century." Here images of workers with modern multi-spindle carving machines and routers were shown alongside hand carving finishers, again intended to make the craft skills of the makers clear to the viewer (Figure 8.2).

One of the most noteworthy features of furniture's visual culture at this time was the increasing use of celebrities to link products with particular markets and lifestyles. Individual celebrities continued to endorse furniture products. This was because "Celebrities have particular configurations of meanings that cannot be found elsewhere" (McCracken 1988: 107). The reason for this, according to McCracken, is that "The consumer suddenly 'sees' that the cultural meanings contained in the people, objects, and contexts of the advertisement are also contained in the product. Well-crafted advertisements enable this essentially metaphoric transference. Badly crafted advertisements do not" (314). Hence the celebrity image is crucial to the message.

Film stars dominated, with examples including the American Mengel (*c*. 1877–*c*. 1960) furniture company's 1949 advertisement for an eighteenth-century inspired bedroom suite used by Joan Crawford (1904–77) in the film *Flamingo Road* (1949), and another with Doris Day (1924–) linked to her film *My Dream is Yours* (1949). Lane's hope chests (see above) were advertised using a teenaged Shirley Temple as a model, in a campaign targeted at GIs and absentee sweethearts of the Second World War, whilst MGM star Kathryn Grayson (1922–2010) endorsed Chromecraft (1946–) dinette sets in the *Ladies Home Journal*. In a different vein, moviegoers continued to see film sets reflecting particular interior styles. For example, *The Fountainhead* (1949), a film based on Ayn Rand's novel, depicted the modernist architect Howard Rourke's apartment as a Wrightian studio that expressed a vision of Modernism in its furnishings that would have appeared very advanced to 1949 audiences.

The celebrities did not only come from popular culture. The American Drexel company's (1903–)1949 Precedence range mentioned Edward Wormley (1907–95) as designer, and in the same year another American company

How the Twentieth Century

brings you the

Eighteenth Century

Extremely interesting developments have quietly been going on in the Drexel furniture factories. Some years ago Drexel analysed the truth about what people wanted in furniture. The conclusions were something like this: people didn't like machine-made furniture because it was often ill-designed, ill-proportioned, ill-finished. Yet most people couldn't afford the alternatives – antiques, or expensive hand-made reproductions that cost nearly as much as the antiques themselves. Wasn't there some way of giving people beautiful reproductions inexpensively? Yes, there might be, if machines could be devised that could be used as skilfully as the hand tools of Old World cabinet-makers, yet which performed their tasks in multiple fashion and with scientific precision.

Drexel set out to obtain such machines. Sometimes they had to be specially invented. Often they were invented by the Drexel craftsmen themselves. Today, a trip through the Drexel factories is a review of endless little miracles of production, in which science and craftsmanship have joined hands.

First there is Drexel's modern method of seasoning wood. In a neat little control-room are a few coils, levers, thermostats and charts. These control the temperature and moisture of the great kilns where every bit of wood used for Drexel furniture is seasoned – yes, even the wood used for crating it! Drexel furniture is so satisfactory in your home because in every square inch of the wood a proper percentage of moisture has been left. Such precision was impossible in the old days of natural seasoning.

Then comes the actual cabinet-making. Here a multitude of machines aid the craftsmen in their tasks. Electric power lifts heavy loads for them and applies the precise pressure needful to ensure perfect veneering. Compressed air pushes the sides of drawers together as deftly as the most skilful hands could do it. All the tedious drudgery of sandpapering wood to a smooth finish is eliminated – electric power guides the sand-paper more diligently than could the most tireless workman, and produces a surface like satin. Horizontal steel plungers, electrically-driven, punch perfect dowel-holes – it is impossible for those holes to be anything but perfect!

Perhaps most ingenious of all are the master-carvers. These machines, many feet long, capable of carving 18 bed-posts at a time, are so nicely balanced that a child's finger could control them. They carve the lovely shell, waterleaf, acanthus, sheaf, and other 18th century designs as delicately as the master's hand of old.

There is still much hand-work in the making of Drexel furniture. Most of the eighteen final operations that produce the color, depth and glow of the Drexel finish are performed by hand. And there are many operations, both hand and power, that we have not space to touch upon. But we hope we've given you some idea of how Drexel can bring your furniture as beautiful as that of the eighteenth century craftsman, at a fraction of the price.

LOOK FOR THE DREXEL SEAL ON EACH PIECE

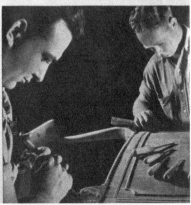

FIGURE 8.2 A page from a catalog of Drexel reproduction furniture. Photograph courtesy of the Canadian Centre for Architecture, Montréal.

Widdicombe (1858–c. 1960) advertised a Scandinavian-style lounge suite citing Terence Harold Robsjohn-Gibbings (1905–76) as the designer. These associations gave the product a certain cachet and reinforced the visual image with a fashionable designerly context. Importantly, they were only meaningful to a particular group of cognoscenti with access to this type of cultural capital.

A different visual experience was reported in the news magazine *Pathfinder* (published weekly 1894–54 for rural American readers). In an illustrated report on Alex Girard's (1907–93) exhibition *For Modern Living* at the Detroit Institute of Arts the scene was visualized for readers:

> Up the richly carpeted ramp, viewers walk up to a dining room done by Alvar Aalto; past two studies [by] Bruno Mathsson and Jean Risom and a bedroom and living-room representing a variety of designers; then up another level to a space furnished by Charles Eames; and finally to a small balcony overlooking George Nelson's living area. The quiet simplicity of the rooms and the gentle tones of symphonic music have people talking in whispers. Sighed one woman: "I'd like to live here."
>
> *(Pathfinder*, October 5, 1949)

For Britain, the decade was mainly remembered as one of rationing, "make do and mend," and the government-controlled Utility scheme for furniture and furnishings. Although there was a whiff of whimsy and frivolity in the second half of the decade, it was rare. The government's Utility scheme furniture was publicized in catalogs that were as bland and uninspiring as the furniture itself. However, the products were influenced by the Arts and Crafts movement's ideals, in conjunction with a restrained Modernism that was seen, in a younger generation, as important in breaking the hold of tradition on British design.

The establishment of the British Design Council's publication *Design* in 1949 continued to spread the visual gospel of "good design." At a grassroots level, and arguably more realistically, the book *Modern Homes Illustrated*, published in 1947 for a popular market, suggested that homemakers should choose from an eclectic range of furnishing opportunities including built-in, antique, reproduction, Utility, garden, and painted furniture.

Two examples of British visual culture playing a didactic role occurred in the later 1940s. The first was a poster titled *Design in Everyday Things—The Development of the Chair*, showing the visual history of the chair in sixteen images produced by the Army Education Service in 1946. Second was a television program, part of a series on design, called *What's in a Chair?* that saw "Gordon Russell (1892–1980), the distinguished furniture designer who had been recently appointed Director of the Council of Industrial Design, discuss the chair in relation to materials, methods of manufacture, social habits, and occupational requirements with [well-known British designers] Frank Austin and H.J. Cutler. Specialist craftsmen are seen at work on different types of chair, each showing a particular type of construction" (*Radio Times*, October 24, 1947). The limited number of TV sets in Britain at the time (in 1948 just 14,500 sets) made this an elite visual experience.

1950S: MODERNISM AND POSTWAR CONFIDENCE

The 1950s were a decade of contrasts, but one in which modern furniture design eventually took center stage. Nonetheless, markets and tastes remained very varied under this umbrella term. For example, manufacturers who wanted to engage consumers with cutting-edge modern design knew that this was a sophisticated market. The 1952 American company Erwin-Lambeth's (1901–87) advertisement for upholstered furniture was dominated by a full-frame photograph of an Egyptian princess' sculpted head from the Berlin Museum, along with an extract from an obscure poem "The Rock in El Ghor" by John Greenleaf Whittier (1807–92). The modernist sofa on sale is modestly illustrated in small scale in the background, a clear case of an appeal to an educated elite. The degree of sophistication among the furniture-buying public in the Western world was varied though. A 1951 advertisement by American maker Knoll (1938–), which was simply promoting the brand, has the logo emblazoned over a close-up photograph of a set of stacking chair legs, which created an abstract image of simple curved components. A later advertisement by the furniture manufacturers Herman Miller (1923–) for their lounger designed by Eames in 1957, on the other hand, showed a young boy sitting in the chair with a toy plane and was captioned "It's a man's chair." Bearing in mind the links between text and image, we can perhaps read the idea of heirloom in the product. In 1958 Knoll advertised a red Saarinen "Womb" chair with a grimy chimney sweep, complete with brushes, sitting in it. This visually startling advert ran on the inside front cover of the *New Yorker*'s anniversary issue every year from 1958 to 1971. It is an intriguing image by graphic designer Herbert Matter (1907–84), apparently based on a chimney sweep from his native Switzerland, but in any event it is an eye-catching and memorable image due to the visual juxtaposition of a seemingly incompatible relationship.

Middle-road and popular furniture of the 1950s was also visually promoted in a variety of ways but with completely different rhetoric. Whereas the more stylish furniture offered clever codings, the mainstream manufacturers continued with visuals of celebrity endorsements that had been popular in the prewar period. For example, the "I Love Lucy suite" made by the American company Johnson Carper (Roanoke, VA) from 1953 advertised: "For only $198 you could purchase the bedroom suite created especially for Lucy and Desi's TV show!" The tie-in with popular television culture could not be more obvious. In the same year, the American Mengel furniture maker introduced the Prismata collection designed by Raymond Loewy (1893–1966). The advertisement illustrates the product range with lots of white space and an asymmetric graphic layout, but also it has an inset photo of the designer, again referring to the designer's image as one of status and trust. The structure of the advert emphasizes the various parts of the image to assist decoding.

In Britain, a major event that was to influence the first part of the decade was the 1951 Festival of Britain. This spawned a new style of furniture that was sometimes called Contemporary. The London store Liberty showed Modernism and the contemporary style in a 1951 advertisement that presented an assemblage of modern furniture designs on a white background, which suggested lifestyle references rather than particular objects. This trend in visual merchandising of lifestyles rather than specific products was to develop throughout the second half of the century.

One of the other important cultural events of the decade was the *Design in Scandinavia* exhibition of objects for the home, set up in 1954. It was an important traveling exhibition that brought Scandinavian Modern design to the attention of America. Culturally, it presented a refined Modernism that was in tune with many American tastes. Importantly, it encouraged US manufacturers to develop ranges in the same idiom. Although the products varied, the advertising and visuals were clearly targeted. In 1952 the Baker Furniture Company (1893–) promoted a typical "Scandinavian" dining group designed by the Dane Finn Juhl (1912–89), but very incongruously the photograph and the brief text was placed in a rococo-style frame, not unlike an eighteenth-century trade card. This was clearly another instance of a nod to the past. In complete contrast to this traditional image and evidently appealing to a younger audience, the Lane Company advertised their "Scandinavian [dining] range" in 1959 with humor, including a stereotypical Viking complete with horned helmet, sitting at a dining table.

The work of American designer Jens Risom (1916–2016) is an interesting case of the adaption of Scandinavian design. In the early 1950s Risom worked with renowned photographer Richard Avedon (1923–2004) to produce a series of advertisements titled, "The Answer is Risom!" The advertisements had one piece of furniture shown in use against a white seamless background with no extraneous details, with a model or two people in an overt pose. Production values are clearly important in displaying the visual message. In another example, prominent photographer Ezra Stoller (1915–2004) shot the 1948 Herman Miller Collection catalog of mid-century modern masterpieces in black-and-white. His use of cropping techniques, dramatic lighting effects, and unusual angles all made this appeal to a very different audience from the one to which newspaper adverts were selling furniture simply on the basis of price.

Yet other visuals reflect the differing tastes of the time. Depictions of the familiar American Barcalounger (Barcalo Manufacturing Company, Buffalo, New York) easy recliner chair, for instance, often employed a sense of humor in the 1950s. The cartoonist Charles Addams (1912–88) designed a Father's Day advertisement with a giant cartoon figure and a chair with the catch line "I understand you have Barcaloungers to fit everybody." Addams also illustrated a number of other ads including a Father Christmas sitting in the chair, and one with a dog looking at the chair in a shop window with the line "How much is that Barcalounger in the window." This was a reference to a popular contemporary 1953 song titled "How much is that doggy in the window."

Another individual chair to relax in was the American Contour Chair-Lounge (Contour Chair Company, St. Louis, Missouri). Developed in the late 1940s, it was initially advertised with large amounts of text as a therapeutic chair, complete with testimonials from doctors. The effective qualities were promoted in an advertisement from 1951 that had the headline in a white horror-dripping font on a black background saying "The Case of the Aching Back"—clearly making a link to the horror-film posters of the same era. The lower image shows the relaxed woman who has solved the case by buying the Contour chair. The chair was also featured in advertisements for other products, such as vinyl coverings, and as a prop for photo shoots. Earl Theisen (1903–73) photographed one in the early 1950s for *Look* magazine (published biweekly 1937–71 in Des Moines, Iowa) that featured Marilyn Monroe (1926–62) lying on it. These visual endorsements vicariously made reference to a desirable lifestyle image.

During the decade, the images used in advertising changed rapidly. In 1952 an advert for the American Kuehne Manufacturing Co. who began producing dinette sets at Mattoon, Illinois, in the 1930s, shows a drawn and colored image of a couple looking at the set in a shop window from the street outside with the caption "You designed this dinette," quite straightforward and easy to read in terms of the rhetoric of the image. By 1959 the Laverne company's (founded *c.* 1938) "invisible chair" advertisement shows a photograph of a young boy sprawling paint over the back of the well-known acrylic chair. The caption reads, "The next sound you hear will not be a mother screaming." The lower text mentions that the chair is recommended for "reading Proust or watching *Open End*" (a respected US talk show). The contrast in approach between a modern, yet easily recognizable, steel and melamine dinette set and the latest challenging chair designs is obvious. In 1951 the first IKEA furniture catalog was issued, which represented the beginning of a completely new approach to furniture selling and buying.

1960S: VARIETY IS THE SPICE OF LIFE

The Pop furniture design of the 1960s was all about image. Although made in 1956, the famous collage by Richard Hamilton (1922–2011) titled "Just what is it that makes today's homes so different, so appealing?" seems to represent the culture of the age. With an image of a contemporary open-plan lounge taken from a flooring advert in the *Ladies Home Journal* (founded 1883, published monthly until 2014 when it became quarterly) the image encapsulates the consumer boom of the 1960s using advertising clips to build the scene and represent the commercialization of culture.

In 1962 the first Sunday newspaper color supplement began to reflect British lifestyles in both advertising and editorial content. Companies such as Habitat (1964) in the United Kingdom, IKEA (1958) in Sweden, and Crate and Barrel (1962) in the United States, offered good, simple furnishings and home products based on a number of stylistic tendencies that included a reformed Modernism, a farmhouse style, and watered-down Pop imagery—any of which could define an individual lifestyle. Indeed these types of businesses returned to the advertising and display of merchandise in "lifestyle vignettes" that showed groups of objects in loose room settings so the display encouraged the purchase of a ready-made lifestyle (Plate 29).

In 1966 British retail chain Habitat launched their first catalog—a hand-drawn, black-and-white broadsheet. By 1969 they were producing a ninety-page mail-order catalog with color photographs and by 1973 the catalog had become more of a lifestyle magazine with goods photographed in real locations and models using the furniture with accessories to match a lifestyle image.

One of the seminal images of this period was the 1963 publicity shot of the infamous model Christine Keeler (1942–) by Lewis Morley (1925–2013) where she posed naked on a chair. Although often described as the Arne Jacobsen (1902–71) model 3107 design for Danish company Fritz Hansen, the chair in the photograph is actually a copy of this. Nevertheless, as a signifier of contemporary modernity it works as a generic image and it is only enthusiasts who forensically analyze the image. Interestingly, the image was adopted many times in later years and even in a 1999 episode of *The Simpsons* with Homer in place of Keeler. An interesting decoding project!

The use of mid-century classics in advertisements for non-furniture products was also evident in the 1960s. The association with a well-known design (at least to the cognoscenti) was manifest. For example, the American Simpson Company's advertisement for plywood wall cladding showed a room set with a Harry Bertoia wire chair being used by children eating. Eero Aarnio's (1932–) stunning white globe chair was used in an American advertisement for Rael-Brook cotton shirts with the male model posing by the chair but with a female hand offering a telephone receiver from deep within the chair. The same chair, all in red, was also used as a foil for a British carpet advertisement for Naylor Ltd., again with the connotations of modernity. In another instance, the chair can be seen in a 1962 advertisement along with the famous Arco lamp and Pastilli chair in an advertisement titled "What sort of man reads Playboy?" In 1962, the Eero Saarinen Tulip table was used in a Tupperware advertisement as a prop for the display of their plastic containers. All these images created implied connotations of the particular products as representing both modernity and style credibility.

More difficult to unpick are visuals such as the Cannon towel advertisements from 1962 with towels draped over a Saarinen Tulip chair alongside a nineteenth-century rococo revival Belter chair. The final instance, a 1968 advertisement for the International Paper Corp., is a double-page spread with a man sitting on a spotted cardboard chair designed by Peter Murdoch (1940–) atop a hill photographed from below. Although seeming to promote the company generically, the image and symbolism of a Pop design classic was surely not lost on the viewer.

The range of illustrated advertisements produced during the 1960s demonstrates the wide range of products available to the consumers. The Scandinavian theme continued in an amusing 1961 advertisement for Jens Risom with half the space taken by a close up of a large image of a "Danish pastry" with a lot of text and a very small image of a Risom designed desk and chair. In the following year the Danish Royal Cado system (a wall-mounted shelving system) illustrated goods being stored in a cupboard in an "inhibited" manner and a contrasting image of the Cado system with an eclectic collection out on display and "exhibited" in the advertisement; again an appeal to a lifestyle choice.

In another vein Herman Miller devised two contrasting advertisements. The first entitled "Beware of imitations" featured Eames's designs on a poster made to look as if it was pasted on a brick wall reminiscent of a "Wanted" bill. Designed to draw attention to "copies" it again linked into well-known populist imagery related to the film and TV representations of the Wild West. In contrast, a 1962 cover of a Herman Miller catalog shows a set of silhouettes of the outlines of some of their well-known chairs that creates an effect like an Alexander Calder (1898–1976) mobile. Again it was aimed at customers who would make the connection with these apparently abstract symbols and "see" the furniture by a process of gestalt.

Knoll furniture and their adverts were a touchstone of modernity during the period. In 1964 an advertisement shows a split image with one side showing raw glass fibers and the other a finished Tulip chair. The style of image changed again when in 1969 the Tulip chair was shown on a black background with a model outfitted with a fashionable knotted dress, stainless steel visor, and knitted top, with the tag line that the chair was on show in both the Museum of Modern Art and the Knoll showrooms. The appeal of these images to a particular cultural group was obvious.

At the top of the cultural capital pyramid was an advert from 1967 for John Stuart Inc. (high-end retail showrooms in Grand Rapids and New York) showing a Purist painting by Le Corbusier on a white background space with some short text to connect Corbusier's ideas with the company's elite interior projects. It really did assume some prior knowledge of art and design on the part of the reader to take any reasonable meaning from the advert.

In North America, popular cultural tastes were reflected in a range of examples. The 1964 Bassett advertisement for the French provincial *Provencaux* range "Speaks French in style and your language in price." A depiction of the suite in a room setting was complete with a smiling Gendarme in a collaged image just to make sure the connection was made. A different approach was in a 1966 Barcalounger chair advert that showed a wood-framed recliner vaguely reminiscent of an Eames piece but with a woman lounging in it and straplined "The chair Raymond Loewy designed for your Barcalounger break." This is interesting, as these chairs were usually aimed at a male market, so it may represent a change in attitudes to gender issues.

Film has already been seen as a component of visual culture that has important connections with furniture. The 1960s were no exception with perhaps the most famous example being *2001: A Space Odyssey* directed by Stanley Kubrick (1928–99). This featured the amoeba-like shaped Djinn furniture covered with stretch fabric in bright colors by French designer Olivier Mourgue (1939–) that furnished the space hotel. Other chairs used in film sets include the 1966 TV series *Star Trek* with its apparent use of Saarinen's Tulip chair but actually a derivative made by Burke Inc. of Dallas with a star-shaped pedestal. In television, Eero Aarnio's Ball or Globe chair (see also above) was featured in the enigmatic British television series *The Prisoner* (1967–8). The design has been associated with the widespread appeal of space travel in the period, but other imagery may be conjured up, including the technological future and even references to the potential isolation within modern society. Finally, who can forget the unusual bathtub sofa in the 1961 film *Breakfast at Tiffany's*? This product is available today as both a reproduction and as a case study in DIY upcycling!

1970S: POPULAR CULTURE AND CONSUMPTION

The loose influence of Scandinavia continued into the 1970s as many middle-range manufacturers continued to sell teak-finished furniture often as a vague reinterpretation of the real thing.

An interesting diversion in design terms, however, was the Toledo range produced by British company Younger Furniture from 1972. This collection relied on an adaptation of a Spanish style. Often photographed on ceramic tiles with accessories reminiscent of Spanish interiors, it offered consumers a link to the exotic, even if it was only a reminder of a fortnight's holiday on the Costa Brava.

One noteworthy example of an approach that seriously considered popular visual culture is the 1976 Renwick Gallery exhibition titled *Signs of Life: Symbols in the American City*. One of the sections was about the use of signs and symbols in the home (furnishings, decoration, architectural style, and details). Mock-ups of suburban interiors showed just how eclectic average American homes could be. A room that had examples of products and designs derived from Regency, Art Deco, Renaissance, and Georgian models, all in the same space, was a clear challenge to architects and designers, but offered a glimpse of the actual furnishings of a great many homes.

Quite similar as a symbol of contemporary visual culture, was the TV set of British director Mike Leigh's celebrated play *Abigail's Party* of 1977. The main living room was furnished with reproduction Breuer "Cesca" chairs, a mahogany-colored room divider, an orange leather-type suite on a wooden frame that was loosely Scandinavian in inspiration, and all this was complemented by an onyx and gilt framed coffee table. Again in this vein is the controversial American sitcom *All in the Family* (1971–9) about everyday people dealing with actual and often-sensitive issues. This series featured a wing chair of vaguely eighteenth-century style as the seat of the main, rather bigoted protagonist, Archie Bunker. The chair is now in the collection of the Smithsonian Museum along with that of his long-suffering wife. A fascinating example of the visual imagery of popular culture made permanent.

Another interesting case study of the various approaches to visual culture was the promotion of the American La-Z-Boy recliner. In 1970 and again in 1971 La-Z-Boy featured a Scrooge character in their advertisements running up to Christmas. The strapline explained the link with the well-known Dickensian character "Even Scrooge would have been happy with a La-Z-Boy!" The 1972 La-Z-Boy adverts changed and featured drawings in a Norman Rockwell style reflecting aspects of popular American culture. A little later, the adverts featured endorsements by American football quarterback Joe Namath in a variety of situations. This clearly made links with popular culture and the main male market for the chair. However, the identity of the chair with white Anglo-Saxon males was challenged by the company advert in *Ebony* magazine (December 1974) published monthly since 1945, with an image of a (Black) woman using the recliner in a sophisticated interior. This reference to changing cultures in advertisements was again demonstrated in a 1974 *House Beautiful* La-Z-Boy chair advertisement with an image of Uncle Sam as in his 1917 recruiting poster ("I want you") but this time he was reclining on the chair with the line "La-Z-Boy wants you to save energy." This was evidently an appeal to Americans to save energy during a worldwide energy crisis, as well as a reference to the comfort of the chair itself.

Whilst companies such as Herman Miller and Knoll developed a somewhat visually consistent corporate modernist market in the architect-led furnishing sector, the domestic furniture market remained wildly varied. The American Thomasville's 1970 advertisements for their Coronado range, for example, were based loosely on Spanish baroque originals while the 1972 Baker advertisement made references to eighteenth-century trade cards by describing the business as "Cabinet Makers." Finally, an introductory Canadian IKEA advertisement of 1977 was based on a comic magazine layout with sequential hand-drawn scenes of the progress of a purchase. These brief examples reflect the eclectic and un-homogenized nature of the visual culture of furniture.

1980–99: POSTMODERNISM

The variety and range of tastes associated with furniture remained as many of the major and minor styles of the 1980s were placed under the umbrella term of Postmodernism. This included versions of Modernism, eclectic mixes, and nostalgia. In 1981, for instance, the British Laura Ashley catalog was launched with a version of the English country house look. On the other hand, a taste for the individual and unusual was being met by businesses such as the Hollywood based Phyllis Morris whose outrageous and individualist furniture perfectly met the demands of Hollywood-lifestyle aspirants. A classic Postmodern image with its wit, irony, and deflation of a modernist icon is the 1994 image of the Eameses' recliner by graphic designer Alan Fletcher (1931–2006), who collaged various printed floral textile patterns onto the chair for the cover of the Italian magazine *Domus* (April 1994), founded in 1928 and mostly published monthly.

Modernism was not far away though. In 1983 Kartel advertised their plastic Bartoli chair and Tube Table shown in three different scene settings, namely, Traditional, Contemporary, and Country Kitchen, as if to capture the potential variety of moods. In 1990 the Haller Company in Japan showed an advertisement with full-length black-and-white images of the named designers Mario Bellini (1935–) and Antonio Citterio (1950–) standing next to their chairs. Modernism and the power of a name had not gone away.

In a completely different image, a 1997 advertisement for Stickley furniture showed a regular dining set superimposed on a background of the famous Flatiron building in New York. The caption reads "every piece [of furniture] an architectural gem for your home." However, during the 1990s the American Harden Furniture Company was still using images of aproned craftsmen in a variety of situations apparently visually reflecting Arts and Crafts ideals in a postmodern world.

The way that furniture from a few decades ago (sometimes called vintage) was used in films of the 1990s demonstrates something of the growing sophistication of visual culture when 1960s furniture can make a statement. For example, in the 1996 film *Mars Attacks!* there is a classic Eero Aarnio Ball chair and in the 1997 *Austin Powers* film the character Dr. Evil uses an Ox chair by Hans Wegner (1914–2007) and the Lips sofa by Salvador Dali (1904–89). An even more famous instance is the use of the 1968 Ovalia chair by Henrik Thor-Larsen (1932–) in the 1997 film *Men in Black*. The retro-futuristic images chime with both the viewers and the context.

The visual power of a chair is featured in the TV sitcom *Frasier* (1993–2004). The title character's Eames recliner chair in the smart Seattle apartment was in direct contrast to a worn and grubby recliner brought into the apartment by his father (Plate 30). Much was made of the contrast, both visually and emotionally. In a similar vein but as a documentary series from 1991, the British

"Signs of the Times" TV documentary and subsequent book by Nicholas Barker (1955–) and photographs by Martin Parr (1952–) exposed the relationship that the ordinary British person had with their furniture and furnishings. The result was a revealing and sometime humorous portrait of the taste of a country equally at home with the country house look, an Italian lifestyle feel, Nordic rusticity, or high-tech Modernism.

The broadcasting and publishing media were also responsible for an upsurge in the popularity of furnishings as a topic for all. Whether it was the Martha Stewart shows, IKEA's advertising pleas to "chuck out your chintz," reality television makeover programs, or any of the home magazines that flourished in the decade, there was an enormous interest in visualizing interior design, decoration, and furnishings from all groups of people. Visual culture also references changes in society. In 1994 the American Deutsch agency made a series of short advertising films for IKEA. One of its groundbreaking commercials showed two men shopping for a dining room table—the first time a gay couple had been depicted on an American TV spot. Other commercials in the campaign represent a recently divorced mother and a heterosexual couple with an adopted son.

Visualizing furniture *in extremis* is evident in Furniture Land South in Jamestown, North Carolina, where the retailer displays the largest tallboy in the United States. At a height of 185 feet (56 meters) this reproduction eighteenth-century style object stands outside the premises, not only as a statement of the business but also perhaps as an "ironic" sign of postmodern visualization.

2000S: THE DIGITAL AGE

In this digital age we are bombarded with images that make up our visual culture. In terms of furniture we see representations of objects and spaces in imagery via online magazines, web pages, blogs, films, etc. So whether our taste is retro, vintage, modern, or cutting edge there will be well-illustrated websites devoted to that topic. Despite this, the approach to talking about and marketing furniture has many similarities with the previous century. Promotion of furniture series with tenuous celebrity associations included the Elvis Range by Vaughan-Bassett Furniture Co. in 2002 that offered a "Love Me Tender" bed and a "Burning Love" heart-shaped mirror. In addition to Elvis's gaudier side, the lines named "Hollywood" and "Graceland" were planned to appeal to a wider array of fans. Having a point-of-sale display with an image of Elvis Presley (1935–77) and the legend "Elvis is in the building" it is not hard to see the connections between the visual, textual, and cultural. The theme continues with the Humphrey Bogart (2002) and Ernest Hemingway (2000) collections by Thomasville, while the contemporary actress Brooke Shields (1965–) was used to promote La-Z-Boy recliners and other products in 2010 TV and press advertisements particularly aimed at women with families.

Eclectic reinterpretation of furniture classics by well-known celebrities or designers in other fields includes Martha Stewart's (1941–) signature Lily Pond collection for Bernhardt & Co. in 2004 modeled after her shingle-style home in East Hampton on Long Island. Similarly, fashion designer Oscar de la Renta's (1932–2014) Century furniture collection of 2002 was a reinterpretation of classic styles based on eighteenth-century Regency and Chinese originals. Another example is the Laura Ashley (1925–85) range for the American Kincaid Company in the 2000s: "Exuding the gentle essence of European country cottage living" although offering eighteenth-century-inspired mahogany dining rooms and cream painted bedroom suites (Sturlyn n.d.).

In the twenty-first century, films continue to be an interesting source of furniture imagery but again often using classic or retro objects. The film *Down with Love* (2003) features the Saarinen womb chair but in baby pink upholstery, *Casino Royale* (2006) uses the steely Barcelona chair and Aeron chair, while the sets for *Sex and the City 2* (2010) were featured in *Elle Décor* magazine, with stills of studio shots and links to where to buy the furniture.

Placing branded furniture in television programs was nothing new and a great example is found in the 2000 TV show *Friends* (Episode 11, Series 6) called "The one with the apothecary's table." It features a striking product placement including a table by the company Pottery Barn, a US chain of home furnishers whose resulting sales were impressive. In computer games there was also an attempt to use furniture symbols. The *Sims3* (2009) series, for example, offers players virtual furniture to complete their virtual houses including a "Dr Pepper lips sofa in fushia" (*sic*). Salvador Dali would surely find this amusing.

IKEA are great exponents of the visual, whether it is the IKEA virtual furniture in the *Sims2* (2004), a life simulation video game, or the 2012 "Banksy style" street graffiti in Milan as part of the IKEA "People bring Design to Life" campaign. The employment of visual imagery that links to popular culture remains key to their strategy. Applications of photo-realistic imaging of objects on the web are also now part of the marketing armory of furnishers. The IKEA Company began to use computer-generated imagery (CGI) in 2005 with one image in the catalog. In 2010, the first "virtual room" was created and by 2013 around 12 percent of the images used in the catalog and website were CGI. As of 2014, 75 percent of product images (i.e., white background images) and 35 percent of non-product images across all IKEA communications are fully computer-generated (CG Society n.d.).

The use of augmented reality was introduced in the 2013 edition of the IKEA catalog. This allowed all interactive content to be "read" by scanning a symbol on the catalog with a mobile device. In 2014 the catalog included an app that puts an object into a real-time photographic image of the reader's individual space. Interestingly, IKEA, at least for the moment, continues to use its catalog as its main visual marketing tool. In 2013 the company printed 212 million copies of the IKEA catalog in twenty-nine languages and sixty-two editions (IKEA 2013) (Plate 31).

With over seven hundred million hits in a Google search for "furniture" (January 2015) the impact of the internet cannot be underestimated. Designboom, founded in 1999, is the world's first and most popular digital architecture and design magazine. Whether it is online magazines such as *Dezeen* (n.d.), the Martha Stewart *Living* magazine app, the amazing selection of videos on YouTube, or simply "The Chair Blog," in twenty years the web has become all but ubiquitous in the realm of visualizing furniture as nearly all else.

This brief journey through the many and various manifestations of the visual culture of twentieth-century furniture has confirmed the importance of the image itself, the role of the viewer, and the perception of the images; and through this, the power of cultural context in our engagement with furniture.[1]

CHAPTER NINE

Verbal Representations

ANJA BAUMHOFF

Verbal representations of furniture in twentieth-century culture have appeared in numerous forms such as radio programs, film, digital media, TV, novels, manuals, or in the context of photography.[1] Advertisements allow for a close analysis of taste, identity, lifestyle, or questions of gender, class, and ethnicity. They also highlight matters around consumption, social conventions, and customs and represent a wide variety of patterns of meaning. While this analysis will include audible sources it will also make use of printed advertising to complement the scarce audio files, which were rarely archived (Leech 1966; Reimann 2012: 483).

Because of the influence of material culture studies on the field of the decorative arts it is now common to use furniture as a means of investigating concepts such as order, identity, or consumption. Furniture offers numerous opportunities for analyzing human behavior, values, and thought because it functions on several levels at once—as a symbol, as part of the daily rituals performed in the home, and in connection with identity and taste formation. The commercial success of a piece of furniture depends on the preferences of the consumer, something experts like architects, designers, and all kinds of reformers have long tried to influence. Since the second half of the nineteenth century the number of publications dealing with interior design and housing has been on the rise, demonstrating the increasingly prominent role of tastemakers in a culture where the consumption of goods has become evermore important on a symbolic level. Shaping people's taste has become an important part of many professions, although no one can really say how influential these experts actually are.

Researching the verbal representation of furniture also reflects media history because new technical possibilities were swiftly taken up by the advertising industry. Radio distinguishes itself from other media because of its oral nature and the fact that people listen to it in a variety of circumstances. Often, though not always, the context determines the content. The reception of radio content varies a lot and listeners seldom concentrate fully on what is said and broadcast. It is well known that radio listeners pick up very little of the program's content. Radio advertisements thus fight for people's attention in the first place and entertainment is an important means to make people "tune in." In addition, radio spots for furniture are often characterized by short sentences and crystal clear messages (Fock 1992: 266–9). Radio adverts are thus rather limited in what they can achieve and today verbal furniture advertisements are used mainly in support of a brand or to announce a sale. While the radio provides a great way to reach people at home the internet offers new modes of communication with consumers. However, audio advertisements are still around because they are easy to make and cheap to produce, while pictures require more expertise, especially if 3D techniques become the new standard.

Advertising has come a long way and the experiences of the printed media also informed the development within the realm of the radio. By 1900 advertising was a well-established profession. Film and radio were still in their infancy and exhibitions were a popular way in which people could familiarize themselves with contemporary trends in furniture design. Newspapers and journals such as *Homes and Gardens*, *Good Housekeeping*, *Ideal Home*, *The Listener*, and *Picture Post* also spread information quickly. Despite this guidance most people preferred their interior to be one of various historical styles and reproduction furniture remained the backbone of the industry. Styles not only ranged broadly from the sixteenth to the late eighteenth century but also Arts and Crafts furniture was advertised and sold to those who could afford it. These period furniture designs reflected revivalism and demonstrated an interest in antiques. These choices were connected to concepts relating to the making of cultural capital, highlighting the buyers' concern about their perceived status (Bourdieu [1984] 2010). Because of the dominance of historical furniture styles and their sometimes hideous mixtures, reformers in England as well as on the Continent already began to target this disarray in the nineteenth century. The world exhibitions, starting with the Crystal Palace in England in 1851, played a key role in inspiring this reassessment. The early reformers intended not only to raise the standard of living but also people's taste as well to introduce true and lasting values into the homes of the nation—an endeavor that emerged in England, and other countries soon followed its lead.

One nation that was particularly enthusiastic about this reform was Germany and the man who exemplifies this best is the author, diplomat, and architect

Hermann Muthesius (1861–1927). Arriving in London in 1896 as a cultural attaché to the German embassy he set out to report in great detail about English architecture and design. His stay resulted in a three-volume work published in 1904/5 under the title *The English House* and became very influential. The book's importance is highlighted by the fact that it is still on the market and was recently reprinted.[2] By spreading the ideals of the English Arts and Crafts movement Muthesius influenced German taste profoundly. He much preferred English design to the dominant historicist style in his homeland. Muthesius particularly disliked the architecture of the late nineteenth century with its pretentious façades and overbearing ornamentation. From the Arts and Crafts he learned to emphasize function, a respect for materials, and the thought that less design is essentially good design. He also experienced the potential of the English Industrial Revolution.

Back in the German Reich he founded the Werkbund—the German Association of Craftsmen—a connection of artists, architects, designers, and industrialists. Muthesius used the Werkbund organization to argue in favor of mass production while many of his colleagues resisted the idea at the time and opted for a more individualistic path that would allow for greater artistic freedom. At the Werkbund exhibition in Cologne in 1914, these positions unforgettably clashed:

> Although the appearance of many of the products and buildings endorsed a predominantly functional aesthetic, there was nonetheless quite a profusion of styles and approaches on show: something of the neo-Baroque was evident [...], (as well as) reminiscences of Jugendstil [...], Neoclassicism [...], and Expressionism [...], all of which contrasted strongly with the clean, functional, modern lines of Walter Gropius's Administration Building and Model Factory.
>
> (Woodham 1997: 23)

This stylistic eclecticism provided the background for a heated debate about artistic freedom and mass production and the future direction of industrial design and finally of the Werkbund itself (Schwartz 1996). The young Werkbund member Walter Gropius (1883–1969) was at this point in time still in favor of artistic individualism and consequently opposed to Muthesius. He chose to follow the Belgian architect Henry van de Velde (1863–1957) who was heading the opposition. Later van de Velde became vital in establishing Gropius as his successor in Weimar and thus as director of the Bauhaus. Ten years after the Werkbund debate Gropius would finally change his mind when he gave out the slogan: "art and technology—a new unity"—knowing very well that the "new unity" was not so new after all. While Muthesius's views took time to spread they did shape German modern design profoundly.

Besides Muthesius there were other reformers such as the writer Ferdinand Avenarius (1856–1923), founder of the journal *Der Kunstwart* (Heidelberg Historic Literature—digitized 1900). In his text for the exhibition Volkstümliche Ausstellung für Haus und Herd (Popular Exhibition for Home and Hearth) Avenarius presented his "Ten Commandments" on how to furnish one's home (Avenarius 1900: 341–4; Muthesius 1974: 157). The matter at hand, he explained, was not only dear to his heart but sacred since it concerned the family and thus the heart of the nation. Interestingly enough his first commandment concerned functionality. "Richte Dich zweckmäßig ein!" (Furnish your home purposefully!), he demanded. Furnish it so that you can afford it and make it reflect your personality and your style, he continued. He strongly recommended not buying imitations and particularly disliked birch wood that was painted to look like oak. If unable to afford oak furniture, he suggested buying pine instead and letting it look like pine and nothing else but pine.

Authenticity and individual choice are concepts that are already apparent in his text although he does not use this terminology. The moral attitude that would figure prominently in the design and architectural debates of the twentieth century is evident here as well as in many contemporary Arts and Crafts advertisements. The latter showed a tendency toward austerity and helped to pave the way to the modern ideology of apparently "honest" and "truthful" furniture and architecture (Figure 9.1). This outlook together with the idea of the honesty of materials—a concept dear to the likes of Le Corbusier and Gropius—was an idea that had been around since the nineteenth century. Considering that Modernism fought vehemently against nineteenth-century attitudes toward architecture and design this is remarkable. In many ways Avenarius captured the spirit of functionalism in his early Ten Commandments. But contrary to reformers like Avenarius and Muthesius many furniture buyers on the Continent preferred the more cheerful Art Nouveau style to the Arts and Crafts.

Also at the turn of the century a book from Sweden started its journey around the world and influenced the taste of the Continent profoundly. Its legacy can still be recognized today in IKEA design. The painter Carl Larsson (1853–1919) and his wife Karin (née Bergöö, 1859–1928) published their bestselling book *Ett hem* (Our Home) in 1899, translated into German under the title *Haus in der Sonne*. It sold 40,000 copies in the first few months. In it Larsson depicted family life with his wife Karin and their children. His watercolors exhibited a simple, colorful, and cheerful version of the Arts and Crafts style that could easily include period furniture. It was a paradigmatic change and suggested to the fascinated public that interior design was not necessarily a matter of decency and status but could also be regarded as a place for creativity and for individual choices. Swedish designers were admired all over Europe, especially after 1930, enjoying the reputation of being:

FIGURE 9.1 Schaub, Die Welt am laufenden Band, 1932–4(?). BHA Inv. no. 2011/73.29.20. Photograph courtesy of Bauhaus Archiv Berlin.

leaders in the field [...]. It was with admiration and not a little envy that British Modernists walked around the site of the Stockholm Exhibition of 1930, and with a sense of resignation that British critics acknowledged the superiority of the Swedish pavilion over the British at the Paris Exposition Universelle seven years later.

(Naylor 1990: 163, 171)

A compatible relationship between design and the crafts, as well as the integration of both into society, made the situation in Sweden unique.

Britain had its own discourse on interior design, which accelerated once the Ideal Home Exhibition series, starting in 1908, marked a heightened interest in styles and inspired new forms of decoration. The *Daily Mail* explained that "all the world and her husband" came to these exhibitions, which had been set up with the idea in mind of "principally assisting married folk and their families. It has been felt that no home can be really ideal unless it contains one man, one woman, and, if possible, one baby, or else a good substitute" (Ryan 1997: 26, 28). Alongside the home products the exhibitions liked to display interiors from other cultures partly to demonstrate how advanced the national design was (32). The 1926 exhibition, for example, showed "Old Kitchens of the Nations." Besides England the examples concerned Sweden, Spain, Holland, Denmark, and France and presented rural traditional kitchens. "In the catalogue the French kitchen was characterized as being overfull of furniture, while the Danish kitchen was noted as being very bright and gay" (49). The American kitchen displayed characteristics of the Shaker style and provided a contrast to the other ones because of its modern features.

Meanwhile, on the Continent, French design was conquered by Art Nouveau, which was followed by Art Deco. The Art Deco style developed before the First World War and had its high point in the 1920s only to be superseded by the sleek International Style. But its influence on French furniture design was limited since the modern movement was international and socialist in outlook. The moral implications of socialist design entailed that furniture had to be affordable, easy to clean, and user-friendly. Because the modern movement operated in a political climate that was critical of these ideals it had to be "converted into 'moderne' in order that it should be acceptable" (Greenhalgh 1990a: 163, 81, 53).

Since the turn of the century German design was slowly improving in shape and form. Around 1910 the Arts and Crafts exhibition took place at the Paris Salon d'Automne. Thirteen rooms were displayed of which twelve were done by German designers, all of whom were members of the Vereinigung für Angewandte Kunst (Munich Union for the Applied Arts), among them well-known names such as Bruno Paul (1874–1968) and Richard Riemerschmid (1868–1957). People carefully assessed the artifacts on display and came to a favorable conclusion. German products became more desirable, saleable, and popular and that resulted in a heightened competition with other European designers. The furniture industry became more international as well, a development that reflected the worldwide appeal of Art Deco. Germany, however, remained slightly distant from Art Deco since this fun-loving style did not carry a lot of "meaning." Modernism indeed had other lectures on offer for the country of Goethe and Schiller and, soon to come, Hitler.

England meanwhile focused on mass production while trying to uphold the spirit of craftsmanship. In Sweden, however, the Arts and Crafts ideal was put into practice with more ease, as the success of Swedish products in the 1950s and 1960s demonstrates. Here ideological questions mattered less and thus an aesthetic, as well as pragmatic, approach was taken. This resulted in an implementation of the Arts and Crafts ideal that went hand in hand with an efficient housing policy of the Swedish Social Democratic government. The fact that Swedish design managed to integrate itself in a unique way into society made its example difficult to copy and England could not keep up with this success.

Obviously there was a gap between the choices of the ordinary furniture buyer and the intentions of architects and designers who were trying to modernize the home and its interiors. Public taste was difficult to improve even though there were countless attempts to do so all over Europe. The Viennese architect Adolf Loos (1870–1933) was among those educators who had long argued in favor of Modernism in his many pamphlets and articles of which "Ornament and Crime" (1908) is the most prominent one (Stewart 2000: 173). Even writers and philosophers such as Walter Benjamin (1892–1940), Berthold Brecht (1898–1956), and Karl Kraus (1874–1936) commented on the design developments (Benjamin 1982: 292). Furniture slowly deserved to become part of the *feuilleton* culture, which eventually led to a build-up of design collections. This was the time when the American art historian Alfred H. Barr (1902–81) visited Europe and went to see the Bauhaus. Barr became the founding director of the Museum of Modern Art in New York, and this trip motivated him to break with tradition and include product design into the new art museum. Simultaneously, art historian Sigfried Giedion (1888–1968) wrote about the changes in interior design (Giedion 1929) and started to prepare his significant book on mechanization (Giedion 1948). Like Barr he was an acquaintance of Bauhaus founder Walter Gropius and all three of them became important supporters who helped Bauhaus-Modernism to finally "take command" (Giedion 1948).

The impetus with which Modernism came along provoked a lot of resistance especially where functionality was involved. While many of the early bourgeois reformers originally aimed their polemics at the middle classes the Modernists now tried to include the lower classes as well. Affordable housing, a new kind of functional interior design, rationalization of housework, fresh air, and sunlight became the key components. The young Bauhaus designer Marcel Breuer (1902–81) might also have favored classlessness when he designed the cantilever chair "Wassily," which used fewer materials and therefore could have become an affordable chair. He promoted it with an image of a faceless woman who wore one of the beautiful masks from Oskar Schlemmer's (1888–1943) stage play. Her anonymity communicated the idea that she was representing the species rather than an individual person with a distinctive face. The chair was a beautiful translation of the ideal of functionality and consumer usage into product design.

Advertising was still in its infancy at the time and the Bauhaus opened a department for it in the mid-1920s. The young Herbert Bayer (1900–1985) would head it and later became the artistic director of the renowned Dorland advertising agency in Berlin (Plate 32). Most Bauhaus products were promoted in an austere and minimalist style. Everything should be designed with its use in mind and no ornament was required to decorate this functionalist dream. This steel-and-glass type of aesthetic contrasted with the mainstream of the profession where few furniture makers "sought to clear away the Victorian legacy" (Denby 1971: 34) and most manufacturers still advertised the company name with a few tangible models. Others used multiple images jam-packed into advertisements without much text. These collages were simple to produce, inexpensive, and mostly done in-house. Their purpose remained to convey factual information that could be grasped at a glance.

Exhibitions remained the best tool for people to experience various styles of living. One example for this was the exhibition in Weimar in 1923, which featured the newly built "Haus am Horn" with its radical interior design. It created a lot of dispute. The art critic Paul Westheim (1886–1963) wrote in the journal *Kunstblatt*:

> Three days in Weimar and one can never look at a square again for the rest of one's life. [...] The ultimate of Bauhaus ideals: the individual square. Talent is a square, genius an absolute square. The "Stijl" people have put on a protest exhibition in Jena—they claim to possess the only true squares.
> (Wingler 1986: 69)

In Britain and France, meanwhile, Art Deco offered a more consumer-friendly style. Film was the medium that popularized it, quickly stimulating exhibition designers to create interior settings that would stir people's imagination. Three-dimensional display clearly triumphs over print when it comes to furniture. Art Deco influenced not only the style of the visual arts but also of architecture, fashion as well as product design between 1910 and 1939. It originated in France and came to represent the glamor of the golden 1920s in America as well. Its modern form showed fine craftsmanship and was decorated with rich materials. It embodied extravagance, luxury, enthusiasm, and faith in social and technological progress.

Holland cultivated its own modern movement. The De Stijl group, in combination with neoplasticism, was a driving force in the early twentieth century. Piet Mondrian, one of the most prominent protagonists of abstract art, coined the term neoplasticism to characterize his paintings. He divided the canvas into horizontal and vertical lines and preferred primary colors. By leaving his paintings without a frame they could connect with the surrounding white walls and become an architectural element of the room. As De Stijl and neoplasticism was more radical and advanced it had a profound influence on the Bauhaus. The success of De Stijl came not only through works of art or its many pamphlets and texts (De Stijl had its own journal by the same name as did the Bauhaus) and exhibitions but through commissions. The Rietveld Schröder House in Utrecht serves as a supreme case of a highly influential monument for modern architecture with its fabulous and colorful interior design.[3] It is one of the most radical examples of classical Modernism of the period. An example of similarly radical design can be found in Dessau where the Bauhaus erected several buildings. They were widely published, filmed, and open to the public. With it the Bauhaus attempted to create the living conditions for the New Man—the ultimate aim of all the Bauhaus' endeavors (Baumhoff 2009: 198; Keim 2012: 149).

While the Bauhaus aimed to create the new architecture for the new man it essentially reached backward in time to the idea of the total work of art and the Gothic cathedral. The Bauhaus Manifesto explained: "The ultimate aim of all visual arts is the complete building!" (Wingler 1986: 39). This was a revolutionary statement in that it subjected all art, including the Arts and Crafts, in support of architecture. Stylewise it focused the color palette on primary colors and Bauhaus advertisements were real eye-catchers because of their difference to the conventional commercials.

While neither De Stijl nor the Bauhaus used much film or radio technology just yet, broadcasting did increase after the First World War, even though radio advertisements were still sporadic in the early days of the media. Picture advertisements remained the most common source of information. After 1933 a radio (Volksempfänger) wireless set was subsidized and widely distributed so that the radio had become part of every German household after the Second World War (Marßolek and von Saldern 1989: 382). Other European countries showed a similar development.

Listeners were influenced not only by commercials but also by advisory programs of which quite a few were aimed at housewives: radio programs such as "radio hour" (*Funkstunde*), for example, informed women about "Hauseinrichtung in England und bei uns" (Interior Decor in England and at Home), or about topics like "Die enge Wohnung" (The Small Flat), or "Genie und Alltag: der schöpferische Mensch im Dienste der Hauswirtschaft" (Genius and the Everyday: Creativity in the Service of the Household Economy) (Lacey 1996: 66). The radio also reported on exhibitions like Heim und Technik (Home and Technology) in Munich in September 1929:

In 21 ideal flats the exhibition displayed the latest architectural designs, installation of amenities, and [...] labor-saving technology. The remit of the exhibition and of the radio programs which it influenced was to bridge the gap perceived between the advanced state of the technological infrastructure of the world at large and the backward, unreformed state of most private homes.

(Lacey 1996: 153)

Radio as a medium connected the public with the private domain and was naturally susceptible to political influence. It made women a primary target who would soon support Hitler's rise to power in great numbers (Bridenthal 1984). Radio was thus an important means for infiltrating the private sphere even though topics such as "how to decorate your home" seemed harmless. But they helped pave the way for political influence. Historian Paul Betts concludes:

Whereas the radio was exploited by the Nazis as an instrument of radical collectivization and accelerated social modernization, its housing was conversely stylized as a familiar emblem of social stability and private pleasure.

(2004: 45)

The usage of a novel medium does not inevitably reflect back on an advanced style of life.

Modernism's challenge began slowly to fade once open-minded parts of the middle classes started to embrace the design. An example of this is Erwin Piscator (1893–1966), a friend of the poet Bertholt Brecht and director of the Berliner Volksbühne, the "people's stage" (Droste, Ludewig, and Bauhuas Archiv 2001: 74–80). His ultra-modern home displays a clear segregation between the man's room and the woman's bedroom. His room has sports facilities in it—a sack filled with sand for boxing exercise in the morning—while the woman's bedroom is characterized by a dressing table and a beautiful mirror. His beauty was more or less internal—health and fitness—while hers was external and makeup related and thus reflects some of the gender stereotypes of the period. The contrast of this kind of interior design to the average bourgeois household was stark and underlined that he belonged to a new species, the New Man, which Modernism tried to bring about. Piscator appears as an incarnation of this concept. The modern interior design of his apartment thus provided another stage for the theatre producer in that it framed him in celluloid.

Today it is difficult to assess the impact modern design had at the time but historian Helmut Lethen points out that many people experienced "the immediate confrontation with modernity as a freezing shock" (Lethen 2002: ix). Broad public rejection and a certain exclusivity made it interesting for a small number of artists and writers who could afford it and to whom it provided an aura of distinction. While individuals played an important role in making modern design acceptable, exhibitions also continued to play a key role. One of the most interesting furniture displays of the interwar years was exhibited at the Weissenhof estate in 1927 in Stuttgart. The international exhibition showcased the best avant-garde homes with the most recent interior design trends and generated a lot of publicity. Here the Dutch architect Mart Stam (1899–1986) displayed the first tubular steel furniture. The cantilever chair was designed to be mass produced but because the public denounced it as "cold," tubular steel chairs became an icon for the upper-middle classes. They could afford it at a time when they were still handmade.

For almost half a century Modernism was rejected by the masses despite the many pamphlets that promised them improved and affordable living conditions. Instead the lower classes aspired to the nineteenth-century bourgeois lifestyle with its heavy drapery and dark wooden furniture, which seemed to elevate them above their class. Thus it is no surprise that Le Corbusier's (1887–1965) request to construct a house like a "machine for living in" did not inspire much enthusiasm. The lack of coziness was only one issue among many. As Tim Benton put it, modernist ideology did not fulfill the basic needs of the user: functionalism "was the key flaw in the nightmare that was Modernism" (Benton 1990: 40).[4]

Advertisements, both aural and printed, rarely reflected these discussions since their aim never changed: to motivate people to buy. But the question remains: how could a style that few people liked come to dominate the design of the twentieth century? One reason is connected to the shake up of the Second World War, when people wished to distance themselves from the past. Changing the look of one's home was one of the means that helped to achieve that—at least in Germany. Britain, however, as the winner of the war, remained in most parts committed to furniture of the traditional kind. Only slowly did Modernism establish itself here too as the dominant paradigm (Marcus 1998: 7) by embracing the International Style: an anonymous kind of style—the style beyond all styles characterized by materials such as glass, concrete, and steel.

While Scandinavian furniture developed along similar lines it never seemed so reduced to its bare essentials. It did not require any ideology or manifesto to explain its intentions. Scandinavian design appeared as cheerful, natural, simple, and beautiful. However, these traits hardly influenced the advertisements. Visually the furniture trade remained one of the more traditionalist areas in most countries but Scandinavia until the 1960s (Edwards 1994).

In England the public was sensitized to interior design debates when Modernism emerged on the horizon and the new style was experienced as foreign (Holder 1990: 123–44). The BBC harbored reservations toward European Modernism and many listeners shared this sentiment. The Director of British Ideal Furniture Co. Ltd. wrote about the broadcast of a countryman's visit to the British Industries Fair in 1935:

He is supposed to be in the furniture section and remarked that he is glad to see exhibitors are showing the old-fashioned wooden furniture instead of modern steel, referring to the latter as tables which look as if they going to collapse, and chairs which are not comfortable to sit in.[5]

More complaints like this were made.[6] Because of sentiments like this one functionalism seemed to be a sensible design for the poor and it found its way into the Utility scheme during the Second World War (Attfield 1999). Thus Modernism became associated with affordable furniture for those who could afford nothing else.

Italy, however, was in a different situation. By the end of the 1940s an Italian modern furniture movement had emerged. In the 1950s women's and home magazines celebrated the benefits of the fitted kitchen and praised the new labor-saving household appliances. "The 'ideal home' of those boom years—unlike its counterpart of a decade earlier, which was much more concerned with the basic necessities of everyday life—now contained a version of the American 'dream kitchen' as seen in Hollywood films and American TV soap operas" (Sparke 1990: 190). However, the domestic products associated with the economic miracle and the "'heroic' years of Italian modern design were aimed at an essentially bourgeois market, both at home and abroad" (190). Increasingly this concept of modernity was connected to luxury with furnishings dominating the scene. Its success helped Italy to enter into foreign markets. "As American-style consumerism became further entrenched within Italian society, items of furnishing turned increasingly into fetishized commodities rather than simple elements within the interior landscape" (191). This can be seen in magazines of the time like *Stile Industria* or the 1950s exhibitions at the Milan Triennale in 1951 and 1954. Here the sculptural values and the aesthetic pleasure played a bigger role than their function. A particular middle-class style emerged that turned the Italian design of those years into prestigious artifacts for people with money and perceived taste. In this light it may not be surprising that Italy saw the emergence of the counter-design or anti-design movement in the late 1960s. While precious design objects had helped to carry modern design and the lifestyle of consumption into the domestic as well as the foreign markets, young designers—many of whom were architects by training—now turned to a more holistic approach. Environmental aspects became more important and with it a utopian vision of design. But this tendency ultimately remained exclusive.

While Italy saw the rise of the modern furniture movement in the late 1940s, architects and designers in Germany, the Netherlands, and France were discussing furniture in the context of the minimum standard of living. The Second World War had made this issue urgent because of a dramatic shortage of materials. In England the Wartime Social Survey Unit for the Board of Trade recommended a minimum standard for furniture. This included half an easy chair per person, one-third of a wardrobe for each member of the household, half a chest of drawers, a bed, and a straight chair (Edwards 2005: 235). This did not help to increase the popularity of the modern style. The company that finally managed to give Modernism a better image was IKEA. It turned it into the ultimate style in the sense of the Bauhaus: a style that is no style any more but seems to consist of pure function. Unsurprisingly Britain resisted its lure for a very long time. Only in 1987 did IKEA finally come to England, after it had already made it to Switzerland, Germany, France, Saudi Arabia, Japan, the United States, and Australia, among others. By that time its founder Ingvar Kamprad (1926–) had already retired (Woodham 2004: 209).

Once IKEA expanded into the continental market it began with Switzerland and moved from there to West Germany. It was not accidental that the firm preferred the West to the East. The German Democratic Republic (GDR) was off limits to IKEA even though most companies had resumed their advertising activities soon after the war and no one had the intention of building a wall just yet. Manufacturers in the East showcased their products in newspapers and magazines, along with the popular direct-mail advertising, to reach out to consumers. GDR commercials tried to build a connection to familiar prewar products and brands while the West embarked on a love affair with American culture. In both German states: "The idealized '50s home represented both continuity with and a break from the Nazi past" (Betts 2004: 228).

In East Germany home product advertising was stimulated by the establishment of the Handelsorganisation (State Trade Organization)—the so-called Free Stores. Otherwise the Socialist Unity Party of Germany (SED), which governed the GDR for forty-three years, put consumer needs last. Consequently, "the neglect of consumer goods production also meant that little attention was paid to advertising" (Kaminsky 2007: 263). However, the uprising of 1953 sent a wake-up call to the Communist Party and put living conditions on the political agenda. "Improving individual consumption" was the new slogan and soon the first journal for advertisers appeared. *Neue Werbung* (New Advertising) was supposed to draw attention to the achievements of the socialist state and communicate them to the public (264). Henceforth it was more a political organ than a journal for product advertising. Seldom were enough products available and even the less well-liked ones always landed in the hands of a needy shopper.

But East German designers had their own perspective on things. A reference work for advertising described the differences between socialist and capitalist advertising from their perspective this way:

Socialist advertising truthfully informs consumers about the real benefits of goods and services without the exaggeration typical of capitalist advertising.

> It does not manipulate consumers by trying to convince them that a given product offers additional benefits, such as an increase in prestige. Customers are given information intended to facilitate a fact-based purchasing decision. They should not allow themselves to get carried away by emotionally driven impulse purchases that they may later regret.
>
> (Kaminsky 2007: 265)

However, many East German consumers would have liked to get carried away more often.

In 1959 the GDR aired its first TV commercial on the two official channels. Under the name *TausendTeleTips* (One Thousand Television Tips), over four thousand commercials were broadcast from that year until advertising was eventually banned in 1976 (Kaminsky 2007: 265). Considering the social, political, and economic circumstances it is surprising that the GDR had advertisements at all. The true reason was that advertising "was to provide tangible proof of the advantages of socialism over capitalism" (Gries 2003: 216). Despite the party's promises and gradual improvements in supply, the GDR economy never produced enough goods to satisfy the demand. What remained were products that were advertised but that were hardly ever available. Therefore one advertising agency was enough and it was part of the central bureau of the SED (231). Thus the party could use the advertisements as an alternative form of political propaganda. East German furniture from the 1960s and 1970s was characterized by the slogan that functionality was beautiful and hence cozy, a supposition that only started to ring true in the early 1980s (Godau 1994: 109).

Because of the great consumer demand little advertising of interior design was done. In the context of a housing shortage it was a privilege to move into one of the new buildings that the country started to erect in the 1970s consisting of prefabricated building blocks (*Plattenbau*). Meanwhile GDR radio tried to educate the consumer and improve their taste, an endeavor complemented in print journals such as *Kultur im Heim* (Culture in the Home). The party tried hard to turn its population into a more cultured one while at the same time avoiding so-called individual aberrations of different tastes (Marßolek and von Saldern 1989: 371).

In West Germany the Werkbund was revived after the Second World War and continued its work to promote *Die Gute Form* (Good Form). This was necessary indeed because a poll claimed that 60 percent of West Germans preferred a style called "Gelsenkirchner Baroque," which was the favorite style of the petit bourgeoisie of the 1930s (Betts 2004: 94). The 1950s saw another style become very popular: the organic "Nierentisch" design, a kidney-shaped table, usually small and on three legs decorated with various colors or patterns. Clearly this was a rejection of functionalism and a popular vote for a more playful and cheerful design. It also implied a rejection of the Werkbund's "good design" philosophy, which in turn made the Werkbund push harder in promoting what they called good design—modern, "honest," and functional. In the following years the Werkbund supported the opening of several design schools (*Werkkunstschulen*) and started to publish the journal *Baukunst und Werkform* as well as *Werk und Zeit*. In this way it continued to spread the gospel of "good design" and spearheaded the creation of design centers to promote their ideas. In addition it tried to influence the public with exhibitions and showrooms (96). Despite their success many members of the Werkbund felt disappointed. While they intended to change society they came to realize that they had merely changed the face of consumer goods (97). The marketplace had the power to absorb their moral intentions and for a long time it seemed that not much of it entered into the mainstream. However, in the long run the Werkbund, and its offspring the German Design Council, influenced the design of companies such as Bosch, WMF, Rasch, and Braun as well as the Bauhaus and its successor the Ulm Institute of Design. And Ulm had a strong impact on the design philosophy of Jonathan Ives from Apple.

The Ulm Institute of Design (1953–68) aimed to develop a rationalist design philosophy in architecture, interior design, and related areas to implant its vision of social reform (Selle 1994: 290). By employing a scientific approach they created a new way to advance design. Part of this was a distinct new form of product photography (Figure 9.2).

FIGURE 9.2 Hans Gigelot, Radio, 1955. HfG Ulm. BHA, Inv. no. 85234. Photograph courtesy of Bauhaus Archiv Berlin.

Comparing Ulm's product photography for Braun with the more typical photography style used to advertise other 1950s consumer [goods, A.B.] [...] helps illuminate the uniqueness of Ulm's aesthetic strategies. Whereas the conventional Nierentisch design commodity was almost always pictured with bold dynamic lines, often situated in domestic living rooms with smiling women on hand to "harmonize" the ambience of consumer excitement, the Braun products were patently de-fetishized, featured alone against cool, unalluring blank backgrounds in frontal, shadowless "still lives" that accentuated the functional product designs themselves. Rarely did these ads suggest cosy domestic settings; smiling housewives were never on hand to "sensualize" the products. [...] Ulm's work for Braun was a bold venture in engineering a corporate identity based on the denial of commodity fetishism and the more "secular" qualities of sober functionalism and technical performance.

(Betts 2004: 163–5)

One company that took some of these lessons up to popularize them was the European furniture dealer Interlübke. In the 1970s the company advertised the slogan "Interlübke turns living at home into a great experience," which referred to their "Environment 121." The process of living should move into the forefront. The byline was translated into Dutch, French, and English as "an event" and as "a completely new experience" (Möller 1981: 30–1). This straightforward language is typical for furniture retailers with the exception of IKEA, a company that has the courage to play with words. Their word creations helped to increase their image as a creative enterprise and they managed to appear as something other than just another furniture retailer (Schöberl 2005; Vogel 2008: 127). Interlübke, however, did not want to alienate its customers with terms they might misunderstand and therefore stuck to a no-nonsense approach like most furniture companies in Europe. One newspaper called their style "Mondrian-like," which of course ennobled their products (Möller 1981: 31). While their advertising aimed at the upper-middle class it depicted a kind of modern design that was nevertheless traditional in style and content. Depictions of gender roles underline the conventionality of this approach. The Interlübke advert pictured women in white, light green, and pink colors in the kitchen, living room, or bedroom while men were shown behind a desk in a brown and white work-like context (41). The company advertised its furniture as a system. Their arrangements represented regularity and equilibrium, and the company promised their customers that with Interblübke good taste was guaranteed. Aesthetically it was almost a "total system" (43). Like IKEA the Interlübke adverts did not depict furniture but rather an environment. While IKEA assumed that people would combine their furniture with other items, Interlübke aimed to style the whole living space. This gave IKEA a certain openness that companies like Interlübke did not promote.

Today IKEA uses multimedia to advertise its products and issues a new catalog every year. It is so far the only furniture catalog that is mentioned in the mainstream media. It is reviewed in papers such as the *Guardian* or the *Süddeutsche Zeitung* and was recently assessed by the distinguished literary critic Hellmuth Karasek (1934–2015).[7] This move underlined the company's appeal in Germany, which is IKEA's biggest market.

IKEA is common in all European states. In 2015 it entertained the British public by playing with the term "notebook" under the title "Experience the Power of a BookBook" (IKEA Singapore 2014). The Bookbook is the IKEA catalog, which is treated in this advertisement as a serious competitor of the notebook to demonstrate its advantages against the digital "book." This came at a time when sales in eBooks are dropping. The firm is clearly aware of the newest social and cultural trends.

The intelligent IKEA advertisements differ greatly from those of other furniture manufacturers or retailers. A typical example of the informative but dull advertisements of other companies can be demonstrated with a representative example of a big local furniture dealer from Berlin. In a radio commercial for Möbel Hübner the humor is simplistic to reach a large audience.

Paul: Yes, yes Pauline. We shall go to Möbel-Hübner. They sell nice furniture cheaply.

Pauline: You see, Paul. This is the only matter where we shall always agree: Going to Möbel-Hübner has always been the right thing to do.

Paul: Quite right. Their buyers are always 100% satisfied!

Pauline: Mr. Hübner is a really nice guy, don't you think?

Paul: Absolutely. He is really giving his all and his staff too: helping you to purchase the right thing, showing you around.

Pauline: And the variety.

Paul: And their low prices!

Pauline: And the free delivery.

Paul: And the easy way to pay.

Pauline: And their wonderful service when they deliver everything for free.

Paul: How right you are.[8]

Here the company's name is frequently repeated to make it more memorable. While the message is clear the overall impact is mind numbing. Other IKEA competitors, however, were even more reductive in their advertisements. Generally television and radio marketing tends to be based on the same jingle and on similar strategies (Schöberl 2005: 38). This approach is not only less expensive but is also believed to increase brand recognition.

IKEA uses smarter ways to advertise its products and engages in all kinds of media. In 1997 the company announced that it considered the home as the most important place in the world. This hit a nerve in England. Especially popular was the "Not For Sale" sign that the slogan depicted. IKEA successfully sent out the message that it understood the importance of the private sphere and wanted to help improve it and not merely make a profit. This is typical for IKEA advertisements (Jungblut 2006; Mazur 2013: 29). Entertainment, storytelling, and jokes in their commercial promotion are the firm's hallmarks. But jokes can easily be offensive so this kind of advertisement is not without risk and needs to adjust style and content to the various countries. Because IKEA is everywhere on the globe except in Africa this is a huge task.

IKEA's multimedia campaign included films such as "Dinner with the Limps." Here IKEA presents an Asian family inviting other children home. The mother talks casually about her needs in this specific situation and it becomes clear: it is not the company that is the expert but the user.

IKEA's film advertising campaigns in Europe deploy pop music and children to attract the buyer. In "Playing with my Friends," a French music video by IKEA from 2012, the music's lyrics were written and composed specifically for this 2.6 minute dance film. The short film starts with a dreamlike section in the kitchen where the girl plays grown-up and starts to set the table; she is expecting guests. They enter one by one and each child has a gigantic toy in tow. A strange little party starts with a funny role reversal. The kids take the lead and the large toys follow. Meanwhile the teddy, the robot, and the giant ape help her to prepare the party and to cook the food before they burst into an ecstatic dance. The film ends with the giant toys sitting down at the dinner table together with the kids. The camera then moves to a mirror on the wall that reflects the scene and suddenly reveals that these toys are actually family members in disguise. This film moves away from the idea of selling furniture and appliances and indicates that IKEA wants to be more than just a furniture retailer. While it is unmistakably an IKEA film, the movie blurs the genre between advertisement and entertainment. It is something adults and children could enjoy together and watch just for fun. It makes it harder to doubt IKEA's good intentions.

Only in Germany are the advertisements somewhat less playful. A no-nonsense way of imparting information depicts grown-ups explaining to the observer how to organize life in tiny spaces. Here IKEA prefers to emphasize its good carbon footprint. They try to hit the common ground in each country.

The abovementioned films and adverts have one thing in common—they treat adults and children in a similar fashion. Their main aim is to target families of all shapes and sizes. This way IKEA reaches out to young consumers who often have a say in the buying process. Going to IKEA has become a family adventure where kids try out the furniture as well. And the company tends to address mature consumers by appealing to their children first. This makes IKEA more entertaining and gives them an excuse to treat grown-ups in a harmless, seemingly noncommercial fashion. It makes the company look less profit-making and businesslike than it really is. With this trick IKEA is positioning itself as a kind of fellow family member; someone people feel connected to—a brand that is attached to intimate family memories. IKEA tries to establish a bond so that people will shop there in the future. This is underlined by their inhouse installations, which strive to create the impression of a "lived in" environment:

> We understand how important the knowledge of home furnishing is. How homes look, how homes feel. The experienced photographers at IKEA have been working with the interior designers on re-creating this feel for fifteen to twenty years, some of them. We needed to translate that knowledge over to the 3D artists who were tech-savvy but in some cases coming directly from school. We needed them to understand the kind of feel we wanted the images to convey. It was very hard at the beginning.
>
> (CG Society n.d.)

In its psychology IKEA's marketing is very advanced and unlike any other company, let alone any furniture brand.

Being globally successful means that IKEA sells the same items everywhere despite the differences in tradition and taste in various countries. It is not located in a specific place and therefore pays hardly any tax (Hentschel 2015). But there is one big difference in comparison with Google or Starbucks. IKEA is a company that projects a distinct national image. Its brand colors are taken from the Swedish flag and it does not sell design—it sells Swedish design. While IKEA celebrates ethnic diversity and different lifestyles it nonetheless conveys the impression of a set identity. In addition to desirable products and competitive prices IKEA set up restaurant areas (Småland) to provide cheap fast food that increases the attraction for its customers. And since the rise of DIY culture the fact that its furniture needs to be assembled seems to be a welcome challenge. All of this turns shopping at IKEA into a specific experience.[9]

But there are examples that prove that selling furniture could be done differently and that word of mouth is the ultimate way of promoting something new. The Irish furniture designer Eileen Gray (1878–1976) demonstrates the point. Her work counts among the most advanced furniture design of the twentieth century. She was a friend of the architect Le Corbusier and like him spent most of her life in France. Because her furniture did not aim at the mass market she hardly ever advertised it. Through her connections with the rich and famous she got the chance to design furniture first in an Art Deco style and later with modern minimalist elegance. The materials she used were valuable and expensive. She started out with exotic lacquer. From there she moved on to design complete apartments, for instance that of Madame Lévy in Paris. Here she did everything from lamps to carpets to wallpaper, including the furniture, thus creating a total work of art. For this apartment she built the famous Bibendum chair, the Serpent chair, and the Pirogue Boat Bed and decorated the surrounding walls with tribal art. After this became a triumph she opened a small shop in Paris under the name Jean Desert where she exhibited her work. She also took part in national furniture exhibitions but never had her designs mass produced nor did she try to increase her sales by advertising her products. Her enormous success only becomes apparent today. After almost one hundred years many of her designs are still on the market—for example, the table E1027, which has turned into a mass product and currently sells on the internet for about one hundred euros. This is an example that furniture does not necessarily need to be advertised. It does not need to be non-elitist or to be explicitly designed for mass consumption to become a widespread commodity. Similar to Le Corbusier, her furniture is nowadays widely available and represents the style of classical Modernism together with names like Mies van der Rohe or Marcel Breuer. These designers are so popular that they stand for furniture design of the highest quality that has almost the aura of a piece of art. Icons like that don't need advertising. They appear effortlessly in the visual cultural context of our time.

Furniture advertising has come a long way and reflects the technological development of the media. All over Europe visual representation must tie in to the new media possibilities, as well as national characteristics, social bonds, and psychological profiles of the consumers. However, the idea of selling an environment instead of a single piece of furniture has turned IKEA into a market leader worldwide. The company set an example that most other firms were unable to follow. IKEA's widespread market presence makes it possible to conclude that in the early twenty-first century in Europe consumer profiles resemble each other more than they differ. IKEA's market success merely reflects this phenomenon.

NOTES

Introduction

1   The father Charles Arpel was played by Jean-Pierre Zola; Adrienne Servantie was Mme. Arpel; as the uncle, Tati revived his alter ego Monsieur Hulot.

2   *Mon Oncle* won the Special Prize at Cannes in 1958 and the Best Foreign Picture Oscar in 1959. Controversies arose around Tati's playful remarks after a pontifical audience at the Vatican and his rebuff of Warner Brothers' offer to fund a Tati western, preferring to make "Monsieur Hulot goes East." Tati was probably invoking his desire to return to France rather than Soviet sympathies; nonetheless, the matter escalated into accusations of communist leanings in a climate of Cold War tensions (Bellos 2012: 224–6). The set design was realized as a complete house in Studios de la Victorine near Nice.

3   The malfunctioning metal fish water feature and controlling geometric paving in colored materials recall gardens of the Villa Noailles in Hyères, France, of 1928 designed by Gabriel Guevrekian (1892–1968) and the architect Robert Mallet-Stevens (1886–1945). The black wire chairs suggest the "DKR" (Dining Height / K-wire Shell / R-wire Rod-iron base) 1950 designed by Charles (1907–78) and Ray (née Kaiser, 1912–88) Eames manufactured by Banner Metals of California for the Herman Miller Furniture Company, Zeeland, Michigan; and the 1952 "diamond" chair designed by Harry Bertoia (1915–78) manufactured by Knoll Associates New York. The "Model 44" (Saturn chair) designed by Geneviève Dangles and Christian De France (b.1929–), star of the Salon des Arts Ménagers exhibition of 1957, is also intimated (artnet n.d.-b).

4   The reincarnation of the villa Arpel at the Venice Biennale in 2014 won a Special Jury award. Catherine Mallet, director of Les Modillons, a contemporary art center in Vindelle, Angoulême, also adopted Madame Arpel's phrase as the title of a 2012 exhibition exploring modern conceptualizations of place-making (Dreyfus 2012).

5   For example in the United Kingdom: the Furniture Society, the Regional Furniture Society, and the Design History Society.

6   The monthly woman's magazine *Modern Priscilla*, edited by Frank S. Guild and Miss Beulah F. Kellogg, was in circulation from 1887 to 1930. In 1925 the subscription

rate was $2 per year or 20 cents per copy at the newsstand with a circulation of 600,000. Advice books on cooking (1924) and home furnishing (1925) were also printed by the firm (*Newsstand* 1925).

7   *Kunstwart* was supported by future members of the Deutscher Werkbund, including the architect-designer Peter Behrens (1868–1940), the critic Hermann Muthesius (1861–1927), and the museum director Alfred Lichtwark (1852–1914).

8   The chairs were manufactured by A.L. Colombo, trade name "Columbus." Terragni also commissioned a variation of the *Lariana* chair for the Sant'Elia preschool in Como instilling this fascist tensile posture in the next generation (Rusconi and Zanchetti 2013: 158).

9   The company was founded in 1945 by Frank (1911–88) and Theresa (1913–2010) Caplan, authors of *The Power of Play* (1973).

10   The Museum of Modern Art hosted the *Stockholm Builds* exhibition in 1941, which promoted the park commissioner Holger Blom's role in creating the play environments of the Tessin estate in Stockholm, Sweden (Burkhalter 2014).

11   The Vittas, a Franco-Piedmontese Jewish family of bankers and silk merchants, built the Villa la Sapinère in Evian-les-Bains amidst the spectacle of alpine scenery and seasonal high society on the banks of Lake Léman.

12   Perhaps the most famous elements of Joseph Vitta's collection were *The Death of Sardanapalus* by Eugène Délacroix (1798–1863) sold to the Louvre in 1922 as well as two vast donations, which form the basis of the Musée Délacroix Paris and the Musée des Beaux Arts Chéret Nice (Nimmen 2014). Vitta also collected Asian decorative art and commissioned much contemporary design.

13   Begun during the lifetime of the father, Baron Jonas Vitta (1820–92), the villa and its furnishing were realized in consultation with the women of the household. Nimmen (2014: n. 48) cites a recent exhibition catalog, which demonstrates that Baroness Hélène Vitta was more instrumental in the commissioning of the jardinières from Auguste Rodin (1840–1917) than has been recognized (Blanchetière 2009: 206).

14   The guests at their marriage on September 18, 1899, included members of the Rothschild and Noailles dynasties and Proust (*Gil Blas*, September 27, 1899: 2; Charton 2014). Foà's specimen collecting in Africa for the Paris Natural History Museum and his books about his game-hunting travels earned him the Legion d'Honneur. Upon the death of her son Jean (1902–46), president of Air France and a fighter pilot who died of his wounds, Fanny Foà donated the villa to a foundation (ADAPT), which has continued her lifelong work supporting the rehabilitation of disabled deportees and wounded aviators and their families in his memory (General Bassault's letter of support for Fanny Foà's candidacy for Chevalier de la Légion d'Honneur November 16, 1948; Archives Nationales 1870).

15   The actresses are identified as Beaudin and Raffard performing in *La visite de M. le Curé* (Menier family album Musée D'Orsay, PHO 1986 129 1 64).

16   John Snr (1826–93) and John Jnr (1847–1919) who founded a billiard table company in Bombay were champion players and authors on the game (Billiard & Snooker Heritage Collection n.d.). Charles recounted how his sister Emily, who might be the woman in the photograph, borrowed gentleman's evening dress to watch her brother's championship match where women were not admitted ("Two Books on Billiards" 1912: 20).

17   Musée D'Orsay, PHO 1987 36 100. The "mace" was recommended to women players as it vouchsafed the exposing posture of leaning into the table (Phelan

[1859] 1874: 44). The respectable gentility of Berkeley's main oeuvre took the form of photocollage.

18 £5 and 5s equated to £300 in 2005 or fifteen days of a builder's wages in 1900 (The National Archives n.d.).

Chapter 1

1 The examples discussed in this chapter can be found in the design collections of major international museums including the V&A, https://www.vam.ac.uk, the Museum of Modern Art, https://www.moma.org, and the Vitra Design Museum, https://www.design-museum.de (all accessed May 22, 2021).

2 A number of authors have identified the roots of modernist thinking in the design reform of the nineteenth century, by identifying in the work of A.W.N. Pugin, John Ruskin, Henry Cole, and William Morris, among others, a concern for principled design for manufacture often concerned with notions of honesty and quality, artifice and sham (Pevsner [1936] 2005; Wainwright 1990; Lubbock 1995).

Chapter 2

1 Furniture is defined here as objects that are primarily functional but with aesthetic qualities, which are found in or around human habitations, workplaces, and places of concourse, performing three broad and frequently overlapping functions: provision of physical comfort (seating and sleeping), work and social concourse (seating, desks, and tables), and the ordering of other material culture (storage).

2 Smith and Rogers (2006: 13, 16) note the peak of the East End furniture trade from 1860 to 1945; Agius (1978: 154) that two-thirds of the cabinetmakers listed in the national 1881 census were working in London, mainly in the East End.

3 The distinction between hardwoods and softwoods is fundamentally botanical but is employed to group timbers broadly by density as a working material. Hardwoods are those angiosperm tree species with enclosed seeds; softwoods gymnosperm species with uncovered seeds. Hardwood is composed of pores that generally give rise to a more fibrous composition than the tubular composition of softwood. French polishing is a process that involves the application of shellac, the resinous substance extruded by the *kerria lacca* insect on trees in India and Thailand, dissolved in ethanol.

4 Molesworth (1858: 17–39) dates the powered circular saw to *c.* 1790 and the patenting of rotary planing and molding machines to 1793, as also the use of saws to produce dovetails.

5 Plywood refers to a board made up of thin layers of wood, often produced by rotary peeling of the log, glued together with grain direction alternating with each layer. This gives the board greater stability than solid timber, avoiding shrinkage and warping. American patents were filed for such layered board in 1865 and 1868. The term "plywood" first appeared *c.* 1919 (Logie 1947: 76).

6 The number of employees is noted in the March 1902 edition of the *Grand Falls Furniture Record*. Butterfly keys are small visible pieces of timber inserted to join two boards.

7 A distinction can be drawn between glues, the "drying" action of which by loss of solvent is potentially reversible, and cements that set through an irreversible change in molecular structure. Casein cement had been known from *c.* 1870, and was used for First World War aircraft. Synthetic resins—urea formaldehyde, phenol formaldehyde—were developed as adhesives from *c.* 1930 (Logie 1947: 84).

8   Spray finishes were not introduced without labor and health problems. In Britain
    NAFTA successfully campaigned for the continued employment of traditional
    polishers in this new technology, and an amendment to the Factories and
    Workshops Act ensured safer working with potentially toxic spray solvents (Reid
    1986: 125–6).
9   Acid catalyzed and pre-catalyzed lacquers containing formaldehyde and melamine,
    among other hard wearing resins, have been developed in the later twentieth century
    (Edwards 1994: 86).
10 The introduction of chip- or particle board led to greater standardization of
    production, the establishment of specialist volume producers, and a subsequent
    diminution of employment. In Britain in 1968, 3.8 percent of furniture manufacturing
    companies were responsible for over 50 percent of the output. Unions accepted
    the principle of the interchange ability of skills, thus effectively ending furniture-
    making specialisms (Reid 1986: 167–9).
11 *Bricolage* is a French term denoting encountered, pre-used materials, therefore likely
    to lead to an incidental rather than highly planned composition. Their apparent
    incompatibility can be employed as cultural commentary. A *bricoleur* can therefore
    be one who deliberately subverts the original meanings of materials (Hebdige 1979:
    102–6).

Chapter 3

1   The Werkstätten had workshops in Munich, Berlin, Hamburg, Cologne, and
    Bremen. See also for the word Typenmöbel *DWDS* (n.d.).
2   The pieces were reconstructed and manufactured by the Wittmann firm in Austria
    in the late 1990s.

Chapter 5

1   The "public realm" here means space or settings that "support and facilitate public
    life and social interaction" (Carmona, de Magalhães, and Hammond 2008: 137).
    "Civic space" concerns the ceremonial or institutional aspects of the public realm
    (Scott Brown 1990: 22).
2   A style of planting low-height flowers in colorful geometric designs popularized in
    the mid-to-late nineteenth century. As carpet bedding became associated with public
    parks and squares by the early twentieth century, the style became associated with
    "bad taste" among the social elite.
3   Olmsted, considered the "father" of landscape architecture, designed Central Park
    (1858–61).
4   A style of architecture and planning known as Beaux Arts after the renowned École
    des Beaux-Arts in Paris where many architects from Europe and the United States
    were trained.
5   Although developers often specify stone, metal, or marble furniture for their vandal-
    proof and durable properties.
6   For example the elegant, sculptural stone benches designed by Spanish designer
    Oscar Tusquets (1941–).
7   Inclusive design is design that addresses everyone's needs, irrespective of culture,
    race, gender, ability, and other differences.
8   The "third space" is the environment where digital technologies allow us to work
    outside the home and the workplace.

Chapter 6

1 This room was part of the future Museum of the Colonies building designed by the architect Albert Laprade (1883–1978), now known as the Palais de la Porte Dorée since the non-European collections were moved to the Quai Branly Museum in Paris in 2006.

2 The École Boulle founded in 1886 in rue de Reuilly, named after André-Charles Boulle (1642–1732) cabinetmaker to Louis XIV, is situated near the famous furniture making district of the "faubourg Saint Antoine" in Paris. The chair frames made by the École Boulle shown in 1925 were covered in tapestry upholstery woven in wool and silk (seven threads to a centimeter) by nine weavers at the Gobelins. Earlier volumes in this series examine the significance of the foundation and preeminence of the French royal manufactures of tapestry known as Gobelins.

3 For the 1925 exhibition, Ruhlmann had coordinated a team to create the "Townhouse of a Collector" whilst members of the Societé des artistes décorateurs devised the French Embassy installation. Both teams designed elegant furniture in a spectrum of exquisite materials and forms suited to the different functions of the rooms of these fictive mansions: formal receptions; sport and smoking; office and library work; a lady's rest and toilette. Leading French department stores also promoted their newly founded interior design services to more middle-class budgets through adaptable single-room displays, such as the "La Maîtrise" pavilion under the artistic direction of Maurice Dufrêne (1876–1955) at the Galleries Lafayette (Possémé 1999: 131–66). Pomone, the interior design studio of the Bon Marché department store; Studium-Louvre at Les Grands Magasins du Louvre; and Primavera for le Printemps each had pavilions designed by fashionable modern architects in which to house the model rooms created by their studio's art direction.

4 This short-lived project involved many members of the American Union of Decorative Artists and Craftsmen (AUDAC) such as Norman Bel Geddes (1893–1958), Donald Deskey (1894–1989), Paul Frankl (1886–1958), Frank Lloyd Wright (1867–1959), and Gilbert Rohde (1894–1944).

5 The Museum of Ornament would later evolve into the Victoria and Albert Museum in South Kensington.

6 Author of nine architectural history books including *Australia's Home* (1952); curator of *The Modern Home exhibition* 1949 in Melbourne.

Chapter 8

1 Twentieth-century furniture advertisements may be found on many websites including eBay, the Internet archive, Advertising Archives, and Pinterest.

Chapter 9

1 I would like to thank my employers, the Hochschule Hannover, for their kind support. Muriel Favre and Marion Gillum from the Deutsches Rundfunkarchiv (DRA) in Frankfurt provided valuable sources, which Antonia Halsch helped to transcribe. Many thanks to Matthew Chipping from the BBC Written Archives Centre, the British Library as well as the Bauhaus-Archiv-Berlin and the Staatsbibliothek Berlin.

2 Republished 1999 in Berlin by Gebr. Mann. See Rahman (n.d.).

3 The house was commissioned by Mrs. Truus Schröder-Schrader and designed and built by architect-designer Gerrit Rietveld. Today it is a museum and part of UNESCO World Heritage.

4   If one compares the press coverage Walter Gropius collected for his settlement
     plans in Dessau-Törten it is obvious that his young competitor Leopold Fischer
     received more praise for his since he seemed to have a much better understanding
     of the needs of those for whom he designed for (Becker et al. n.d.).
5   Letter from the managing director to the secretary of the BBC, February 18, 1935.
     BBC Written Archives Centre file "R34/18: Advertising in Programs, British Ideal
     Furniture Co Ltd."
6   See for example the 1950 correspondence at the BBC Written Archives Centre
     file "R34/17: Advertising in Programs, British Furniture Manufactures Federated
     Associations."
7   The film is from 2015 and was called "Die kleinen Freunden des Alltags" (The little
     Pleasures of Every Day Life) (IKEA Switzerland 2015).
8   Möbel-Hübner-Werbeplatte: Paul und Pauline Neugebauer. Deutsches Rundfunk
     Archiv, Frankfurt am Main, no. 2905050: "Pauline: Komm mit zu Möbel-Hübner!"
     created by Ludwig Manfred Lommel.
9   Interview about IKEA with Hendrik Schröder, Professor of Marketing at the
     University of Duisburg-Essen. "40 Jahre Ikea Deutschland—Ein Erfolgskonzept."
     Deutsches Rundfunk Archiv Frankfurt a.M., archive no. F055108.

BIBLIOGRAPHY

2001: A Space Odyssey (1968), [Film] Dir. Stanley Kubrick, USA: Metro-Goldwyn-Mayer (MGM) and Stanley Kubrick Productions.

Aalto, Alvar (1978), *Sketches*, edited by Göran Schildt, Cambridge, MA: MIT Press.

Abigail's Party (1977), [TV Programme], *Play For Today*, BBC1, November 1.

Acheson, E.D., R.H. Cowdell, E. Hadfield and R.G. Macbeth (1968), "Nasal Cancer in Woodworkers in the Furniture Industry," *British Medical Journal*, 8 (2): 587–96.

Adamson, Glenn (2013), "Substance Abuse: The Postmodern Surface," in Glenn Adamson and Victoria Kelley (eds.), *Surface Tensions: Surface, Finish and the Meaning of Objects*, Manchester, UK: Manchester University Press.

Agius, Pauline (1978), *British Furniture 1880–1915*, Woodbridge, UK: Antique Collectors' Club.

Ajani, Judith (2011), "The Global Wood Market, Wood Resource Productivity and Price Trends: An Examination with Special Attention to China," *Environmental Conservation*, 38 (1): 53–63.

Albaret, Céleste (1973), *Monsieur Proust: Souvenirs recueillis par Georges Belmont*, Paris: Éditions Robert Laffont.

Alexander, Christopher, Sara Ishikawa, and Murray Silverstein (1977), *A Pattern Language*, New York: Oxford University Press.

All in the Family (1971–9), [TV program] Columbia Broadcasting System (CBS).

Anderson, Benedict (1983), *Imagined Communities: Reflections on the Origin and Spread of Nationalism*, London: Verso.

Andrews, John (2005), *Arts and Crafts Furniture*, Woodbridge, UK: Antique Collectors' Club.

Angus Ross (2015), "Public Art: Woldsway." Available online: https://www.angusross.co.uk/commissions/outdoors-and-garden (accessed June 9, 2021).

Appleton, Jay (1975), *The Experience of Landscape*, London: John Wiley.

Archives Nationales (1870), "Patronymes: Lieux de naissance." Available online: https://www.leonore.archives-nationales.culture.gouv.fr/ui/notice/143818 (accessed June 9, 2021).

Architectural Association (n.d.), "Hooke Park." Available online: http://www.aaschool.ac.uk/AASCHOOL/HOOKEPARK/hooke.php (accessed July 4, 2015).

Archives Nationales, Fanny Vitta Foà dossier (n.d.). Available online: culture.gouv.fr (accessed February 2, 2016).

Armanni, Vittorio (1998), "AL Colombo A Milanese Engineering Company: From Metal Tubing to Vehicle Frames and Tubular Furniture 1919–1931," in Anty Pansera (ed.), *Flessibili Splendori: Imobili in tubulare metallica. Il casa Columbus*, Milan: Electa.

Armstrong, Isobel (2008), *Victorian Glassworlds: Glass Culture and the Imagination 1830–1880*, Oxford: Oxford University Press.

Art at Runnymede (n.d.). Available online: http://artatrunnymede.com (accessed November 23, 2015).

artnet (n.d.-a), "Charles Edouard Boutibonne (French, 1816–1897)." Available online: http://www.artnet.com/artists/charles-edouard-boutibonne/4 (accessed May 25, 2021).

artnet (n.d.-b), "Past Auction." Available online: http://www.artnet.com/artists/christian-defrance-and-genevi%C3%A8ve-dangles/two-rare-lounge-chairs-mod-saturne-designed-by-ILv6JyMeToLQw-hR3ggbGQ2 (accessed May 25, 2021).

Ashbee, Charles R. (1938), "*Memoirs*," unpublished typescript, vol. 4, Victoria and Albert Museum Library.

Ashford-Down, Harold (1931), *The Art of Window Display; A Complete Guide to Modern Methods of Shop Window Publicity, Shop Lighting Interior Display and the Work of the Display Man*, London: Sir Isaac Pitman and Sons.

Atkinson, Paul (2010), *Computer*, London: Reaktion Books.

Attfield, Judy (1999), *Utility Reassessed: The Role of Ethics in the Practice of Design*, Manchester, UK: Manchester University Press.

Augé, Marc ([1995] 2008), *Non-places: An Introduction to Supermodernity*, London: Verso.

Auslander, Leora (1998), *Taste and Power: Furnishing Modern France*, Berkeley: University of California Press.

Austin Powers: International Man of Mystery (1997), [Film] Dir. Jay Roach, USA: Copelia International.

Avenarius, Ferdinand (1900), "Zehn Gebote zur Wohnungseinrichtung," *Der Kunstwart*, 13 (9) (February): 341–4.

Aynsley, Jeremy (2006), "The Modern Period Room—A Contradiction in Terms?," in Penny Sparke, Brenda Martin, and Trevor Keeble (eds.), *The Modern Period Room: The Construction of the Exhibited Interior 1870–1950*, 8–30, Abingdon, UK: Routledge.

Ayto, John (2009), *From the Horse's Mouth: Oxford Dictionary of English Idioms*, Oxford: Oxford University Press.

Bachelard, Gaston (1964), *The Poetics of Space*, Boston: Beacon Press.

Bailey, Colin, Philip Conisbee, and Thomas Gaehtgens (2003), *The Age of Watteau, Chardin and Fragonard: Masterpieces of French Genre Painting*, New Haven, CT: Yale University Press.

Bargiel, Réjane (2014), "Chez le baron Vitta, l'affichiste Jules Chéret devient décorateur," in Ville d'Evian, *Joseph Vitta Passion de collection*, 89–94, Paris: Somogy éditions d'art.

Barnes, Carolyn, Barbara Hall, and Simon Jackson (2009), "Relaxed and Comfortable: The Australian Pavlion at Expo '67," *Design Issues*, 25 (1): 80–93.

Baroni, Daniele (1978), *Gerrit Thomas Rietveld Furniture*, London: Academy Editions.

Barron, Stephanie and Maurice Tuchman, eds. (1981), *The Avant-Garde in Russia, 1910–1930: New Perspectives*, Cambridge, MA: MIT Press.

Barthes, Roland (1957), *Mythologies*, Paris: Éditions du Seuil.

Bauhaus Online (n.d.), "African Chair." Available online: http://bauhaus-online.de/en/atlas/werke/african-chair (accessed May 16, 2015).

Baumhoff, Anja (2009), "Zum Mythos der sachlichen Form: Paul Klee und Piet Mondrian," in Anja Baumhoff and Magdalena Droste (eds.), *Mythos Bauhaus: Zwischen Selbsterfindung und Enthistorisierung*, Berlin: Reimer.

Becker, Fritz, Irene Below, Peter Koitzsch, Wolfgang Paul, Sandra Striebing, Juliane Vierich, and Frank Wolter (n.d.), *Leopold Fischer Architekt der Moderne*, Dessau-Roßlau: Funk Verlag Bernhard Hein e.K. Available online: http://bauhausverein.de/uploads/files/180310_Publikation%20Leopold%20Fischer.pdf (accessed May 25, 2021).

Bellos, David (2012), *Jacques Tati*, New York: Random House.

Benjamin, Walter (1982), *Das Passagen-Werk (1927–1940)*, Frankfurt: Suhrkamp.

Bennett, Daryl (2005), *Shapland & Petter Ltd. of Barnstaple: Arts and Crafts Furniture in Devon*, Barnstaple, UK: Museum of Barnstaple and North Devon.

Benton, Charlotte, Tim Benton, and Ghislane Wood, eds. (2003), *Art Deco 1910–39*, London: V&A Publications.

Benton, Tim (1990), "The Myth of Function," in Paul Greenhalgh (ed.), *Modernism in Design*, London: Reaktion Books.

Benton, Tim (2006a), "Modernism and Nature," in Christopher Wilk (ed.), *Modernism: Designing a New World, 1914–1939*, 311–39, London: V&A Publications.

Benton, Tim (2006b), *The Modernist Home*, London: V&A Publications.

Betts, Paul (2004), *The Authority of Everyday Objects: A Cultural History of West German Industrial Design*, Berkeley: University of California Press.

Beuttinger, E. (1904), "Ausstellung der Dresdener Werkstätten für Handwerkskunst," *Innendekoration*, 15: 163. Translation available online: https://www.mackintosh-architecture.gla.ac.uk/catalogue/pdf/M224.pdf (accessed June 9, 2021).

Bhaba, Homi K., ed. (1990), *Nations and Narrative*, London: Routledge.

Bibliothèque Nationale de France (2012), *1929–1956 Union des Artistes Modernes: La Naissance du Design en France*. Available online: http://www.bnf.fr/documents/biblio_uam.pdf (accessed October 20, 2015).

Bijker, Wiebe E., ed. (2012), *The Social Construction of Technological Systems: New Directions in the Sociology of the History of Technology*, Cambridge, MA; London: MIT Press.

The Billiard Player: A Journal for the Public and Private Billiard Room (1903a), "Billiard Room Gossip," (July): 79.

The Billiard Player: A Journal for the Public and Private Billiard Room (1903b), "How to Take Care of a Billiard Table," (July): 94–5.

The Billiard Player: A Journal for the Public and Private Billiard Room (1903c), "The B.P. Bijou Tables," (July): 220–1.

Billiard & Snooker Heritage Collection (n.d.), "Past Masters." Available online: https://snookerheritage.co.uk/normans-articles/past-masters/ (accessed May 25, 2021).

Blanchetière, François (2009), "Le Gout du Baron Vitta," in François Blanchetière and Jean-Paul Bouillon (eds.), *Rodin: Les Arts décoratifs*, 205–13, Paris: Éditions Alternatives.

Bloom Hiesinger, Kathryn, ed. (1988), *Art Nouveau in Munich: Masters of Jugendstil*, Munich: Prestel/Philadelphia Museum of Art.

"BM TRADA Highlights Plywood Testing Findings" (2015), *TTJ*, June 25. Available online: http://www.ttjonline.com/news/bm-trada-highlights-plywood-testing-findings-4609064 (accessed May 21, 2021).

Bogner, Dieter and Peter Noever, eds. (2001), *Frederick J. Kiesler Endless Space*, Vienna: Hatje Cantz Verlag.

Bouillon, Jean-Paul (1979), "An Artistic Collaboration: Bracquemond and Baron Vitta," *Bulletin of the Cleveland Museum of Art*, (November): 311–19.

Bourdieu, Pierre (1979), *Distinction: A Social Critique of the Judgement of Taste*, Paris: Les Editions de Minuit.

Bourdieu, Pierre ([1984] 2010), *Distinction: A Social Critique of the Judgement of Taste. Translated by Richard Nice, with a new introduction by Tony Bennett*, London: Routledge.

Bouillon, Jean-Paul (2014), "Vitta et Bracquemond, un moment d'art privilégié," in Ville d'Evian, *Joseph Vitta Passion de collection*, 66–84, Paris: Somogy éditions d'art.

Branzi, Andrea (1984), *The Hot House: Italian New Wave Design*, London: Thames and Hudson.

Breakfast at Tiffany's (1961), [Film] Dir. Blake Edwards, USA: Jurow-Shepherd Productions.

Breuer, Marcel (1926), *ein bauhaus-film fünf jahre lang*, Bauhaus Archiv, Berlin.

Breuer, Marcel ([1928] 2012), "Metal Furniture and Spatiality," in Catherine Ince, Lydia Yee, and Juliette Desgorgues (eds.), *Bauhaus Art as Life*, London: Koenig Books in association with the Barbican Art Gallery.

Breward, Christopher and Ghislaine Wood, eds. (2012), *British Design from 1948: Innovation in the Modern Age*, London: V&A Publishing.

Brewer, E. Cobham (1970), *Dictionary of Phrase and Fable: Centenary Edition revised by Ivor H. Evans*, London: Cassell.

Bridenthal, Renate (1984), "Professional Housewives," in Renate Bridenthal, Anita Grossmann, and Marion Kaplan (eds.), *When Biology Became Destiny: Women in Weimar and Nazi Germany*, 131–52, New York: Monthly Review Press.

British Furniture Confederation (n.d.), "About the British Furniture Confederation." Available online: http://www.britishfurnitureconfederation.org.uk/about_furniture_industry.php (accessed July 1, 2015).

Brooklyn Museum Archives (1954), Records of the Department of Public Information. Press releases.

Brown, Bill, ed. (2004), *Things*, Chicago: University of Chicago.

Brüderlin, Markus and Annelie Lütgens, eds. (2008), *Interieur, Exterieur: Living in Art: From Romantic Interior Painting to the Home Design of the Future*, Ostfildern: Hatje Cantz Verlag.

Brunhammer, Yvonne (2002), "Le décor du Palais des Colonies: Du côté des arts décoratifs," in Germain Viatte and Dominique François (eds.), *Le palais des colonies histoire du musée des arts d'Afrique et d'Océanie*, 127–79, Paris: Réunion des Musées Nationaux.

Bryden, I. and J. Floyd (1999), *Domestic Space: Reading the Interior in Nineteenth-century Britain and America*, Manchester, UK: Manchester University Press.

Bullock, Nicholas (2002), *Building the Post-War World: Modern Architecture and Reconstruction in Britain*, London: Routledge.

Burgess, Joanne C. (1993), "Timber Production, Timber Trade and Tropical Deforestation," *Ambio*, 22 (2/3): 136–43.

Burke, Peter (2001), *Eye-witnessing, the Use of Images as Historical Evidence*, London: Reaktion Books.

Burke, Peter ([2004] 2015), *What Is Cultural History?*, Cambridge, UK: Polity.

Burkhalter, Gabriela (2014), "When Play Got Serious," *Tate Etc.*, (31) (July 18). Available online: https://www.tate.org.uk/tate-etc/issue-31-summer-2014/when-play-got-serious (accessed February 2, 2016).

Burton, Benedict (1983), *The Anthropology of World's Fairs San Francisco's Panama Pacific International Exposition of 1915*, London: Scolar Press.

The Cabinet Maker and Art Furnisher (1895), December 16 (186): 133–64.

Calloway, Stephen (1988), *Twentieth-Century Decoration: The Domestic Interior from 1900 to the Present Day*, London: Weidenfeld and Nicholson.

Campbell, Margaret (1999), "From Cure Chair to 'Chaise Longue': Medical Treatment and the Form of the Modern Recliner," *Journal of Design History*, 12 (4): 327–43.

Caradoc, R.L. (1934), *Sales-increasing Window Display Schemes for Furnishers*, London: The Furnishing World.

Carlano, Annie and Bobbie Sumberg (2006), *Sleeping Around: The Bed from Antiquity to Now*, Seattle: University of Washington Press with Museum of International Folk Art Santa Fe.

Carmona, Matthew, Claudio de Magalhães, and Leo Hammond eds. (2008), *Public Space: the Management Dimension*, London: Routledge.

Carmona, Matthew, Steven Tiesdell, Tim Heath, and Taner Oc (2010), *Public Places Urban Spaces: The Dimensions of Urban Design*, Oxford: Architectural Press.

Carruthers, Annette (1992), *Edward Barnsley and his Workshop*, Oxford: White Cockade Publishing.

Carter, Christopher (2015), *Rhetorical Exposures. Confrontation and Contradiction in US Social Documentary Photography*, Tuscaloosa: University of Alabama Press.

Case, Gerald Otley (1934), *British Guiana Timbers*, London: Metcalfe & Cooper.

Casino Royale (2006), [Film] Dir. Martin Campbell, USA: Columbia Pictures.

Castillo, Greg (2010), *Cold War on the Home Front: The Soft Power of Midcentury Design*, Minneapolis: University of Minnesota Press.

Catalogue de l'exposition structures gonflables, mars 1968: précédé d'un Essai sur technique et société, de Considérations inactuelles sur le gonflable et de Particularité des structures gonflables (1968). Available online: https://aap68.yale.edu/catalogue-de-lexposition-structures-gonflables-mars-1968-precede-dun-essai-sur-technique-et-societe (accessed August 8, 2015).

Center for Design Planning (1976, 1979), *Streetscape Equipment Sourcebook*, Washington, DC: ULI-the Urban Land Institute.

CG Society (n.d.), "Building 3d with IKEA." Available online: http://www.cgsociety.org/index.php/CGSFeatures/CGSFeatureSpecial/building_3d_with_ikea (accessed October 18, 2015).

Chapman, Arthur (1922), "Cheating the Park Bench," *Outlook*, July 12: 457.

Charton, Ariane (2014), "Un mécène méconnu," *L'Arche*, May 2. Available online: https://larchemag.fr/2014/05/02/1096/un-mecene-meconnu/ (accessed January 26, 2016)

Chion, Michael (2006), *The Films of Tati*, Lancaster, UK: Guernica Editions.

Cieraad, Irene, ed. (1999), *At Home: An Anthropology of Domestic Space*, Syracuse: Syracuse University Press.

Collectif Cochenko (n.d.). Available online: http://www.cochenko.fr/Collectif-Cochenko (accessed February 25, 2015).

Collins, Michael and Andreas Papadakis (1989), *Post-Modern Design*, London: Academy Editions.

Colombino, Laura (2012), "The House as Skin: J.G. Ballard, Existentialism, and Archigram's Mini-Environments," *European Journal of English Studies*, 16 (1): 21–31.

Colomina, Beatriz (1996), *Privacy and Publicity: Modern Architecture as Mass Media*, Cambridge, MA: MIT Press.

Colomina, Beatriz (1998), "The Exhibitionist House," in R. Ferguson (ed.), *At the End of the Century: One Hundred Years of Architecture*, 126–66, Los Angeles: Museum of Contemporary Art; New York: Harry N. Abrams.

Colomina, Beatriz (2004), "Unbreathed Air 1956," *Grey Room*, (15) (Spring): 28–59.

Colwell, David (n.d.), "About." Available online: http://www.davidcolwell.com/about.html (accessed September 5, 2015).

Conrad, Peter (1999), *Modern Times Modern Places: Life & Art in the 20th Century*, London: Thames & Hudson.

Conway, Hazel (1982), *Ernest Race*, London: Design Council.

Cook, Peter (1999), *Archigram*, Princeton, NJ: Princeton University Press.

Cooper Hewitt Museum (1994), "Garden Notebook: A History of Central Park through a Handful of Benches," *New York Times*, July 7. Available online: http://www.nytimes.com/1994/07/07/garden/garden-notebook-the-history-of-central-park-through-a-handful-of-benches.html (accessed December 12, 2014).

Cooper Marcus, Clare and Carolyn Francis, eds. (1998), *People Places: Design Guidelines for Urban Open Space*, New York: John Wiley.

Cork, Richard (1991), "Art in the City," in Mark Fisher and Ursula Owen (eds.), *Whose Cities?*, 131–41, London: Penguin.

Cotton, Bernard (1990), *The English Regional Chair*, Woodbridge, UK: Antique Collectors' Club.

Council for Industrial Design/Design Council (1963–83), *Street Furniture from Design Index*, London: CoID; Design Council.

Cranz, Galen (2000), *The Chair: Rethinking Culture, Body and Design*, New York: W.W. Norton and Co.

Crawford, Alan (2005), *C.R. Ashbee: Architect, Designer & Romantic Socialist*, New Haven, CT: Yale University Press.

Csikszentmihalyi, Mihaly and Eugene Rochberg-Halton (1981), *The Meaning of Things*, Cambridge: Cambridge University Press.

Cullen, Gordon (1967), "A Study of Rotterdam," *Architectural Review*, 141 (839): 43–9.

Cullen, Gordon (2002), *The Concise Townscape*, Oxford: Architectural Press.

Cupers, Kenny (2014), *The Social Project: Housing Postwar France*, Minneapolis: University of Minnesota Press.

Curtis, L. (1997), *Lloyd Loom: Woven Fibre Furniture*, rev. edn., London: Salamander.

Davidson, Cathy and Linda Wagner-Martin (1995), *The Oxford Companion to Women's Writing in the United States*, Oxford: Oxford University Press.

Davies, Kevin (1998), "Finmar and the Furniture of the Future: The Sale of Alvar Aalto's Plywood Furniture in the UK, 1934–1939," *Journal of Design History*, 11 (2): 145–56.

Davies, Kevin (1997), "Scandinavian Furniture in Britain: Finmar and the UK Market 1949–52," *Journal of Design History*, 10 (1): 39–52.

Davies, M. (1998), *City of Quartz: Excavating the Future in Los Angeles*, London: Random House.

Deese, Martha (1992), "Gerald Summers and the Makers of Simple Furniture," *Journal of Design History*, 5 (2): 183–205.

Dell, Simon (1999), "The Consumer and the Making of the "Exposition Internationale des Arts Décoratifs et Industriels Modernes 1907–1925," *Journal of Design History*, 12 (4): 311–25.

Denby, Elaine (1971), *What's in a Room: Some Aspects of Interior Design*, Manuscript from the BBC Radio 3 broadcast from June 10, London: BBC Publications.

Denney, Matthew (1999), "Utility Furniture and the Myth of Utility," in Judy Attfield (ed.), *Utility Reassessed: The Role of Ethics in the Practice of Design*, 110–24, Manchester, UK: Manchester University Press.

De Reyniès, Nicole (1987), *Le mobilier domestique: Vocabulaire typologique*, 2 vols., Paris: Imprimérie Nationale.

Deshairs, Léon (1925), *Intérieurs et couleurs, France: cinquante planches en couleurs*, Paris: A Lévy.

Designboom (n.d.). Available online: http://www.designboom.com/ (accessed February 23, 2016).

Dew, Josie (2006), *Saddled at Sea: A 15,000 Mile Journey to New Zealand by Russian Freighter*, London: Little, Brown & Co.

Dezeen (n.d.). Available online: http://dezeen.com (accessed February 23, 2016).

Dieckmann, Erich and Karl Keller (1925), *Möbel Der Staatlichen Bauhochschule Weimar*, Weimar: Staatliche Bauhochschule.

Dinner at Eight (1933), [Film] Dir. George Cukor, USA: Metro-Goldwyn-Mayer (MGM).

Doesburg, Theo van (1919), "XXII. aanteekeningen bij een leunstoel van rietveld," *De Stijl*, 2: 11.

Doesburg, Theo van (1920), "Schilderkunst van giorgio de chirico en een stoel van rietveld," *De Stijl*, 3 (5): 46.

Doherty, Joe, Volker Busch-Geertsema, Vita Karpuskiene, Jukka Korhonen, Eoin O'Sullivan, Ingrid Sahlin, Agostino Petrillo, and Julia Wygnanska (2008), "Homelessness and Exclusion: Regulating Public Space in European Cities," *Surveillance and Society*, 5 (3): 290–314. Available online: https://www.researchgate.net/publication/239934314_Homelessness_and_Exclusion_Regulating_Public_Space_in_European_Cities (accessed June 9, 2021).

Down with Love (2003), [Film] Dir. Peyton Reed. USA: Fox 2000 Pictures.

Drabble, Margaret (1991), "A Vision of the Real City," in Mark Fisher and Ursula Owen(eds.), *Whose Cities?*, 32–42, London: Penguin.

Drexler, Arthur (1973), *Charles Eames: Furniture from the Design Collection*, New York: Museum of Modern Art.

Dreyfus, Alain (2012), "Habitats du bonheur aux Mobillons." Available online: http://www.artnet.fr/magazine/expositions/DREYFUS/c-est-si-pratique-tout-communique-aux-modillons.asp (accessed June 9, 2021).

Droste, Magdalena, Manfred Ludewig, and Bauhaus Archiv, eds. (2001), *Marcel Breuer: Design*, Cologne: Taschen Publications.

Duck and Cover (1951), [Film] Dir. Anthony Rizzo, USA: United States Federal Civil Defense Administration; Archer Productions, Inc. USA.

Duncan, Alastair (1992), *Art Deco Furniture: The French Designers*, London: Thames and Hudson.

Dunnett, H. McG. (1951), "Furniture Since the War," *Architectural Review*, 109 (651): 150–66.

Dunstan, Simon (1984), *Flak Jackets, 20th-Century Military Body Armour*, Oxford: Osprey Books.

Durso, Joseph (1999), "Joe DiMaggio, Yankee Clipper, Dies at 84," *New York Times*, March 9. Available online: https://www.nytimes.com/1999/03/09/sports/joe-dimaggio-yankee-clipper-dies-at-84.html (accessed May 21, 2021).

DWDS (n.d.), s.v. "Typenmöbel." Available online: https://www.dwds.de/wb/Typenm%C3%B6bel (accessed May 22, 2021).

Eastlake, Charles L. (1869), *Hints on Household Taste in Furniture, Upholstery and Other Details*, London: Longmans Green.

Editors of Encyclopedia Britannica (2013), "Melamine," *Encyclopedia Britannica*, February 20. Available online: https://www.britannica.com/science/melamine (accessed October 18, 2015).

Editors of Encyclopedia Britannica (2018), "Realschule," *Encyclopedia Britannica*, May 17. Available online: https://www.britannica.com/topic/Realschule (accessed October 18, 2015).

Edwards, Clive (1994), *Twentieth-Century Furniture: Materials, Manufacture and Markets*, Manchester, UK: Manchester University Press.

Edwards, Clive (2005), *Turning Houses into Homes: A History of the Retail and Consumption of Domestic Furnishings*, London: Ashgate.

Edwards, Clive (2014), "*Multum in Parvo*: 'A Place for Everything and Everything in its Place'. Modernism, Space-Saving Bedroom Furniture and the Compactom Wardrobe," *Journal of Design History*, 27 (1): 17–37.

Edwards, Clive and Treve Rosoman (2006), *British Furniture: 1600–2000*, London: The Intelligent Layman's Publishers.

Eliel, Carol, Françoise Ducros, Tag Gronberg, and Los Angeles County Museum of Art (2001), *L'Esprit Nouveau: Purism in Paris, 1918–1925*, Los Angeles: Los Angeles County Museum of Art in association with Harry N. Abrams.

End Furniture Poverty (n.d.). Available online: http://endfurniturepoverty.org (accessed November 22, 2016).

Evans, Stuart (2006), "Furniture for Small Houses," *Furniture History*, 42: 193–205. https://www.jstor.org/stable/23410081.

Expo '67 (1967), *Terre des hommes: Man and His World; Official Guide*, Montreal.

Expo '67 (n.d.). Available online: http://collectionsearch.nma.gov.au/collections/Expo%2067 (accessed June 9, 2021).

Fallan, Kjetil (2010), *Design History: Understanding Theory and Method*, Oxford: Berg.

Ferry, Emma (2003), "'Decorators May Be Compared to Doctors' An Analysis of Rhoda and Agnes Garrett's *Suggestions for Household Decoration in Painting Woodwork and Furniture* (1876)," *Journal of Design History*, 16 (1): 15–33.

Fiell, Charlotte and Peter Fiell (2012), *Chairs: 1000 Masterpieces of Modern Design, 1800 to the Present Day*, London: Goodman Books.

Filipová, Marta, ed. (2015), *Cultures of International Exhibitions 1840–1940: Great Exhibitions in the Margins*, Farnham, UK: Ashgate.

Flamingo Road (1949), [Film] Dir. Michael Curtiz, USA: Michael Curtiz Productions and Warner Bros.

Fleig, Karl (1975), *Alvar Aalto*, London: Thames and Hudson.

Floré, Freddie and Mil De Kooning (2003), "The Representation of Modern Domesticity in the Belgian Section of the Brussels World's Fair of 1958," *Journal of Design History*, 16 (4): 319–40.

Flores, Oscar Salinas (2014), "Organic Design MoMA 1940: The Breath of Modernity Arrives in Latin America," *Revista KEPES*, 11 (10): 195–208.

Flusser, Vilém (1999), *The Shape of Things: A Philosophy of Design*, London: Reaktion books.

Fock, Matthias (1992), *Werbung für den PC: Vergleichende Analyse der Anzeigen- und Hörfunkwerbung*, Frankfurt: Peter Lang.

Forest Stewardship Council (n.d.), "About FSC." Available online: http://www.fsc-uk. org/about-fsc.2.htm (accessed May 21, 2021).

Forgács, Eva (2012), "Reinventing the Bauhaus: The 1923 Bauhaus Exhibition as a Turning Point in the Direction of the School," in Catherine Ince and Lydia Yee (eds.), *Bauhaus Art as Life*, London: Koenig Books and Barbican Centre.

Forty, Adrian (1986), *Objects of Desire: Design and Society 1750–1980*, London: Thames & Hudson.

Forty, Adrian (1989), "Of Cars, Clothes and Carpets: Design Metaphors in Architectural Thought: The First Banham Memorial Lecture," *Journal of Design History*, 2 (1): 1–14.

Foucault, Michel (1984), *Of Other Spaces, Heterotopias*. Available online: http:// foucault.info/doc/documents/heterotopia/foucault-heterotopia-en-html (accessed May 12, 2015).

The Fountainhead (1949), [Film] Dir. King Vidor, USA: Warner Bros.

Fourastié, Jean (1979), *Les Trente Glorieuses, ou la révolution invisible de 1946 à 1975*, Paris: Fayard.

Frampton, Kenneth (1998), "Industrialization and the Crises in Architecture," in Michael Hayes (ed.), *Oppositions Reader: Selected Readings from a Journal for Ideas and Criticism in Architecture 1973–84*, 39–64, New York: Princeton Architectural Press.

Frampton, Kenneth (2001), *Le Corbusier*, London: Thames & Hudson.

Frasier (1993–2004), [TV Program] USA: Grub Street Productions, Paramount Television, Grammnet Productions.

Frayling, Christopher (2010), *Henry Cole and the Chamber of Horrors: The Curious Origins of the Victoria and Albert Museum*, London: V&A Publishing.

Friedman, Marilyn (2007), "Defining Modernism at the American Designer's Gallery, New York," *Studies in the Decorative Arts*, 14 (2): 79–116.

Friends (1994–2004), [TV program] USA: Warner Brothers Television.

Froissart Pezone, Rosella and Catherine Méneux (2006), "Des 'arts décoratifs' à un 'art social' sous la direction de l'architecte," in Ville de Nancy, *Roger Marx, un critique aux côtés de Gallé, Monet, Rodin, Gauguin ...*, 228–30, Nancy: Arts Lys.

Fry, Roger (1932), "Appendix Memorandum by Mr Roger Fry," in *Art and Industry Report of the committee appointed by the Board of Trade under the Chairmanship of Lord Gorrell on the production and exhibition of articles of good design and everyday use*, London: HMSO.

Future City (2014), "Skystation." Available online: http://futurecity.co.uk/portfolio/ skystation-riverlight/ (accessed May 21, 2021).

Gallé, Émile (2014), *Émile Gallé*, New York: Parkstone International.

Garner, Philippe (2006), *Eileen Gray: Design and Architecture, 1878–1976*, London: Taschen.

Garnwell, Lynn (2015), *Mathematics and Art: A Cultural History*, Princeton, NJ: Princeton University Press.

Geddes, Patrick (1900), "The Closing Exhibition—Paris 1900," *Contemporary Review*, 78 (419): 653–8.

Gehl, Jan (1971), *Life Between Buildings*, Copenhagen: Danish Architectural Press.

Giedion, Sigfried (1929), *Befreites Wohnen*, Zurich: Orell Füssli.

Giedion, Sigfried (1948), *Mechanization Takes Command: A Contribution to Anonymous History*, Oxford: Oxford University Press.

Gilbert, Nicolas L., Mireille Guay, Denis Gauvin, Benoît Lévesque, Russell N. Dietz, and Cecilia C. Chan (2008), "Air Change Rate and Concentration of Formaldehyde in Residential Indoor Air," *Atmospheric Environment*, 42 (10): 2424–8.

Gimson, Ernest (n.d.), "Harry Peach and Dryad," Leicester Museums Websites. Available online: http://gimson.leicester.gov.uk/leicester-designers/harry-peach-and-dryad/ (accessed July 1, 2015).

Girouard, Mark (1978), *Life in the English Country House: A Social and Architectural History*, New Haven, CT: Yale University Press.

Gleiniger, Andrea (2000), "Marcel Breuer," in Jeannine Fiedler, Peter Feierabend, and Ute Ackermann (eds.), *Bauhaus*, Cologne: Könemann.

Gloag, John (1969), *A Short Dictionary of Furniture*, revised and enlarged edition, London: George Allen and Unwin.

Godau, Marion (1994), "Die Innenraumgestaltung in der DDR," in Kerstin Dörhöfer (ed.), *Wohnkultur und Plattenbau. Beispiele aus Berlin und Budapest*, 105–20, Berlin: Reimer.

Grace's Guide (2017), "De Vilbiss Co." Available online: https://www.gracesguide.co.uk/De_Vilbiss_Co (accessed June 3, 2021).

Grace's Guide (2020), "Pel." Available online: http://www.gracesguide.co.uk/Pel (accessed May 21, 2021).

Greenberg, Cara (1999), *Op to Pop: Furniture of the 1960s*, New York: Little, Brown and Company.

Greenhalgh, Paul (1990a), "The Struggles within French Furniture, 1900–1930," in Paul Greenhalgh (ed.), *Modernism in Design*, 54–84, London: Reaktion Books.

Greenhalgh, Paul, ed. (1990b), *Modernism in Design*, London: Reaktion Books.

Greenhalgh, Paul (2000), *Art Nouveau 1900–1914*, London: V&A Publications.

Greensted, Mary (1980), *Gimson and the Barnsleys*, London: Evans Brothers.

Green woodwork (n.d.), "Homepage." Available online: http://www.greenwoodwork.co.uk (accessed July 1, 2015).

Grier, Katherine (1997), *Culture and Comfort: Parlor Making and Middle Class Identity, 1850–1930*, Washington, DC: Smithsonian Institution Press.

Gries, Rainer (2003), *Produkte als Medien: Kulturgeschichte der Produktkommunikation in der Bundesrepublik und der DDR*, Leipzig: Leipziger Universitätsverlag.

Gronberg, Tag (1998), *Design on Modernity: Exhibiting the City in 1920s Paris*, Manchester, UK: Manchester University Press.

Gronberg, Tag (2007), *Vienna: City of Modernity, 1890–1914*, Oxford: Peter Lang.

Guffey, Elizabeth (2006), *Retro: The Culture of Revival*, London: Reaktion Books.

Günther, Sonja (1982), "Richard Riemerschmid und die Dresdener Werkstätten für Handwerkskunst," in Nerdinger Winfried (ed.), *Richard Riemerschmid: Vom Jugendstil zum Werkbund. Werke und Dokumente*, 34–8, Munich: Prestel Verlag.

Haddow, Robert (1997), *Pavilions of Plenty: Exhibiting America Culture Abroad in the 1950s*, Washington, DC: Smithsonian Institution.

Hall, Stuart (1997), *Representation: Cultural Representations and Signifying Practices*, London: Sage.

Hall, Stuart, David Morley, and Kuan-Hsing Chen (1996), *Stuart Hall: Critical Dialogues in Cultural Studies*, London: Routledge.

Hansen, Per (2006), "Networks; Narratives and New Markets: The Rise and Decline of Danish Modern Furniture Design 1930–1970," *Business History Review*, 80 (3): 449–83.

Harris, John (2007), *Moving Rooms: The Trade in Architectural Salvage*, New Haven, CT: Yale University Press.

Hart, Imogen (2010), *Arts and Crafts Objects*, Manchester, UK: Manchester University Press.

Havard, Henri (1887–9), *Dictionnaire de l'ameublement et de la décoration depuis de XIIIe siècle jusqu'à nos jours*, 3 vols, plus 1 vol. of plates, Paris: Maison Quantin.

Hayward, Helena (1965), *World Furniture: An Illustrated History*, London: Hamlyn.

Hayward Gallery (1995), *Art and Power: Europe under the Dictators 1930–45*, London: Thames and Hudson.

Hebdige, Dick (1979), *Subculture: Meaning of Style*, London: Routledge.

Heidelberg Historic Literature—digitized (1900), *The Art Warden: A Survey of all Areas of Beauty; Monthly Booklets for Art, Literature and Life*, February 13. https://doi.org/10.11588/diglit.7960.

Hensel, Michael and Achim Menges (2006), "Material and Digital Design Synthesis," *Architectural Design*, 76: 88–95. https://doi.org/10.1002/ad.244.

Hentschel, Karl-Martin (2013), *Ein Dschungel namens IKEA*, December 13. Available online: http://www.attac.de/fileadmin/user_upload/Kampagnen/konzernbesteuerung/Fotos/Recherche_IKEA.pdf (accessed January 15, 2016)

Hentschel, Karl-Martin (2015), "IKEA. Zahlst Du noch oder hinterziehst Du schon?," *Blätter für deutsche und internationale Politik*, 1: 101–8. Available online: https://www.blaetter.de/archiv/jahrgaenge/2015/januar/ikea-zahlst-du-noch-oder-hinterziehst-du-schon?print (accessed January 15, 2016).

Herring, Eleanor (2014), "Joining the Modern World: A Study of Street Furniture Design in Postwar Britain," in Anna Calvera and Helena Barbosa (eds.), *Tradition, Transition, Trajectories: Major or Minor Influences? Proceedings of the 9th conference of the International Committee of Design History and Design Studies*, 551–6, Aveiro: Universidade de Aveiro Editora.

Herring, Eleanor (2016), *Street Furniture Design: Contesting Modernism in Post-War Britain*, London: Bloomsbury.

Herrington, Susan (2013), *Cornelia Hahn Oberlander: Making the Modern Landscape*, Charlottesville: University of Virginia Press.

Heuvel, Dirk van den and Max Risselda (2004), *Alison and Peter Smithson—From the House of the Future to a House of Today*, Rotterdam: 010 Publishers.

Hirschler, Édmond (1874), *Le billard au XIXième siècle et son influence sur les moeurs: étude*, Marseille: Bibliothèque du monde élégante.

History (2009), "Marilyn Monroe Marries Joe DiMaggio," A&T Television Networks, November 13. Available online: http://www.history.com/this-day-in-history/marilyn-monroe-marries-joe-dimaggio (accessed May 26, 2015).

Hjorth, Herman (1937), *Machine Woodworking*, Milwaukee, WI: Bruce Publishing Company.

Hobsbawm, Eric and Terrance Ranger (1983), *The Invention of Tradition*, Cambridge: Cambridge University Press.

Holder, Julian (1990), "'Design in Everyday Things': Promoting Modernism in Britain, 1912–1944," in Paul Greenhalgh (ed.), *Modernism in Design*, 123–44, London: Reaktion Books.

Hollingsworth, Andrew (2008), *Danish Modern*, London: Gibbs M. Smith.

Holschbach, Susanne (1995), "Wohnen im Reich der Zeichen. Wohnmodelle der 70er, 80er und 90er Jahre," *Kunstforum*, 130 (May–July): 159–89.

"Home, Sweet Home of the Future" (1928), *Popular Mechanics*, (June): 923–7.

Hongxing, Zhang and Lauren Parker (2008), *China Design Now*, London: V&A Publishing.

Hosain, Attia ([1961] 1988), *Sunlight on a Broken Column*, London: Virago Press.

Hoskins, Stephen (2013), *3D Printing for Artists, Designers and Makers*, London: Bloomsbury.

Hoskyns, Teresa (2014), *The Empty Place: Democracy and Public Space*, Abingdon, UK: Routledge.

Hours, Véronique, Fabien Maudit, Jérémie Souteyrat, and Manuel Tardits (2014), *L'archipel de la maison. Une architecture domestique au Japon*, Paris: Le Lézard Noir.

Howarth, Dan (2015), "Responsive Street Furniture Adapts Public Spaces to Improve Pedestrians' Needs," *Dezeen*, May 3. Available online http://www.dezeen.com/2015/05/03/responsive-street-furniture-ross-atkins-jonathan-scott-marshalls-designs-of-the-year-2015/ (accessed May 6, 2015).

Howsyourdad (2006), s.v. "Brixton Briefcase," *Urban Dictionary*, March 22. Available online: https://www.urbandictionary.com/define.php?term=brixton%20briefcase (accessed June 6, 2021).

Humphrey, Z. (1911), "On a Bench in the Park," *Outlook*, 97 (1): 37.

Huxley, A. (1954), *The Doors of Perception*, London: Chatto & Windus.

Huxtable, Ada Louise (1959), "Street Furniture," *Horizon*, 2 (2): 105–12.

IKEA (2013), "IKEA Group Yearly Summary FY13." Available online: https://www.ikea.com/gb/en/files/pdf/fa/f1/faf12afa/ikea-group-yearly-summary-2013.pdf (accessed May 21, 2021).

IKEA Singapore (2014), "Experience the Power of a Bookbook™," YouTube, September 3. Available online: https://www.youtube.com/watch?v=MOXQo7nURs0 (accessed November 13, 2015).

IKEA Switzerland (2015), "Hellmuth Karasek rezensiert den IKEA Katalog," YouTube, August 20. Available online: https://www.youtube.com/watch?v=8mP0hwWEiko (accessed December 15, 2015).

IKEA (n.d.), "Soft Toys for Education." Available online: http://www.ikea.com/gb/en/good-cause-campaign/soft-toys-for-education/index.html (accessed December 1, 2015).

Isenstadt, Sandy (2006), *The Modern American House: Spaciousness and Middle Class Identity*, Cambridge: Cambridge University Press.

Itex Furniture (n.d.). Available online: http://itexfurniture.com (accessed July 1, 2015).

Jackson, Lesley (1998), *The Sixties: Decade of Design Revolution*, London: Phaidon Press.

Jackson, Lesley (2001), *Robin and Lucienne Day: Pioneers of Contemporary Design*, London: Mitchell Beazley.

Jackson, Lesley (2008), *From Atoms to Patterns: Crystal Structure Designs from the 1951 Festival of Britain*, Shepton Beauchamp: Richard Dennis Publications in association with the Wellcome Collection.

Jackson, Lesley (2013), *Modern British Furniture: Design Since 1945*, London: V&A Publishing.

Jacobs, Jane (1961), *The Death and Life of Great American Cities*, New York: Random House.

Jameson, Frederic (1991), *Postmodernism, or, The Cultural Logic of Late Capitalism*, London: Verso.

Jencks, Charles. A. (1977), *The Language of Post-Modern Architecture*, London: Academy Editions.

Jenkins, David (2005), *Norman Foster: Works 2*, London: Prestel.

Jenkins, Jennifer (1996), "The Kitsch Collections and 'The Spirit in Furniture' Cultural Reform and National Culture in Germany," *Social History*, 21 (2): 123–41.

Jonsson, Anna and Nicolai J. Foss (2011), "International Expansion through Flexible Replication: Learning from the Internationalization Experience of IKEA," *Journal of International Business Studies*, 42 (9): 1079–102.

Jordan, Robert Furneaux (1972), *Le Corbusier*, London: Dent.

Jungbluth, Rüdiger (2006), *Die 11 Geheimnisse des IKEA-Erfolgs*, Frankfurt: Campus Verlag.

Kafka, Franz (1938), *Amerika*. Available online: https://archive.org/details/amerika00fran_0/page/n3/mode/2up (accessed May 12, 2015).

Kaminsky, Anne (2007), "'True advertising means promoting a good thing through a good form': Advertising in the German Democratic Republic," in Pamela E. Swett, S. Jonathan Wiesen, and Jonathan R. Zatlin (eds.), *Selling Modernity. Advertising in Twentieth-Century Germany*, 262–86, Durham, NC: Duke University Press.

Kauffmann, Edgar, Jr. (1950), *What is Modern Design*, New York: Museum of Modern Art.

Kautonen, Mika (1996), "Emerging Innovative Networks and Milieux: The Case of the Furniture Industry in the Lahti Region of Finland," *European Planning Studies*, 4 (4): 439–56.

Keim, Christiane (2012), "Performative Räume—Verführerische Bilder—Montierte Blicke. Zur Konstruktion von Geschlecht im Interieur," in Stefan Moebius and Sophia Prinz (eds.), *Das Design der Gesellschaft: Zur Kultursoziologie des Designs*, 143–62, Bielefeld: Transkript.

Kerb (2004), s.v. "Ghetto Blaster," *Urban Dictionary*, November 27. Available online: https://www.urbandictionary.com/define.php?term=ghetto%20blaster (accessed June 6, 2021).

Kiaer, Christina (2005), *Imagine No Possessions: The Socialist Objects of Russian Constructivism*, Cambridge, MA: MIT Press.

Kiesler, Frederick J. (1949), *Manifeste du Corréalisme ou les états unis de l'art plastique*, Bologne: Editions de l'architecture d'Aujourd'hui.

Kinchin, Julliet and Aidan O'Connor, eds. (2012), *Century of the Child Growing by Design 1900–2000*, New York: Museum of Modern Art.

Kingsley, Mary H. (1897), *Travels in West Africa: Congo Français, Corisco and Cameroons*, London: Macmillan & Co.

Kirkham, Pat (1988), *The London Furniture Trade 1700–1870*, London: Furniture History Society.

Kirkham, Pat (1995), *Charles and Ray Eames: Designers of the Twentieth Century*, Cambridge, MA: MIT Press.

Kirkham, Pat (2009), "New Environments for Modern Living: 'At home' with the Eameses," in Penny Sparke, Anne Massey, Trevor Keeble, and Brenda Martin (eds.), *Designing the Modern Interior: From the Victorians to Today*, 171–82, Oxford: Berg.

The Kiss (1929), [Film] Dir. Jacques Feyder, USA: Metro-Goldwyn-Mayer (MGM).

Knott, Stephen (2015), *Amateur Craft: History and Theory*, London: Bloomsbury Academic.

Koomen, Philip (2004), "A Sustainable Approach to Furniture Design," *The Designer*, Chartered Society of Designers, 21: 8–9.

Koppensteiner, Suzanne, ed. (2003), *Secession: The Architecture*, Vienna: Remprint.

Kostelnick, Charles and David Roberts (2011), *Designing Visual Language: Strategies for Professional Communicators*, Boston: Longman.

Kristofferson, Sara and William Jewson (2014), *Design by IKEA: A Cultural History*, London: Bloomsbury.

Kuper, Marijke and Lex Reitsma (2012), *Rietveld's Chair*, Rotterdam: nai010 publishers.

Lacey, Kate (1996), *Feminine Frequencies Gender, German Radio, and the Public Sphere, 1923–1945*, Ann Arbor: University of Michigan Press.

Lalanne, Antoine (1866), *Le billard*, Paris: Auguste Aubry librarie éditeur.

Lange, Christiane (2006), *Ludwig Mies van der Rohe & Lilly Reich: Furniture and Interiors*, Ostfildern: Hatje Cantz.

Larrochelle, Jean-Jacques (2014), "La villa Arpel, décor de Jacques Tati, vedette du pavilion français à la Biennale de Venise," *Le Monde*, April 19.

Larsson, Carl ([1899] 1976), *Our Home*, London: Methuen.

Latour, Bruno (2005), *Reassembling the Social: An Introduction to Actor-Network-Theory*, Oxford: Oxford University Press.

Lazaj, Jehanne and Bruno Ythier, eds. (2012), *Tapisseries 1925 Aubusson, Beauvais, Les Gobelins à l'Exposition Internationale des Arts Décoratifs Paris*, Toulouse: Éditions Privat.

Leavitt, Sarah A. (2002), *From Catherine Beecher to Martha Stewart: A Cultural History of Domestic Advice*, Chapel Hill: University of North Carolina Press.

Le Corbusier (1925), *L'Art Décoratif d'Aujourd'hui*, Paris: G. Crès.

Le Corbusier ([1925] 1980), *L'Art Décoratif d'Aujourd'hui. Collection de "L'Esprit Nouveau". Collection "Architectures" dirigée par François Hébert-Stevens*, Paris: Les Éditions Arthaud.

Le Corbusier ([1925] 1987), *Decorative Art of Today*, trans. James Dunnett, London: Architectural Press.

Le Corbusier, ([1925].1970), *Towards A New Architecture*, trans. Frederick Etchells, London: Architectural Press.

Leech, Geoffrey N. (1966), *English in Advertising: A Linguistic Study of Advertising in Great Britain*, London: Longmans.

Lees-Maffei, Grace (2001), "From Service to Self-Service: Advice Literature as Design Discourse, 1920–1970," *Journal of Design History*, 14 (3): 187–206.

Lees-Maffei, Grace (2014), *Design at Home: Domestic Advice Books in Britain and the USA since 1945*, Abingdon, UK: Routledge.

Lees-Maffei, Grace and Kjetil Fallen, eds. (2013), *Made in Italy: Rethinking a Century of Italian Design*, London: Bloomsbury.

Lefebvre, Henri (1991), *The Production of Space*, Oxford: Blackwell.

Lefebvre, Henri (2000), "Space and Politics," in Eleaonore Kofman and Elisabeth Lebas (eds.), *Writings on Cities*, 185–204, Oxford: Blackwell.

Lethaby, William (1890), *Plain Furniture*, London: The Workers' Guild.

Lethen, Helmut (2002), *Cool Conduct: The Culture of Distance in Weimar Germany*, trans. Don Reneau, Berkeley: University of California Press.

Lévi-Strauss, C. (1962), *La pensée sauvage*, Paris: Plon.

Lewis, S. (1935), *It Can't Happen Here*, New York: Triangle Books. Available online: https://archive.org/details/itcanthappenhere0000unse/page/n5/mode/2up (accessed June 6, 2021).

The Life of Napoleon (1909), [Film] Dir. J. Stuart Blackton, USA: Vitagraph Company.

Limbert, Charles (1992), *Limbert Arts and Crafts Furniture: The Complete 1903 Catalog*, New York: Dover Publications.

Lizon, Peter (1997), "Bentwood," in Joanna Banham (ed.), *Encyclopaedia of Interior Design*, Abingdon, UK: Routledge.

Lodder, Christina (2006), "Searching for Utopia," in Christopher Wilk (ed.), *Modernism: Designing a New World, 1914–1939*, 23–69, London: V&A Publications.

Logan, Thad (2001), *The Victorian Parlour: A Cultural Study*, Cambridge: Cambridge University Press.

Logie, Gordon (1947), *Furniture from Machines*, London: G. Allen and Unwin.

Long, Veronique (2009), "Les collectionneurs juifs parisiens sous la Troisième République," *Archives Juives*, 42 (1): 84–104. Available online:https://www.cairn.info/revue-archives-juives1-2009-1-page-84.htm (accessed May 21, 2021).

Loos, Adolf ([1908] 1998), *Ornament and Crime: Selected Essays*, London: Ariadne.

Lovelock, James (1995), *The Ages of Gaia: A Biography of Our Living Earth*, New York: Norton.

Low, S., D. Taplin, and S. Sheld (2009), *Rethinking Urban Space: Public Parks and Cultural Diversity*, Austin: University of Texas Press.

Lubbock, Jules (1995), *The Tyranny of Taste: The Politics of Architecture and Design in Britain, 1550–1960*, New Haven, CT: Yale University Press.

Lynn, Greg (1999), *Animate Form*, New York: Princeton Architectural Press.

Maatje, Christian (2000), *Verkaufte Luft. Die Kommerzialisierung des Rundfunks. Hörfunkwerbung in Deutschland (1923–1936)*, Potsdam: Verlag für Berlin-Brandenburg.

MacCarthy, Fiona (2004), "William Richard Lethaby," *Oxford Dictionary of National Biography*, September 23. https://doi.org/10.1093/ref:odnb/34503.

McCracken, Grant (1988), *Culture and Consumption: New Approaches to the Symbolic Character of Consumer Goods and Activities*, Bloomington: Indiana University Press.

McCracken, Grant (2005), *Culture and Consumption II: Markets, Meaning, and Brand Management*, Bloomington: Indiana University Press.

McDonald, Gay (2008), "The 'Advance' of American Postwar Design in Europe: MoMA and the 'Design for Use, USA' Exhibition 1951–1953," *Design Issues*, 24 (2): 1–27.

Máčel, Otakar (2006), *2100 Metal Chairs: A Typology by Otakar Máčel*, Rotterdam: Van Hezik-fonds 90 publishers.

Macguire, Patrick and Jonathan Woodham (1997), *Design and Cultural Politics in Post-War Britain: The Britain Can Make It Exhibition of 1946*, London: Leicester University Press.

McLeod, Mary, ed. (2003), *Charlotte Perriand: An Art of Living*, New York: Harry N. Abrams.

Marcus, George H. (1998), *Design in the Fifties: When Everyone Went Modern*, Munich: Prestel.

Marcus, George H. (2000), *Le Corbusier: Inside the Machine for Living*, New York: Monacelli Press.

Margetts, Martina (2006), *Tord Boontje*, New York: Rizzoli International Publications.

Margolin, Victor (2015), *World History of Design*, London: Bloomsbury.

Mars Attacks! (1996), [Film] Dir. Tim Burton, USA: Warner Brothers and Tim Burton Productions.

Mårtenson, Rita (1981), "Innovations in Multinational Retailing: IKEA on the Swedish, Swiss, German and Austrian Furniture Markets," Ph.D. diss.,University of Gothenburg.

Marßolek, Inge and Adelheid von Saldern, eds. (1989), *Zuhören und Gehörtwerden. Radio in der DDR der fünfziger Jahre. Zwischen Lenkung und Ablenkung*, Tübingen: Edition Diskord.

Marx, Roger (1902a), "Essais de rénovation ornementale: La salle de billard d'une villa moderne," *Gazette des Beaux-Arts*, 18 (3) (May): 409–24.

Marx, Roger (1902b), "Une salle de billard et une galerie modernes," *Art et décoration*, 12 (July): 1–13.

Marx, Roger (1913), *L'art social*, Paris: E. Fasquelle.

Massey, Anne (2011), *Chair*, London: Reaktion Books.

Matthew, W.P., ed. (1946), *The Practical Home Handyman: A Comprehensive Guide to Constructional and Repair Work About the House*, London: Odhams.

Matthews, Ed (2001), "European League Table of Imports of Illegal Timber," *Friends of the Earth Briefing*. Available online: http://www.foe.co.uk/sites/default/files/downloads/league_table_tropical_timber.pdf (accessed October 21, 2015)

Maurois, A. (1931), *"Sur le Vif" L'Exposition Coloniale*, Paris.

Mawson, T.H. (1911), *Civic Art. Studies in Town Planning Parks Boulevards and Open Spaces*, London: Batsford.

Mayes, L.J. (1960), *The History of Chairmaking in High Wycombe*, London: Routledge & Kegan Paul.

Mazur, Jennie (2013), *Die "schwedische" Lösung. Eine kultursemiotisch orientierte Untersuchung der IKEA-Werbespots in Deutschland*, Würzburg: Königshausen & Neumann.

Meikle, Jeffrey L. (2005), *Design in the USA*, Oxford: Oxford University Press.

Men in Black (1997), [Film] Dir. Barry Sonnenfeld, USA: Columbia Pictures.

Merleau-Ponty, Maurice ([1945] 1962), *Phenomenology of Perception*, trans. Colin Smith, London: Routledge.

Mikhailov, Boris (1999), *Case History*, Zurich: Scalo Publishers.

Miller, Daniel (1987), *Material Culture and Mass Consumption*, Oxford: Blackwell.

Miller, Wilbur R. (2012), *The Social History of Crime and Punishment in America: An Encyclopedia*, 5 vols., London: Sage Publications.

Mingxin, Bao and Lu Lijun (2008), "A Brief History of Chinese Fashion Design," in Zhang Hongxing, Lauren Parker, and Beth McKillop (eds.), *China Design Now*, 106–9, London: V&A Publishing.

Minton, Anna (2006), *The Privatisation of Public Space*, London: RICS Report. Available online: http://www.annaminton.com/privatepublicspace.pdf (accessed May 6, 2015).

Mirzoeff, Nicholas (1999), *An Introduction to Visual Culture*, London: Routledge.

Mitchell, Lynne and Elizabeth Burton (2006), *Inclusive Urban Design: Streets for Life*, Oxford: Elsevier.

Molesworth, G.L. (1858), "On the Conversion of Wood by Machinery," *Minutes of the Proceedings*, 17: 17–39, London: Institute of Civil Engineers.

Möller, Heino R. (1981), *Innenräume/Außenwelten. Studien zur Darstellung bürgerlicher Privatheit in Kunst und Warenwerbung*, Gießen: Anabas.

Mo Mo Wo: Women's Creativity since the Modern Movement (n.d.). Available online: http://www.momowo.eu/ (accessed September 1, 2015).

Moors, Anneke (2006), *Simply Droog: 10 + 3 years of Creating Innovation and Discussion*, Amsterdam: Droog.

Morris, William (1887), "How We Live and How We Might Live," in *Commonweal*. Available online: https://www.marxists.org/archive/morris/works/1884/hwl/hwl.htm (accessed October 21, 2015).

Morris and Co. (*c*. 1912), *Specimens of Furniture and Interior Decoration*, London.

Morris Contract Furniture (n.d.), "About Us." Available online: http://www. morrisfurniture.co.uk/about_us/ (accessed June 4, 2021).

Morsiani, Paola and Trevor Smith, eds. (2005), *Andrea Zittel: Critical Space*, Munich: Prestel Publishing.

Morton, Patricia (2000), *Hybrid Modernities: Architecture and Representation at the 1931 Colonial Exposition, Paris*, Cambridge, MA: MIT Press.

Mulford Robinson, Charles (1904), *Modern Civic Art or The City Made Beautiful*, London: G.P. Putnam & Sons.

Mumford, Lewis (1945), *The Culture of Cities*, London: Secker & Warburg.

Mundt, Barbara (1998), *Architekten als Designer. Beispiele in Berlin. Kunstgewerbemuseum des Staatlichen Museen zu Berlin*, Munich: Hirmer Verlag GmbH.

Musée D'Orsay (2008), *Alexandre Charpentier (1856–1909) Naturalisme et Art Nouveau*, Paris: Éditions Nicolas Chaudun.

The Museum of Modern Art ([1999] 2004), *MoMA Highlights*, New York: The Museum of Modern Art.

Muthesius, Hermann ([1904–5] 1979), *The English House*, edited by Janet Seligman, London: Crosby, Lockwood, Staples.

Muthesius, Stefan (1974), *Das englische Vorbild. Eine Studie zu den deutschen Reformbewegungen in Architektur, Wohnbau und Kunstgewerbe im späteren 19. Jahrhundert*, Munich: Prestel.

Muzi, C. (2010), "Diana Cabeza," *Art Nexus*, 9 (78): 96–101.

My Dream is Yours (1949), [Film] Dir. Michael Curtiz, USA: Michael Curtiz Productions and Warner Bros.

Myerson, Jeremy (1992), *Gordon Russell: Designer of Furniture, 1892–1992*, London: Design Council/Gordon Russell Limited.

Myerson, Jeremy (1995), *Makepeace: A Spirit of Adventure in Craft and Design*, London: Conran Octopus.

Nakashima, George (2012), The Soul of a Tree: A Master Woodworker's Reflections, New York: Kodansha Publishing.

Naylor, Gillian (1985), *The Bauhaus Reassessed: Sources and Design Theory*, London: The Herbert Press.

Naylor, Gillian (1990), "Swedish Grace … or the Acceptable Face of Modernism?," in Paul Greenhalgh (ed.), *Modernism in Design*, 164–83, London: Reaktion Books.

Naylor, Gillian (2000), "Secession in Vienna," in Paul Greenhalgh (ed.), *Art Nouveau 1890–1914*, 164–84, London: V&A Publications.

Newman, Oscar (1973), *Defensible Space: People and Design in the Violent City*,
    London: Architectural Press.
Nerdinger Winfried (1982), *Richard Riemerschmid. Vom Jugendstil zum Werkbund.
    Werke und Dokumente*, Munich: Prestel Verlag.
Newsstand (1925). Available online: https://news.uwf.edu/english-department-
    launches-1925-virtual-newsstand-web-site/ (accessed February 2, 2016).
Nimmen, Jane van (2014), "Exhibition Review *Joseph Vitta: Passion de collection*,"
    13 (2). Available online: http://www.19thc-artworldwide.org/autumn14/nimmen-
    reviews-joseph-vitta-passion-de-collection (accessed January 7, 2016)
Noever, Peter, ed. (2006), *The Yearning for Beauty: The Wiener Werkstätte and the
    Stoclet House*, MAK Vienna: Hatje Cantz Verlag.
Noyes, Eliot (1941), *Organic Design in Home Furnishings*, New York: The Museum of
    Modern Art.
Nye, Joseph, Jr. (2005), "Public Diplomacy and Soft Power," *Annals of the American
    Academy of Political and Social Science*, 616: 94–109.
Obniski, Monica (2007), "Exhibiting Modernity Through the Lens of Tradition in
    Gilbert Rohde's Design for Living Interior," *Journal of Design History*, 20 (3):
    227–42.
OED Online (2021a), s.v. "Chair." Available online: https://www.oed.com/view/Entry/
    30215?rskey=3EJn9r&result=1&isAdvanced=false#eid (accessed June 6, 2021).
OED Online (2021b), "Coming Out." Available online: https://www.oed.com/view/
    Entry/416963?rskey=MPK36q&result=3&isAdvanced=false#eid (accessed June
    6, 2021).
OED Online (2021c), "Electric Chair." Available online https://www.oed.com/view/
    Entry/60253?redirectedFrom=electric+chair#eid5821289 (accessed June 6, 2021).
Ogata, Amy (2013), *Designing the Creative Child: Playthings and Places in Midcentury
    America*, Minneapolis: University of Minnesota Press.
Oldenzeil, Ruth and Karin Zachman, eds. (2009), *The Cold War Kitchen:
    Americanization, Technology and European Users*, Cambridge, MA: MIT Press.
O'Mahony, Claire (2010), "Cubist Chameleons: André Mare, the Camoufleurs, and
    the Canons of Art History," *Journal of War and Culture Studies*, 3 (1): 11–35.
Ostergard, Derek, ed. (1987), *Bent Wood and Metal Furniture: 1850–1946*, New York:
    American Federation of Arts.
"Outdoor Seats: A Competition for Manufacturers" (1953), *Design*, 54: 30–2.
Overy, Paul (1991), *De Stijl*, London: Thames and Hudson.
Overy, Paul (2004), "Visions of the Future and the Immediate Past: The Werkbund
    Exhibition, Paris 1930," *Journal of Design History*, 17 (4): 337–57.
Palais de Lumière (2014), *Joseph Vitta: Passion de collection*, Paris: Somogy éditions
    d'art.
Panayotou, Theodore and Peter S. Ashton (1992), *Not by Timber Alone: Economics
    and Ecology for Sustaining Tropical Forests*, Washington, DC: Island Press.
Parker, Lauren (2008), "Shanghai: Dream City," in Zhang Hongxing, Lauren Parker,
    and Beth McKillop (eds.), *China Design Now*, 90–100, London: V&A Publishing.
Pattou, Albert Brace and Clarence Lee Vaughn (1944), *Furniture Finishing, Decoration
    and Patching*, Chicago: Frederick J. Drake & Company.
Pautz, Michelle (2002), "The Decline in Average Weekly Cinema Attendance," *Issues
    in Political Economy*, (11). Available online: https://ecommons.udayton.edu/pol_
    fac_pub/25/ (accessed June 9, 2021).

Pearson, Paul David (1978), *Alvar Aalto and the International Style*, London: Mitchell.

Peer, Shany (1998), *France on Display: Peasants, Provincials and Folklore in the 1937 Paris World's Fair*, Albany: State University of New York Press.

Penson (n.d.). Available online: http://www.penson.co (accessed February 2, 2016).

Pevsner, Nikolaus ([1936] 2005), *Pioneers of Modern Design: From William Morris to Walter Gropius*, New Haven, CT: Yale University Press.

Pevsner, Nikolaus (1939), "The History of Plywood up to 1914," *Architectural Review*, 86: 129–30.

Pfeffer-Lévy, Géraldine, Dominique Darbois, and Granville Fields (1998), *Jean Prouvé*, Paris: Galerie Jousse Seguin, Galerie Enrico Navarra.

Phelan, Michael ([1859] 1874), *The Game of Billiards*, New York: D. Appleton and Co.

Phillips, Barty (1984), *Conran and the Habitat Story*, London: Weidenfeld and Nicholson.

Pick, Frank (1934), "The Design of the Street," in John Gloag (ed.), *Design in Modern Life*, 97–110, London: Allen & Unwin.

Pirc, Andreja and Richard Vlosky (2010), "A Brief Overview of the U.S. Furniture Industry," *Louisiana Forest Products Development Center Working Paper #89*. Available online: http://www.lfpdc.lsu.edu/publications/working_papers/wp89.pdf (accessed October 10, 2015).

Playtime (1967), [Film] Dir: Jacques Tati, France: Specta Films and Jolly Film.

Popp, Joseph (1916), *Bruno Paul: Mit 319 Abbildungen von Häusern und Wohnungen*, Munich: F. Bruckmann A.G.

Porter, Julia and Sally MacDonald (1990), "Fabricating Interiors: Approaches to the History of Domestic Furnishing at the Geffrye Museum," *Journal of Design History*, 3 (2/3): 175–82.

Possémé, Évelyne (1999), *Le Mobilier Français 1910–1930: Les Années 25*, Paris: Éditions Massin.

Powell, A. et al. (2017), *Pink Floyd: Their Mortal Remains*, London: V&A Publishing.

Power, Dominic and Johan Jansson (2011), "Constructing Brands from the Outside? Brand Channels, Cyclical Clusters and Global Circuits," in Andy Pike (ed.), *Brands and Branding Geographies*, 150–64, Cheltenham: Edward Elgar Publishing.

Praz, Mario (1964), *An Illustrated History of Interior Decoration: From Pompeii to Art Nouveau*, London: Thames and Hudson.

Priscilla Publishing Co. (1925), *Modern Priscilla Home Furnishing Book*, Boston: Priscilla Publishing Company.

The Prisoner (1967–8), [TV Program] ITC and Everyman Films.

Proust, Marcel ([1906] 1987), *On Reading Ruskin*, translated and edited by Jean Autret, William Burford, and Phillip J. Wolfe, New Haven, CT: Yale University Press.

Radice, Mario (1936), "Le decorazioni," *Quadrante*, 35/36 (October): 33.

"Quality in Town and Country" (1995), *Urban Design*, 53.

Quinn, Bradley (2004), *Mid Century Modern: Interiors, Furniture, Design Details*, London: Conran Octopus.

Radice, Barbara (1985), *Memphis: Research, Experiences, Results, Failures and Successes of New Design*, London: Thames and Hudson.

Radice, Barbara (1993), *Ettore Sottsass: A Critical Biography*, London: Thames and Hudson.

Rahman, Shaikh H. (n.d.), *English House: An Evolutionary Wonder*. Available online: https://www.academia.edu/10658140/English_house_an_evolutionary_wonder (accessed June 9, 2021).

Ramakers, Remy and Gijs Bakker, eds. (1998), *Droog Design: Spirit of the Nineties*, Rotterdam: 010 Publishers.

Rasch, Brüder (1981), *Material, Konstruktion, Form 1926–1930*, Düsseldorf: Edition Marzona.

Rasch, Heinz and Bodo Rasch (1928), *Der Stuhl*, Stuttgart: Akademischer Verlag, Dr Fritz Wedekind & Co.

Reed, Christopher (2004), *Bloomsbury Rooms: Modernism, Subculture and Domesticity*, New Haven, CT: Yale University Press.

Reid, Hew (1986), *The Furniture Makers: A History of Trade Unionism in the Furniture Trade, 1865–1972*, Oxford: Malthouse.

Reid, Susan (2008), "'Our kitchen is just as good': Soviet Responses to the American National Exhibition in Moscow," in David Crowley and Jane Pavitt (eds.), *Cold War Modern Design 1945–70*, 154–63, London: V&A Publishing.

Reimann, Sandra (2012), "Zugänge zu Korpora deutscher Werbung," in Nina Janich (ed.), *Handbuch Werbekommunikation: Sprachwissenschaftliche und interdisziplinäre Zugänge*, 483–93, Tübingen: Francke.

Reimer, Suzanne and Deborah Leslie (2004), "Identity, Consumption and the Home," *Home Cultures*, 1: 187–208.

Reimer, Suzanne and Philip Pinch (2013), "Geographies of the British Government's Wartime Utility Furniture Scheme 1940–45," *Journal of Historical Geography*, 39: 99–112.

Rejali, Darius (2009), *Torture and Democracy*, Princeton, NJ: Princeton University Press.

Relf, Edward (1987), *The Modern Urban Landscape*, London: Croom Helm.

Rietveld, Gerrit (1919), "Aantekeening bij een kinderstoel (bijlage no. XVIII)," *De Stijl*, 2 (9): 102.

Rifkin, Jeremy (2012), "The Third Industrial Revolution: How the Internet, Green Electricity, and 3-D Printing are Ushering in a Sustainable Era of Distributed Capitalism," *World Financial Review*, March 3. Available online: https://worldfinancialreview.com/the-third-industrial-revolution-how-the-internet-green-electricity-and-3-d-printing-are-ushering-in-a-sustainable-era-of-distributed-capitalism/ (accessed June 9, 2021).

Rifkind, David (2012), *The Battle for Modernism: Quadrante and the Politicization of Architectural Discourse in Fascist Italy*, Vicenza: Centro Internazionale di Studi di Architettura Andrea Palladio, Marsilio.

Riley, Terrence and Edward Eigen (1995), "Between the Museum and the Marketplace: Selling Good Design," in John Szarkowski and John Elderfield (eds.), *The Museum of Modern Art at Mid-Century: At Home and Abroad*, 151–75, New York: Harry Abrams.

Roberts, C. (1901), *Billiards for everybody*, London.

Rogers, Richard (1997), *Cities for a Small Planet*, London: Faber & Faber.

Rosenzweig, Roy and Elizabeth Blackmar (1992), *The Park and the People: A History of Central Park*, Ithaca, NY: Cornell University Press.

Ross, Phyllis (2004), "Merchandising the Modern: Gilbert Rohde at Herman Miller," *Journal of Design History*, 17 (4): 359–76.

Rossi, Catherine (2011), "Making Memphis: 'Glue Culture' and Postmodern Production Strategies," in Glenn Adamson and Jane Pavitt (eds.), *Postmodernism: Style and Subversion, 1970–1990*, 160–65, London: V&A Publishing.

Rudolph, Nicole (2014), "Model Homes: Negotiating Interiors in Postwar France," *Interiors*, 5 (2): 239–56.

Rudolph, Nicole (2015), *At Home in Postwar France: Modern Mass Housing and the Right to Comfort*, New York: Berghahn.

Rüegg, Arthur (2012), *Le Corbusier: Furniture and Interiors 1905–1965*, Zurich: Schiedegger and Spiess; Paris: Fondation Le Corbusier.

Rüegg, Arthur (2014), *Le Corbusier Furniture and Interiors 1905–1965: The Complete Catalogue Raisonné*, London: Asin.

Rusconi, Paolo and Giorgio Zanchetti (2013), *The Thirties: The Arts in Italy beyond Fascism*, Florence: Giunti Editore; Fondazione Palazzo Strozzi.

Ruskin, John ([1865] 1949), "Of Queen's Gardens," in *Sesame and Lilies: Two Lectures*, London: Smith, Elder & Co.

Russell, Gordon and Jacques Groag (1947), *The Story of Furniture*, London: Puffin Books.

Rutsky, R.L. (1999), *High Technē: Art and Technology from the Machine Aesthetic to the Posthuman*, Minneapolis: University of Minnesota Press.

Ryan, Deborah (1997), *The Ideal Home Through the Twentieth Century*, London: Hazar.

Rybczynski, Witold (1986), *Home: A Short History of an Idea*, New York: Viking.

Samuel, Raphael (2012), *Theatres of Memory: Past and Present in Contemporary Culture*, London: Verso.

Sand, Jordan (2013), "Tropical Furniture and Bodily Comportment in Colonial Asia," *Positions: east asia cultures critique*, 21 (1): 95–132.

Schöberl, Sabrina (2005), "Vergleichende Werbung und ihre Wirkung auf den Rezipienten am Fallbeispiel Mömax versus IKEA," BA thesis, University of Vienna.

Schorske, Carl (1980), *Fin-de-siècle Vienna: Politics and Culture*, London: Weidenfeld and Nicholson.

Schumaker, Thomas (1991), *Surface and Symbol: Giuseppe Terragni and the Architecture of Italian Rationalism*, New York: Princeton Architectural Press; London: ADT.

Schwartz, Frederick J. (1996), *The Werkbund. Design Theory and Mass Culture before the First World War*, New Haven, CT: Yale University Press.

Science Museum Group (n.d.), "Wurlitzer Simplex Multi-selector Juke Box Model 41." Available online: https://collection.sciencemuseumgroup.org.uk/objects/co117297/wurlitzer-simplex-multi-selector-juke-box-model-41 (accessed June 6, 2021).

Scott Brown, Denise (1990), "Public Realm, Public Sector and The Public Interest in Urban Design," *Architectural Design*, 60 (1–2): 21–9.

Searl, Marjorie B. and Marie Via (1994), *Head, Heart, and Hand: Elbert Hubbard and the Roycrofters*, Rochester, NY: University of Rochester Press.

Seckendorf, Eva von (2000), "The Joinery and Fitting Shop," in Jeannine Fiedler, Peter Feierabend, and Ute Ackermann (eds.), *Bauhaus*, Cologne: Könemann.

Second Report from the Select Committee of the House of Lords on the Sweating System: With Proceedings, Minutes of Evidence and Appendix (1888), London: HMSO.

Seike, Kiyosi and Charles S. Terry (1964), *Contemporary Japanese Houses*, vol. 1, Tokyo: Kodansha.

Selle, Gert (1994), *Geschichte des Design in Deutschland*, Frankfurt: Campus.

Servas, Lois and Gordon Olsen (1987), *Steelcase: The First 75 Years*, Grand Rapids MI: Steelcase.

Sex and the City 2 (2010), [Film] Dir. Michael Patrick King, USA: Home Box Office (HBO).

Shane, Grahame (1983), "The Street in the Twentieth Century," *Cornell Journal of Architecture*, 2: 20–41.

Sharp, Dennis, Tim Benton, and Barbie Campbell Cole (1977), *Pel and Tubular Steel Furniture of the Thirties*, London: Architectural Press.

Sheridan, Michael (1951), "The Past and the Future," *Ideal Home Magazine*: 132–7.

Shoreditch College (1998–2017), "History." Available online: http://www. shoreditchcollege.org/pages/history.html (accessed July 1, 2015).

Siegfried, Susan (1995), *The Art of Louis Léopold Boilly: Modern Life in Napoleonic France*, New Haven, CT: Yale University Press.

Simmel, Georg ([1896] 2010), "Berliner Gewerbe-Ausstellung," *Die Zeit*, July 25: 56; translated in Alexander Geppert, *Fleeting Cities: Imperial Expositions in Fin-de-Siècle Europe*, 283–5, trans. Sam Whimster, Basingstoke, UK: Palgrave Macmillan.

Simon Thomas, Mienke (2008), *Dutch Design: A History*, London: Reaktion.

Sims2 (2004), [Computer Game] Electronic Arts.

Sims3 (2009), [Computer Game] Electronic Arts.

Single Standard (1929), [Film] Dir. John S Robertson, USA: Metro-Goldwyn-Mayer (MGM).

Smith, Courtenay and Sean Topham (2002), *Extreme Houses*, Munich: Prestel.

Smith, Joanna and Ray Rogers (2006), *Behind the Veneer: The South Shoreditch Furniture Trade and its Buildings*, Swindon, UK: English Heritage.

Smith, Llewellyn (1927), *Reports on the Present Position and Tendencies of the Industrial Arts as Indicated at the International Exhibition of Modern Decorative and Industrial Arts, Paris, 1925*, London: Department of Overseas Trade.

Smith, Terry (1993), *Making the Modern: Industry, Art, and Design in America*, London: University of Chicago Press.

The Social Life of Small Urban Spaces (1988) [Film] Dir. William H. Whyte, USA, Direct Cinema. Available online: https://archive.org/details/SmallUrbanSpaces (accessed May 6, 2015).

Sparke, Penny (1982), *Ettore Sottsass Jr.*, London: Design Council.

Sparke, Penny (1986a), *An Introduction to Design & Culture in the Twentieth Century*, London: Routledge.

Sparke, Penny (1986b), *Furniture Twentieth-Century Design*, London: Harper Collins.

Sparke, Penny, ed. (1986c), *Did Britain Make It? British Design in Context 1946–86*, London: Design Council.

Sparke, Penny (1988), *Italian Design: 1870 to the Present*, London: Thames & Hudson.

Sparke, Penny (1990), "'A home for Everybody?': Design, Ideology and the Culture of the Home in Italy, 1945–1972," in Paul Greenhalgh (ed.), *Modernism in Design*, 185–203, London: Reaktion Books.

Sparke, Penny (1995), *As Long as It's Pink: The Sexual Politics of Taste*, London: Pandora.

Sparke, Penny (2005), *Elsie de Wolfe: The Birth of Modern Interior Decoration*, New York: Acanthus Press.

Sparke, Penny (2008), *The Modern Interior*, London: Reaktion Books.

Sparke, Penny (2013), "Ettore Sottsass and Critical Design in Italy, 1965–1985," in Grace Lees-Maffei and Kjetil Fallen (eds.), *Made in Italy: Rethinking a Century of Italian Design*, 59–72, London: Bloomsbury.

Sparke, Penny and Anne Massey (2013), *Biography, Identity and the Modern Interior*, Farnham, UK: Ashgate.

Sparke, Penny, Brenda Martin, and Trevor Keeble, eds. (2006), *The Modern Period Room: The Construction of the Exhibited Interior 1870–1950*, London: Routledge.

Starr, Ruth (2013), "Seizo Sugawara, Maitre Lacquer," in Cloé Pitiot (ed.), *Eileen Gray*, 43–6, Kilmainham: Irish Museum of Modern Art; Paris: Centre Pompidou.

Star Trek (1966–9), [TV program] aired September 8, 1966, on NBC.

Steadman, Philip (1979), *The Evolution of Designs: Biological Analogy in Architecture and the Applied Arts*, Cambridge: Cambridge University Press.

Steffen, Dagmar and Jochen Gros (2003), "Technofactory versus Mini-Plants: Potentials for a Decentralized Sustainable Furniture Production." Available online: https://jochen-gros.de/A/Virtuelle_Produktion_files/technofactory%20miniplants_1.pdf (accessed June 9, 2021).

Stenebo, Johan (2010), *Die Wahrheit über IKEA*, Frankfurt: Campus.

Stewart, Janet (2000), *Fashioning Vienna: Adolf Loos's Cultural Criticism*, London: Routledge.

Stickley, Gustav (1909), "The Motif of Mission," in Herbert E. Binstead (ed.), *The Furniture Styles*, 179–87, London: Sir I. Pitman.

Stickley, Gustav ([1912, 1915] 1991), *The 1912 and 1915 Gustav Stickley Craftsman Furniture Catalogs*, Philadelphia: Athenaeum of Philadelphia; New York: Dover.

Studio 11 (1967), [TV program] Caroline Jones interview with James Maccormick, Australia: ABC. Available online: https://www.youtube.com/watch?v=fcXKU9_IKo4 (accessed February 19, 2016).

Sturlyn (n.d.), "Features and Benefits. Available online: http://hi.atgimg.com/pdf/2044/80-82_sturlyn_featuresandbenefits.pdf (accessed February 23, 2016).

Swett, Pamela E., Jonathan Wiesen, and Jonathan R. Zatlin, eds. (2007), *Selling Modernity: Advertising in Twentieth-Century Germany*, Durham, NC: Duke University Press.

Tanizaki, Junchirō ([1933] 2001), *In Praise of Shadows*, translated by Thomas Harper and Edward G. Seidensticker, London: Vintage Books.

Taragin, Davira Spiro (1989), *Furniture by Wendell Castle*, New York: Hudson Hills Press; Detroit Institute of Arts.

Taut, Bruno ([1937] 1958), *Houses and People of Japan*, Tokyo: Sanseido.

Taylor, Tom (1903), "New Lights on Billiards," *The Billiard Player: A Journal for the Public and Private Billiard Room*, 1 (1) (July): 18–20.

Teague, Walter Dorwin (1940), *Design This Day*, New York: Harcourt Brace and Co.

Terragni, Giuseppe (1936), "La costruzione della Casa del Fascio di Como," *Quadrante rivista mensile*, 14 (35/36) (October): 5–27. Available online: http://digitale.bnc.roma.sbn.it/tecadigitale/ (accessed February 2, 2016).

The National Archives (n.d.), "Currency Converter: 1270–2017." Available online: https://www.nationalarchives.gov.uk/currency-converter/ (accessed May 25, 2021).

Thoreau, Henry David ([1849] 1980), *Walden and "Civil Disobedience,"* New York: New American Library.

Tigerman, Bobbye (2007), "'I Am Not a Decorator': Florence Knoll, the Knoll Planning Unit and the Making of the Modern Office," *Journal of Design History*, 20 (1): 61–74.

Todd, Robert H., Dell K. Allen, and Leo Alting (1994), *Manufacturing Processes Reference Guide*, Industrial Press.

Topp, Leslie (1997), "An Architecture for Modern Nerves: Josef Hoffmann's Purkersdorf Sanatorium," *Journal of the Society of Architectural Historians*, 56 (4): 414–37.

Troy, Nancy J. (1983), *The De Stijl Environment*, Cambridge, MA: MIT Press.

Troy, Nancy J. (1991), *Modernism and the Decorative Arts. Art Nouveau to Le Corbusier*, New Haven, CT: Yale University Press.

Tryon, Warren S. (1961), *My Native Land, Life in America, 1790–1870*, Chicago: University of Chicago Press.

Tschudi-Madsen, Stephan (1967), *Art Nouveau*, London: Weidenfeld and Nicolson.

Tuan, Yuan-Fan (1977), *Space and Place: The Perspective of Experience*, Minneapolis: University of Minnesota Press.

Turner, Tom (1996), *City as Landscape: A Post-Postmodern View of Design and Planning*, London: E. and F.N. Spon.

"Two Books on Billiards" (1912), *The Spectator*, June 1: 20. Available online: http://archive.spectator.co.uk (accessed February 2, 2016).

Uffelen, Chris van (2010), *Street Furniture*, Salenstein: Braun Publishing.

UN Agenda 21 (1992). Available online: https://sustainabledevelopment.un.org/content/documents/Agenda21.pdf (accessed June 3, 2021).

Uricchio, William and Roberta E. Pearson (1993), *Reframing Culture: The Case of the Vitagraph Quality Films*, Princeton, NJ: Princeton University Press.

Vaughan, Anthony (1984), *The Vaughans: East End Furniture Makers*, London: Inner London Education Authority.

Veasey, Christine (*c.* 1935), *Good Furnishing*, London: Times Furnishing Co.

Vegesack, Alexander von (1996), *100 Masterpieces from the Vitra Design Museum Collection*, Weil-am-Rhein: Vitra Design Museum.

Vegesack, Alexander von, Brigitta Pauley, and Peter Ellenberg (1996), *Thonet: Classic Furniture in Bent Wood and Tubular Steel*, London: Hazar.

Venturi, Robert ([1966] 2002), *Complexity and Contradiction in Architecture*, New York: Museum of Modern Art.

Vidler, Anthony (1996 "Homes for Cyborgs," in Christopher Reed (ed.), *Not at Home: The Suppression of Domesticity in Modern Art and Architecture*, 161–78, London: Thames and Hudson.

Viegut Al Shihabi, Diane (2013), "Capitol Furniture Types of Beaux-Arts Architect: Design Hierarchy Reveals Meaning," *Journal of Interior Design*, 38 (1) (March): 33–48.

Vitra (2021), "Miniatures Collection: Vitra Design Museum, 1820–2011." Available online: http://www.vitra.com/en-us/product/miniatures-collection (accessed May 22, 2021).

Vitra Design Museum (n.d.), "Landi Chair / Landi, 1938." Available online: http://collectiononline.design-museum.de/#/en/object/44478?_k=11k4fl (accessed June 4, 2021).

Vladislavic, Ivan, ed. (2014), *Mikhael Subotzky & Patrick Waterhouse: Ponte City*, Göttingen: Steidl.

Vogel, Michael (2008), "Wortbildung in der Werbung—Grundlagen und empirische Untersuchungen zu IKEA-Katalogen," BA thesis, Justus Liebig University Gießen.

Wainwright, Clive (1990), "The Legacy of the Nineteenth Century," in Paul Greenhalgh (ed.), *Modernism in Design*, 26–40, London: Reaktion Books.

Walker, John (1989), *Design History and the History of Design*, London: Pluto Press.

Walter S. Mackay & Co. (*c.* 1910), *Quaint Furniture: Carpets, Furniture, Draperies*, Oakland, CA.

Wanders, Marcel (1999), *Design for a New Age*, Rotterdam: 010 Publishers.

Warner, Charles (1910), *Home Decoration*, London: T. Werner Laurie.

Waugh, Evelyn ([1945] 1973), *Brideshead Revisited*, Boston: Little, Brown & Co.

Weisberg, Gabriel (1979), "Baron Vitta and the Bracquemond/Rodin Mirror," *Bulletin of the Cleveland Museum of Art*, (November): 298–310.

West, C.D. and S.A. Sinclair (1991), "Technological Assessment of the Wood Household Furniture Industry," *Forest Products Journal*, 41 (4): 11–18.

Westheim, Paul (1923), "Comments on the 'Squaring' of the Bauhaus," *Das Kunstblatt*, 7.

Whiteley, Nigel (2003), *Reyner Banham: Historian of the Immediate Future*, Cambridge, MA: MIT Press.

Wildenberg, Thomas, ed. (1944), *Aircrewman's Gunnery Manual*, "Sperry Retractable Ball Turret," transcribed and formatted for the HyperWar Foundation. Available online: http://www.ibiblio.org/hyperwar/USN/ref/AirGunnery/TURRETS5.html (accessed May 10, 2015).

Wilk, Christopher (1981), *Marcel Breuer: Furniture and Interiors*, New York: Museum of Modern Art.

Wilk, Christopher (2006a), *Modernism: Designing a New World: 1914–1939*, London: V&A Publications.

Wilk, Christopher (2006b), "Sitting on Air," in Christopher Wilk (ed.), *Modernism: Designing a New World, 1914–1939*, 225–47, London: V&A Publications.

Williams, Gareth (2006), *The Furniture Machine: Furniture since 1990*, London: V&A Publications.

Williams, Gareth (2009), *Telling Tales: Fantasy and Fear in Contemporary Design*, London: V&A Publications.

Wilson, Kristina (2010), "Designing the Modern Family at the Fairs," in Robert Rydell and Laura Burd Schiavo (eds.), *Designing Tomorrow America's World Fairs of the 1930s*, 141–58, New Haven, CT: Yale University Press.

Wingler, Hans Maria (1986), *Bauhaus: Weimar, Dessau, Berlin, Chicago*, London: MIT Press.

Winton, Alexandra Griffith (2004), "'A Man's House Is His Art' the Walker Art Center's 'Idea House' Project and the Marketing of Domestic Design 1941–7," *Journal of Design History*, 17 (4): 377–96.

Wise, Arthur (1951), "The Festival is the Present," *Ideal Home Magazine*: 42–7.

Wolff, Janet (1990), "The Culture of Separate Spheres: The Role of Culture in 19th Century Public and Private Life," in *Feminine Sentences: Essays on Women and Culture*, 12–33, Cambridge, UK: Polity.

Wood, Ghislaine, ed. (2007), *Surreal Things: Surrealism and Design*, London: V&A Publications.

Woodham, Jonathan M. (1997), *Twentieth-Century Design*, Oxford: Oxford University Press.

Woodham, Jonathan M. (2004), *A Dictionary of Modern Design*, Oxford: Oxford University Press.

Worpole, Ken (2000), *Here Comes the Sun: Architecture and Public Space in Twentieth-Century European Culture*, London: Reaktion.

Wosk, Julie (2001), *Women and the Machine: Representations from the Spinning Wheel to the Electronic Age*, Baltimore: Johns Hopkins University Press.

Wright, Frank Lloyd (1901), "The Art and Craft of the Machine," address given to the
    Chicago Arts and Crafts Society. Available online: http://www.learn.columbia.edu/
    courses/arch20/pdf/art_hum_reading_50.pdf (accessed October 21, 2015).
Wright, Virginia (1997), *Modern Furniture in Canada 1920–1970*, Toronto: University
    of Toronto Press.
Yasuko, Suga (2004), "Designing the Morality of Consumption: 'Chamber of Horrors'
    at the Museum of Ornamental Art 1852–3," *Design Issues*, 20 (4): 43–56.
Yerbury, Francis R. (1947), *Modern Homes Illustrated*, London: Odhams Press.
Zahar, Marcel. (1931), "L'Architecture [de l'Exposition Coloniale]," *Renaissance de
    l'art*, 14 (8): 223–8.
Zhixian, Yin (2008), "Home: A Chinese Middle-Class Concept," in Zhang Hongxing,
    Lauren Parker, and Beth McKillop (eds.), *China Design Now*, 101–5, London: V&A
    Publishing.
Zittel (n.d.), "Projects." Available online: https://www.zittel.org/ (accessed May 22,
    2021).

INDEX